Front. PASTORALS. p. 7.

When weary reapers quit the sultry field,
And, crown'd with corn, their thanks to Ceres yield.

THE

POETICAL WORKS

OF

ALEXANDER POPE.

EDITED BY THE REV. H. F. CARY, M.A.

A New Edition carefully Revised.

TO WHICH IS PREFIXED,

A BIOGRAPHICAL NOTICE.

WITH ILLUSTRATIONS BY JOHN GILBERT.

NEW YORK:
D. APPLETON & CO., 443 & 445 BROADWAY,
AND 16 LITTLE BRITAIN, LONDON.
1867.

CONTENTS.

MISCELLANIES—*continued.*

EPITAPHS:

ALEXANDER POPE.

ALEXANDER, the only child of Alexander Pope, by Editha, daughter of William Turner, Esquire, of York, was born in Lombard-street, London, on the twenty-first of May, 1688. His father, having amassed a fortune of about twenty thousand pounds by his business as a linen-draper, retired to Binfield, in Windsor Forest; and being a Roman Catholic, and therefore, as it is said, unwilling to trust the government with his money, spent the greater part of it before his death.

At the age of eight, Pope was placed under the care of a priest, in Hampshire, and instructed at once in the rudiments of Greek and Latin: from thence he was removed to a school at Twyford, near Winchester; and afterwards to one in the neighbourhood of Hyde Park Corner.

Being a weak and sickly child, he passed most of his time in reading, and in making verses, a propensity in which he was encouraged by his father. Ogilby's "Homer" and Sandys's "Ovid" were amongst his favourite books. Of his earliest attempts at verse, the "Ode on Solitude" only remains. He had the good sense to destroy the rest.

Spence tells us that Waller, Spenser, and Dryden were Pope's great favourites, in the order they are named, in his first reading, and till he was about twelve years old. He says himself, that he learned versification from Dryden. In his youthful poem of "Alcander," he imitated every poet—Cowley, Milton, Spenser, Statius, Virgil, Homer. In a few years he had dipped into a great number of the English, French, Italian, Latin, and Greek poets. "This I did," he says, "without any design except to amuse myself; and got the languages by hunting after the stories in the several poets. I read—rather than read the books—to get the languages. I followed everywhere as my fancy led me, and was like a boy gathering flowers in the woods and fields, just as they fell in his way. These five or six years I looked upon as the happiest in my life."

When near London, he went to the playhouses; and, in imitation of what he saw there, formed a drama out of the "Iliad," to be represented by his schoolfellows. At Will's Coffee-House he had a sight of Dryden, a yet greater curiosity to him than the actors.

At sixteen he wrote his "Pastorals," which were not printed till 1709, when they appeared in a poetical Miscellany. In that year his "Essay on Criticism" was composed; and two years after, the "Rape of the Lock," which was also published in a miscellany, and at first consisted of only three hundred and fifty lines; but being afterwards embellished with the machinery, was extended to more than double the length. The fancy and elegance of this work placed him at the head of all his poetical competitors.

In 1713 he completed "Windsor Forest," which had been begun at the age of sixteen; and, relying on the high reputation he had obtained, put forth proposals for a subscription to an English version of the "Iliad." His imitations of Chaucer, and translations from the Latin poets, had already prepared him for this task; yet his spirits were so much weighed down at the prospect of it, that he complained of his rest being broken by painful dreams, and wished somebody would hang him. In rather more than five years the formidable work was completed, and met with a success hitherto unexampled in this country, having brought him a profit somewhat exceeding five thousand pounds.

His next engagement was an edition of Shakspere; but he had no skill in verbal criticism, and failed accordingly. The part in which he acquitted himself best was the Preface.

He now undertook a translation of the "Odyssey." For this he called in the assistance of Broome and Fenton; the former of whom contributed eight, and the latter four books. After finishing it in 1725, and reaping a second harvest of gain from Homer, he resolved thenceforward to desist from the labour of translating. But a habit begun so early, and continued so long, was not entirely to be laid aside. The "Imitations" he published from time to time of the Epistles and Satires of Horace and of Donne, are copies not much less faithful to their originals, than his version of the two great epic poems of antiquity. All his other works, derived from his own invention, were now confined to moral or satirical subjects; the "Essay on Man," the "Satires and Epistles," and the "Dunciad." The last of these, consisting of three books, was published in 1728. About two years before his death he added a fourth, after having remodelled the whole, and injudiciously substituted the lively Cibber for the laborious Theobald as the hero. In 1740 he amused himself by editing a selection of Latin poems, by Italian writers, in two volumes.

The history of Pope's Works is nearly that of his life. When he had collected the subscriptions and other profits accruing from his Homer, he prevailed on his father to dispose of his estate at Binfield, and purchase a house at Twickenham, to which he removed with his parents. Here, with the exception of occasional visits to London, Oxford, Bath, and the houses of his friends, he continued to reside for the remainder of his days. Ill health always prevented him from travelling to other countries, for which the desire never left him. Some of his leisure hours at home were diverted by the care of ornamenting his house and gardens, and forming a grotto under the highway that intersected his grounds.

In November, 1717, his father died, at the age of seventy-five. . In 1733 he lost his mother, at the age of ninety-three, whom, in her declining years, he had nursed with the most assiduous tenderness. After her death, his affections centred in Martha Blount, with whom, and her sister Teresa, his acquaintance had commenced in infancy; this friendship continued throughout his life. His attachment to another female, Lady Mary Wortley Montagu, terminated most unpleasantly; in rejection and scorn on one side, and in anger and revenge on the other. The part of Pope's character which we contemplate with most pain, is his sensitiveness to injury, either real or imagined; yet it is to this disposition that our language is indebted for the finest models of a keen and polished satire. As he was violent in his animosities, so he was ardent and sincere in his affections. The friends in whose conversation he most delighted, were, Gay, Swift, Parnell, Jervas the painter, Arbuthnot, Atterbury, Harley, and St. John. He was early introduced to the notice of the great, and continued to mix in their society, without any compromise of integrity or independence: with many of those yet more eminent for wit or literature, he was united by the closer bond of sympathy and mutual endearment. No English poet has ever risen from so humble a beginning, to so great personal distinction.

He died on the thirtieth of May, 1744, after suffering much from his complaints, yet with so little pain at last, that those about him could not distinguish the time at which he expired. On receiving the last sacraments from the priest, he said, "There is nothing that is meritorious but virtue and friendship, and indeed friendship itself is only a part of virtue."

He appears to have been at no time free from some species of bodily weakness or malady, of which a head-ache was the constant symptom. In person he was diminutive and deformed: when a child, he had a pleasing and even beautiful countenance: in more advanced life the best feature was his eye, the lustre of which was remarkable. His bust, by Roubilliac, exhibits an extremely eager and sarcastic expression in the lips, strongly indicative of his character.

It may afford subject for reflection, that by a diligent cultivation of one natural talent, seldom much esteemed so long as the possessor of it is living, a puny misshapen and sickly being, unfit for any active employment of life, and rarely quitting the roof of his parents, became a stay to those parents in their old age, the restorer of their fortunes, the pride of their house; courted by the powerful and wealthy; the dread of his enemies; and one of the chief ornaments of his age and country.

It is well said, that Pope saw nature only dressed

by art; he judged of beauty by fashion; he sought for truth in the opinions of the world; he judged of the feelings of others by his own. The capacious soul of Shakspere had an intuitive and mighty sympathy with whatever could enter into the heart of man in all possible circumstances. Pope had an exact knowledge of all that he himself loved or hated, wished or wanted. Milton has winged his daring flight from heaven to earth, through Chaos and old Night. Pope's muse never wandered with safety, but from his library to his grotto, or from his grotto into his library back again. His mind dwelt with greater pleasure on his own garden than on the garden of Eden; he could describe the faultless whole-length mirror that reflected his own person, better than the smooth surface of the lake that reflects the face of heaven—a piece of cut-glass or a pair of paste buckles with more brilliance and effect than a thousand dew-drops glittering in the sun. He would be more delighted with a patent lamp than with "the pale reflex of Cynthia's brow," that fills the skies with its soft silent lustre, that trembles through the cottage window, and cheers the watchful mariner on the lonely wave. In short, he was the poet of personality and of polished life. That which was the nearest to him, was the greatest; the fashion of the day bore sway in his mind over the immutable laws of nature.

He lived in the smiles of fortune, and basked in the favour of the great. In his smooth and polished verse, we meet with no prodigies of nature, but with miracles of wit; the thunders of his pen are whispered flatteries; its forked lightnings, pointed sarcasm; for "the gnarled oak," he gives us "the soft myrtle;" for rocks, and seas, and mountains, —artificial grass-plots, gravel-walks, and trickling rills;

for earthquakes and tempests,—the breaking of a flower-pot, or the fall of a china-jar; for the tug and war of the elements, or the deadly strife of the passions, we have

"Calm contemplation and poetic ease."

Yet within this retired and narrow circle, how much—and that how exquisite—was contained! What discrimination, what wit, what delicacy, what fancy, what lurking spleen, what elegance of thought, what pampered refinement of sentiment! It is like looking at the world through a microscope, where everything assumes a new character and a new consequence,—where things are seen in their minutest circumstances and slightest shades of difference; where the little becomes gigantic, the deformed beautiful, and the beautiful deformed. The wrong end of the magnifier is, to be sure, held to everything, but still the exhibition is highly curious, and we know not whether to be most pleased or surprised.

The "Rape of the Lock" is the most exquisite specimen of *filigree* work ever invented. It is admirable in proportion as it is made of nothing. It is all gauze and silver spangles: the most glittering appearance is given to everything,—to paste, pomatum, billets-doux and patches. Airs, languid airs, breathe around; the atmosphere is perfumed with affectation. A toilet is described with the solemnity of an altar raised to the goddess of vanity; and the history of a silver bodkin is given with all the pomp of heraldry. No pains are spared, no profusion of ornament, no splendour of poetic diction, to set off the meanest things. The balance between the concealed irony and the assumed gravity is as nicely trimmed as the balance of power in Europe. You hardly know whether to laugh or to weep. It is the triumph of insignificance, the apotheosis of foppery and folly. It is the perfection of the mock-heroic!

Abelard and Eloisa is fine as a poem; it is finer as a piece of high-wrought eloquence. No woman could be supposed to write a better love-letter in verse. The tears shed are drops gushing from the heart; the words are burning sighs breathed from the soul of love.

Hazlitt agrees with Johnson, that the "Essay on Man," though a work of great labour and long consideration, was not the happiest of Pope's performances.

THE AUTHOR'S PREFACE

I AM inclined to think that both the writers of books, and the readers of them, are generally not a little unreasonable in their expectations. The first seem to fancy the world must approve whatever they produce, and the latter to imagine that authors are obliged to please them at any rate. Methinks, as, on the one hand, no single man is born with a right of controlling the opinions of all the rest; so, on the other, the world has no title to demand, that the whole care and time of any particular person should be sacrificed to its entertainment. Therefore I cannot but believe that writers and readers are under equal obligations for as much fame, or pleasure, as each affords the other.

Every one acknowledges, it would be a wild notion to expect perfection in any work of man: and yet one would think the contrary was taken for granted, by the judgment commonly passed upon poems. A critic supposes he has done his part, if he proves a writer to have failed in an expression, or erred in any particular point: and can it then be wondered at, if the poets in general seem resolved not to own themselves in any error? For as long as one side will make no allowances, the other will be brought to no acknowledgments.

I am afraid this extreme zeal on both sides is ill placed; poetry and criticism being by no means the universal concern of the world, but only the affair of idle men who write in their closets, and of idle men who read there.

Yet sure, upon the whole, a bad author deserves better usage than a bad critic; for a writer's endeavour, for the most part, is to please his readers, and he fails merely through the misfortune of an ill judgment; but such a critic's is to put them out of humour: a design he could never go upon without both that and an ill temper.

I think a good deal may be said to extenuate the fault of bad poets. What we call a genius, is hard to be distinguished, by a man himself, from a strong inclination; and if his genius be ever so great, he cannot at first discover it any other way, than by giving way to that prevalent propensity which renders him the more liable to be mistaken. The only method he has is to make the experiment by writing, and appealing to the judgment of others: now if he happens to write ill (which is certainly no sin in itself) he is immediately made an object of ridicule. I wish we had the humanity to reflect that even the worst authors might, in their endeavour to please us, deserve something at our hands. We have no cause to quarrel with them but for their obstinacy in persisting to write; and this too may admit of alleviating circumstances. Their particular friends may be either ignorant or insincere; and the rest of the world in general is too well-bred to shock them with a truth, which generally their booksellers are the first that inform them of. This happens not till they have spent too much of their time to apply to any profession which might better fit their talents; and till such talents as they have are so far discredited as to be but of small service to them. For (what is the hardest case imaginable) the reputation of a man generally depends upon the first steps he makes in the world; and people will establish their opinion of us, from what we do at that season when we have least judgment to direct us.

On the other hand, a good poet no sooner communicates his works with the same desire of information, but it is imagined he is a vain young creature given up to the ambition of fame; when perhaps the poor man is all the while trembling with the fear of being ridiculous. If he is made to hope he may please the world, he falls under very unlucky circumstances; for, from the moment he prints, he must expect to hear no more truth than if he were a prince or a beauty. If he has not very good sense (and indeed there are twenty men of wit for one man of sense), his living thus in a course of flattery may put him in no small danger of becoming a coxcomb: if he has, he will consequently have so much diffidence as not to reap any great satisfaction from his praise; since, if it be given to his face, it can scarce be distinguished from flattery, and if in his absence, it is hard to be certain of it. Were he sure to be commended by the best and most knowing, he is as sure of being envied by the worst and most ignorant, which are the majority; for it is with a fine genius as with a fine fashion, all those are displeased at it who are not able to follow it: and it is to be feared that esteem will seldom do any man so much good, as ill-will does him harm. Then there is a third class of people, who make the largest part of mankind, those of ordinary or indifferent capacities: and these (to a man) will hate or suspect him: a hundred honest gentlemen will dread him as a wit, and a hundred innocent women as a satirist. In a word, whatever be his fate in poetry, it is ten to one but he must give up all the reasonable aims of life for it. There are indeed some advantages accruing from a genius to poetry, and they are all I can think of: the agreeable power of self-amusement when a man is idle or alone; the privilege of being admitted into the best company; and the freedom of saying as many careless things as other people, without being so severely remarked upon.

I believe, if any one, early in his life, should contemplate the dangerous fate of authors, he would scarce be of their number on any consideration. The life of a wit is a warfare upon earth; and the present spirit of the learned world is such, that to attempt to serve it (any way) one must have the constancy of a martyr, and a resolution to suffer for its sake. I could wish people would believe, what I am pretty certain they will not, that I have been much less concerned about fame than I durst declare till this occasion, when methinks I should find more credit than I could heretofore: since my writings have had their fate already, and it is too late to think of prepossessing the reader in their favour. I would plead it as some merit in me, that the world has never been prepared for these trifles by prefaces, biassed by recommendation, dazzled with the names of great patrons, wheedled with fine reasons and pretences, or troubled with excuses. I confess it was want of consideration that made me an author; I writ because it amused me; I corrected because it was as pleasant to me to correct as to write; and I published because I was told, I might please such as it was a credit to please. To what degree I have done this, I am really ignorant; I had too much fondness for my productions to judge of them at first, and too much judgment to be pleased with them at last. But I have reason to think they can have no reputation which will continue long, or which deserves to do so; for they have always fallen short, not only of what I read of others, but even of my own ideas of poetry.

If any one should imagine I am not in earnest, I desire him to reflect that the ancients (to say the least of them) had as much genius as we; and that to take more pains, and employ more time, cannot fail to produce more complete pieces. They constantly applied themselves not only to that art, but to that single branch of an art, to which their talent was most powerfully bent; and it was the business of their lives to correct and finish their works for posterity. If we can pretend to have used the same industry, let us expect the same immortality; though if we took the same care, we should still lie under a further misfortune: they writ in languages that became universal and everlasting, while ours are extremely limited both in extent and in duration. A mighty foundation for our pride! when the utmost we can hope, is but to be read in one island, and to be thrown aside at the end of one age.

All that is left us is to recommend our productions by the imitation of the ancients: and it will be found true, that in every age, the highest character for sense and learning has been obtained by those who have been most indebted to them. For, to say truth, whatever is very good sense, must have been common sense in all times; and what we call learning, is but the knowledge of the sense of our predecessors. Therefore they who say our thoughts are not our own, because they resemble the ancients, may as well say our faces are not our own because they are like our fathers: and indeed it is very unreasonable, that people should expect us to be scholars, and yet be angry to find us so.

I fairly confess that I have served myself all I could by reading; that I made use of the judgment of authors dead and living; that I omitted no means in my power to be informed of my errors, both by my friends and enemies: but the true reason these pieces are not more correct, is owing to the consideration how short a time they, and I, have to live: one may be ashamed to consume half one's days in bringing sense and rhyme together: and what critic can be so unreasonable, as not to leave a man time enough for any more serious employment, or more agreeable amusement?

The only plea I shall use for the favour of the public is, that I have as great respect for it as most authors have for themselves; and that I have sacrificed much of my own self-love for its sake, in preventing not only many mean things from seeing the light, but many which I thought tolerable. I would not be like those authors who forgive themselves some particular lines for the sake of a whole poem, and *vice versâ* a whole poem for the sake of some particular lines. I believe no one qualification is so likely to make a good writer, as the power of rejecting his own thoughts; and it must be this (if anything) that can give me a chance to be one. For what I have published, I can only hope to be pardoned; but for what I have burned, I deserve to be praised. On this account the world is under some obligation to me, and owes me the justice in return, to look upon no verses as mine that are not inserted in this collection. And perhaps nothing could make it worth my while to own what are really so, but to avoid the imputation of so many dull and immoral things as, partly by malice and partly by ignorance, have been ascribed to me. I must further acquit myself of the presumption of having lent my name to recommend any miscellanies, or works of other men; a thing I never thought becoming a person who has hardly credit enough to answer for his own.

In this office of collecting my pieces, I am altogether uncertain, whether to look upon myself as a man building a monument, or burying the dead.

If time shall make it the former, may these poems (as long as they last) remain as a testimony, that their author never made his talents subservient to the mean and unworthy ends of party or self-interest; the gratification of public prejudices, or private passions; the flattery of the undeserving, or the insult of the unfortunate. If I have written well, let it be considered that 'tis what no man can do without good sense, a quality that not only renders one capable of being a good writer, but a good man. And if I have made any acquisition in the opinion of any one under the notion of the former, let it be continued to me under no other title than that of the latter.

But if this publication be only a more solemn funeral of my remains, I desire it may be known that I die in charity, and in my senses; without any murmurs against the justice of this age, or any mad appeals to posterity. I declare I shall think the world in the right, and quietly submit to every truth which time shall discover to the prejudice of these writings; not so much as wishing so irrational a thing, as that everybody should be deceived merely for my credit. However, I desire it may then be considered, that there are very few things in this collection which were not written under the age of five-and-twenty: so that my youth may be made (as it never fails to be in executions) a case of compassion. That I was never so concerned about my works as to vindicate them in print; believing, if anything was good, it would defend itself, and what was bad could never be defended. That I used no artifice to raise or continue a reputation, depreciated no dead author I was obliged to, bribed no living one with unjust praise, insulted no adversary with ill language; or, when I could not attack a rival's works, encouraged reports against his morals. To conclude, if this volume perish, let it serve as a warning to the critics, not to take too much pains for the future to destroy such things as will die of themselves; and a *memento mori* to some of my vain contemporaries the poets, to teach them that, when real merit is wanting, it avails nothing to have been encouraged by the great, commended by the eminent, and favoured by the public in general.

Nov. 10, 1716.

PASTORALS,

WITH

A DISCOURSE ON PASTORAL POETRY.[1]

WRITTEN IN THE YEAR MDCCIV.

Rura mihi et rigui placeant in vallibus amnes,
Flumina amem, sylvasque, inglorius!—*Virg.*

THERE are not, I believe, a greater number of any sort of verses than of those which are called Pastorals; nor a smaller than of those which are truly so. It therefore seems necessary to give some account of this kind of poem, and it is my design to comprise in this short paper the substance of those numerous dissertations that critics have made on the subject, without omitting any of their rules in my own favour. You will also find some points reconciled, about which they seem to differ, and a few remarks, which, I think, have escaped their observation.

The original of poetry is ascribed to that age which succeeded the creation of the world: and as the keeping of flocks seems to have been the first employment of mankind, the most ancient sort of poetry was probably *pastoral.*[2] It is natural to imagine, that the leisure of those ancient shepherds admitting and inviting some diversion, none was so proper to that solitary and sedentary life as singing; and that in their songs they took occasion to celebrate their own felicity. From hence a poem was invented, and afterwards improved to a perfect image of that happy time; which, by giving us an esteem for the virtues of a former age, might recommend them to the present. And since the life of shepherds was attended with more tranquillity than any other rural employment, the poets chose to introduce their persons, from whom it received the name of Pastoral.

[1] Written at sixteen years of age.
[2] Fontenelle's Disc. on Pastorals.

A pastoral is an imitation of the action of a shepherd, or one considered under that character. The form of this imitation is dramatic, or narrative, or mixed of both;[1] the fable simple, the manners not too polite nor too rustic; the thoughts are plain, yet admit a little quickness and passion, but that short and flowing: the expression humble, yet as pure as the language will afford; neat, but not florid; easy, and yet lively. In short, the fable, manners, thoughts, and expressions, are full of the greatest simplicity in nature.

The complete character of this poem consists in simplicity,[2] brevity, and delicacy; the two first of which render an eclogue natural, and the last delightful.

If we would copy nature, it may be useful to take this idea along with us, that pastoral is an image of what they call the golden age. So that we are not to describe our shepherds as shepherds at this day really are, but as they may be conceived then to have been; when the best of men followed the employment. To carry this resemblance yet further, it would not be amiss to give these shepherds some skill in astronomy, as far as it may be useful to that sort of life. And an air of piety to the gods should shine through the poem, which so visibly appears in all the works of antiquity: and it ought to preserve some relish of the old way of writing; the connexion should be loose, the narrations and descriptions short,[3] and the periods concise. Yet it is not sufficient that the sentences only be brief, the whole eclogue should be so too. For we cannot suppose poetry in those days to have been the business of men, but their recreation at vacant hours.

But with a respect to the present age, nothing more conduces to make these composures natural, than when some knowledge in rural affairs is discovered.[4] This may be made to appear rather done by chance than on design and sometimes is best shown by inference; lest by too, much study to seem natural, we destroy that easy simplicity from whence arises the delight. For what is inviting in this sort of poetry proceeds not so much from

1 Heinsius in Theocr. 2 Rapin de Carm. Past. p. 2.
3 Rapin, Reflex. sur l'Art Poet. d'Arist. p. 2. Refl. xxvii.
4 Pref. to Virg. Past. in Dryd. Virg.

the idea of that business, as of the tranquillity of a country life.

We must therefore use some illusion to render a pastoral delightful; and this consists in exposing the best side only of a shepherd's life, and in concealing its miseries.[1] Nor is it enough to introduce shepherds discoursing together in a natural way; but a regard must be had to the subject; that it contain some particular beauty in itself, and that it be different in every eclogue. Besides, in each of them a designed scene or prospect is to be presented to our view, which should likewise have its variety.[2] This variety is obtained in a great degree by frequent comparisons, drawn from the most agreeable objects of the country; by interrogations to things inanimate; by beautiful digressions, but those short; sometimes by insisting a little on circumstances; and lastly, by elegant turns on the words, which render the numbers extremely sweet and pleasing. As for the numbers themselves, though they are properly of the heroic measure, they should be the smoothest, the most easy and flowing imaginable.

It is by rules like these that we ought to judge of pastoral. And since the instructions given for any art are to be delivered as that art is in perfection, they must of necessity be derived from those in whom it is acknowledged so to be. It is therefore from the practice of Theocritus and Virgil (the only undisputed authors of pastoral) that the critics have drawn the foregoing notions concerning it.

Theocritus excels all others in nature and simplicity. The subjects of his Idyllia are purely pastoral; but he is not so exact in his persons, having introduced reapers[3] and fishermen as well as shepherds. He is apt to be too long in his descriptions, of which that of the cup in the first pastoral is a remarkable instance. In the manners he seems a little defective, for his swains are sometimes abusive and immodest, and perhaps too much inclining to rusticity; for instance, in his fourth and fifth Idyllia. But 'tis enough that all others learnt their excellencies

1 Fontenelle's Disc. of Pastorals.
2 See the forementioned Preface.
3 ΘΕΡΙΣΤΑΙ, Idyl. x. and ΑΛΙΕΙΣ, Idyl. xxi.

from him, and that his dialect alone has a secret charm in it, which no other could ever attain.

Virgil, who copies Theocritus, refines upon his original; and in all points, where judgment is principally concerned, he is much superior to his master. Though some of his subjects are not pastoral in themselves, but only seem to be such; they have a wonderful variety in them, which the Greek was a stranger to.[1] He exceeds him in regularity and brevity, and falls short of him in nothing but simplicity and propriety of style; the first of which perhaps was the fault of his age, and the last of his language.

Among the moderns, their success has been greatest who have most endeavoured to make these ancients their pattern. The most considerable genius appears in the famous Tasso and our Spenser. Tasso in his Aminta has as far excelled all the pastoral writers, as in his Gierusalemme he has outdone the epic poets, of his country. But as this piece seems to have been the original of a new sort of poem, the Pastoral Comedy, in Italy, it cannot so well be considered as a copy of the ancients. Spenser's Calendar, in Mr. Dryden's opinion, is the most complete work of this kind which any nation has produced ever since the time of Virgil.[2] Not but that he may be thought imperfect in some few points. His eclogues are somewhat too long, if we compare them with the ancients. He is sometimes too allegorical, and treats of matters of religion in a pastoral style, as the Mantuan had done before him. He has employed the lyric measure, which is contrary to the practice of the old poets. His stanza is not still the same, nor always well chosen. This last may be the reason his expression is sometimes not concise enough; for the Tetrastic has obliged him to extend his sense to the length of four lines, which would have been more closely confined in the couplet.

In the manners, thoughts, and characters, he comes near to Theocritus himself; though, notwithstanding all the care he has taken, he is certainly inferior in his dialect: for the Doric had its beauty and propriety in the time of Theocritus; it was used in part of Greece, and frequent in

1 Rapin, Refl. on Arist. part. ii. refl. xxvii.—Pref. to the Ecl. in Dryden's Virg. 2 Dedication to Virg. Ecl.

the mouths of many of the greatest persons: whereas the old English and country phrases of Spenser were either entirely obsolete, or spoken only by people of the lowest condition. As there is a difference betwixt simplicity and rusticity, so the expression of simple thoughts should be plain, but not clownish. The addition he has made of a Calendar to his eclogues, is very beautiful; since by this, besides the general moral of innocence and simplicity, which is common to other authors of pastoral, he has one peculiar to himself; he compares human life to the several seasons, and at once exposes to his readers a view of the great and little worlds, in their various changes and aspects. Yet the scrupulous division of his pastorals into months, has obliged him either to repeat the same description, in other words, for three months together; or, when it was exhausted before, entirely to omit it: whence it comes to pass that some of his eclogues (as the sixth, eighth, and tenth, for example) have nothing but their titles to distinguish them. The reason is evident, because the year has not that variety in it to furnish every month with a particular description, as it may every season.

Of the following eclogues I shall only say that these four comprehend all the subjects which the critics upon Theocritus and Virgil will allow to be fit for pastoral: that they have as much variety of description, in respect of the several seasons, as Spenser's; that in order to add to this variety, the several times of the day are observed, the rural employments in each season or time of day, and the rural scenes or places proper to such employments; not without some regard to the several ages of man, and the different passions proper to each age.

But after all, if they have any merit, it is to be attributed to some good old authors, whose works as I had leisure to study, so I hope I have not wanted care to imitate.

These Pastorals were written at the age of sixteen, and then passed through the hands of Mr. Walsh, Mr. Wycherley, G. Granville afterwards Lord Lansdown, Sir William Trumbal, Dr. Garth, Lord Halifax, Lord Somers, Mr. Mainwaring, and others. All these gave our author the greatest encouragement, and particularly Mr. Walsh, whom Mr. Dryden, in his postscript to Virgil, calls the best critic of his age. "The author (says he) seems to have a particular genius for this kind of poetry, and a judgment that much exceeds his years. He has taken very freely from the ancients. But what he has mixed of his own with theirs is no way inferior to what he has taken from them. It is not flattery at all to say, that Virgil had written nothing so good at his age. His preface is very judicious and learned."

SPRING:

THE FIRST PASTORAL, OR

Damon.

TO SIR WILLIAM TRUMBAL.

First in these fields I try the silvan strains,
Nor blush to sport on Windsor's blissful plains:
Fair Thames, flow gently from thy sacred spring,
While on thy banks Sicilian Muses sing;
Let vernal airs through trembling osiers play,
And Albion's cliffs resound the rural lay.
You, that too wise for pride, too good for power,
Enjoy the glory to be great no more,
And, carrying with you all the world can boast,
To all the world illustriously are lost!
O let my muse her slender reed inspire,
Till in your native shades you tune the lyre:
So when the nightingale to rest removes,
The thrush may chant to the forsaken groves,
But charm'd to silence, listens while she sings,
And all the aerial audience clap their wings.
Soon as the flocks shook off the nightly dews,
Two swains, whom love kept wakeful, and the muse,
Pour'd o'er the whitening vale their fleecy care,
Fresh as the morn, and as the season fair:

The dawn now blushing on the mountain's side,
Thus Daphnis spoke, and Strephon thus replied.

DAPHNIS.

Hear how the birds, on every blooming spray,
With joyous music wake the dawning day!
Why sit we mute, when early linnets sing,
When warbling Philomel salutes the spring?
Why sit we sad, when Phosphor shines so clear,
And lavish nature paints the purple year?

STREPHON.

Sing then, and Damon shall attend the strain,
While yon slow oxen turn the furrow'd plain,
Here the bright crocus and blue violet glow,
Here western winds on breathing roses blow.
I'll stake yon lamb, that near the fountain plays,
And from the brink his dancing shade surveys.

DAPHNIS.

And I this bowl, where wanton ivy twines,
And swelling clusters bend the curling vines:
Four figures rising from the work appear,
The various seasons of the rolling year;
And what is that, which binds the radiant sky,
Where twelve fair signs in beauteous order lie?

DAMON.

Then sing by turns, by turns the Muses sing;
Now hawthorns blossom, now the daisies spring,
Now leaves the trees, and flowers adorn the ground;
Begin, the vales shall every note rebound.

STREPHON.

Inspire me, Phœbus, in my Delia's praise,
With Waller's strains, or Granville's moving lays!
A milk-white bull shall at your altars stand,
That threats a fight, and spurns the rising sand.

DAPHNIS.

O Love! for Sylvia let me gain the prize,
And make my tongue victorious as her eyes:
No lambs or sheep for victims I'll impart,
Thy victim, Love, shall be the shepherd's heart.

STREPHON.

Me gentle Delia beckons from the plain,
Then hid in shades, eludes her eager swain;
But feigns a laugh, to see me search around,
And by that laugh the willing fair is found.

DAPHNIS.

The sprightly Sylvia trips along the green,
She runs, but hopes she does not run unseen;
While a kind glance at her pursuer flies,
How much at variance are her feet and eyes!

STREPHON.

O'er golden sands let rich Pactolus flow,
And trees weep amber on the banks of Po;
The Thames bright shores the brightest beauties yield,
Feed here my lambs, I'll seek no distant field.

DAPHNIS.

Celestial Venus haunts Idalia's groves;
Diana Cynthus, Ceres Hybla loves;
If Windsor-shades delight the matchless maid,
Cynthus and Hybla yield to Windsor-shade.

STREPHON.

All nature mourns, the skies relent in showers,
Hush'd are the birds, and closed the drooping flowers;
If Delia smile, the flowers begin to spring,
The skies to brighten, and the birds to sing.

DAPHNIS.

All nature laughs, the groves are fresh and fair,
The sun's mild lustre warms the vital air;
If Sylvia smiles, new glories gild the shore,
And vanquish'd nature seems to charm no more.

STREPHON.

In spring the fields, in autumn hills I love,
At morn the plains, at noon the shady grove,
But Delia always; absent from her sight,
Nor plains at morn, nor groves at noon delight.

DAPHNIS.

Sylvia's like autumn ripe, yet mild as May,
More bright than noon, yet fresh as early day;

Even spring displeases, when she shines not here;
But blest with her, 'tis spring throughout the year.

STREPHON.

Say, Daphnis, say, in what glad soil appears
A wondrous tree that sacred monarchs bears;
Tell me but this, and I'll disclaim the prize,
And give the conquest to thy Sylvia's eyes.

DAPHNIS.

Nay tell me first, in what more happy fields
The thistle springs, to which the lily yields:
And then a nobler prize I will resign;
For Sylvia, charming Sylvia, shall be thine.

DAMON.

Cease to contend, for, Daphnis, I decree,
The bowl to Strephon, and the lamb to thee:
Blest swains, whose nymphs in every grace excel;
Blest nymphs, whose swains those graces sing so well!
Now rise, and haste to yonder woodbine bowers,
A soft retreat from sudden vernal showers;
The turf with rural dainties shall be crown'd,
While opening blooms diffuse their sweets around.
For see! the gathering flocks to shelter tend,
And from the Pleiads fruitful showers descend.

SUMMER:

THE SECOND PASTORAL, OR

Alexis.

The scene of this pastoral by the river side, suitable to the heat of the season; the time, noon.

TO DR. GARTH,

AUTHOR OF "THE DISPENSARY."

A SHEPHERD'S boy (he seeks no better name)
Led forth his flocks along the silver Thame,
Where dancing sunbeams on the waters play'd,
And verdant alders form'd a quivering shade.
Soft as he mourn'd, the streams forgot to flow,
The flocks around a dumb compassion show,

The Naiads wept in every watery bower,
And Jove consented in a silent shower.
Accept, O GARTH! the Muse's early lays,
That adds this wreath of ivy to thy bays;
Hear what from Love unpractised hearts endure,
From Love, the sole disease thou canst not cure.
Ye shady beeches, and ye cooling streams,
Defence from Phœbus', not from Cupid's beams,
To you I mourn, nor to the deaf I sing,
The woods shall answer, and their echo ring.
The hills and rocks attend my doleful lay,
Why art thou prouder and more hard than they?
The bleating sheep with my complaints agree,
They parch'd with heat, and I inflamed by thee.
The sultry Sirius burns the thirsty plains,
While in thy heart eternal winter reigns.
Where stray ye, Muses, in what lawn or grove,
While your Alexis pines in hopeless love?
In those fair fields where sacred Isis glides,
Or else where Cam his winding vales divides?
As in the crystal spring I view my face,
Fresh-rising blushes paint the watery glass;
But since those graces please thy eyes no more,
I shun the fountains which I sought before.
Once I was skill'd in every herb that grew,
And every plant that drinks the morning dew;
Ah, wretched shepherd, what avails thy art,
To cure thy lambs, but not to heal thy heart!
Let other swains attend the rural care,
Feed fairer flocks, or richer fleeces shear:
But nigh yon mountain let me tune my lays,
Embrace my love, and bind my brows with bays.
That flute is mine which Colin's tuneful breath
Inspired when living, and bequeath'd in death:
He said; Alexis, take this pipe, the same
That taught the groves my Rosalinda's name:
But now the reeds shall hang on yonder tree,
For ever silent, since despised by thee.
Oh! were I made by some transforming power
The captive bird that sings within thy bower!
Then might my voice thy listening ears employ,
And I those kisses he receives enjoy.
And yet my numbers please the rural throng,
Rough satyrs dance, and Pan applauds the song:

The nymphs, forsaking every cave and spring,
Their early fruit and milk-white turtles bring!
Each amorous nymph prefers her gifts in vain,
On you their gifts are all bestow'd again.
For you the swains their fairest flowers design,
And in one garland all their beauties join;
Accept the wreath which you deserve alone,
In whom all beauties are comprised in one.
See what delights in silvan scenes appear!
Descending gods have found Elysium here.
In woods bright Venus with Adonis stray'd,
And chaste Diana haunts the forest-shade.
Come, lovely nymph, and bless the silent hours,
When swains from shearing seek their nightly bowers;
When weary reapers quit the sultry field,
And crown'd with corn their thanks to Ceres yield.
This harmless grove no lurking viper hides,
But in my breast the serpent Love abides.
Here bees from blossoms sip the rosy dew,
But your Alexis knows no sweets but you.
O deign to visit our forsaken seats,
The mossy fountains, and the green retreats!
Where'er you walk, cool gales shall fan the glade,
Trees, where you sit, shall crowd into a shade:
Where'er you tread the blushing flowers shall rise,
And all things flourish where you turn your eyes.
O! how I long with you to pass my days,
Invoke the Muses, and resound your praise!
Your praise the birds shall chant in every grove,
And winds shall waft it to the powers above.
But would you sing, and rival Orpheus' strain,
The wondering forests soon should dance again,
The moving mountains hear the powerful call,
And headlong streams hang listening in their fall!
But see, the shepherds shun the noon-day heat,
The lowing herds to murmuring brooks retreat,
To closer shades the panting flocks remove;
Ye gods! and is there no relief for love?
But soon the sun with milder rays descends
To the cool ocean, where his journey ends.
On me Love's fiercer flames for ever prey,
By night he scorches, as he burns by day.

AUTUMN:

THE THIRD PASTORAL, OR

Hylas and Aegon.

This pastoral consists of two parts, like the eighth of Virgil:
The Scene, a Hill; the Time, at Sunset.

TO MR. WYCHERLEY,

A FAMOUS AUTHOR OF COMEDIES; OF WHICH THE MOST CELEBRATED WERE THE "PLAIN DEALER" AND "COUNTRY WIFE."

BENEATH the shade a spreading beech displays,
Hylas and Ægon sung their rural lays;
This mourn'd a faithless, that an absent love,
And Delia's name and Doris' fill'd the grove.
Ye Mantuan nymphs, your sacred succour bring;
Hylas and Ægon's rural lays I sing.
  Thou, whom the Nine with Plautus' wit inspire,
The art of Terence, and Menander's fire;
Whose sense instructs us, and whose humour charms,
Whose judgment sways us, and whose spirit warms!
Oh, skill'd in nature! see the hearts of swains,
Their artless passions, and their tender pains.
  Now setting Phœbus shone serenely bright,
And fleecy clouds were streak'd with purple light;
When tuneful Hylas with melodious moan,
Taught rocks to weep, and made the mountains groan.
  Go, gentle gales, and bear my sighs away!
To Delia's ear the tender notes convey.
As some sad turtle his lost love deplores,
And with deep murmurs fills the sounding shores;
Thus, far from Delia, to the winds I mourn
Alike unheard, unpitied, and forlorn.
  Go, gentle gales, and bear my sighs along!
For her, the feather'd choirs neglect their song:
For her, the limes their pleasing shades deny;
For her, the lilies hang their heads and die.
Ye flowers that droop, forsaken by the spring,
Ye birds that, left by summer, cease to sing,
Ye trees that fade when autumn-heats remove,
Say, is not absence death to those who love?
  Go, gentle gales, and bear my sighs away!
Cursed be the fields that cause my Delia's stay;

Fade every blossom, wither every tree,
Die every flower, and perish all, but she.
What have I said? where'er my Delia flies,
Let spring attend, and sudden flowers arise;
Let opening roses knotted oaks adorn,
And liquid amber drop from every thorn.
   Go, gentle gales, and bear my sighs along!
The birds shall cease to tune their evening song,
The winds to breathe, the waving woods to move,
And streams to murmur, ere I cease to love.
Not bubbling fountains to the thirsty swain,
Not balmy sleep to labourers faint with pain,
Not showers to larks, nor sunshine to the bee,
Are half so charming as thy sight to me.
   Go, gentle gales, and bear my sighs away!
Come, Delia, come; ah, why this long delay?
Thro' rocks and caves the name of Delia sounds,
Delia! each cave and echoing rock rebounds.
Ye powers, what pleasing frenzy soothes my mind!
Do lovers dream, or is my Delia kind?
She comes, my Delia comes! Now cease my lay,
And cease, ye gales, to bear my sighs away!
   Next Ægon sung, while Windsor groves admired;
Rehearse, ye Muses, what yourselves inspired.
   Resound, ye hills, resound my mournful strain!
Of perjured Doris, dying I complain!
Here, where the mountains, lessening as they rise
Lose the low vales, and steal into the skies;
While labouring oxen, spent with toil and heat,
In their loose traces from the field retreat:
While curling smoke from village-tops are seen,
And the fleet shades glide o'er the dusky green.
   Resound, ye hills, resound my mournful lay!
Beneath yon poplar oft we pass'd the day;
Oft on the rind I carved her amorous vows,
While she with garlands hung the bending boughs;
The garlands fade, the vows are worn away;
So dies her love, and so my hopes decay.
   Resound, ye hills, resound my mournful strain!
Now bright Arcturus glads the teeming grain,
Now golden fruits on loaded branches shine,
And grateful clusters swell with floods of wine;
Now blushing berries paint the yellow grove;
Just gods! shall all things yield returns but love?

Resound, ye hills, resound my mournful lay!
The shepherds cry, "Thy flocks are left a prey"—
Ah! what avails it me, the flocks to keep,
Who lost my heart while I preserved my sheep.
Pan came, and ask'd what magic caused my smart,
Or what ill eyes malignant glances dart?
What eyes but hers, alas, have power to move!
And is there magic but what dwells in love!
Resound, ye hills, resound my mournful strains!
I'll fly from shepherds, flocks, and flowery plains,
From shepherds, flocks, and plains, I may remove,
Forsake mankind, and all the world—but love!
I know thee, Love! on foreign mountains bred,
Wolves gave thee suck, and savage tigers fed.
Thou wert from Etna's burning entrails torn,
Got by fierce whirlwinds, and in thunder born!
Resound, ye hills, resound my mournful lay!
Farewell, ye woods, adieu the light of day!
One leap from yonder cliff shall end my pains,
No more, ye hills, no more resound my strains!
Thus sung the shepherds till the approach of night,
The skies yet blushing with departing light,
When falling dews with spangles deck'd the glade,
And the low sun had lengthen'd every shade.

WINTER:

THE FOURTH PASTORAL, OR

Daphne.

TO THE MEMORY OF MRS. TEMPEST.

LYCIDAS.

Thyrsis, the music of that murmuring spring
Is not so mournful as the strains you sing;
Nor rivers winding through the vales below,
So sweetly warble, or so smoothly flow.
Now sleeping flocks on their soft fleeces lie,
The moon, serene in glory, mounts the sky,
While silent birds forget their tuneful lays,
Oh sing of Daphne's fate, and Daphne's praise!

THYRSIS.

Behold the groves that shine with silver frost,
Their beauty wither'd, and their verdure lost.

Here shall I try the sweet Alexis' strain,
That call'd the listening Dryads to the plain?
Thames heard the numbers as he flow'd along,
And bade his willows learn the moving song.

LYCIDAS.

So may kind rains their vital moisture yield,
And swell the future harvest of the field.
Begin; this charge the dying Daphne gave,
And said, "Ye shepherds, sing around my grave!"
Sing, while beside the shaded tomb I mourn,
And with fresh bays her rural shrine adorn.

THYRSIS.

Ye gentle Muses, leave your crystal spring,
Let nymphs and silvans cypress garlands bring;
Ye weeping Loves, the stream with myrtles hide,
And break your bows, as when Adonis died;
And with your golden darts, now useless grown,
Inscribe a verse on this relenting stone:
"Let nature change, let heaven and earth deplore,
"Fair Daphne's dead, and love is now no more!"
'Tis done, and nature's various charms decay,
See gloomy clouds obscure the cheerful day!
Now hung with pearls the dropping trees appear,
Their faded honours scatter'd on her bier.
See, where on earth the flowery glories lie,
With her they flourish'd, and with her they die.
Ah what avail the beauties nature wore?
Fair Daphne's dead, and beauty is no more!
For her the flocks refuse their verdant food,
The thirsty heifers shun the gliding flood,
The silver swans her hapless fate bemoan,
In notes more sad than when they sing their own;
In hollow caves sweet echo silent lies,
Silent, or only to her name replies;
Her name with pleasure once she taught the shore,
Now Daphne's dead, and pleasure is no more!
No grateful dews descend from evening skies,
Nor morning odours from the flowers arise;
No rich perfumes refresh the fruitful field,
Nor fragrant herbs their native incense yield.
The balmy zephyrs, silent since her death,
Lament the ceasing of a sweeter breath;

The industrious bees neglect their golden store!
Fair Daphne's dead, and sweetness is no more!
No more the mounting larks, while Daphne sings,
Shall, listening in mid-air, suspend their wings;
No more the birds shall imitate her lays,
Or, hush'd with wonder, hearken from the sprays:
No more the streams their murmurs shall forbear,
A sweeter music than their own to hear;
But tell the reeds, and tell the vocal shore,
Fair Daphne's dead, and music is no more!
Her fate is whisper'd by the gentle breeze,
And told in sighs to all the trembling trees;
The trembling trees, in every plain and wood,
Her fate remurmur to the silver flood;
The silver flood, so lately calm appears
Swell'd with new passion, and o'erflows with tears;
The winds, and trees, and floods, her death deplore,
Daphne, our grief! our glory now no more!
But see! where Daphne, wondering, mounts on high
Above the clouds, above the starry sky!
Eternal beauties grace the shining scene,
Fields ever fresh, and groves for ever green!
There, while you rest in amaranthine bowers,
Or from those meads select unfading flowers,
Behold us kindly, who your name implore,
Daphne, our goddess, and our grief no more!

LYCIDAS.

How all things listen while thy muse complains!
Such silence waits on Philomela's strains,
In some still evening, when the whispering breeze
Pants on the leaves, and dies upon the trees.
To thee, bright goddess, oft a lamb shall bleed,
If teeming ewes increase my fleecy breed.
While plants their shade, or flowers their odours give
Thy name, thy honour, and thy praise shall live!

THYRSIS.

But see, Orion sheds unwholesome dews;
Arise! the pines a noxious shade diffuse;
Sharp Boreas blows, and nature feels decay,
Time conquers all, and we must Time obey.
Adieu, ye vales, ye mountains, streams, and groves,
Adieu, ye shepherds' rural lays and loves;
Adieu, my flocks; farewell, ye silvan crew;
Daphne, farewell; and all the world adieu!

MESSIAH,

A SACRED ECLOGUE:

IN IMITATION OF

Virgil's Pollio.

IN reading several passages of the prophet Isaiah, which foretell the coming of Christ and the felicities attending it, I could not but observe a remarkable parity between many of the thoughts, and those in the Pollio of Virgil. This will not seem surprising, when we reflect that the eclogue was taken from a Sibylline prophecy on the same subject. One may judge that Virgil did not copy it line by line, but selected such ideas as best agreed with the nature of pastoral poetry, and disposed them in that manner which served most to beautify his piece. I have endeavoured the same in this imitation of him, though without admitting anything of my own; since it was written with this particular view, that the reader, by comparing the several thoughts, might see how far the images and descriptions of the Prophet are superior to those of the Poet. But as I fear I have prejudiced them by my management, I subjoin the passages of Isaiah, and those of Virgil, under the same disadvantage of a literal translation.

"*Now the Virgin returns, now the kingdom of Saturn returns, now a new progeny is sent down from high heaven. By means of thee, whatever reliques of our crimes remain shall be wiped away, and free the world from perpetual fears. He shall govern the earth in peace, with the virtues of his father.*"—VIRGIL, Ecl. iv.

"*Behold, a Virgin shall conceive and bear a son.*"—Isaiah, ch. vii. "*Unto us a Child is born, unto us a Son is given; the Prince of Peace: of the increase of his government, and of his peace, there shall be no end. Upon the throne of David, and upon his kingdom, to order and to establish it with judgment, and with justice, for ever and ever.*"—Ch. ix.

"*For thee, O Child, shall the earth, without being tilled, produce her early offerings; winding ivy, mixed with* Baccar, *and* Colocasia, *with smiling* Acanthus. *Thy cradle shall pour forth pleasing flowers about thee.*"—Ecl. iv.

"*The wilderness and the solitary place shall be glad, and the desert shall rejoice, and blossom as the rose.*"—Isaiah, ch. xxxv. "*The glory of Lebanon shall come unto thee, the fir-tree, the pine-tree, and the box together, to beautify the place of my sanctuary.*"—Ch. lx.

"*Oh come and receive the mighty honours; the time draws nigh, O beloved offspring of the Gods, O great increase of Jove! The uncultivated mountains send shouts of joy to the stars, the very rocks sing in verse, the very shrubs cry out, A God, a God!*"—Ecl. iv.

"*The voice of him that crieth in the wilderness, Prepare ye the way of the Lord! make straight in the desert a high way for our God! Every valley shall be exalted, and every mountain and hill shall be made low, and the crooked shall be made straight, and the rough places plain.*"—Isaiah, ch. xl. "*Break forth into singing, ye mountains! O forest, and every tree therein! for the Lord hath redeemed Israel.*"—Ch. iv.

"*The fields shall grow yellow with ripened ears, and the red grape shall hang upon the wild brambles, and the hard oak shall distil honey like dew.*" —Ecl. iv.

"*The parched ground shall become a pool, and the thirsty land springs of water. In the habitation where dragons lay shall be grass, and reeds, and rushes.*"—Isaiah, ch. xxxv. "*Instead of the thorn shall come up the fir-tree, and instead of the brier shall come up the myrtle-tree.*"—Ch. lv.

"*The goats shall bear to the fold their udders distended with milk; nor shall the herds be afraid of the greatest lions. The serpent shall die, and the herb that conceals poison shall die.*"—Ecl. iv.

"*The wolf shall dwell with the lamb, and the leopard shall lie down with the kid, and the calf, and the young lion, and the fatling together; and a little child shall lead them.—And the lion shall eat straw like the ox. And the sucking child shall play on the hole of the asp, and the weaned child shall put his hand on the den of the cockatrice.*"—Isaiah, ch. xi.

Ye nymphs of Solyma! begin the song:
To heavenly themes sublimer strains belong.
The mossy fountains, and the silvan shades,
The dreams of Pindus and the Aonian maids,
Delight no more—O Thou my voice inspire
Who touched Isaiah's hallowed lips with fire!
Rapt into future times, the bard begun:
A Virgin shall conceive, a Virgin bear a Son!
From Jesse's root behold a branch arise,
Whose sacred flower with fragrance fills the skies:
The ethereal spirit o'er its leaves shall move,
And on its top descends the mystic dove.
Ye heavens! from high the dewy nectar pour,
And in soft silence shed the kindly shower!
The sick and weak the healing plant shall aid,
From storms a shelter, and from heat a shade.
All crimes shall cease, and ancient fraud shall fail;
Returning Justice lift aloft her scale;
Peace o'er the world her olive wand extend,
And white-robed Innocence from heaven descend.
Swift fly the years, and rise the expected morn!
Oh spring to light, auspicious Babe, be born!
See Nature hastes her earliest wreaths to bring,
With all the incense of the breathing spring:
See lofty Lebanon his head advance,
See nodding forests on the mountains dance:
See spicy clouds from lowly Saron rise,
And Carmel's flowery top perfumes the skies!

Hark! a glad voice the lonely desert cheers;
Prepare the way! a God, a God appears:
A God, a God! the vocal hills reply,
The rocks proclaim the approaching Deity.
Lo, earth receives him from the bending skies!
Sink down, ye mountains, and, ye valleys, rise;
With heads declined, ye cedars, homage pay;
Be smooth, ye rocks; ye rapid floods, give way;
The Saviour comes! by ancient bards foretold!
Hear him, ye deaf, and all ye blind, behold!
He from thick films shall purge the visual ray,
And on the sightless eyeball pour the day:
'Tis he the obstructed paths of sound shall clear,
And bid new music charm the unfolding ear:
The dumb shall sing, the lame his crutch forego,
And leap exulting like the bounding roe.
No sigh, no murmur the wide world shall hear,
From every face he wipes off every tear.
In adamantine chains shall Death be bound,
And Hell's grim tyrant feel the eternal wound.
As the good shepherd tends his fleecy care,
Seeks freshest pasture and the purest air,
Explores the lost, the wandering sheep directs,
By day o'ersees them, and by night protects,
The tender lambs he raises in his arms,
Feeds from his hand, and in his bosom warms;
Thus shall mankind his guardian care engage,
The promised Father of the future age.
No more shall nation against nation rise,
Nor ardent warriors meet with hateful eyes,
Nor fields with gleaming steel be covered o'er,
The brazen trumpets kindle rage no more;
But useless lances into scythes shall bend,
And the broad falchion in a ploughshare end.
Then palaces shall rise; the joyful son
Shall finish what his short-lived sire begun;
Their vines a shadow to their race shall yield,
And the same hand that sow'd, shall reap the field.
The swain, in barren deserts with surprise
See lilies spring, and sudden verdure rise;
And start, amidst the thirsty wilds, to hear
New falls of water murmuring in his ear.
On rifted rocks, the dragon's late abodes,
The green reed trembles, and the bulrush nods.

Waste sandy valleys, once perplex'd with thorn,
The spiry fir and shapely box adorn;
To leafless shrubs the flowering palms succeed,
And odorous myrtle to the noisome weed.
The lambs with wolves shall graze the verdant mead,
And boys in flowery bands the tiger lead;
The steer and lion at one crib shall meet,
And harmless serpents lick the pilgrim's feet.
The smiling infant in his hand shall take
The crested basilisk and speckled snake,
Pleased the green lustre of the scales survey,
And with their forky tongue shall innocently play.
Rise, crown'd with light, imperial Salem, rise![1]
Exalt thy towery head, and lift thy eyes!
See, a long race thy spacious courts adorn;
See future sons, and daughters yet unborn,
In crowding ranks on every side arise,
Demanding life, impatient for the skies!
See barbarous nations at thy gates attend,
Walk in thy light, and in thy temple bend;
See thy bright altars throng'd with prostrate kings,
And heap'd with products of Sabean springs,
For thee Idume's spicy forests blow,
And seeds of gold in Ophir's mountains glow.
See heaven its sparkling portals wide display,
And break upon thee in a flood of day.
No more the rising sun shall gild the morn,
Nor evening Cynthia fill her silver horn;
But lost, dissolved in thy superior rays,
One tide of glory, one unclouded blaze
O'erflow thy courts; the Light himself shall shine
Reveal'd, and God's eternal day be thine!
The seas shall waste, the skies in smoke decay,
Rocks fall to dust, and mountains melt away;
But fix'd his word, his saving power remains;
Thy realm for ever lasts, thy own MESSIAH reigns!

[1] The thoughts of Isaiah, which compose the latter part of the poem, are wonderfully elevated, and much above those general exclamations of Virgil, which make the loftiest parts of his Pollio.

MESSIAH. p. 26.

Boys in flowery bands the tiger lead.

WINDSOR FOREST.

Thy Forest, Windsor! and thy green retreats,
At once the Monarch's and the Muses' seats.

WINDSOR FOREST.

TO THE RIGHT HONOURABLE

GEORGE LORD LANSDOWN.

This poem was written at two different times: the first part of it, which relates to the country, in the year 1704, at the same time with the Pastorals; the latter part was not added till the year 1713, in which it was published.

Thy forest, Windsor, and thy green retreats,
At once the monarch's and the Muses' seats,
Invite my lays. Be present, silvan maids!
Unlock your springs, and open all your shades.
Granville commands; your aid, O muses, bring!
What muse for Granville can refuse to sing?
The groves of Eden, vanish'd now so long,
Live in description, and look green in song;
These, were my breast inspired with equal flame,
Like them in beauty, should be like in fame.
Here hills and vales, the woodland and the plain,
Here earth and water seem to strive again;
Not chaos-like, together crush'd and bruised,
But, as the world, harmoniously confused;
Where order in variety we see,
And where, though all things differ, all agree.
Here waving groves a chequer'd scene display,
And part admit, and part exclude the day;
As some coy nymph her lover's warm address
Nor quite indulges, nor can quite repress.
There, interspersed in lawns and opening glades,
Thin trees arise that shun each other's shades.
Here in full light the russet plains extend;
There, wrapt in clouds, the bluish hills ascend.
Even the wild heath displays her purple dyes,
And midst the desert fruitful fields arise,
That crown'd with tufted trees and springing corn,
Like verdant isles the sable waste adorn.
Let India boast her plants, nor envy we
The weeping-amber, or the balmy-tree,
While by our oaks the precious loads are borne,
And realms commanded which those trees adorn.
Not proud Olympus yields a nobler sight,
Though gods assembled grace his towering height,

Than what more humble mountains offer here,
Where, in their blessings, all those gods appear.
See Pan with flocks, with fruits Pomona crown'd,
Here blushing Flora paints the enamelled ground,
Here Ceres' gifts in waving prospect stand,
And, nodding, tempt the joyful reaper's hand;
Rich Industry sits smiling on the plains,
And peace and plenty tell, a STUART reigns.
Not thus the land appear'd in ages past,
A dreary desert, and a gloomy waste,
To savage beasts and savage laws a prey,
And kings more furious and severe than they;
Who claim'd the skies, dispeopled air and floods,
The lonely lords of empty wilds and woods:
Cities laid waste, they storm'd the dens and caves,
(For wiser brutes were backward to be slaves:)
What could be free when lawless beasts obey'd,
And even the elements a tyrant sway'd?
In vain kind seasons swell'd the teeming grain,
Soft showers distill'd, and suns grew warm in vain;
The swain with tears his frustrate labour yields,
And famish'd dies amidst his ripen'd fields.
What wonder then, a beast or subject slain
Were equal crimes in a despotic reign?
Both doom'd alike, for sportive tyrants bled,
But while the subject starved, the beast was fed.
Proud Nimrod first the bloody chase began,
A mighty hunter, and his prey was man:
Our haughty Norman boasts that barbarous name,
And makes his trembling slaves the royal game.
The fields are ravish'd[1] from the industrious swains,
From men their cities, and from gods their fanes:
The levelled towns with weeds lie covered o'er;
The hollow winds through naked temples roar;
Round broken columns clasping ivy twined;
O'er heaps of ruin stalk'd the stately hind;
The fox obscene to gaping tombs retires,
And savage howlings fill the sacred quires.
Awed by his nobles, by his commons curst,
The oppressor ruled tyrannic where he durst,
Stretch'd o'er the poor and church his iron rod,
And served alike his vassals and his God.

[1] Alluding to the destruction made in the New Forest by William I.

Whom even the Saxon spared, and bloody Dane,
The wanton victims of his sport remain.
But see, the man, who spacious regions gave
A waste for beasts, himself denied a grave!
Stretch'd on the lawn his second hope survey,
At once the chaser, and at once the prey:
Lo, Rufus, tugging at the deadly dart,
Bleeds in the forest like a wounded hart.
Succeeding monarchs heard the subjects' cries,
Nor saw displeased the peaceful cottage rise:
Then gathering flocks on unknown mountains fed,
O'er sandy wilds were yellow harvests spread,
The forest wondered at the unusual grain,
And secret transports touch'd the conscious swain.
Fair Liberty, Britannia's Goddess, rears
Her cheerful head, and leads the golden years.
  Ye vigorous swains! while youth ferments your [blood,
And purer spirits swell the sprightly flood,
Now range the hills, the gameful woods beset,
Wind the shrill horn, or spread the waving net.
When milder autumn summer's heat succeeds,
And in the new-shorn field the partridge feeds,
Before his lord the ready spaniel bounds,
Panting with hope, he tries the furrow'd grounds;
But when the tainted gales the game betray,
Couch'd close he lies, and meditates the prey;
Secure they trust the unfaithful field beset,
Till hovering o'er them sweeps the swelling net.
Thus (if small things we may with great compare)
When Albion sends her eager sons to war,
Some thoughtless town, with ease and plenty blest,
Near, and more near, the closing lines invest;
Sudden they seize the amazed defenceless prize,
And high in air Britannia's standard flies.
  See from the brake the whirring pheasant springs,
And mounts exulting on triumphant wings:
Short is his joy; he feels the fiery wound,
Flutters in blood, and panting beats the ground.
Ah! what avail his glossy, varying dyes,
His purple crest, and scarlet-circled eyes,
The vivid green his shining plumes unfold,
His painted wings, and breast that flames with gold?
  Nor yet, when moist Arcturus clouds the sky,
The woods and fields their pleasing toils deny.

To plains with well-breathed beagles we repair,
And trace the mazes of the circling hare:
(Beasts, urged by us, their fellow beasts pursue,
And learn of man each other to undo.)
With slaughtering guns the unwearied fowler roves,
When frosts have whitened all the naked groves;
Where doves in flocks the leafless trees o'ershade,
And lonely woodcocks haunt the watery glade
He lifts the tube, and levels with his eye;
Straight a short thunder breaks the frozen sky:
Oft, as in airy rings they skim the heath,
The clamorous lapwings feel the leaden death:
Oft, as the mounting larks their notes prepare,
They fall, and leave their little lives in air.
In genial spring, beneath the quivering shade,
Where cooling vapours breathe along the mead,
The patient fisher takes his silent stand,
Intent, his angle trembling in his hand;
With looks unmoved, he hopes the scaly breed,
And eyes the dancing cork and bending reed.
Our plenteous streams a various race supply,
The bright-eyed perch, with fins of Tyrian dye,
The silver eel, in shining volumes roll'd,
The yellow carp, in scales bedropp'd with gold,
Swift trouts, diversified with crimson stains,
And pikes, the tyrants of the watery plains.
Now Cancer glows with Phœbus' fiery car:
The youth rush eager to the silvan war,
Swarm o'er the lawns, the forest walks surround,
Rouse the fleet hart, and cheer the opening hound.
The impatient courser pants in every vein,
And pawing, seems to beat the distant plain:
Hills, vales, and floods, appear already cross'd,
And ere he starts, a thousand steps are lost.
See the bold youth strain up the threatening steep,
Rush through the thickets, down the valleys sweep,
Hang o'er their coursers' heads with eager speed,
And earth rolls back beneath the flying steed.
Let old Arcadia boast her ample plain,
The immortal huntress, and her virgin-train;
Nor envy, Windsor, since thy shades have seen
As bright a goddess, and as chaste a queen;
Whose care like hers, protects the silvan reign,
The earth's fair light, and empress of the main.

Here too, 'tis sung, of old Diana stray'd,
And Cynthus' top forsook for Windsor shade;
Here was she seen o'er airy wastes to rove,
Seek the clear spring, or haunt the pathless grove;
Here arm'd with silver bows, in early dawn,
Her buskin'd virgins traced the dewy lawn.
Above the rest a rural nymph was famed,
Thy offspring, Thames! the fair Lodona named,
(Lodona's fate, in long oblivion cast,
The Muse shall sing, and what she sings shall last.)
Scarce could the goddess from her nymph be known,
But by the crescent and the golden zone.
She scorn'd the praise of beauty, and the care;
A belt her waist, a fillet binds her hair;
A painted quiver on her shoulder sounds,
And with her dart the flying deer she wounds.
It chanced, as eager of the chase, the maid
Beyond the forest's verdant limits stray'd,
Pan saw and loved, and burning with desire
Pursued her flight, her flight increased his fire.
Not half so swift the trembling doves can fly,
When the fierce eagle cleaves the liquid sky;
Not half so swiftly the fierce eagle moves, [doves;
When through the clouds he drives the trembling
As from the god she flew with furious pace,
Or as the god, more furious, urged the chase,
Now fainting, sinking, pale, the nymph appears;
Now close behind his sounding steps she hears;
And now his shadow reach'd her as she run,
His shadow lengthen'd by the setting sun;
And now his shorter breath with sultry air,
Pants on her neck, and fans her parting hair.
In vain on Father Thames she calls for aid,
Nor could Diana help her injured maid.
Faint, breathless, thus she pray'd, nor pray'd in vain;
"Ah Cynthia! ah—though banish'd from thy train,
Let me, O let me, to the shades repair,
My native shades—there weep and murmur there."
She said, and melting as in tears she lay,
In a soft silver stream dissolved away.
The silver stream her virgin coldness keeps,
For ever murmurs, and for ever weeps;
Still bears the name the hapless virgin bore,
And bathes the forest where she ranged before.

In her chaste current oft the goddess laves,
And with celestial tears augments the waves.
Oft in her glass the musing shepherd spies
The headlong mountains and the downward skies,
The watery landscape of the pendant woods,
And absent trees that tremble in the floods;
In the clear azure gleam the flocks are seen,
And floating forests paint the waves with green,
Through the fair scene roll slow the lingering streams,
Then foaming pour along, and rush into the Thames.
Thou, too, great father of the British floods!
With joyful pride survey'st our lofty woods;
Where towering oaks their growing honours rear,
And future navies on thy shores appear.
Not Neptune's self from all her streams receives
A wealthier tribute than to thine he gives.
No seas so rich, so gay no banks appear,
No lake so gentle, and no spring so clear.
Nor Po so swells the fabling poet's lays,
While led along the skies his current strays,
As thine, which visits Windsor's famed abodes,
To grace the mansion of our earthly gods:
Nor all his stars above a lustre show,
Like the bright beauties on thy banks below;
Where Jove, subdued by mortal passion still,
Might change Olympus for a nobler hill.
Happy the man whom this bright court approves,
His sovereign favours, and his country loves:
Happy next him, who to these shades retires,
Whom nature charms, and whom the Muse inspires:
Whom humbler joys of home-felt quiet please,
Successive study, exercise, and ease.
He gathers health from herbs the forest yields,
And of their fragrant physic spoils the fields:
With chemic art exalts the mineral powers,
And draws the aromatic souls of flowers:
Now marks the course of rolling orbs on high;
O'er figured worlds now travels with his eye;
Of ancient writ unlocks the learned store,
Consults the dead, and lives past ages o'er:
Or wandering thoughtful in the silent wood,
Attends the duties of the wise and good,
To observe a mean, be to himself a friend,
To follow nature, and regard his end;

Or looks on heaven with more than mortal eyes,
Bids his free soul expatiate in the skies,
Amid her kindred stars familiar roam,
Survey the region, and confess her home!
Such was the life great Scipio once admired,
Thus Atticus, and TRUMBAL thus retired.
  Ye sacred Nine! that all my soul possess,
Whose raptures fire me, and whose visions bless,
Bear me, oh bear me to sequester'd scenes,
The bowery mazes, and surrounding greens;
To Thames's banks which fragrant breezes fill,
Or where ye Muses sport on Cooper's Hill.
(On Cooper's Hill eternal wreaths shall grow
While lasts the mountain, or while Thames shall flow.)
I seem through consecrated walks to rove,
I hear soft music die along the grove:
Led by the sound, I roam from shade to shade,
By godlike poets venerable made;
Here his first lays majestic DENHAM sung:
There the last numbers flow'd from COWLEY's[1] tongue.
O early lost! what tears the river shed,
When the sad pomp along his banks was led!
His drooping swans on every note expire,
And on his willows hung each Muse's lyre.
  Since fate relentless stopp'd their heavenly voice,
No more the forests ring, or groves rejoice;
Who now shall charm the shades, where COWLEY strung
His living harp, and lofty DENHAM sung?
But hark! the groves rejoice, the forest rings!
Are these revived? or is it GRANVILLE sings!
'Tis yours, my Lord, to bless our soft retreats,
And call the Muses to their ancient seats;
To paint anew the flowery silvan scenes,
To crown the forest with immortal greens,
Make Windsor-hills in lofty numbers rise,
And lift her turrets nearer to the skies;
To sing those honours you deserve to wear,
And add new lustre to her silver star.
  Here noble SURREY[2] felt the sacred rage,
SURREY, the GRANVILLE of a former age;

[1] Mr. Cowley died at Chertsey, on the borders of the forest, and was from thence conveyed to Westminster.

[2] Henry Howard, Earl of Surrey, one of the first refiners of the English poetry, who flourished in the time of Henry VIII.

Matchless his pen, victorious was his lance,
Bold in the lists, and graceful in the dance:
In the same shades the Cupids tuned his lyre,
To the same notes, of love, and soft desire:
Fair Geraldine, bright object of his vow,
Then fill'd the groves, as heavenly Mira now.
Oh would'st thou sing what heroes Windsor bore,
What kings first breathed upon her winding shore,
Or raise old warriors, whose adored remains
In weeping vaults her hallow'd earth contains!
With Edward's[1] acts adorn the shining page,
Stretch his long triumphs down through every age,
Draw monarchs chain'd, and Crecy's glorious field,
The lilies blazing on the regal shield:
Then, from her roofs when Verrio's colours fall,
And leave inanimate the naked wall,
Still in thy song should vanquish'd France appear,
And bleed for ever under Britain's spear.
Let softer strains ill-fated Henry[2] mourn,
And palms eternal flourish round his urn.
Here o'er the Martyr-King the marble weeps,
And, fast beside him, once-fear'd Edward[3] sleeps:
Whom not the extended Albion could contain,
From old Belerium to the northern main,
The grave unites; where e'en the great find rest,
And blended lie the oppressor and the opprest!
Make sacred Charles's tomb for ever known,
(Obscure the place, and uninscribed the stone.)
Oh fact accurst! what tears has Albion shed,
Heavens, what new wounds! and how her old have bled!
She saw her sons with purple death expire,
Her sacred domes involved in rolling fire,
A dreadful series of intestine wars,
Inglorious triumphs and dishonest scars.
At length great ANNA said—"Let discord cease!"
She said,—the world obey'd, and all was peace!
In that blest moment, from his oozy bed
Old father Thames advanced his reverend head;
His tresses dropp'd with dews, and o'er the stream
His shining horns diffused a golden gleam;

[1] Edward III. was born here.
[2] Henry VI. [3] Edward IV.

Graved on his urn appear'd the moon, that guides
His swelling waters, and alternate tides;
The figured streams in waves of silver roll'd,
And on her banks Augusta rose in gold.
Around his throne the sea-born brothers stood,
Who swell with tributary urns his flood,
First the famed authors of his ancient name,
The winding Isis and the fruitful Thame:
The Kennet swift, for silver eels renown'd;
The Loddon slow, with verdant alders crown'd;
Cole, whose dark streams his flowery islands lave;
And chalky Wey, that rolls a milky wave;
The blue, transparent Vandalis appears;
The gulfy Lee his sedgy tresses rears;
And sullen Mole, that hides his diving flood;
And silent Darent, stain'd with Danish blood.
  High in the midst, upon his urn reclined
(His sea-green mantle waving with the wind)
The god appear'd; he turned his azure eyes
Where Windsor-domes and pompous turrets rise;
Then bow'd and spoke; the winds forget to roar,
And the hush'd waves glide softly to the shore.
  "Hail, sacred Peace! hail, long-expected days,
That Thames's glory to the stars shall raise!
Though Tiber's streams immortal Rome behold,
Though foaming Hermus swells with tides of gold,
From heaven itself though sevenfold Nilus flows,
And harvests on a hundred realms bestows;
These now no more shall be the Muse's themes,
Lost in my fame, as in the sea their streams.
Let Volga's banks with iron squadrons shine,
And groves of lances glitter on the Rhine,
Let barbarous Ganges arm a servile train;
Be mine the blessings of a peaceful reign.
No more my sons shall dye with British blood
Red Iber's sands, or Ister's foaming flood:
Safe on my shore each unmolested swain
Shall tend the flocks, or reap the bearded grain;
The shady empire shall retain no trace
Of war or blood, but in the silvan chase;
The trumpet sleep, while cheerful horns are blown,
And arms employ'd on birds and beasts alone.
Behold! the ascending villas on my side
Project long shadows o'er the crystal tide;

Behold! Augusta's glittering spires increase,
And temples[1] rise, the beauteous works of peace.
I see, I see, where two fair cities bend
Their ample bow, a new Whitehall ascend!
There mighty nations shall inquire their doom,
The world's great oracle in times to come;
There kings shall sue, and suppliant states be seen
Once more to bend before a BRITISH QUEEN.
  Thy trees, fair Windsor! now shall leave their woods,
And half thy forests rush into thy floods,
Bear Britain's thunder, and her cross display,
To the bright regions of the rising day;
Tempt icy seas, where scarce the waters roll,
Where clearer flames glow round the frozen pole;
Or under southern skies exalt their sails,
Led by new stars and borne by spicy gales!
For me the balm shall bleed, and amber flow,
The coral redden, and the ruby glow,
The pearly shell its lucid globe infold,
And Phœbus warm the ripening ore to gold.
The time shall come, when free as seas or wind
Unbounded Thames shall flow for all mankind;
Whole nations enter with each swelling tide,
And seas but join the regions they divide;
Earth's distant ends our glory shall behold,
And the new world launch forth to seek the old.
Then ships of uncouth form shall stem the tide,
And feather'd people crowd my wealthy side,
And naked youths and painted chiefs admire
Our speech, our colour, and our strange attire!
Oh stretch thy reign, fair Peace! from shore to shore,
Till conquest cease, and slavery be no more;
Till the freed Indians in their native groves
Reap their own fruits, and woo their sable loves.
Peru once more a race of kings behold,
And other Mexicos be roof'd with gold.
Exiled by thee from earth to deepest hell,
In brazen bonds shall barbarous discord dwell;
Gigantic pride, pale terror, gloomy care,
And mad ambition, shall attend her there;
There purple vengeance, bathed in gore, retires,
Her weapons blunted, and extinct her fires;

[1] The fifty new churches.

There hated envy her own snakes shall feel,
And persecution mourn her broken wheel;
There faction roar, rebellion bite her chain,
And gasping furies thirst for blood in vain."
  Here cease thy flight, nor with unhallow'd lays
Touch the fair fame of Albion's golden days:
The thoughts of gods let GRANVILLE's verse recite,
And bring the scenes of opening fate to light.
My humble muse, in unambitious strains,
Paints the green forests and the flowery plains,
Where peace, descending, bids her olive spring,
And scatters blessings from her dove-like wing.
Even I more sweetly pass my careless days,
Pleased in the silent shade with empty praise;
Enough for me, that to the listening swains
First in these fields I sung the silvan strains.

ODE ON ST. CECILIA'S DAY,

MDCCVIII.

AND OTHER PIECES FOR MUSIC.

I.

DESCEND, ye Nine! descend and sing;
The breathing instruments inspire,
Wake into voice each silent string,
And sweep the sounding lyre!
    In a sadly-pleasing strain
    Let the warbling lute complain:
        Let the loud trumpet sound,
        Till the roofs all around
        The shrill echoes rebound;
While in more lengthen'd notes and slow,
The deep, majestic, solemn organs blow.
    Hark! the numbers soft and clear
    Gently steal upon the ear;
    Now louder, and yet louder rise,
    And fill with spreading sounds the skies:
Exulting in triumph now swell the bold notes,
In broken air, trembling, the wild music floats;

Till, by degrees, remote and small,
The strains decay,
And melt away,
In a dying, dying fall.

II.

By music, minds an equal temper know,
Nor swell too high, nor sink too low.
If in the breast tumultuous joys arise,
Music her soft, assuasive voice applies;
Or, when the soul is press'd with cares,
Exalts her in enlivening airs.
Warriors she fires with animated sounds;
Pours balm into the bleeding lover's wounds:
Melancholy lifts her head,
Morpheus rouses from his bed,
Sloth unfolds her arms and wakes,
Listening Envy drops her snakes;
Intestine war no more our passions wage,
And giddy factions hear away their rage.

III.

But when our country's cause provokes to arms
How martial music every bosom warms!
So when the first bold vessel dared the seas,
High on the stern the Thracian raised his strain,
While Argo saw her kindred trees
Descend from Pelion to the main.
Transported demi-gods stood round,
And men grew heroes at the sound,
Inflamed with glory's charms;
Each chief his sevenfold shield display'd,
And half unsheathed the shining blade:
And seas, and rocks, and skies rebound
To arms! to arms! to arms!

IV.

But when, through all the infernal bounds
Which flaming Phlegethon surrounds,
Love, strong as death, the poet led
To the pale nations of the dead.
What sounds were heard,
What scenes appear'd,
O'er all the dreary coasts!

Dreadful gleams,
Dismal screams,
Fires that glow,
Shrieks of woe,
Sullen moans,
Hollow groans,
And cries of tortured ghosts!
But, hark! he strikes the golden lyre;
And see! the tortured ghosts respire,
See, shady forms advance!
Thy stone, O Sisyphus, stands still,
Ixion rests upon his wheel,
And the pale spectres dance;
The Furies sink upon their iron beds,
And snakes uncurl'd hang listening round their heads.

V.

By the streams that ever flow,
By the fragrant winds that blow
O'er the Elysian flowers;
By those happy souls who dwell
In yellow meads of asphodel,
Or amaranthine bowers;
By the heroes' armed shades,
Glittering through the gloomy glades;
By the youths that died for love,
Wandering in the myrtle grove,
Restore, restore Eurydice to life:
Oh take the husband, or return the wife!

He sung, and hell consented
To hear the poet's prayer;
Stern Proserpine relented,
And gave him back the fair.
Thus song could prevail
O'er death, and o'er hell,
A conquest how hard and how glorious!
Though fate had fast bound her
With Styx nine times round her,
Yet music and love were victorious.

VI.

But soon, too soon, the lover turns his eyes:
Again she falls, again she dies, she dies!

How wilt thou now the fatal sisters move?
No crime was thine, if 'tis no crime to love.
Now under hanging mountains,
Beside the falls of fountains,
Or where Hebrus wanders,
Rolling in meanders,
All alone,
Unheard, unknown,
He makes his moan;
And calls her ghost,
For ever, ever, ever lost!
Now with furies surrounded,
Despairing, confounded,
He trembles, he glows,
Amidst Rhodope's snows:
See, wild as the winds, o'er the desert he flies;
Hark! Hæmus resounds with the Bacchanals' cries—
Ah see, he dies!
Yet even in death Eurydice he sung,
Eurydice still trembled on his tongue,
Eurydice the woods,
Eurydice the floods,
Eurydice the rocks, and hollow mountains rung.

VII.

Music the fiercest grief can charm,
And fate's severest rage disarm;
Music can soften pain to ease,
And make despair and madness please:
Our joys below it can improve,
And antedate the bliss above.
This the divine Cecilia found,
And to her Maker's praise confined the sound.
When the full organ joins the tuneful choir,
The immortal powers incline their ear;
Borne on the swelling notes our souls aspire,
While solemn airs improve the sacred fire;
And angels lean from heaven to hear.
Of Orpheus now no more let poets tell,
To bright Cecilia greater power is given;
His numbers raised a shade from hell,
Hers lift the soul to heaven.

TWO CHORUSES

TO THE TRAGEDY OF BRUTUS.

CHORUS OF ATHENIANS.

STROPHE I.

Ye shades, where sacred truth is sought;
Groves, where immortal sages taught;
Where heavenly visions Plato fired,
And Epicurus lay inspired!
In vain your guiltless laurels stood
Unspotted long with human blood.
War, horrid war, your thoughtful walks invades,
And steel now glitters in the Muses' shades.

ANTISTROPHE I.

Oh heaven-born sisters! source of art!
Who charm the sense, or mend the heart;
Who lead fair virtue's train along,
Moral truth, and mystic song!
To what new clime, what distant sky,
Forsaken, friendless, shall ye fly?
Say, will ye bless the bleak Atlantic shore?
Or bid the furious Gaul be rude no more?

STROPHE II.

When Athens sinks by fates unjust,
When wild barbarians spurn her dust;
Perhaps even Britain's utmost shore
Shall cease to blush with strangers' gore,
See arts her savage sons control,
And Athens rising near the pole!
Till some new tyrant lifts his purple hand,
And civil madness tears them from the land.

ANTISTROPHE II.

Ye gods! what justice rules the ball?
Freedom and arts together fall;
Fools grant whate'er ambition craves,
And men, once ignorant, are slaves.
Oh cursed effects of civil hate,
In every age, in every state!
Still, when the lust of tyrant power succeeds,
Some Athens perishes, some Tully bleeds.

CHORUS OF YOUTHS AND VIRGINS

SEMICHORUS.

Oh tyrant Love! hast thou possest
The prudent, learn'd, and virtuous breast?
Wisdom and wit in vain reclaim,
And arts but soften us to feel thy flame.
Love, soft intruder, enters here,
But entering learns to be sincere.
Marcus with blushes owns he loves,
And Brutus tenderly reproves.
Why, virtue, dost thou blame desire,
Which nature has imprest,
Why, nature, dost thou soonest fire
The mild and generous breast?

CHORUS.

Love's purer flames the gods approve;
The gods and Brutus bend to love:
Brutus for absent Portia sighs,
And sterner Cassius melts at Junia's eyes.
What is loose love? a transient gust,
Spent in a sudden storm of lust,
A vapour fed from wild desire,
A wandering, self-consuming fire.
But Hymen's kinder flames unite,
And burn for ever one;
Chaste as cold Cynthia's virgin light,
Productive as the sun.

SEMICHORUS.

O source of every social tie,
United wish, and mutual joy!
What various joys on one attend,
As son, as father, brother, husband, friend!
Whether his hoary sire he spies,
While thousand grateful thoughts arise;
Or meets his spouse's fonder eye;
Or views his smiling progeny:
What tender passions take their turns,
What home-felt raptures move!
His heart now melts, now leaps, now burns,
With reverence, hope, and love.

CHORUS.

Hence guilty joys, distastes, surmises,
Hence false tears, deceits, disguises,
Dangers, doubts, delays, surprises;
Fires that scorch, yet dare not shine:
Purest love's unwasting treasure,
Constant faith, fair hope, long leisure,
Days of ease, and nights of pleasure;
Sacred Hymen! these are thine.

ODE ON SOLITUDE.

Happy the man, whose wish and care
A few paternal acres bound,
Content to breathe his native air
In his own ground.

Whose herds with milk, whose fields with bread,
Whose flocks supply him with attire,
Whose trees in summer yield him shade,
In winter fire.

Blest, who can unconcern'dly find
Hours, days, and years, slide soft away,
In health of body, peace of mind,
Quiet by day,

Sound sleep by night; study and ease,
Together mixt; sweet recreation:
And innocence, which most does please
With meditation.

Thus let me live, unseen, unknown,
Thus unlamented let me die,
Steal from the world, and not a stone
Tell where I lie.

THE DYING CHRISTIAN TO HIS SOUL.

Ode.

I.

VITAL spark of heavenly flame!
Quit, oh quit this mortal frame!
Trembling, hoping, lingering, flying
Oh the pain, the bliss of dying!
Cease, fond nature, cease thy strife,
And let me languish into life!

II.

Hark! they whisper; angels say,
Sister spirit, come away!
What is this absorbs me quite?
Steals my senses, shuts my sight,
Drowns my spirits, draws my breath?
Tell me, my soul, can this be death?

III.

The world recedes; it disappears!
Heaven opens on my eyes! my ears
With sounds seraphic ring:
Lend, lend your wings! I mount! I fly!
O Grave! where is thy victory?
O Death! where is thy sting?

AN ESSAY ON CRITICISM.

Written in the year 1709.

I.

'Tis hard to say, if greater want of skill
Appear in writing or in judging ill;
But, of the two, less dangerous is the offence
To tire our patience, than mislead our sense.
Some few in that, but numbers err in this,
Ten censure wrong for one who writes amiss;
A fool might once himself alone expose,
Now one in verse makes many more in prose.
'Tis with our judgments as our watches, none
Go just alike, yet each believes his own.
In poets as true genius is but rare,
True taste as seldom is the critics' share;
Both must alike from Heaven derive their light,
These born to judge, as well as those to write.
Let such teach others who themselves excel,
And censure freely who have written well.
Authors are partial to their wit, 'tis true,
But are not critics to their judgment too?
Yet if we look more closely, we shall find
Most have the seeds of judgment in their mind:
Nature affords at least a glimmering light;
The lines, though touch'd but faintly are drawn right.
But as the slightest sketch, if justly traced,
Is by ill-colouring but the more disgraced,
So by false learning is good sense defaced:
Some are bewilder'd in the maze of schools,
And some made coxcombs nature meant but fools.
In search of wit these lose their common sense,
And then turn critics in their own defence:
Each burns alike, who can, or cannot write,
Or with a rival's or a eunuch's spite.
All fools have still an itching to deride,
And fain would be upon the laughing side.
If Mævius scribble in Apollo's spite,
There are who judge still worse than he can write.
Some have at first for wits, then poets pass'd,
Turn'd critics next, and proved plain fools at last.

Some neither can for wits nor critics pass,
As heavy mules are neither horse nor ass.
Those half-learn'd witlings, numerous in our isle,
As half-form'd insects on the banks of Nile;
Unfinish'd things, one knows not what to call,
Their generation's so equivocal:
To tell them, would a hundred tongues require,
Or one vain wit's, that might a hundred tire.
But you who seek to give and merit fame,
And justly bear a critic's noble name,
Be sure yourself and your own reach to know,
How far your genius, taste, and learning go;
Launch not beyond your depth, but be discreet,
And mark that point where sense and dulness meet.
Nature to all things fix'd the limits fit,
And wisely curb'd proud man's pretending wit.
As on the land while here the ocean gains,
In other parts it leaves wide sandy plains;
Thus in the soul while memory prevails,
The solid power of understanding fails:
Where beams of warm imagination play,
The memory's soft figures melt away.
One science only will one genius fit;
So vast is art, so narrow human wit:
Not only bounded to peculiar arts,
But oft in those confined to single parts.
Like kings we lose the conquests gain'd before,
By vain ambition still to make them more:
Each might his several province well command,
Would all but stoop to what they understand.
First follow Nature, and your judgment frame
By her just standard, which is still the same:
Unerring NATURE, still divinely bright,
One clear, unchanged, and universal light,
Life, force, and beauty, must to all impart,
At once the source, and end, and test of Art.
Art from that fund each just supply provides;
Works without show, and without pomp presides:
In some fair body thus the informing soul
With spirits feeds, with vigour fills the whole,
Each motion guides, and every nerve sustains;
Itself unseen, but in the effects remains.
Some, to whom Heaven in wit has been profuse,
Want as much more, to turn it to its use;

For wit and judgment often are at strife,
Though meant each other's aid, like man and wife.
'Tis more to guide, than spur the Muses' steed;
Restrain his fury, than provoke his speed;
The winged courser, like a generous horse,
Shows most true mettle when you check his course.
  Those RULES of old discover'd, not devised,
Are nature still, but nature methodized;
Nature, like liberty, is but restrain'd
By the same laws which first herself ordain'd.
  Hear how learn'd Greece her useful rules indites,
When to repress, and when indulge our flights:
High on Parnassus' top her sons she show'd,
And pointed out those arduous paths they trod;
Held from afar, aloft, the immortal prize,
And urged the rest by equal steps to rise.
Just precepts thus from great examples given,
She drew from them what they derived from heaven.
The generous critic fann'd the poet's fire,
And taught the world with reason to admire.
Then Criticism the Muse's handmaid proved,
To dress her charms, and make her more beloved:
But following wits from that intention stray'd,
Who could not win the mistress, woo'd the maid;
Against the poets their own arms they turn'd,
Sure to hate most the men from whom they learn'd.
So modern 'pothecaries, taught the art
By doctors' bills to play the doctor's part,
Bold in the practice of mistaken rules,
Prescribe, apply, and call their masters fools.
Some on the leaves of ancient authors prey,
Nor time nor moths e'er spoil so much as they.
Some drily plain, without invention's aid,
Write dull receipts how poems may be made.
These leave the sense, their learning to display,
And those explain the meaning quite away. [steer,
  You then whose judgment the right course would
Know well each ANCIENT's proper character;
His fable, subject, scope, in every page;
Religion, country, genius of his age:
Without all these at once before your eyes,
Cavil you may, but never criticise.
Be Homer's works your study and delight,
Read them by day, and meditate by night;

Thence form your judgment, thence your maxims bring,
And trace the Muses upward to their spring.
Still with itself compared, his text peruse;
And let your comment be the Mantuan Muse.
When first young Maro in his boundless mind
A work to outlast immortal Rome design'd,
Perhaps he seem'd above the critic's law,
And but from nature's fountain scorn'd to draw:
But when to examine every part he came,
Nature and Homer were, he found, the same.
Convinced, amazed, he checks the bold design:
And rules as strict his labour'd work confine,
As if the Stagirite o'erlook'd each line.
Learn hence for ancient rules a just esteem;
To copy nature is to copy them.
Some beauties yet no precepts can declare,
For there's a happiness as well as care.
Music resembles poetry: in each
Are nameless graces which no methods teach,
And which a master-hand alone can reach.
If, where the rules not far enough extend,
(Since rules were made but to promote their end)
Some lucky licence answer to the full
The intent proposed, that licence is a rule.
Thus Pegasus, a nearer way to take,
May boldly deviate from the common track.
Great wits sometimes may gloriously offend,
And rise to faults true critics dare not mend;
From vulgar bounds with brave disorder part,
And snatch a grace beyond the reach of art,
Which, without passing through the judgment, gains
The heart, and all its end at once attains.
In prospects thus, some objects please our eyes,
Which out of nature's common order rise,
The shapeless rock, or hanging precipice.
But though the ancients thus their rules invade,
(As kings dispense with laws themselves have made,)
Moderns, beware! or if you must offend
Against the precept, ne'er transgress its end;
Let it be seldom, and compell'd by need;
And have, at least, their precedent to plead.
The critic else proceeds without remorse,
Seizes your fame, and puts his laws in force.
I know there are, to whose presumptuous thoughts
Those freer beauties, even in them, seem faults.

Some figures monstrous and misshaped appear,
Consider'd singly, or beheld too near,
Which, but proportioned to their light or place,
Due distance reconciles to form and grace.
A prudent chief not always must display
His powers, in equal ranks, and fair array,
But with the occasion and the place comply,
Conceal his force, nay, seem sometimes to fly.
Those oft are stratagems which errors seem,
Nor is it Homer nods, but we that dream.
  Still green with bays each ancient altar stands,
Above the reach of sacrilegious hands;
Secure from flames, from envy's fiercer rage,
Destructive war, and all-involving age.
See from each clime the learn'd their incense bring!
Hear, in all tongues consenting pæans ring!
In praise so just let every voice be join'd,
And fill the general chorus of mankind.
Hail, bards triumphant! born in happier days;
Immortal heirs of universal praise!
Whose honours with increase of ages grow,
As streams roll down, enlarging as they flow;
Nations unborn your mighty names shall sound
And worlds applaud that must not yet be found!
O may some spark of your celestial fire,
The last, the meanest of your sons inspire,
(That on weak wings, from far, pursues your flights;
Glows while he reads, but trembles as he writes)
To teach vain wits a science little known,
To admire superior sense, and doubt their own!

II.

  Of all the causes which conspire to blind
Man's erring judgment, and misguide the mind,
What the weak head with strongest bias rules,
Is *pride*, the never-failing vice of fools.
Whatever nature has in worth denied,
She gives in large recruits of needful pride;
For as in bodies, thus in souls, we find
What wants in blood and spirits, swell'd with wind
Pride, where wit fails, steps in to our defence,
And fills up all the mighty void of sense.
If once right reason drives that cloud away,
Truth breaks upon us with resistless day.

Trust not yourself; but your defects to know
Make use of every friend—and every foe.
A *little learning* is a dangerous thing;
Drink deep, or taste not the Pierian spring:
There shallow draughts intoxicate the brain,
And drinking largely sobers us again.
Fired at first sight with what the Muse imparts,
In fearless youth we tempt the heights of arts,
While from the bounded level of our mind,
Short views we take, nor see the lengths behind;
But more advanced, behold with strange surprise
New distant scenes of endless science rise!
So pleased at first the towering Alps we try,
Mount o'er the vales and seem to tread the sky,
The eternal snows appear already pass'd,
And the first clouds and mountains seem the last:
But, those attain'd, we tremble to survey
The growing labours of the lengthen'd way,
The increasing prospect tires our wandering eyes,
Hills peep o'er hills, and Alps on Alps arise!
A perfect judge will read each work of wit
With the same spirit that its author writ:
Survey the WHOLE, nor seek slight faults to find
Where nature moves, and rapture warms the mind;
Nor lose for that malignant dull delight,
The generous pleasure to be charm'd with wit.
But in such lays as neither ebb nor flow,
Correctly cold, and regularly low,
That shunning faults, one quiet tenor keep;
We cannot blame indeed—but we may sleep.
In wit, as nature, what affects our hearts
Is not the exactness of peculiar parts;
'Tis not a lip, or eye, we beauty call,
But the joint force and full result of all.
Thus when we view some well-proportioned dome,
(The world's just wonder, and even thine, O Rome!)
No single parts unequally surprise,
All comes united to the admiring eyes;
No monstrous height, or breadth, or length appear;
The whole at once is bold, and regular.
Whoever thinks a faultless piece to see,
Thinks what ne'er was, nor is, nor e'er shall be.
In every work regard the writer's end,
Since none can compass more than they intend;

And if the means be just, the conduct true,
Applause, in spite of trivial faults, is due.
As men of breeding, sometimes men of wit,
To avoid great errors, must the less commit;
Neglect the rules each verbal critic lays,
For not to know some trifles is a praise.
Most critics, fond of some subservient art,
Still make the whole depend upon a part:
They talk of principles, but notions prize,
And all to one loved folly sacrifice.
  Once on a time, La Mancha's knight, they say,
A certain bard encountering on the way,
Discoursed in terms as just, with looks as sage,
As e'er could Dennis, of the Grecian stage;
Concluding all were desperate sots and fools,
Who durst depart from Aristotle's rules.
Our author, happy in a judge so nice,
Produced his play, and begg'd the knight's advice;
Made him observe the subject, and the plot,
The manners, passions, unities: what not?
All which, exact to rule, were brought about,
Were but a combat in the lists left out.
"What! leave the combat out?" exclaims the knight;
Yes, or we must renounce the Stagirite.
"Not so, by Heaven!" (he answers in a rage)
"Knights, squires, and steeds, must enter on the stage."
So vast a throng the stage can ne'er contain.
"Then build a new, or act it in a plain."
  Thus critics of less judgment than caprice,
Curious not knowing, not exact but nice,
Form short ideas; and offend in arts
(As most in manners) by a love to parts.
  Some to *conceit* alone their taste confine,
And glittering thoughts struck out at every line;
Pleased with a work where nothing's just or fit;
One glaring chaos and wild heap of wit.
Poets, like painters, thus, unskill'd to trace
The naked nature and the living grace,
With gold and jewels cover every part,
And hide with ornaments their want of art.
True wit is nature to advantage dress'd;
What oft was thought, but ne'er so well express'd;
Something, whose truth, convinced at sight we find,
That gives us back the image of our mind.

As shades more sweetly recommend the light,
So modest plainness sets off sprightly wit.
For works may have more wit than does 'em good,
As bodies perish through excess of blood.
Others for *language* all their care express,
And value books, as women men, for dress:
Their praise is still,—The style is excellent;
The sense they humbly take upon content.
Words are like leaves; and where they most abound,
Much fruit of sense beneath is rarely found:
False eloquence, like the prismatic glass,
Its gaudy colours spreads on every place;
The face of nature we no more survey,
All glares alike, without distinction gay:
But true expression, like the unchanging sun,
Clears and improves whate'er it shines upon,
It gilds all objects, but it alters none.
Expression is the dress of thought, and still
Appears more decent, as more suitable;
A vile conceit in pompous words express'd
Is like a clown in regal purple dress'd:
For different styles with different subjects sort,
As several garbs with country, town, and court.
Some by old words to fame have made pretence,
Ancients in phrase, mere moderns in their sense;
Such labour'd nothings, in so strange a style,
Amaze the unlearn'd and make the learned smile.
Unlucky, as Fungoso in the play,
These sparks with awkward vanity display
What the fine gentleman wore yesterday;
And but so mimic ancient wits at best,
As apes our grandsires, in their doublets drest.
In words, as fashions, the same rule will hold;
Alike fantastic, if too new, or old:
Be not the first by whom the new are tried,
Nor yet the last to lay the old aside.
But most by numbers judge a poet's song,
And smooth or rough, with them, is right or wrong:
In the bright Muse, though thousand charms conspire,
Her voice is all these tuneful fools admire;
Who haunt Parnassus but to please their ear,
Not mend their minds; as some to church repair,
Not for the doctrine, but the music there.

These equal syllables alone require,
Though oft the ear the open vowels tire;
While expletives their feeble aid do join;
And ten low words oft creep in one dull line:
While they ring round the same unvaried chimes,
With sure returns of still expected rhymes:
Where'er you find "the cooling western breeze,"
In the next line, it "whispers through the trees:"
If crystal streams "with pleasing murmurs creep,"
The reader's threaten'd (not in vain) with "sleep:"
Then, at the last and only couplet fraught
With some unmeaning thing they call a thought,
A needless Alexandrine ends the song,
That, like a wounded snake, drags its slow length along.
Leave such to tune their own dull rhymes, and know
What's roundly smooth, or languishingly slow;
And praise the easy vigour of a line,
Where Denham's strength and Waller's sweetness join.
True ease in writing comes from art, not chance,
As those move easiest who have learn'd to dance.
'Tis not enough no harshness gives offence,
The sound must seem an echo to the sense.
Soft is the strain when Zephyr gently blows,
And the smooth stream in smoother numbers flows;
But when loud surges lash the sounding shore,
The hoarse, rough verse should like the torrent roar:
When Ajax strives some rock's vast weight to throw,
The line too labours, and the words move slow:
Not so, when swift Camilla scours the plain,
Flies o'er the unbending corn, and skims along the main.
Hear how Timotheus' varied lays surprise,
And bid alternate passions fall and rise!
While at each change the son of Libyan Jove
Now burns with glory, and then melts with love;
Now his fierce eyes with sparkling fury glow,
Now sighs steal out, and tears begin to flow:
Persians and Greeks like turns of nature found,
And the world's victor stood subdued by sound!
The power of music all our hearts allow,
And what Timotheus was, is DRYDEN now.
Avoid extremes; and shun the fault of such,
Who still are pleased too little or too much.

At every trifle scorn to take offence,
That always shows great pride or little sense:
Those heads, as stomachs, are not sure the best
Which nauseate all, and nothing can digest.
Yet let not each gay turn thy rapture move:
For fools admire, but men of sense approve:
As things seem large which we through mist descry,
Dulness is ever apt to magnify.
Some foreign writers, some our own despise;
The ancients only, or the moderns prize.
Thus wit, like faith, by each man is applied
To one small sect, and all are damn'd beside.
Meanly they seek the blessing to confine,
And force that sun but on a part to shine,
Which not alone the southern wit sublimes,
But ripens spirits in cold northern climes;
Which from the first has shone on ages past,
Enlights the present, and shall warm the last;
Though each may feel increases and decays,
And see now clearer and now darker days.
Regard not then if wit be old or new,
But blame the false, and value still the true.
Some ne'er advance a judgment of their own,
But catch the spreading notion of the town;
They reason and conclude by precedent,
And own stale nonsense which they ne'er invent.
Some judge of authors' names, not works, and then
Nor praise nor blame the writings, but the men.
Of all this servile herd, the worst is he
That in proud dulness joins with quality.
A constant critic at the great man's board,
To fetch and carry nonsense for my lord.
What woful stuff this madrigal would be,
In some starved hackney sonneteer, or me!
But let a lord once own the happy lines,
How the wit brightens! how the style refines!
Before his sacred name flies every fault,
And each exalted stanza teems with thought!
The vulgar thus through imitation err;
As oft the learn'd by being singular;
So much they scorn the crowd, that if the throng
By chance go right, they purposely go wrong;
So schismatics the plain believers quit,
And are but damn'd for having too much wit.

Some praise at morning what they blame at night;
But always think the last opinion right.
A Muse by these is like a mistress used,
This hour she's idolized, the next abused;
While their weak heads, like towns unfortified,
'Twixt sense and nonsense daily change their side.
Ask them the cause; they're wiser still, they say;
And still to-morrow's wiser than to-day.
We think our fathers fools, so wise we grow;
Our wiser sons, no doubt, will think us so.
Once school-divines this zealous isle o'erspread;
Who knew most sentences, was deepest read;
Faith, gospel, all, seem'd made to be disputed,
And none had sense enough to be confuted:
Scotists and Thomists now in peace remain,
Amidst their kindred cobwebs in Duck-lane.[1]
If faith itself has different dresses worn,
What wonder modes in wit should take their turn?
Oft, leaving what is natural and fit,
The current folly proves the ready wit;
And authors think their reputation safe,
Which lives as long as fools are pleased to laugh.
  Some valuing those of their own side or mind,
Still make themselves the measure of mankind:
Fondly we think we honour merit then,
When we but praise ourselves in other men.
Parties in wit attend on those of state,
And public faction doubles private hate.
Pride, malice, folly, against Dryden rose,
In various shapes of parsons, critics, beaux;
But sense survived when merry jests were past,
For rising merit will buoy up at last.
Might he return, and bless once more our eyes,
New Blackmores and new Milbourns must arise:
Nay, should great Homer lift his awful head,
Zoilus again would start up from the dead.
Envy will merit, as its shade, pursue;
But like a shadow, proves the substance true:
For envied wit, like Sol eclipsed, makes known
The opposing body's grossness, not its own.
When first that sun too powerful beams displays,
It draws up vapours which obscure its rays;

[1] A place where old and second-hand books were sold formerly, near Smithfield.

But even those clouds at last adorn its way,
Reflect new glories, and augment the day.
  Be thou the first true merit to befriend;
His praise is lost, who stays till all commend.
Short is the date, alas, of modern rhymes,
And 'tis but just to let them live betimes.
No longer now that golden age appears,
When patriarch-wits survived a thousand years:
Now length of fame (our second life) is lost,
And bare threescore is all e'en that can boast;
Our sons their fathers' failing language see,
And such as Chaucer is, shall Dryden be.
So when the faithful pencil has design'd
Some bright idea of the master's mind,
Where a new world leaps out at his command,
And ready nature waits upon his hand:
When the ripe colours soften and unite,
And sweetly melt into just shade and light;
When mellowing years their full perfection give,
And each bold figure just begins to live,
The treacherous colours the fair art betray,
And all the bright creation fades away!
  Unhappy wit, like most mistaken things,
Atones not for that envy which it brings.
In youth alone its empty praise we boast,
But soon the short-lived vanity is lost:
Like some fair flower the early spring supplies,
That gaily blooms, but even in blooming dies.
What is this wit, which must our cares employ?
The owner's wife, that other men enjoy;
Then most our trouble still when most admired,
And still the more we give, the more required;
Whose fame with pains we guard, but lose with ease,
Sure some to vex, but never all to please;
'Tis what the vicious fear, the virtuous shun,
By fools 'tis hated, and by knaves undone!
  If wit so much from ignorance undergo,
Ah let not learning too commence its foe!
Of old, those met rewards who could excel,
And such were praised who but endeavour'd well:
Though triumphs were to generals only due,
Crowns were reserved to grace the soldiers too.
Now, they who reach Parnassus' lofty crown,
Employ their pains to spurn some others down;

And while self-love each jealous writer rules,
Contending wits become the sport of fools:
But still the worst with most regret commend,
For each ill author is as bad a friend.
To what base ends, and by what abject ways,
Are mortals urged through sacred lust of praise!
Ah ne'er so dire a thirst of glory boast,
Nor in the critic let the man be lost.
Good-nature and good sense must ever join;
To err is human, to forgive—divine.
 But if in noble minds some dregs remain
Not yet purged off, of spleen and sour disdain;
Discharge that rage on more provoking crimes,
Nor fear a dearth in these flagitious times.
No pardon vile obscenity should find,
Though wit and art conspire to move your mind;
But dulness with obscenity must prove
As shameful sure as impotence in love.
In the fat age of pleasure, wealth, and ease,
Sprung the rank weed, and thrived with large increase:
When love was all an easy monarch's care;
Seldom at council, never in a war:
Jilts ruled the state, and statesmen farces writ:
Nay, wits had pensions, and young lords had wit:
The fair sat panting at a courtier's play,
And not a mask went unimproved away:
The modest fan was lifted up no more,
And virgins smiled at what they blush'd before.
The following licence of a foreign reign
Did all the dregs of bold Socinus drain;
Then unbelieving priests reform'd the nation,
And taught more pleasant methods of salvation;
Where heaven's free subjects might their rights dispute,
Lest God himself should seem too absolute:
Pulpits their sacred satire learn'd to spare,
And vice admired to find a flatterer there!
Encouraged thus, wit's Titans braved the skies,
And the press groan'd with licensed blasphemies
These monsters, critics! with your darts engage,
Here point your thunder, and exhaust your rage!
Yet shun their fault, who, scandalously nice,
Will needs mistake an author into vice;
All seems infected that the infected spy,
As all looks yellow to the jaundiced eye.

III.

LEARN then what MORALS critics ought to show,
For 'tis but half a judge's task, to know.
'Tis not enough, taste, judgment, learning, join;
In all you speak, let truth and candour shine:
That not alone what to your sense is due
All may allow: but seek your friendship too.
Be silent always, when you doubt your sense;
And speak, though sure, with seeming diffidence:
Some positive, persisting fops we know,
Who, if once wrong, will needs be always so;
But you, with pleasure own your errors past,
And make each day a critique on the last.
'Tis not enough your counsel still be true;
Blunt truths more mischief than nice falsehoods do;
Men must be taught as if you taught them not,
And things unknown proposed as things forgot.
Without good-breeding truth is disapproved;
That only makes superior sense beloved.
Be niggards of advice on no pretence:
For the worst avarice is that of sense.
With mean complacence ne'er betray your trust,
Nor be so civil as to prove unjust.
Fear not the anger of the wise to raise;
Those best can bear reproof, who merit praise.
'Twere well might critics still this freedom take,
But Appius reddens at each word you speak,
And stares, tremendous[1] with a threatening eye,
Like some fierce tyrant in old tapestry.
Fear most to tax an honourable fool,
Whose right it is, uncensured, to be dull;
Such, without wit, are poets when they please,
As without learning they can take degrees.
Leave dangerous truths to unsuccessful satires,
And flattery to fulsome dedicators,
Whom, when they praise, the world believes no more,
Than when they promise to give scribbling o'er.

1 This picture was taken to himself by John Dennis, a furious old critic by profession, who, upon no other provocation, wrote against this essay and its author, in a manner perfectly lunatic: for as to the mention made of him in ver. 270, he took it as a compliment, and said it was treacherously meant to cause him to overlook this abuse of his person.

'Tis best sometimes your censure to restrain,
And charitably let the dull be vain:
Your silence there is better than your spite,
For who can rail so long as they can write?
Still humming on, their drowsy course they keep,
And lash'd so long, like tops, are lash'd asleep.
False steps but help them to renew the race,
As, after stumbling, jades will mend their pace.
What crowds of these, impenitently bold,
In sounds and jingling syllables grown old,
Still run on poets in a raging vein,
Even to the dregs and squeezing of the brain,
Strain out the last dull droppings of their sense,
And rhyme with all the rage of impotence.
  Such shameless bards we have; and yet 'tis true,
There are as mad, abandon'd critics too.
The bookful blockhead ignorantly read,
With loads of learned lumber in his head,
With his own tongue still edifies his ears,
And always listening to himself appears.
All books he reads, and all he reads assails,
From Dryden's Fables down to D'Urfey's Tales.
With him most authors steal their works, or buy;
Garth did not write his own Dispensary.[1]
Name a new play, and he's the poet's friend,
Nay, show'd his faults—but when would poets mend?
No place so sacred from such fops is barr'd,
Nor is Paul's church more safe than Paul's church-yard:
Nay, fly to altars; there they'll talk you dead;
For fools rush in where angels fear to tread.
Distrustful sense with modest caution speaks,
It still looks home, and short excursions makes;
But rattling nonsense in full volleys breaks,
And never shock'd, and never turn'd aside,
Bursts out, resistless, with a thundering tide.
  But where's the man who counsel can bestow,
Still pleased to teach, and yet not proud to know?
Unbiass'd, or by favour or by spite;
Not dully prepossess'd, nor blindly right;

[1] A common slander at that time in prejudice of that deserving ithor. Our poet did him this justice, when that slander most preiled; and it is now (perhaps the sooner for this very verse) dead and rgotten.

Though learn'd, well-bred; and though well-bred, sincere;
Modestly bold, and humanly severe;
Who to a friend his faults can freely show,
And gladly praise the merit of a foe?
Blest with a taste exact, yet unconfined;
A knowledge both of books and human kind;
Generous converse; a soul exempt from pride;
And love to praise, with reason on his side?
Such once were critics; such the happy few,
Athens and Rome in better ages knew.
The mighty Stagirite first left the shore,
Spread all his sails, and durst the deeps explore;
He steer'd securely, and discover'd far,
Led by the light of the Mæonian star.
Poets, a race long unconfined and free,
Still fond and proud of savage liberty,
Received his laws; and stood convinced 'twas fit,
Who conquer'd nature should preside o'er wit.
Horace still charms with graceful negligence,
And without method talks us into sense;
Will, like a friend, familiarly convey
The truest notions in the easiest way.
He, who, supreme in judgment as in wit,
Might boldly censure, as he boldly writ,
Yet judged with coolness, though he sung with fire;
His precepts teach but what his works inspire.
Our critics take a contrary extreme,
They judge with fury, but they write with phlegm:
Nor suffers Horace more in wrong translations
By wits, than critics in as wrong quotations.
See Dionysius Homer's thoughts refine,
And call new beauties forth from every line!
Fancy and art in gay Petronius please,
The scholar's learning with the courtier's ease.
In grave Quintilian's copious work, we find
The justest rules and clearest method join'd:
Thus useful arms in magazines we place,
All ranged in order, and disposed with grace,
But less to please the eye, than arm the hand,
Still fit for use, and ready at command.
Thee, bold Longinus! all the Nine inspire,
And bless their critic with a poet's fire.
An ardent judge, who, jealous in his trust,
With warmth gives sentence, yet is always just:

Whose own example strengthens all his laws;
And is himself that great sublime he draws.
  Thus long succeeding critics justly reign'd,
Licence repress'd, and useful laws ordain'd.
Learning and Rome alike in empire grew;
And arts still follow'd where her eagles flew;
From the same foes at last both felt their doom,
And the same age saw learning fall and Rome.
Then tyranny with superstition join'd,
As that the body, this enslaved the mind;
Much was believed, but little understood,
And to be dull was construed to be good;
A second deluge learning thus o'errun,
And the monks finish'd what the Goths begun.
  At length Erasmus, that great injured name,
(The glory of the priesthood and the shame!)
Stemm'd the wild torrent of a barbarous age,
And drove those holy Vandals off the stage.
But see! each muse, in Leo's golden days,
Starts from her trance, and trims her withered bays,
Rome's ancient genius, o'er its ruins spread,
Shakes off the dust, and rears his reverend head.
Then sculpture and her sister-arts revive;
Stones leap'd to form, and rocks began to live;
With sweeter notes each rising temple rung;
A Raphael painted, and a Vida sung.
Immortal Vida! on whose honour'd brow
The poet's bays and critic's ivy grow:
Cremona now shall ever boast thy name,
As next in place to Mantua, next in fame!
  But soon by impious arms from Latium chased,
Their ancient bounds the banish'd Muses pass'd.
Thence arts o'er all the northern world advance,
But critic-learning flourish'd most in France;
The rules a nation, born to serve, obeys;
And Boileau still in right of Horace sways.
But we, brave Britons, foreign laws despised,
And kept unconquer'd, and uncivilized;
Fierce for the liberties of wit, and bold,
We still defied the Romans, as of old.
Yet some there were, among the sounder few
Of those who less presumed and better knew,
Who durst assert the juster ancient cause,
And here restored wit's fundamental laws.

Such was the Muse,[1] whose rules and practice tell,
"Nature's chief masterpiece is writing well."
Such was Roscommon, not more learn'd than good,
With manners generous as his noble blood;
To him the wit of Greece and Rome was known,
And every author's merit, but his own.
Such late was Walsh—the Muse's judge and friend,
Who justly knew to blame or to commend!
To failings mild, but zealous for desert;
The clearest head, and the sincerest heart.
This humble praise, lamented shade, receive!
This praise at least a grateful muse may give:
The muse, whose early voice you taught to sing,
Prescribed her heights, and pruned her tender wing,
(Her guide now lost) no more attempts to rise,
But in low numbers short excursions tries:
Content, if hence the unlearn'd their wants may view,
The learn'd reflect on what before they knew:
Careless of censure, nor too fond of fame;
Still pleased to praise, yet not afraid to blame;
Averse alike to flatter, or offend;
Not free from faults, nor yet too vain to mend.

1 *Essay on Poetry* by the Duke of Buckingham. Our poet is not the only one of his time who complimented this *Essay* and its noble author. Mr. Dryden had done it very largely, in the dedication to his translation of the Æneid; and Dr. Garth in the first edition of his Dispensary says,

"The Tyber now no courtly Gallus sees,
But smiling Thames enjoys his Normanbys;"

though afterwards omitted, when parties were carried so high in the reign of Queen Anne, as to allow no commendation to an opposite in politics. The duke was all his life a steady adherent to the Church of England party, yet an enemy to the extravagant measures of the court in the reign of Charles II. On which account, after having strongly patronized Mr. Dryden, a coolness succeeded between them on that poet's absolute attachment to the court, which carried him some length beyond what the duke could approve of. This nobleman's true character had been very well marked by Mr. Dryden before:

"The Muse's friend,
Himself a muse. In Sanadrin's debate
True to his prince, but not a slave of state."
ABS. AND ACHIT.

Our author was more happy; he was honoured very young with his friendship, and it continued till his death in all the circumstances of a familiar esteem.

THE RAPE OF THE LOCK

AN HEROI-COMICAL POEM.

Written in the year 1712.

TO MRS. ARABELLA FERMOR.

MADAM,

IT will be in vain to deny that I have some regard for this piece, since I dedicate it to you. Yet you may bear me witness, it was intended only to divert a few young ladies, who have good sense and good humour enough to laugh not only at their sex's little unguarded follies, but at their own. But as it was communicated with the air of a secret, it soon found its way into the world. An imperfect copy having been offered to a bookseller, you had the goodnature for my sake to consent to the publication of one more correct: this I was forced to, before I had executed half my design, for the machinery was entirely wanting to complete it.

The machinery, madam, is a term invented by the critics, to signify that part which the deities, angels, or demons, are made to act in a poem: for the ancient poets are in one respect like many modern ladies; let an action be never so trivial in itself, they always make it appear of the utmost importance. These machines I determined to raise on a very new and odd foundation, the Rosicrucian doctrine of spirits.

I know how disagreeable it is to make use of hard words before a lady; but 'tis so much the concern of a poet to have his works understood, and particularly by your sex, that you must give me leave to explain two or three difficult terms.

The Rosicrucians are a people I must bring you acquainted with. The best account I know of them is in a French book called *Le Comte de Gabalis*, which both in its title and size is so like a novel, that many of the fair sex have read it for one by mistake. According to these gentlemen, the four elements are inhabited by spirits, which they call sylphs, gnomes, nymphs, and salamanders. The gnomes, or demons of earth, delight in mischief; but the sylphs, whose habitation is in the air, are the best-conditioned creatures imaginable. For they say, any mortals may enjoy the most intimate familiarities with these gentle spirits, upon a condition very easy to all true adepts, an inviolate preservation of chastity.

As to the following cantos, all the passages of them are as fabulous as the vision at the beginning, or the transformation at the end (except the loss of your hair, which I always mention with reverence). The human persons are as fictitious as the airy ones; and the character of Belinda, as it is now managed, resembles you in nothing but in beauty.

If this poem had as many graces as there are in your person, or in your mind, yet I could never hope it should pass through the world half so uncensured as you have done. But let its fortune be what it will, mine is happy enough, to have given me this occasion of assuring you that I am, with the truest esteem, Madam,

Your most obedient, humble servant,

A. POPE.

Nolueram, Belinda, tuos violare capillos;
Sed juvat, hoc precibus me tribuisse tuis.—*Mart.*

It appears by this motto, that the following poem was written or published at the lady's request. But there are some further circumstances not unworthy relating. Mr. Caryl (a gentleman who was secretary to Queen Mary, wife of James II., whose fortunes he followed into France, author of the comedy of Sir Solomon Single, and of several translations in Dryden's Miscellanies) originally proposed the subject to him, in a view of putting an end, by this piece of ridicule, to a quarrel that was risen between two noble families, those of Lord Petre and of Mrs. Fermor, on the trifling occasion of his having cut off a lock of her hair. The author sent it to the lady with whom he was acquainted; and she took it so well as to give about copies of it.

CANTO FIRST.

WHAT dire offence from amorous causes springs,
What mighty contests rise from trivial things,
I sing—This verse to CARYL, muse! is due:
This, even Belinda may vouchsafe to view:
Slight is the subject, but not so the praise,
If she inspire, and he approve my lays.
Say what strange motive, goddess! could compel
A well-bred lord to assault a gentle belle?
O say what stranger cause, yet unexplored,
Could make a gentle belle reject a lord?
In tasks so bold can little men engage,
And in soft bosoms dwells such mighty rage?
Sol through white curtains shot a timorous ray,
And oped those eyes that must eclipse the day:
Now lap-dogs give themselves the rousing shake,
And sleepless lovers, just at twelve, awake:
Thrice rung the bell, the slipper knock'd the ground,
And the press'd watch return'd a silver sound.
Belinda still her downy pillow prest,
Her guardian SYLPH prolonged the balmy rest:
'Twas he had summoned to her silent bed
The morning-dream that hover'd o'er her head;
A youth more glittering than a birth-night beau
(That e'en in slumber caused her cheek to glow)
Seem'd to her ear his winning lips to lay,
And thus in whispers said, or seem'd to say:

Fairest of mortals, thou distinguish'd care
Of thousand bright inhabitants of air!
If e'er one vision touch'd thy infant thought,
Of all the nurse and all the priest have taught;
Of airy elves by moonlight shadows seen,
The silver token, and the circled green,
Or virgins visited by angel-powers
With golden crowns and wreaths of heavenly flowers;
Hear and believe! thy own importance know,
Nor bound thy narrow views to things below.
Some secret truths, from learned pride conceal'd,
To maids alone and children are reveal'd:
What though no credit doubting wits may give?
The fair and innocent shall still believe.
Know, then, unnumber'd spirits round thee fly,
The light militia of the lower sky:
These, though unseen, are ever on the wing,
Hang o'er the box, and hover round the ring
Think what an equipage thou hast in air,
And view with scorn two pages and a chair.
As now your own, our beings were of old,
And once enclosed in woman's beauteous mould;
Thence, by a soft transition, we repair
From earthly vehicles to those of air.
Think not, when woman's transient breath is fled,
That all her vanities at once are dead;
Succeeding vanities she still regards,
And though she plays no more, o'erlooks the cards.
Her joy in gilded chariots, when alive,
And love of ombre, after death survive.
For when the fair in all their pride expire,
To their first elements their souls retire:
The sprites of fiery termagants in flame
Mount up, and take a salamander's name.
Soft yielding minds to water glide away,
And sip, with nymphs, their elemental tea.
The graver prude sinks downward to a gnome,
In search of mischief still on earth to roam.
The light coquettes in sylphs aloft repair,
And sport and flutter in the fields of air.
Know further yet; whoever fair and chaste
Rejects mankind, is by some sylph embraced:
For spirits, freed from mortal laws, with ease
Assume what sexes and what shapes they please.

What guards the purity of melting maids,
In courtly balls, and midnight masquerades,
Safe from the treacherous friend, the daring spark,
The glance by day, the whisper in the dark,
When kind occasion prompts their warm desires,
When music softens, and when dancing fires?
'Tis but their sylph, the wise celestials know,
Though honour is the word with men below.
Some nymphs there are, too conscious of their face,
For life predestined to the gnomes' embrace.
These swell their prospects and exalt their pride,
When offers are disdain'd, and love denied:
Then gay ideas crowd the vacant brain,
While peers, and dukes, and all their sweeping train,
And garters, stars, and coronets appear,
And in soft sounds, YOUR GRACE salutes their ear.
'Tis these that early taint the female soul,
Instruct the eyes of young coquettes to roll,
Teach infant-cheeks a hidden blush to know,
And little hearts to flutter at a beau.
Oft, when the world imagine women stray,
The sylphs through mystic mazes guide their way,
Through all the giddy circle they pursue,
And old impertinence expel by new.
What tender maid but must a victim fall
To one man's treat, but for another's ball?
When Florio speaks, what virgin could withstand,
If gentle Damon did not squeeze her hand?
With varying vanities, from every part,
They shift the moving toyshop of their heart;
Where wigs with wigs, with sword-knots sword-knots strive,
Beaux banish beaux, and coaches coaches drive.
This erring mortals levity may call,
Oh, blind to truth! the sylphs contrive it all.
Of these am I, who thy protection claim,
A watchful sprite, and Ariel is my name.
Late, as I ranged the crystal wilds of air,
In the clear mirror of thy ruling star
I saw, alas! some dread event impend,
Ere to the main this morning sun descend,
But heaven reveals not what, or how, or where:
Warn'd by the sylph, oh, pious maid, beware!
This to disclose is all thy guardian can:
Beware of all, but most beware of man!

He said; when Shock, who thought she slept too long,
Leap'd up, and waked his mistress with his tongue.
'Twas then, Belinda, if report say true,
Thy eyes first open'd on a billet-doux;
Wounds, charms, and ardours, were no sooner read,
But all the vision vanish'd from thy head.
And now, unveil'd, the toilet stands display'd,
Each silver vase in mystic order laid.
First, robed in white, the nymph intent adores,
With head uncover'd, the cosmetic powers.
A heavenly image in the glass appears,
To that she bends, to that her eyes she rears;
The inferior priestess, at her altar's side,
Trembling begins the sacred rites of pride.
Unnumber'd treasures ope at once, and here
The various offerings of the world appear;
From each she nicely culls with curious toil,
And decks the goddess with the glittering spoil.
This casket India's glowing gems unlocks,
And all Arabia breathes from yonder box.
The tortoise here and elephant unite,
Tranform'd to combs, the speckled, and the white.
Here files of pins extend their shining rows,
Puffs, powders, patches, bibles, billets-doux.
Now awful beauty puts on all its arms;
The fair each moment rises in her charms,
Repairs her smiles, awakens every grace,
And calls forth all the wonders of her face;
Sees by degrees a purer blush arise,
And keener lightnings quicken in her eyes.
The busy sylphs[1] surround their darling care,
These set the head, and those divide the hair,
Some fold the sleeve, whilst others plait the gown;
And Betty's praised for labours not her own.

CANTO SECOND.

Not with more glories, in the ethereal plain,
The sun first rises o'er the purpled main,
Than, issuing forth, the rival of his beams
Launch'd on the bosom of the silver Thames.

[1] Ancient traditions of the rabbis relate, that several of the fallen angels became amorous of women, and particularize some; among the rest, Asael, who was enamoured with Naamah, the wife of Noah, or of Ham; and who, continuing impenitent, still presides over the women's toilets.

Fair nymphs and well-dress'd youths around her shone,
But every eye was fix'd on her alone.
On her white breast a sparkling cross she wore
Which Jews might kiss, and Infidels adore.
Her lively looks a sprightly mind disclose,
Quick as her eyes, and as unfix'd as those:
Favours to none, to all she smiles extends;
Oft she rejects, but never once offends.
Bright as the sun, her eyes the gazers strike,
And like the sun, they shine on all alike.
Yet graceful ease, and sweetness void of pride,
Might hide her faults, if belles had faults to hide:
If to her share some female errors fall,
Look on her face, and you'll forget 'em all.
This nymph, to the destruction of mankind,
Nourish'd two locks, which graceful hung behind
In equal curls, and well conspired to deck
With shining ringlets the smooth ivory neck.
Love in these labyrinths his slaves detains,
And mighty hearts are held in slender chains.
With hairy springes we the birds betray,
Slight lines of hair surprise the finny prey,
Fair tresses man's imperial race insnare,
And beauty draws us with a single hair.
The adventurous Baron the bright locks admired;
He saw, he wish'd, and to the prize aspired.
Resolved to win, he meditates the way,
By force to ravish, or by fraud betray;
For when success a lover's toil attends,
Few ask, if fraud or force attain'd his ends.
For this, ere Phœbus rose, he had implored
Propitious Heaven, and every power adored,
But chiefly Love—to Love an altar built,
Of twelve vast French romances, neatly gilt.
There lay three garters, half a pair of gloves,
And all the trophies of his former loves;
With tender billets-doux he lights the pyre,
And breathes three amorous sighs to raise the fire.
Then prostrate falls, and begs with ardent eyes
Soon to obtain, and long possess the prize:
The powers gave ear, and granted half his prayer,
The rest, the winds dispersed in empty air.
But now secure the painted vessel glides,
The sunbeams trembling on the floating tides:

While melting music steals upon the sky,
And soften'd sounds along the waters die;
Smooth flow the waves, the zephyrs gently play,
Belinda smiled, and all the world was gay—
All but the sylph; with careful thoughts opprest,
The impending woe sat heavy on his breast.
He summons straight his denizens of air;
The lucid squadrons round the sails repair:
Soft o'er the shrouds aërial whispers breathe,
That seem'd but zephyrs to the train beneath.
Some to the sun their insect-wings unfold,
Waft on the breeze, or sink in clouds of gold;
Transparent forms, too fine for mortal sight,
Their fluid bodies half dissolved in light,
Loose to the wind their airy garments flew,
Thin glittering textures of the filmy dew,
Dipt in the richest tincture of the skies,
Where light disports in ever-mingling dyes;
While every beam new transient colours flings,
Colours that change whene'er they wave their wings.
Amid the circle, on the gilded mast,
Superior by the head, was Ariel placed;
His purple pinions opening to the sun,
He raised his azure wand, and thus begun:—
  Ye sylphs and sylphids, to your chief give ear,
Fays, fairies, genii, elves, and demons, hear!
Ye know the spheres, and various tasks assign'd
By laws eternal to the aërial kind.
Some in the fields of purest ether play,
And bask and whiten in the blaze of day;
Some guide the course of wandering orbs on high,
Or roll the planets through the boundless sky;
Some, less refined, beneath the moon's pale light
Pursue the stars that shoot athwart the night,
Or suck the mists in grosser air below,
Or dip their pinions in the painted bow,
Or brew fierce tempests on the wintry main,
Or o'er the glebe distil the kindly rain;
Others on earth o'er human race preside,
Watch all their ways, and all their actions guide:
Of these the chief the care of nations own,
And guard with arms divine the British throne.
  Our humbler province is to tend the fair,
Not a less pleasing, though less glorious care;

To save the powder from too rude a gale,
Nor let the imprison'd essences exhale;
To draw fresh colours from the vernal flowers;
To steal from rainbows ere they drop in showers
A brighter wash; to curl their waving hairs,
Assist their blushes, and inspire their airs;
Nay oft, in dreams, invention we bestow,
To change a flounce, or add a furbelow.
  This day, black omens threat the brightest fair
That e'er deserved a watchful spirit's care;
Some dire disaster, or by force or slight;
But what, or where, the fates have wrapt in night.
Whether the nymph shall break Diana's law,
Or some frail China jar receive a flaw;
Or stain her honour, or her new brocade;
Forget her prayers, or miss a masquerade;
Or lose her heart, or necklace, at a ball;
Or whether Heaven has doom'd that Shock must fall.
Haste then, ye spirits! to your charge repair:
The fluttering fan be Zephyretta's care;
The drops to thee, Brillante, we consign;
And, Momentilla, let the watch be thine;
Do thou, Crispissa, tend her favourite Lock;
Ariel himself shall be the guard of Shock.
  To fifty chosen sylphs, of special note,
We trust the important charge, the petticoat:
Oft have we known that sevenfold fence to fail,
Though stiff with hoops and arm'd with ribs of whale;
Form a strong line about the silver bound,
And guard the wide circumference around.
  Whatever spirit, careless of his charge,
His post neglects, or leaves the fair at large,
Shall feel sharp vengeance soon o'ertake his sins,
Be stopp'd in vials, or transfix'd with pins;
Or plunged in lakes of bitter washes lie,
Or wedged whole ages in a bodkin's eye:
Gums and pomatums shall his flight restrain,
While clogg'd he beats his silken wings in vain;
Or alum styptics, with contracting power,
Shrink his thin essence like a rivel'd flower:
Or, as Ixion fix'd, the wretch shall feel
The giddy motion of the whirling mill,
In fumes of burning chocolate shall glow,
And tremble at the sea that froths below!

He spoke; the spirits from the sails descend;
Some, orb in orb, around the nymph extend;
Some thread the mazy ringlets of her hair;
Some hang upon the pendants of her ear;
With beating hearts the dire event they wait,
Anxious, and trembling for the birth of fate.

CANTO THIRD.

Close by those meads, for ever crown'd with flowers,
Where Thames with pride surveys his rising towers,
There stands a structure of majestic frame, [name.
Which from the neighbouring Hampton takes its
Here Britain's statesmen oft the fall foredoom
Of foreign tyrants, and of nymphs at home;
Here thou, great Anna! whom three realms obey,
Dost sometimes counsel take—and sometimes tea.
Hither the heroes and the nymphs resort,
To taste awhile the pleasures of a court;
In various talk the instructive hours they pass'd
Who gave the ball, or paid the visit last;
One speaks the glory of the British Queen,
And one describes a charming Indian screen;
A third interprets motions, looks, and eyes;
At every word a reputation dies.
Snuff, or the fan, supplies each pause of chat,
With singing, laughing, ogling, and all that.
Meanwhile, declining from the noon of day,
The sun obliquely shoots his burning ray:
The hungry judges soon the sentence sign,
And wretches hang that jurymen may dine;
The merchant from the Exchange returns in peace,
And the long labours of the toilet cease.
Belinda now, whom thirst of fame invites,
Burns to encounter two adventurous knights,
At ombre singly to decide their doom;
And swells her breast with conquests yet to come.
Straight the three bands prepare in arms to join,
Each band the number of the sacred Nine.
Soon as she spreads her hand, the aërial guard
Descend, and sit on each important card:
First Ariel perch'd upon a Matadore,
Then each according to the rank they bore;

For sylphs, yet mindful of their ancient race,
Are, as when women, wondrous fond of place.
  Behold, four kings, in majesty revered,
With hoary whiskers and a forky beard;
And four fair queens whose hands sustain a flower,
The expressive emblem of their softer power;
Four knaves in garbs succinct. a trusty band,
Caps on their heads, and halberts in their hand;
And party-colour'd troops, a shining train,
Draw forth to combat on the velvet plain.
  The skilful nymph reviews her force with care;
Let spades be trumps! she said, and trumps they were.
  Now move to war her sable Matadores,
In show like leaders of the swarthy Moors.
Spadillio first, unconquerable lord!
Led off two captive trumps, and swept the board.
As many more Manillio forced to yield,
And march'd a victor from the verdant field.
Him Basto follow'd, but his fate more hard
Gain'd but one trump and one plebeian card.
With his broad sabre next, a chief in years,
The hoary majesty of spades appears,
Puts forth one manly leg, to sight reveal'd,
The rest, his many-colour'd robe conceal'd.
The rebel knave, who dares his prince engage,
Proves the just victim of his royal rage.
Even mighty Pam, that kings and queens o'erthrew,
And mow'd down armies in the fights of Loo,
Sad chance of war! now destitute of aid,
Falls undistinguish'd by the victor spade!
  Thus far both armies to Belinda yield.
Now to the Baron Fate inclines the field;
His warlike amazon her host invades,
The imperial consort of the crown of Spades.
The Clubs' black tyrant first her victim died,
Spite of his haughty mien and barbarous pride:
What boots the regal circle on his head,
His giant limbs, in state unwieldy spread;
That long behind he trails his pompous robe,
And, of all monarchs, only grasps the globe?
  The Baron now his Diamonds pours apace;
The embroider'd King who shows but half his face,
And his refulgent queen, with powers combined
Of broken troops an easy conquest find.

Clubs, Diamonds, Hearts, in wild disorder seen,
With throngs promiscuous strow the level green.
Thus when dispersed a routed army runs,
Of Asia's troops, and Afric's sable sons,
With like confusion different nations fly,
Of various habit, and of various dye; -
The pierced battalions disunited fall,
In heaps on heaps; one fate o'erwhelms them all.
The Knave of Diamonds tries his wily arts,
And wins (oh shameful chance!) the Queen of Hearts.
At this, the blood the virgin's cheek forsook,
A livid paleness spreads o'er all her look;
She sees, and trembles at the approaching ill,
Just in the jaws of ruin, and codille.
And now (as oft in some distemper'd state)
On one nice trick depends the general fate;
An Ace of Hearts steps forth; the King, unseen,
Lurk'd in her hand, and mourn'd his captive Queen:
He springs to vengeance with an eager pace,
And falls like thunder on the prostrate Ace.
The nymph exulting fills with shouts the sky;
The walls, the woods, and long canals reply.
Oh, thoughtless mortals! ever blind to fate,
Too soon dejected, and too soon elate.
Sudden these honours shall be snatch'd away,
And cursed for ever this victorious day.
For lo! the board with cups and spoons is crown'd,
The berries crackle, and the mill turns round;
On shining altars of Japan they raise
The silver lamp; the fiery spirits blaze:
From silver spouts the grateful liquors glide,
While China's earth receives the smoking tide:
At once they gratify their scent and taste,
And frequent cups prolong the rich repast.
Straight hover round the fair her airy band;
Some, as she sipp'd, the fuming liquor fann'd,
Some o'er her lap their careful plumes display'd,
Trembling, and conscious of the rich brocade.
Coffee (which makes the politician wise,
And see through all things with his half-shut eyes)
Sent up in vapours to the Baron's brain
New stratagems, the radiant Lock to gain.
Ah cease, rash youth! desist ere 'tis too late,
Fear the just gods, and think of Scylla's fate!

Changed to a bird, and sent to flit in air,
She dearly pays for Nisus' injured hair!
But when to mischief mortals bend their will,
How soon they find fit instruments of ill!
Just then Clarissa drew, with tempting grace,
A two-edged weapon from her shining case:
So ladies in romance assist their knight,
Present the spear, and arm him for the fight.
He takes the gift with reverence, and extends
The little engine on his fingers' ends;
This just behind Belinda's neck he spread,
As o'er the fragrant steams she bends her head.
Swift to the Lock a thousand sprites repair,
A thousand wings, by turns, blow back the hair;
And thrice they twitch'd the diamond in her ear;
Thrice she look'd back, and thrice the foe drew near.
Just in that instant anxious Ariel sought
The close recesses of the virgin's thought:
As on the nosegay in her breast reclined,
He watch'd the ideas rising in her mind,
Sudden he view'd, in spite of all her art,
An earthly lover lurking at her heart.
Amazed, confused, he found his power expired,
Resign'd to fate, and with a sigh retired.
The peer now spreads the glittering forfex wide,
To inclose the Lock; now joins it, to divide.
Even then, before the fatal engine closed,
A wretched sylph too fondly interposed;
Fate urged the shears, and cut the sylph in twain,
(But airy substance soon unites again;)
The meeting points the sacred hair dissever
From the fair head, for ever, and for ever!
Then flash'd the living lightning from her eyes,
And screams of horror rend the affrighted skies;
Not louder shrieks to pitying heaven are cast,
When husbands, or when lap-dogs, breathe their last;
Or when rich China vessels, fallen from high,
In glittering dust and painted fragments lie!
Let wreaths of triumph now my temples twine,
(The victor cried,) the glorious prize is mine!
While fish in streams, or birds delight in air,
Or in a coach-and-six the British fair,
As long as Atalantis shall be read,
Or the small pillow grace a lady's bed,

p. 74.

THE RAPE OF THE LOCK.

The peer now spreads the glittering forfex wide,
To enclose the lock: now joins it, to divide.

While visits shall be paid on solemn days,
When numerous wax-lights in bright order blaze,
While nymphs take treats, or assignations give,
So long my honour, name, and praise, shall live!
What time would spare, from steel receives its date,
And monuments, like men, submit to fate!
Steel could the labour of the gods destroy,
And strike to dust the imperial towers of Troy
Steel could the works of mortal pride confound,
And hew triumphal arches to the ground.
What wonder then, fair nymph! thy hairs should feel
The conquering force of unresisted steel?

CANTO FOURTH.

But anxious cares the pensive nymph oppress'd,
And secret passions labour'd in her breast
Not youthful kings in battle seized alive,
Not scornful virgins who their charms survive,
Not ardent lovers robb'd of all their bliss,
Not ancient ladies when refused a kiss,
Not tyrants fierce that unrepenting die,
Not Cynthia when her manteau's pinn'd awry,
E'er felt such rage, resentment, and despair,
As thou, sad virgin! for thy ravish'd hair.
For, that sad moment, when the sylphs withdrew,
And Ariel weeping from Belinda flew,
Umbriel, a dusky, melancholy sprite,
As ever sullied the fair face of light,
Down to the central earth, his proper scene,
Repair'd to search the gloomy cave of Spleen
Swift on his sooty pinions flits the gnome,
And in a vapour reach'd the dismal dome.
No cheerful breeze this sullen region knows,
The dreaded east is all the wind that blows.
Here in a grotto shelter'd close from air,
And screen'd in shades from day's detested glare,
She sighs for ever on her pensive bed,
Pain at her side, and Megrim at her head
Two handmaids wait the throne: alike in place,
But differing far in figure and in face.
Here stood Ill-nature, like an ancient maid,
Her wrinkled form in black and white array'd,

With store of prayers, for mornings, nights, and noons,
Her hand is fill'd; her bosom with lampoons.
There Affectation, with a sickly mien,
Shows in her cheek the roses of eighteen;
Practised to lisp, and hang the head aside,
Faints into airs, and languishes with pride,
On the rich quilt sinks with becoming woe,
Wrapt in a gown, for sickness, and for show.
The fair ones feel such maladies as these,
When each new night-dress gives a new disease.
A constant vapour o'er the palace flies;
Strange phantoms rising as the mists arise;
Dreadful, as hermits' dreams in haunted shades,
Or bright, as visions of expiring maids.
Now glaring fiends, and snakes on rolling spires,
Pale spectres, gaping tombs, and purple fires:
Now lakes of liquid gold, Elysian scenes,
And crystal domes, and angels in machines.
Unnumber'd throngs on every side are seen,
Of bodies changed to various forms by Spleen.
Here living tea-pots stand, one arm held out,
One bent; the handle this, and that the spout:
A pipkin there, like Homer's tripod, walks;[1]
Here sighs a jar, and there a goose-pie talks;[2]
Men prove with child, as powerful fancy works,
And maids, turn'd bottles, call aloud for corks.
Safe pass'd the gnome through this fantastic band,
A branch of healing spleenwort in his hand.
Then thus address'd the power—Hail, wayward queen!
Who rule the sex to fifty from fifteen:
Parent of vapours and of female wit,
Who give the hysteric, or poetic fit,
On various tempers act by various ways,
Make some take physic, others scribble plays;
Who cause the proud their visits to delay,
And send the godly in a pet to pray.
A nymph there is that all thy power disdains,
And thousands more in equal mirth maintains.
But oh! if e'er thy gnome could spoil a grace,
Or raise a pimple on a beauteous face,

1 See Hom. Iliad, xviii. of Vulcan's walking tripods.

2 Alludes to a real fact, a lady of distinction imagined herself in this condition.

Like citron-waters matrons' cheeks inflame,
Or change complexions at a losing game;
If e'er with airy horns I planted heads,
Or rumpled petticoats, or tumbled beds,
Or caused suspicion when no soul was rude,
Or discomposed the head-dress of a prude,
Or e'er to costive lap-dog gave disease,
Which not the tears of brightest eyes could ease:
Hear me, and touch Belinda with chagrin,
That single act gives half the world the spleen.
The goddess with a discontented air
Seems to reject him, though she grants his prayer.
A wondrous bag with both her hands she binds,
Like that where once Ulysses held the winds;
There she collects the force of female lungs,
Sighs, sobs, and passions, and the war of tongues.
A vial next she fills with fainting fears,
Soft sorrows, melting griefs, and flowing tears.
The gnome rejoicing bears her gifts away,
Spreads his black wings, and slowly mounts to day.
Sunk in Thalestris' arms the nymph he found,
Her eyes dejected, and her hair unbound.
Full o'er their heads the swelling bag he rent,
And all the Furies issued at the vent.
Belinda burns with more than mortal ire,
And fierce Thalestris fans the rising fire.
O wretched maid! she spread her hands, and cried,
(While Hampton's echoes, Wretched maid! replied,)
Was it for this you took such constant care
The bodkin, comb, and essence, to prepare?
For this your locks in paper durance bound?
For this with torturing irons wreathed around?
For this with fillets strain'd your tender head?
And bravely bore the double loads of lead?
Gods! shall the ravisher display your hair,
While the fops envy, and the ladies stare!
Honour forbid! at whose unrivall'd shrine
Ease, pleasure, virtue, all our sex resign.
Methinks already I your tears survey,
Already hear the horrid things they say;
Already see you a degraded toast,
And all your honour in a whisper lost!
How shall I, then, your hapless fame defend?
'Twill then be infamy to seem your friend!

And shall this prize, the inestimable prize,
Exposed through crystal to the gazing eyes,
And heighten'd by the diamond's circling rays,
On that rapacious hand for ever blaze?
Sooner shall grass in Hyde-park Circus grow,
And wits take lodgings in the sound of Bow;
Sooner let earth, air, sea, to chaos fall,
Men, monkeys, lap-dogs, parrots, perish all!
She said; then raging to Sir Plume repairs,
And bids her beau demand the precious hairs:
(Sir Plume, of amber snuff-box justly vain,
And the nice conduct of a clouded cane,)
With earnest eyes, and round, unthinking face,
He first the snuff-box open'd, then the case,
And thus broke out—"My lord, why, what the devil!
"Z—ds! damn the lock! 'fore Gad, you must be civil.
"Plague on't! 'tis past a jest—nay prithee, pox!
"Give her the hair"—he spoke, and rapp'd his box.
It grieves me much (replied the Peer again)
Who speaks so well should ever speak in vain.
But by this lock, this sacred lock, I swear,
(Which never more shall join its parted hair;
Which never more its honours shall renew,
Clipp'd from the lovely head where late it grew,)
That while my nostrils draw the vital air,
This hand, which won it, shall for ever wear.
He spoke, and speaking, in proud triumph spread
The long-contended honours of her head.
But Umbriel, hateful gnome! forbears not so;
He breaks the vial whence the sorrows flow.
Then see! the nymph in beauteous grief appears,
Her eyes half-languishing, half-drown'd in tears;
On her heaved bosom hung her drooping head,
Which with a sigh she raised; and thus she said:
For ever cursed be this detested day,
Which snatch'd my best, my favourite curl away!
Happy! ah ten times happy had I been,
If Hampton-Court these eyes had never seen!
Yet am not I the first mistaken maid,
By love of courts to numerous ills betray'd.
Oh had I rather unadmired remain'd
In some lone isle, or distant northern land;
Where the gilt chariot never marks the way,
Where none learn ombre, none e'er taste Bohea!

There kept my charms concealed from mortal eye,
Like roses, that in deserts bloom and die.
What moved my mind with youthful lords to roam?
Oh had I staid, and said my prayers at home!
'Twas this the morning omens seem'd to tell,
Thrice from my trembling hand the patch-box fell;
The tottering China shook without a wind,
Nay, Poll sat mute, and Shock was most unkind!
A sylph, too, warn'd me of the threats of fate,
In mystic visions, now believed too late!
See the poor remnants of these slighted hairs!
My hands shall rend what even thy rapine spares:
These in two sable ringlets taught to break,
Once gave new beauties to the snowy neck;
The sister-lock now sits uncouth, alone,
And in its fellow's fate foresees its own;
Uncurl'd it hangs, the fatal shears demands,
And tempts, once more, thy sacrilegious hands.
Oh hadst thou, cruel! been content to seize
Hairs less in sight, or any hairs but these!

CANTO FIFTH.

She said: the pitying audience melt in tears;
But Fate and Jove had stopp'd the Baron's ears.
In vain Thalestris with reproach assails,
For who can move when fair Belinda fails?
Not half so fix'd the Trojan could remain,
While Anna begg'd and Dido raged in vain.
Then grave Clarissa graceful waved her fan;
Silence ensued, and thus the nymph began:—
Say, why are beauties praised and honour'd most,
The wise man's passion, and the vain man's toast?
Why deck'd with all that land and sea afford,
Why angels call'd, and angel-like adored?
Why round our coaches crowd the white-gloved beaux,
Why bows the side-box from its inmost rows?
How vain are all these glories, all our pains,
Unless good sense preserve what beauty gains:
That men may say, when we the front-box grace,
Behold the first in virtue as in face!
Oh! if to dance all night, and dress all day,
Charm'd the small-pox, or chased old-age away;

Who would not scorn what housewife's cares produce,
Or who would learn one earthly thing of use?
To patch, nay ogle, might become a saint,
Nor could it sure be such a sin to paint.
But since, alas! frail beauty must decay,
Curl'd or uncurl'd, since locks will turn to grey;
Since, painted or not painted, all shall fade,
And she who scorns a man must die a maid;
What then remains but well our power to use,
And keep good humour still whate'er we lose?
And trust me, dear! good-humour can prevail,
When airs, and flights, and screams, and scolding fail;
Beauties in vain their pretty eyes may roll;
Charms strike the sight, but merit wins the soul.
So spoke the dame, but no applause ensued;
Belinda frown'd, Thalestris call'd her prude.
To arms, to arms! the fierce virago cries,
And swift as lightning to the combat flies.
All side in parties, and begin the attack;
Fans clap, silks rustle, and tough whalebones crack;
Heroes' and heroines' shouts confusedly rise,
And bass and treble voices strike the skies.
No common weapons in their hands are found,
Like gods they fight, nor dread a mortal wound.
So when bold Homer makes the gods engage,
And heavenly breasts with human passions rage;
'Gainst Pallas, Mars; Latona, Hermes arms;
And all Olympus rings with loud alarms:
Jove's thunder roars, heaven trembles all around,
Blue Neptune storms, the bellowing deeps resound:
Earth shakes her nodding towers, the ground gives way,
And the pale ghosts start at the flash of day!
Triumphant Umbriel, on a sconce's height
Clapp'd his glad wings, and sate to view the fight:
Propp'd on their bodkin spears, the sprites survey
The growing combat, or assist the fray.
While through the press enraged Thalestris flies,
And scatters death around from both her eyes,
A beau and witling perish'd in the throng,
One died in metaphor, and one in song.
"O cruel nymph! a living death I bear!"
Cried Dapperwit, and sunk beside his chair.
A mournful glance Sir Fopling upwards cast,
"Those eyes are made so killing!"—was his last.

Thus on Mæander's flowery margin lies
The expiring swan, and as he sings he dies.
When bold Sir Plume had drawn Clarissa down,
Chloe stepp'd in, and kill'd him with a frown;
She smiled to see the doughty hero slain,
But at her smile the beau revived again.
Now Jove suspends his golden scales in air,
Weighs the men's wits against the lady's hair;
The doubtful beam long nods from side to side;
At length the wits mount up, the hairs subside.
See! fierce Belinda on the Baron flies,
With more than usual lightning in her eyes:
Nor fear'd the chief the unequal fight to try,
Who sought no more than on his foe to die.
But this bold lord, with manly strength endued,
She with one finger and a thumb subdued:
Just where the breath of life his nostrils drew,
A charge of snuff the wily virgin threw;
The gnomes direct, to every atom just,
The pungent grains of titillating dust.
Sudden with starting tears each eye o'erflows,
And the high dome re-echoes to his nose.
Now meet thy fate! incensed Belinda cried,
And drew a deadly bodkin from her side.
(The same, his ancient personage to deck,
Her great-great-grandsire wore about his neck,
In three seal-rings; which after, melted down,
Form'd a vast buckle for his widow's gown:
Her infant grandame's whistle next it grew,
The bells she jingled, and the whistle blew;
Then in a bodkin graced her mother's hairs,
Which long she wore, and now Belinda wears.)
Boast not my fall (he cried), insulting foe!
Thou by some other shalt be laid as low.
Nor think, to die dejects my lofty mind;
All that I dread is leaving you behind!
Rather than so, ah! let me still survive,
And burn in Cupid's flames—but burn alive.
Restore the Lock! she cries; and all around,
Restore the Lock! the vaulted roofs rebound.
Not fierce Othello, in so loud a strain,
Roar'd for the handkerchief that caused his pain.
But see how oft ambitious aims are cross'd,
And chiefs contend till all the prize is lost!

The Lock, obtain'd with guilt, and kept with pain,
In every place is sought, but sought in vain:
With such a prize no mortal must be blest,
So Heaven decrees! with Heaven who can contest?
Some thought it mounted to the lunar sphere,
Since all things lost on earth are treasured there.
There heroes' wits are kept in ponderous vases,
And beaux' in snuff-boxes and tweezer-cases;
There broken vows and death-bed alms are found.
And lovers' hearts with ends of riband bound,
The courtier's promises, and sick men's prayers,
The smiles of harlots, and the tears of heirs,
Cages for gnats, and chains to yoke a flea,
Dried butterflies, and tomes of casuistry.
But trust the Muse—she saw it upward rise,
Though mark'd by none but quick, poetic eyes:
(So Rome's great founder to the heavens withdrew,
To Proculus alone confess'd in view:)
A sudden star, it shot through liquid air,
And drew behind a radiant trail of hair.
Not Berenice's locks first rose so bright,
The heavens bespangling with dishevell'd light.
The sylphs behold it kindling as it flies,
And pleased pursue its progress through the skies.
This the beau monde shall from the Mall survey,
And hail with music its propitious ray;
This the blest lover shall for Venus take,
And send up vows from Rosamonda's lake;
This Partridge soon shall view in cloudless skies,
When next he looks through Galileo's eyes;
And hence the egregious wizard shall foredoom
The fate of Louis, and the fall of Rome.
Then cease, bright nymph! to mourn thy ravish'd hair,
Which adds new glory to the shining sphere!
Not all the tresses that fair heads can boast,
Shall draw such envy as the Lock you lost.
For after all the murders of your eye,
When, after millions slain, yourself shall die;
When those fair suns shall set, as set they must,
And all those tresses shall be laid in dust,
This lock the Muse shall consecrate to fame,
And 'midst the stars inscribe Belinda's name.

ELEGY

TO THE MEMORY OF AN UNFORTUNATE LADY.

WHAT beckoning ghost along the moonlight shade
Invites my steps, and points to yonder glade?
'Tis she!—but why that bleeding bosom gored?
Why dimly gleams the visionary sword?
Oh, ever beauteous, ever friendly! tell,
Is it, in heaven, a crime to love too well?
To bear too tender or too firm a heart,
To act a lover's or a Roman's part?
Is there no bright reversion in the sky,
For those who greatly think, or bravely die?
Why bade ye else, ye powers! her soul aspire
Above the vulgar flight of low desire?
Ambition first sprung from your blest abodes;
The glorious fault of angels and of gods:
Thence to their images on earth it flows,
And in the breasts of kings and heroes glows.
Most souls, 'tis true, but peep out once an age,
Dull sullen prisoners in the body's cage:
Dim lights of life, that burn a length of years
Useless, unseen, as lamps in sepulchres;
Like Eastern kings a lazy state they keep,
And, close confined to their own palace, sleep.
From these perhaps (ere nature bade her die)
Fate snatch'd her early to the pitying sky.
As into air the purer spirits flow,
And separate from their kindred dregs below;
So flew the soul to its congenial place,
Nor left one virtue to redeem her race.
But thou, false guardian of a charge too good,
Thou, mean deserter of thy brother's blood!
See on these ruby lips the trembling breath,
These cheeks now fading at the blast of death:
Cold is that breast which warm'd the world before,
And those love-darting eyes must roll no more.
Thus, if eternal justice rules the ball,
Thus shall your wives, and thus your children fall:
On all the line a sudden vengeance waits,
And frequent hearses shall besiege your gates;

There passengers shall stand, and pointing say,
(While the long funerals blacken all the way,)
Lo! these were they, whose souls the Furies steel'd,
And cursed with hearts unknowing how to yield.
Thus unlamented pass the proud away,
The gaze of fools, and pageant of a day!
So perish all, whose breast ne'er learn'd to glow
For others' good, or melt at others' woe.
What can atone (O ever-injured shade!)
Thy fate unpitied, and thy rites unpaid?
No friend's complaint, no kind domestic tear
Pleased thy pale ghost, or graced thy mournful bier.
By foreign hands thy dying eyes were closed,
By foreign hands thy decent limbs composed,
By foreign hands thy humble grave adorn'd,
By strangers honour'd, and by strangers mourn'd!
What though no friends in sable weeds appear,
Grieve for an hour, perhaps, then mourn a year,
And bear about the mockery of woe
To midnight dances, and the public show?
What though no weeping loves thy ashes grace,
Nor polish'd marble emulate thy face?
What though no sacred earth allow thee room,
Nor hallow'd dirge be mutter'd o'er thy tomb?
Yet shall thy grave with rising flowers be drest,
And the green turf lie lightly on thy breast:
There shall the morn her earliest tears bestow,
There the first roses of the year shall blow;
While angels with their silver wings o'ershade
The ground, now sacred by thy reliques made.
So peaceful rests, without a stone, a name,
What once had beauty, titles, wealth, and fame
How loved, how honour'd once, avails thee not,
To whom related, or by whom begot;
A heap of dust alone remains of thee,
'Tis all thou art, and all the proud shall be!
Poets themselves must fall like those they sung,
Deaf the praised ear, and mute the tuneful tongue.
Even he, whose soul now melts in mournful lays,
Shall shortly want the generous tear he pays;
Then from his closing eyes thy form shall part,
And the last pang shall tear thee from his heart,
Life's idle business at one gasp be o'er,
The muse forgot, and thou beloved no more!

PROLOGUE

TO

MR. ADDISON'S TRAGEDY OF CATO.

To wake the soul by tender strokes of art,
To raise the genius, and to mend the heart,
To make mankind, in conscious virtue bold,
Live o'er each scene, and be what they behold:
For this the Tragic Muse first trod the stage,
Commanding tears to stream through every age;
Tyrants no more their savage nature kept,
And foes to virtue wonder'd how they wept.
Our author shuns by vulgar springs to move
The hero's glory, or the virgin's love;
In pitying love, we but our weakness show,
And wild ambition well deserves its woe.
Here tears shall flow from a more generous cause,
Such tears as patriots shed for dying laws:
He bids your breasts with ancient ardour rise,
And calls forth Roman drops from British eyes.
Virtue confess'd in human shape he draws,
What Plato thought, and godlike Cato was:
No common object to your sight displays,
But what with pleasure Heaven itself surveys,
A brave man struggling in the storms of fate,
And greatly falling with a falling state.
While Cato gives his little senate laws,
What bosom beats not in his country's cause?
Who sees him act, but envies every deed?
Who hears him groan, and does not wish to bleed?
Even when proud Cæsar, 'midst triumphal cars,
The spoils of nations, and the pomp of wars,
Ignobly vain, and impotently great,
Show'd Rome her Cato's figure drawn in state;
As her dead father's reverend image pass'd,
The pomp was darken'd, and the day o'ercast;
The triumph ceased, tears gush'd from every eye;
The world's great victor pass'd unheeded by;
Her last good man dejected Rome adored,
And honoured Cæsar's less than Cato's sword.

Britons, attend: be worth like this approved,
And show, you have the virtue to be moved.
With honest scorn the first famed Cato view'd
Rome learning arts from Greece, whom she subdued;
Your scene precariously subsists too long
On French translation, and Italian song.
Dare to have sense yourselves; assert the stage,
Be justly warm'd with your own native rage:
Such plays alone should win a British ear,
As Cato's self had not disdain'd to hear.

EPILOGUE

TO

MR. ROWE'S JANE SHORE.

PRODIGIOUS this! the frail one of our play
From her own sex should mercy find to-day!
You might have held the pretty head aside,
Peep'd in your fans, been serious, thus, and cried,
The play may pass—but that strange creature, Shore,
I can't—indeed now—I so hate a whore—
Just as a blockhead rubs his thoughtless skull,
And thanks his stars he was not born a fool;
So from a sister sinner you shall hear,
"How strangely you expose yourself, my dear!"
But let me die, all raillery apart,
Our sex are still forgiving at their heart;
And, did not wicked custom so contrive,
We'd be the best, good-natured things alive.
There are, 'tis true, who tell another tale,
That virtuous ladies envy while they rail;
Such rage without betrays the fire within;
In some close corner of the soul, they sin;
Still hoarding up, most scandalously nice,
Amidst their virtues a reserve of vice.
The godly dame, who fleshly failings damns,
Scolds with her maid, or with her chaplain crams.
Would you enjoy soft nights and solid dinners?
'Faith, gallants, board with saints, and bed with sinners.

Well, if our author in the wife offends,
He has a husband that will make amends:
He draws him gentle, tender, and forgiving,
And sure such kind good creatures may be living.
In days of old, they pardon'd breach of vows,
Stern Cato's self was no relentless spouse:
Plu—Plutarch, what's his name, that writes his life?
Tells us, that Cato dearly loved his wife:
Yet, if a friend, a night or so, should need her,
He'd recommend her as a special breeder.
To lend a wife, few here would scruple make,
But, pray, which of you all would take her back?
Though with the stoic chief our stage may ring,
The stoic husband was the glorious thing.
The man had courage, was a sage, 'tis true,
And loved his country,—but what's that to you?
Those strange examples ne'er were made to fit ye,
But the kind cuckold might instruct the city:
There, many an honest man may copy Cato,
Who ne'er saw naked sword, or look'd in Plato.
If, after all, you think it a disgrace,
That Edward's Miss thus perks it in your face;
To see a piece of failing flesh and blood,
In all the rest so impudently good;
Faith, let the modest matrons of the town
Come here in crowds, and stare the strumpet down.

SAPPHO TO PHAON.

Translated from Ovid.

Say, lovely youth, that dost my heart command,
Can Phaon's eyes forget his Sappho's hand?
Must then her name the wretched writer prove,
To thy remembrance lost, as to thy love?
Ask not the cause that I new numbers choose,
The lute neglected, and the lyric muse;
Love taught my tears in sadder notes to flow,
And tuned my heart to elegies of woe.
I burn, I burn, as when through ripen'd corn
By driving winds the spreading flames are borne!
Phaon to Ætna's scorching fields retires,
While I consume with more than Ætna's fires!

No more my soul a charm in music finds;
Music has charms alone for peaceful minds.
Soft scenes of solitude no more can please,
Love enters there, and I'm my own disease.
No more the Lesbian dames my passion move,
Once the dear objects of my guilty love;
All other loves are lost in only thine,
Ah, youth, ungrateful to a flame like mine!
Whom would not all those blooming charms surprise,
Those heavenly looks, and dear deluding eyes?
The harp and bow would you like Phœbus bear,
A brighter Phœbus Phaon might appear;
Would you with ivy wreathe your flowing hair,
Not Bacchus self with Phaon could compare:
Yet Phœbus loved, and Bacchus felt the flame,
One Daphne warm'd, and one the Cretan dame;
Nymphs that in verse no more could rival me,
Than even those gods contend in charms with thee.
The Muses teach me all their softest lays,
And the wide world resounds with Sappho's praise.
Though great Alcæus more sublimely sings,
And strikes with bolder rage the sounding strings,
No less renown attends the moving lyre,
Which Venus tunes, and all her loves inspire;
To me what nature has in charms denied,
Is well by wit's more lasting flames supplied.
Though short my stature, yet my name extends
To heaven itself, and earth's remotest ends.
Brown as I am, an Ethiopian dame
Inspired young Perseus with a generous flame;
Turtles and doves of different hues unite,
And glossy jet is pair'd with shining white.
If to no charms thou wilt thy heart resign,
But such as merit, such as equal thine;
By none, alas! by none thou canst be moved;
Phaon alone by Phaon must be loved!
Yet once thy Sappho could thy cares employ,
Once in her arms you centred all your joy:
No time the dear remembrance can remove,
For oh! how vast a memory has love!
My music, then, you could for ever hear,
And all my words were music to your ear.
You stopp'd with kisses my enchanting tongue,
And found my kisses sweeter than my song.

In all I pleased, but most in what was best;
And the last joy was dearer than the rest.
Then with each word, each glance, each motion fired,
You still enjoy'd, and yet you still desired,
Till all dissolving in the trance we lay,
And in tumultuous raptures died away.
The fair Sicilians now thy soul inflame;
Why was I born, ye gods, a Lesbian dame?
But ah! beware, Sicilian nymphs! nor boast
That wandering heart which I so lately lost;
Nor be with all those tempting words abused,
Those tempting words were all to Sappho used.
And you that rule Sicilia's happy plains,
Have pity, Venus, on your poet's pains!
Shall fortune still in one sad tenor run,
And still increase the woes so soon begun?
Inured to sorrow from my tender years,
My parent's ashes drank my early tears;
My brother next, neglecting wealth and fame,
Ignobly burn'd in a destructive flame:
An infant daughter late my griefs increased,
And all a mother's cares distract my breast.
Alas! what more could fate itself impose,
But thee, the last and greatest of my woes?
No more my robes in waving purple flow,
Nor on my hand the sparkling diamonds glow;
No more my locks, in ringlets curl'd, diffuse
The costly sweetness of Arabian dews,
Nor braids of gold the varied tresses bind,
That fly disorder'd with the wanton wind:
For whom should Sappho use such arts as these?
He's gone, whom only she desired to please!
Cupid's light darts my tender bosom move,
Still is there cause for Sappho still to love:
So from my birth the Sisters fix'd my doom,
And gave to Venus all my life to come;
Or, while my muse in melting notes complains,
My yielding heart keeps measure to my strains.
By charms like thine which all my soul have won,
Who might not—ah! who would not be undone?
For those Aurora Cephalus might scorn,
And with fresh blushes paint the conscious morn.
For those might Cynthia lengthen Phaon's sleep,
And bid Endymion nightly tend his sheep.

Venus for those had rapt thee to the skies,
But Mars on thee might look with Venus' eyes.
O scarce a youth, yet scarce a tender boy!
O useful time for lovers to employ!
Pride of thy age, and glory of thy race,
Come to these arms, and melt in this embrace!
The vows you never will return, receive;
And take at least the love you will not give.
See, while I write, my words are lost in tears!
The less my sense, the more my love appears.
Sure 'twas not much to bid one kind adieu,
(At least to feign was never hard to you;)
Farewell, my Lesbian love, you might have said;
Or coldly thus, Farewell, O Lesbian maid!
No tear did you, no parting kiss receive,
Nor knew I then how much I was to grieve.
No lover's gift your Sappho could confer,
And wrongs and woes were all you left with her.
No charge I gave you, and no charge could give,
But this, Be mindful of our loves, and live.
Now by the nine, those powers adored by me,
And Love, the god that ever waits on thee,
When first I heard (from whom I hardly knew)
That you were fled, and all my joys with you,
Like some sad statue, speechless, pale I stood,
Grief chill'd my breast, and stopp'd my freezing blood;
No sigh to rise, no tear had power to flow,
Fix'd in a stupid lethargy of woe;
But when its way the impetuous passion found,
I rend my tresses, and my breast I wound;
I rave, then weep; I curse, and then complain;
Now swell to rage, now melt in tears again.
Not fiercer pangs distract the mournful dame,
Whose first-born infant feeds the funeral flame.
My scornful brother with a smile appears,
Insults my woes, and triumphs in my tears:
His hated image ever haunts my eyes,
And why this grief? thy daughter lives, he cries.
Stung with my love, and furious with despair,
All torn my garments, and my bosom bare,
My woes, thy crimes, I to the world proclaim;
Such inconsistent things are love and shame!
'Tis thou art all my care and my delight,
My daily longing, and my dream by night:

Oh night more pleasing than the brightest day,
When fancy gives what absence takes away,
And, dress'd in all its visionary charms,
Restores my fair deserter to my arms!
Then round your neck in wanton wreath I twine,
Then you, methinks, as fondly circle mine;
A thousand tender words I hear and speak;
A thousand melting kisses give, and take:
Then fiercer joys, I blush to mention these,
Yet, while I blush, confess how much they please.
But when, with day, the sweet delusions fly,
And all things wake to life and joy, but I.
As if once more forsaken, I complain,
And close my eyes to dream of you again:
Then frantic rise, and like some fury rove
Through lonely plains, and through the silent grove;
As if the silent grove, and lonely plains,
That knew my pleasures, could relieve my pains.
I view the grotto, once the scene of love,
The rocks around, the hanging roofs above,
That charm'd me more, with native moss o'ergrown,
Than Phrygian marble, or the Parian stone.
I find the shades that veil'd our joys before;
But, Phaon gone, those shades delight no more.
Here the press'd herbs with bending tops betray
Where oft entwined in amorous folds we lay;
I kiss that earth which once was press'd by you,
And all with tears the withering herbs bedew.
For thee the fading trees appear to mourn,
And birds defer their songs till thy return:
Night shades the groves, and all in silence lie,
All but the mournful Philomel and I:
With mournful Philomel I join my strain,
Of Tereus she, of Phaon I complain.
A spring there is, whose silver waters show,
Clear as a glass, the shining sands below:
A flowery lotos spreads its arms above,
Shades all the banks, and seems itself a grove;
Eternal greens the mossy margin grace,
Watched by the silvan genius of the place:
Here as I lay, and swell'd with tears the flood,
Before my sight a watery virgin stood:
She stood and cried, "O you that love in vain!
Fly hence, and seek the far Leucadian main;

There stands a rock, from whose impending steep
Apollo's fane surveys the rolling deep;
There injured lovers, leaping from above,
Their flames extinguish, and forget to love.
Deucalion once with hopeless fury burn'd,
In vain he loved, relentless Pyrrha scorn'd:
But when from hence he plunged into the main,
Deucalion scorn'd, and Pyrrha loved in vain.
Haste, Sappho, haste! from high Leucadia throw
Thy wretched weight, nor dread the deeps below.
She spoke, and vanish'd with the voice—I rise,
And silent tears fall trickling from my eyes.
I go, ye nymphs! those rocks and seas to prove;
How much I fear, but ah, how much I love!
I go, ye nymphs, where furious love inspires;
Let female fears submit to female fires.
To rocks and seas I fly from Phaon's hate,
And hope from seas and rocks a milder fate
Ye gentle gales, beneath my body blow,
And softly lay me on the waves below!
And thou, kind Love, my sinking limbs sustain,
Spread thy soft wings, and waft me o'er the main,
Nor let a lover's death the guiltless flood profane!
On Phœbus' shrine my harp I'll then bestow,
And this inscription shall be placed below:
"Here she who sung, to him that did inspire,
Sappho to Phœbus consecrates her lyre;
What suits with Sappho, Phœbus, suits with thee;
The gift, the giver, and the god agree."
  But why, alas! relentless youth, ah why,
To distant seas must tender Sappho fly?
Thy charms than those may far more powerful be,
And Phœbus self is less a god to me.
Ah! canst thou doom me to the rocks and sea,
O far more faithless and more hard than they?
Ah! canst thou rather see this tender breast
Dash'd on these rocks than to thy bosom press'd?
This breast, which once, in vain! you liked so well;
Where the loves play'd, and where the muses dwell.
Alas! the muses now no more inspire,
Untuned my lute, and silent is my lyre.
My languid numbers have forgot to flow,
And fancy sinks beneath the weight of woe.

Ye Lesbian virgins, and ye Lesbian dames,
Themes of my verse, and objects of my flames,
No more your groves with my glad songs shall ring,
No more these hands shall touch the trembling string:
My Phaon 's fled, and I those arts resign—
(Wretch that I am, to call that Phaon mine!)
Return, fair youth, return, and bring along
Joy to my soul, and vigour to my song:
Absent from thee, the poet's flame expires;
But ah! how fiercely burn the lover's fires!
Gods! can no prayers, no sighs, no numbers move
One savage heart, or teach it how to love?
The winds my prayers, my sighs, my numbers bear,
The flying winds have lost them all in air!
Or when, alas! shall more auspicious gales
To these fond eyes restore thy welcome sails!
If you return—ah why these long delays?
Poor Sappho dies while careless Phaon stays.
O launch the bark, nor fear the watery plain;
Venus for thee shall smooth her native main.
O launch thy bark, secure of prosperous gales;
Cupid for thee shall spread the swelling sails.
If you will fly—(yet ah! what cause can be,
Too cruel youth, that you should fly from me?)
If not from Phaon I must hope for ease,
Ah let me seek it from the raging seas:
To raging seas unpitied I'll remove,
And either cease to live or cease to love!

ELOISA TO ABELARD.

ARGUMENT.

ABELARD, one of the most celebrated teachers of the twelfth century, both for his extraordinary talents and his misfortunes, was born at Palais, in the neighbourhood of Nantes, in the year 1079. After surpassing many of the greatest scholars of his age, he became a professor of divinity in Paris with great success. He cast his eyes on the fair Heloise, the niece of Fulbert, a canon in the cathedral of Paris, and, determined to gratify his passion, he proposed to Fulbert to receive him into his house as a boarder, and promised to give, in exchange, all the instruction which he might consider his niece might require. The canon, being rather parsimonious, and anxious to see his niece among the stars of her time, agreed to the proposal. Among the things taught by Abelard to his ardent pupil, the art of love was the chief, and in which she soon surpassed her master. The consequence was soon visible, and Fulbert insisted on their marriage. This Abelard, although ordained, consented to; but Heloise, considering that it would be the destruction of Abelard's glory, in a letter tried to dissuade him from it. However, they were married, with the understanding that it was to be kept from the knowledge of the public. Fulbert, jealous of the honour of his family, soon made the fact known, upon which Heloise, in the firmest manner, denied it. Fulbert's unkind treatment of his niece caused Abelard to remove her to the convent of Argenteuil; and Fulbert, fancying that it was intended to make her a nun, in revenge contrived to get introduced into Abelard's bed-room, in the dead of night, two wretches, who mutilated him in a most atrocious manner. The miscreants were punished, the canon disgraced; Heloise took the veil, and Abelard buried his grief and shame under the monastic garment, in the abbey of St. Denis. After some years had passed, the nuns of Argenteuil were expelled, Heloise among them. Abelard, who had built the oratory of Paraclet, gave it to Heloise, whose exemplary conduct procured her universal praise. Abelard died in 1142, and was buried at Paraclet, in a beautiful gothic tomb erected by Heloise, whose remains were interred in the same receptacle twenty-one years after. The tomb was removed to Paris, and placed where it is now to be seen, in the cemetery of Père la Chaise. From the letters which passed between this unfortunate pair, the author was indebted for the sentiments expressed in the poem.

In these deep solitudes and awful cells,
Where heavenly-pensive Contemplation dwells,
And ever-musing Melancholy reigns;
What means this tumult in a vestal's veins?
Why rove my thoughts beyond this last retreat?
Why feels my heart its long-forgotten heat?
Yet, yet I love!—From Abelard it came,
And Eloïsa yet must kiss the name.
Dear fatal name! rest ever unreveal'd,
Nor pass these lips, in holy silence seal'd:
Hide it, my heart, within that close disguise,
Where, mix'd with God's, his loved idea lies:
O write it not, my hand—the name appears
Already written—wash it out, my tears!
In vain lost Eloïsa weeps and prays,
Her heart still dictates, and her hand obeys.
Relentless walls! whose darksome round contains
Repentant sighs, and voluntary pains:
Ye rugged rocks, which holy knees have worn:
Ye grots and caverns shagg'd with horrid thorn!
Shrines! where their vigils pale-eyed virgins keep,
And pitying saints, whose statues learn to weep!
Tho' cold like you, unmoved and silent grown,
I have not yet forgot myself to stone.

All is not Heaven's while Abelard has part,
Still rebel nature holds out half my heart;
Nor prayers nor fasts its stubborn pulse restrain,
Nor tears for ages taught to flow in vain.
Soon as thy letters trembling I unclose,
That well-known name awakens all my woes.
O name, for ever sad! for ever dear!
Still breathed in sighs, still usher'd with a tear.
I tremble, too, whene'er my own I find;
Some dire misfortune follows close behind.
Line after line my gushing eyes o'erflow,
Led through a sad variety of woe:
Now warm in love, now withering in my bloom,
Lost in a convent's solitary gloom!
There stern Religion quench'd the unwilling flame,
There died the best of passions, Love and Fame.
Yet write, oh! write me all, that I may join
Griefs to thy griefs, and echo sighs to thine.
Nor foes nor fortune take this power away;
And is my Abelard less kind than they?
Tears still are mine, and those I need not spare,
Love but demands what else were shed in prayer;
No happier task these faded eyes pursue;
To read and weep is all they now can do.
Then share thy pain, allow that sad relief;
Ah, more than share it! give me all thy grief.
Heaven first taught letters for some wretch's aid,
Some banish'd lover, or some captive maid;
They live, they speak, they breathe what love inspires
Warm from the soul, and faithful to its fires,
The virgin's wish without her fears impart,
Excuse the blush, and pour out all the heart,
Speed the soft intercourse from soul to soul,
And waft a sigh from Indus to the Pole.
Thou know'st how guiltless first I met thy flame,
When Love approach'd me under friendship's name;
My fancy form'd thee of angelic kind,
Some emanation of the all-beauteous Mind.
Those smiling eyes, attempering every ray,
Shone sweetly lambent with celestial day.
Guiltless I gazed, Heaven listen'd while you sung,
And truths divine came mended from that tongue.
From lips like those what precept fail'd to move?
Too soon they taught me 'twas no sin to love:

Back through the paths of pleasing sense I ran,
Nor wish'd an angel whom I loved a man.
Dim and remote the joys of saints I see;
Nor envy them that heaven I lose for thee.
How oft, when press'd to marriage, have I said,
Curse on all laws but those which love has made!
Love, free as air, at sight of human ties,
Spreads his light wings, and in a moment flies.
Let wealth, let honour, wait the wedded dame,
August her deed, and sacred be her fame;
Before true passion all those views remove;
Fame, wealth, and honour! what are you to Love?
The jealous god, when we profane his fires,
Those restless passions in revenge inspires,
And bids them make mistaken mortals groan,
Who seek in love for aught but love alone.
Should at my feet the world's great master fall,
Himself, his throne, his world, I'd scorn 'em all;
Nor Cæsar's empress would I deign to prove;
No, make me mistress to the man I love:
If there be yet another name more free,
More fond than mistress, make me that to thee!
Oh! happy state! when souls each other draw,
When love is liberty, and nature law:
All then is full, possessing and possess'd,
No craving void left aching in the breast:
Ev'n thought meets thought, ere from the lips it part,
And each warm wish springs mutual from the heart.
This sure is bliss (if bliss on earth there be),
And once the lot of Abelard and me.
Alas, how changed! what sudden horrors rise!
A naked lover bound and bleeding lies!
Where, where was Eloïse? her voice, her hand,
Her poniard had opposed the dire command.
Barbarian, stay! that bloody stroke restrain;
The crime was common, common be the pain.
I can no more, by shame, by rage suppress'd—
Let tears and burning blushes speak the rest.
Canst thou forget that sad, that solemn day,
When victims at yon altar's foot we lay?
Canst thou forget what tears that moment fell,
When, warm in youth, I bade the world farewell?
As with cold lips I kiss'd the sacred veil,
The shrines all trembled, and the lamps grew pale:

Heaven scarce believed the conquest it survey'd,
And saints with wonder heard the vows I made.
Yet then, to those dread altars as I drew,
Not on the cross my eyes were fix'd, but you:
Not grace, or zeal, love only was my call,
And if I lose thy love, I lose my all.
Come! with thy looks, thy words relieve my woe,
Those still at least are left thee to bestow.
Still on that breast enamoured let me lie,
Still drink delicious poison from thy eye,
Pant on thy lip, and to thy heart be press'd;
Give all thou canst—and let me dream the rest.
Ah no! instruct me other joys to prize,
With other beauties charm my partial eyes,
Full in my view set all the bright abode,
And make my soul quit Abelard for God.
  Ah think at least thy flock deserves thy care,
Plants of thy hand, and children of thy prayer;
From the false world in early youth they fled,
By thee to mountains, wilds, and deserts led.
You raised these hallow'd walls; the desert smiled,
And Paradise was open'd in the Wild.
No weeping orphan saw his father's stores
Our shrines irradiate, or emblaze the floors;
No silver saints, by dying misers given,
Here bribed the rage of ill-requited Heaven:
But such plain roofs as piety could raise,
And only vocal with the Maker's praise.
In these lone walls (their days' eternal bound)
These moss-grown domes with spiry turrets crown'd
Where awful arches make a noon-day night,
And the dim windows shed a solemn light;
Thy eyes diffused a reconciling ray,
And gleams of glory brighten'd all the day.
But now no face divine contentment wears,
'Tis all blank sadness, or continual tears.
See how the force of others' prayers I try,
(O pious fraud of amorous charity!)
But why should I on others' prayers depend?
Come thou, my father, brother, husband, friend!
Ah let thy handmaid, sister, daughter, move,
And all those tender names in one, thy love!
The darksome pines that o'er yon rocks reclined
Wave high, and murmur to the hollow wind,

The wandering streams, that shine between the hills,
The grots that echo to the tinkling rills,
The dying gales that pant upon the trees,
The lakes that quiver to the curling breeze;
No more these scenes my meditation aid,
Or lull to rest the visionary maid.
But o'er the twilight groves and dusky caves,
Long-sounding aisles, and intermingled graves,
Black Melancholy sits, and round her throws
A death-like silence, and a dread repose:
Her gloomy presence saddens all the scene,
Shades every flower, and darkens every green,
Deepens the murmur of the falling floods,
And breathes a browner horror on the woods.
Yet here for ever, ever must I stay;
Sad proof how well a lover can obey!
Death, only Death, can break the lasting chain;
And here, even then, shall my cold dust remain;
Here all its frailties, all its flames resign,
And wait till 'tis no sin to mix with thine.
Ah wretch! believed the spouse of God in vain,
Confess'd within the slave of love and man.
Assist me, Heaven! but whence arose that prayer?
Sprung it from piety, or from despair?
Even here, where frozen chastity retires,
Love finds an altar for forbidden fires.
I ought to grieve, but cannot what I ought;
I mourn the lover, not lament the fault;
I view my crime, but kindle at the view,
Repent old pleasures, and solicit new;
Now turn'd to Heaven, I weep my past offence,
Now think of thee, and curse my innocence.
Of all affliction taught a lover yet,
'Tis sure the hardest science to forget!
How shall I lose the sin, yet keep the sense?
And love the offender, yet detest the offence?
How the dear object from the crime remove,
Or how distinguish penitence from love?
Unequal task! a passion to resign,
For hearts so touch'd, so pierced, so lost as mine.
Ere such a soul regains its peaceful state,
How often must it love, how often hate!
How often hope, despair, resent, regret,
Conceal, disdain,—do all things but forget!

But let Heaven seize it, all at once 'tis fired;
Not touch'd, but rapt; not waken'd, but inspired!
Oh come! oh teach me nature to subdue,
Renounce my love, my life, myself—and you.
Fill my fond heart with God alone, for he
Alone can rival, can succeed to thee.
How happy is the blameless vestal's lot?
The world forgetting, by the world forgot:
Eternal sunshine of the spotless mind!
Each prayer accepted and each wish resign'd;
Labour and rest, that equal periods keep;
"Obedient slumbers that can wake and weep;"
Desires composed, affections ever even;
Tears that delight, and sighs that waft to heaven.
Grace shines around her with serenest beams,
And whispering angels prompt her golden dreams.
For her the unfading rose of Eden blooms,
And wings of seraphs shed divine perfumes;
For her the spouse prepares the bridal ring,
For her white virgins hymeneals sing,
To sounds of heavenly harps she dies away,
And melts in visions of eternal day.
Far other dreams my erring soul employ,
Far other raptures, of unholy joy:
When at the close of each sad, sorrowing day,
Fancy restores what vengeance snatch'd away,
Then conscience sleeps, and leaving nature free,
All my loose soul unbounded springs to thee.
Oh curst, dear horrors of all-conscious night!
How glowing guilt exalts the keen delight!
Provoking demons all restraint remove,
And stir within me every source of love.
I hear thee, view thee, gaze o'er all thy charms,
And round thy phantom glue my clasping arms.
I wake:—no more I hear, no more I view,
The phantom flies me, as unkind as you.
I call aloud; it hears not what I say:
I stretch my empty arms; it glides away.
To dream once more I close my willing eyes;
Ye soft illusions, dear deceits, arise;
Alas, no more! methinks we wandering go
Through dreary wastes, and weep each other's woe,
Where, round some mouldering tower, pale ivy creeps,
And low-brow'd rocks hang nodding o'er the deeps.

Sudden you mount, you beckon from the skies;
Clouds interpose, waves roar, and winds arise.
I shriek, start up, the same sad prospect find,
And wake to all the griefs I left behind.
  For thee the fates, severely kind, ordain
A cool suspense from pleasure and from pain;
Thy life a long dead calm of fix'd repose;
No pulse that riots, and no blood that glows.
Still as the sea, ere winds were taught to blow,
Or moving spirit bade the waters flow;
Soft as the slumbers of a saint forgiven,
And mild as opening gleams of promised heaven.
  Come, Abelard! for what hast thou to dread
The torch of Venus burns not for the dead.
Nature stands check'd; Religion disapproves;
Even thou art cold—yet Eloïsa loves.
Ah hopeless, lasting flames; like those that burn
To light the dead, and warm the unfruitful urn.
  What scenes appear where'er I turn my view?
The dear ideas, where I fly, pursue,
Rise in the grove, before the altar rise,
Stain all my soul, and wanton in my eyes.
I waste the matin lamp in sighs for thee,
Thy image steals between my God and me,
Thy voice I seem in every hymn to hear,
With every bead I drop too soft a tear.
When from the censer clouds of fragrance roll,
And swelling organs lift the rising soul,
One thought of thee puts all the pomp to flight,
Priests, tapers, temples, swim before my sight:
In seas of flame my plunging soul is drown'd,
While altars blaze, and angels tremble round.
  While prostrate here in humble grief I lie,
Kind, virtuous drops just gathering in my eye,
While praying, trembling, in the dust I roll,
And dawning grace is opening on my soul:
Come, if thou darest, all charming as thou art!
Oppose thyself to Heaven; dispute my heart;
Come, with one glance of those deluding eyes
Blot out each bright idea of the skies;
Take back that grace, those sorrows, and those tears;
Take back my fruitless penitence and prayers;
Snatch me, just mounting, from the blest abode;
Assist the fiends, and tear me from my God!

No, fly me, fly me, far as Pole from Pole;
Rise Alps between us! and whole oceans roll!
Ah, come not, write not, think not once of me,
Nor share one pang of all I felt for thee.
Thy oaths I quit, thy memory resign;
Forget, renounce me, hate whate'er was mine.
Fair eyes, and tempting looks, (which yet I view!)
Long loved, adored ideas, all adieu!
Oh grace serene! oh virtue heavenly fair!
Divine oblivion of low-thoughted Care!
Fresh-blooming Hope, gay daughter of the sky!
And Faith, our early immortality!
Enter, each mild, each amicable guest;
Receive, and wrap me, in eternal rest!
See in her cell sad Eloïsa spread,
Propp'd on some tomb, a neighbour of the dead.
In each low wind methinks a spirit calls,
And more than echoes talk along the walls.
Here, as I watch'd the dying lamps around,
From yonder shrine I heard a hollow sound.
"Come, sister, come! (it said, or seem'd to say)
Thy place is here, sad sister, come away;
Once like thyself, I trembled, wept, and pray'd,
Love's victim then, though now a sainted maid:
But all is calm in this eternal sleep;
Here Grief forgets to groan, and Love to weep,
E'en Superstition loses every fear:
For God, not man, absolves our frailties here."
I come, I come! prepare your roseate bowers,
Celestial palms, and ever-blooming flowers.
Thither, where sinners may have rest, I go,
Where flames refined in breasts seraphic glow:
Thou, Abelard! the last sad office pay,
And smooth my passage to the realms of day:
See my lips tremble, and my eyeballs roll,
Suck my last breath, and catch my flying soul!
Ah no—in sacred vestments may'st thou stand,
The hallow'd taper trembling in thy hand,
Present the cross before my lifted eye,
Teach me at once, and learn of me, to die.
Ah then, thy once-loved Eloïsa see!
It will be then no crime to gaze on me.
See from my cheek the transient roses fly!
See the last sparkle languish in my eye!

Till every motion, pulse, and breath be o'er;
And even my Abelard be loved no more.
O Death all-eloquent! you only prove
What dust we dote on, when 'tis man we love.
Then, too, when fate shall thy fair frame destroy,
(That cause of all my guilt, and all my joy)
In trance ecstatic may thy pangs be drown'd,
Bright clouds descend, and angels watch thee round,
From opening skies may streaming glories shine,
And saints embrace thee with a love like mine.
May one kind grave unite each hapless name,
And graft my love immortal on thy fame!
Then, ages hence, when all my woes are o'er,
When this rebellious heart shall beat no more;
If ever chance two wandering lovers brings
To Paraclet's white walls and silver springs,
O'er the pale marble shall they join their heads;
And drink the falling tears each other sheds;
Then sadly say, with mutual pity moved,
"Oh may we never love as these have loved!"
From the full choir when loud hosannahs rise,
And swell the pomp of dreadful sacrifice,
Amid that scene if some relenting eye
Glance on the stone where our cold relics lie,
Devotion's self shall steal a thought from heaven,
One human tear shall drop, and be forgiven.
And sure if fate some future bard shall join
In sad similitude of griefs to mine,
Condemn'd whole years in absence to deplore,
And image charms he must behold no more;
Such if there be, who loves so long, so well;
Let him our sad, our tender story tell;
The well-sung woes will soothe my pensive ghost;
He best can paint them who shall feel them most.

TRANSLATIONS AND IMITATIONS.

THE following Translations were selected from many others done by the Author in his youth; for the most part, indeed, but a sort of *Exercises*, while he was improving himself in the languages, and carried by his early bent to *Poetry* to perform them rather in verse than prose. Mr. Dryden's *Fables* came out by that time, which occasioned the Translations from Chaucer. They were first separately printed in Miscellanies by J. Tonson and B. Lintot, and afterwards collected in the quarto edition of 1717. The *Imitations of English Authors*, which are added at the end, were done as early, some of them at fourteen or fifteen years old; but having also got into Miscellanies, we have thought it best so to continue them.

THE TEMPLE OF FAME.

WRITTEN IN THE YEAR MDCCXI.

THE hint of the following piece was taken from Chaucer's *House of Fame*. The design is in a manner entirely altered, the descriptions and most of the particular thoughts my own; yet I could not suffer it to be printed without this acknowledgment. The reader who would compare this with Chaucer, may begin with his third Book of *Fame*, there being nothing in the two first books that answers to their title.

This poem is introduced in the manner of the Provençal poets, whose works were for the most part visions or pieces of imagination, and constantly descriptive.

IN that soft season, when descending showers
Call forth the greens, and wake the rising flowers;
When opening buds salute the welcome day,
And earth relenting feels the genial ray;
As balmy sleep had charm'd my cares to rest,
And love itself was banish'd from my breast,
(What time the morn mysterious visions brings,
While purer slumbers spread their golden wings)
A train of phantoms in wild order rose,
And join'd, this intellectual scene compose.

I stood, methought, betwixt earth, seas, and skies;
The whole creation open to my eyes:
In air self-balanced hung the globe below,
Where mountains rise, and circling oceans flow;
Here naked rocks and empty wastes were seen,
There towery cities, and the forests green;
Here sailing ships delight the wandering eyes;
There trees and intermingled temples rise:
Now a clear sun the shining scene displays,
The transient landscape now in clouds decays.
O'er the wide prospect as I gazed around,
Sudden I heard a wild promiscuous sound,
Like broken thunders that at distance roar,
Or billows murmuring on the hollow shore:
Then gazing up, a glorious pile beheld,
Whose towering summit ambient clouds conceal'd.
High on a rock of ice the structure lay,
Steep its ascent, and slippery was the way;
The wondrous rock like Parian marble shone,
And seem'd, to distant sight, of solid stone.
Inscriptions here of various names I view'd,
The greater part by hostile time subdued;
Yet wide was spread their fame in ages past,
And poets once had promised they should last.
Some fresh engraved appear'd of wits renown'd;
I look'd again, nor could their trace be found.
Critics I saw, that other names deface,
And fix their own, with labour, in their place:
Their own, like others, soon their place resign'd,
Or disappear'd, and left the first behind.
Nor was the work impair'd by storms alone,
But felt the approaches of too warm a sun;
For fame, impatient of extremes, decays
Not more by envy than excess of praise.
Yet part no injuries of heaven could feel,
Like crystal faithful to the graving steel:
The rock's high summit, in the temple's shade,
Nor heat could melt, nor beating storm invade.
Their names inscribed unnumber'd ages past
From time's first birth, with time itself shall last;
These ever new, nor subject to decays,
Spread, and grow brighter with the length of days.
So Zembla's rocks (the beauteous work of frost)
Rise white in air, and glitter o'er the coast;

Pale suns, unfelt, at distance roll away,
And on the impassive ice the lightnings play;
Eternal snows the growing mass supply,
Till the bright mountains prop the incumbent sky
As Atlas fix'd, each hoary pile appears,
The gather'd winter of a thousand years.
On this foundation Fame's high temple stands;
Stupendous pile! not rear'd by mortal hands.
Whate'er proud Rome or artful Greece beheld,
Or elder Babylon, its frame excell'd.
  Four faces had the dome,[1] and ev'ry face
Of various structure, but of equal grace:
Four brazen gates, on columns lifted high,
Salute the different quarters of the sky.
Here fabled chiefs in darker ages born,
Or worthies old, whom arms or arts adorn,
Who cities raised, or tamed a monstrous race,
The walls in venerable order grace.
Heroes in animated marble frown,
And legislators seem to think in stone.
  Westward, a sumptuous frontispiece appear'd,
On Doric pillars of white marble rear'd,
Crown'd with an architrave of antique mould,
And sculpture rising on the roughen'd gold.
In shaggy spoils here Theseus was beheld,
And Perseus dreadful with Minerva's shield:
There great Alcides[2] stooping with his toil,
Rests on his club, and holds the Hesperian spoil.
Here Orpheus sings; trees moving to the sound
Start from their roots, and form a shade around:
Amphion there the loud-creating lyre
Strikes, and beholds a sudden Thebes aspire!
Cithæron's echoes answer to his call,
And half the mountain rolls into a wall:
There might you see the lengthening spires ascend,
The domes swell up, and widening arches bend,

[1] The Temple is described to be square, the four fronts with open gates facing the different quarters of the world, as an intimation that all nations of the earth may alike be received into it. The western front is of Grecian architecture: the Doric order was peculiarly sacred to heroes and worthies. Those whose statues are after mentioned, were the first names of old Greece in arms and arts.

[2] This figure of Hercules is drawn with an eye to the position of the famous statue of Farnese.

The growing towers, like exhalations rise,
And the huge columns heave into the skies.
  The eastern front was glorious to behold,
With diamond flaming, and barbaric gold.
There Ninus shone, who spread the Assyrian fame,
And the great founder of the Persian name:[1]
There in long robes the royal Magi stand,
Grave Zoroaster waves the circling wand,
The sage Chaldeans robed in white appear'd,
And Brachmans, deep in desert woods revered.
These stopp'd the moon, and call'd the unbodied shades
To midnight banquets in the glimmering glades;
Made visionary fabrics round them rise,
And airy spectres skim before their eyes;
Of talismans and sigils knew the power,
And careful watch'd the planetary hour.
Superior, and alone, Confucius stood,
Who taught that useful science, to be good.
  But on the south, a long majestic race
Of Egypt's priests[2] the gilded niches grace,
Who measured earth, described the starry spheres,
And traced the long records of lunar years.
High on his car Sesostris struck my view,
Whom sceptred slaves in golden harness drew:
His hands a bow and pointed javelin hold;
His giant limbs are arm'd in scales of gold.
Between the statues obelisks were placed,
And the learn'd walls with hieroglyphics graced.
  Of Gothic structure was the northern side,[3]
O'erwrought with ornaments of barbarous pride:

[1] Cyrus was the beginning of the Persian, as Ninus was of the Assyrian monarchy. The Magi and Chaldeans (the chief of whom was Zoroaster) employed their studies upon magic and astrology, which was in a manner almost all the learning of the ancient Asian people. We have scarce any account of a moral philosopher except Confucius, the great lawgiver of the Chinese, who lived about two thousand years ago.

[2] The learning of the old Egyptian priests consisted for the most part in geometry and astronomy; they also preserved the history of their nation. Their greatest hero upon record is Sesostris, whose actions and conquests may be seen at large in Diodorus, &c. He is said to have caused the kings he vanquished to draw him in his chariot. The posture of his statue, in these verses, is correspondent to the description which Herodotus gives of one of them remaining in his own time.

[3] The architecture is agreeable to that part of the world. The learning of the northern nations lay more obscure than that of the rest;

There huge Colossæ rose, with trophies crown'd,
And Runic characters were graved around.
There sat Zamolxis with erected eyes,
And Odin here in mimic trances dies.
There on rude iron columns, smear'd with blood,
The horrid forms of Scythian heroes stood,
Druids and bards[1] (their once loud harps unstrung)
And youths that died to be by poets sung.
These and a thousand more of doubtful fame,
To whom old fables gave a lasting name,
In ranks adorn'd the temple's outward face;
The wall in lustre and effect like glass,
Which o'er each object casting various dyes,
Enlarges some, and other multiplies:
Nor void of emblem was the mystic wall,
For thus romantic fame increases all.
  The temple shakes, the sounding gates unfold,
Wide vaults appear, and roofs of fretted gold:
Raised on a thousand pillars, wreathed around
With laurel foliage, and with eagles crown'd:
Of bright, transparent beryl were the walls,
The friezes gold, and gold the capitals:
As heaven with stars, the roof with jewels glows,
And ever-living lamps depend in rows.
Full in the passage of each spacious gate,
The sage historians in white garments wait;
Graved o'er their seats the form of Time was found,
His scythe reversed, and both his pinions bound.
Within stood heroes, who through loud alarms
In bloody fields pursued renown in arms,
High on a throne with trophies charged, I view'd
The youth that all things but himself subdued;[2]

Zamolxis was the disciple of Pythagoras, who taught the immortality of the soul to the Scythians. Odin, or Woden, was the great legislator and hero of the Goths. They tell us of him, that, being subject to fits, he persuaded his followers, that during those trances he received inspirations, from whence he dictated his laws; he is said to have been the inventor of the Runic characters.

[1] These were the priests and poets of those people, so celebrated for their savage virtue. Those heroic barbarians accounted it a dishonour to die in their beds, and rushed on to certain death in the prospect of an after-life, and for the glory of a song from their bards in praise of their actions.

[2] Alexander the Great; the tiara was the crown peculiar to the Asian princes; his desire to be thought the son of Jupiter Ammon caused him to wear the horns of that god, and to represent the same upon his coins; which was continued by several of his successors.

His feet on sceptres and tiaras trod,
And his horn'd head belied the Libyan god.
There Cæsar, graced with both Minervas, shone;
Cæsar, the world's great master, and his own;
Unmoved, superior still in every state,
And scarce detested in his country's fate.
But chief were those, who not for empire fought,
But with their toils their people's safety bought:
High o'er the rest Epaminondas stood;
Timoleon, glorious in his brother's blood;[1]
Bold Scipio, saviour of the Roman state;
Great in his triumphs, in retirement great;
And wise Aurelius, in whose well-taught mind
With boundless power unbounded virtue join'd,
His own strict judge, and patron of mankind.
   Much-suffering heroes next their honours claim
Those of less noisy and less guilty fame,
Fair Virtue's silent train: supreme of these
Here ever shines the godlike Socrates:
He whom ungrateful Athens[2] could expel,
At all times just, but when he sign'd the shell:
Here his abode the martyr'd Phocion claims,
With Agis, not the last of Spartan names:
Unconquer'd Cato shows the wound he tore,
And Brutus his ill genius meets no more.
   But in the centre of the hallow'd choir,[3]
Six pompous columns o'er the rest aspire;
Around the shrine itself of Fame they stand,
Hold the chief honours, and the fane command.

[1] Timoleon had saved the life of his brother Timophanes in the battle between the Argives and Corinthians; but afterwards killed him when he affected the tyranny, preferring his duty to his country to all the obligations of blood.

[2] Aristides, who for his great integrity was distinguished by the appellation of *the Just*. When his countrymen would have banished him by the ostracism, where it was the custom for every man to sign the name of the person he voted to exile in an oyster-shell, a peasant, who could not write, came to Aristides to do it for him, who readily signed his own name.

[3] In the midst of the Temple, nearest the throne of Fame, are placed the greatest names in learning of all antiquity. These are described in such attitudes as express their different characters: the columns on which they are raised are adorned with sculptures, taken from the most striking subjects of their works; which sculpture bears a resemblance, in its manner and character, to the manner and character of their writings.

High on the first, the mighty Homer shone;
Eternal adamant composed his throne;
Father of verse, in holy fillets drest,
His silver beard waved gently o'er his breast;
Tho' blind, a boldness in his looks appears:
In years he seem'd, but not impair'd by years.
The wars of Troy were round the pillar seen:
Here fierce Tydides wounds the Cyprian Queen;
Here Hector glorious from Patroclus' fall,
Here dragg'd in triumph round the Trojan wall:
Motion and life did every part inspire,
Bold was the work, and proved the master's fire;
A strong expression most he seem'd to affect,
And here and there disclosed a brave neglect.
A golden column next in rank appear'd,
On which a shrine of purest gold was rear'd;
Finish'd the whole, and labour'd ev'ry part,
With patient touches of unwearied art:
The Mantuan there in sober triumph sate,
Composed his posture, and his looks sedate;
On Homer still he fix'd a reverend eye,
Great without pride, in modest majesty.
In living sculpture on the sides were spread
The Latian wars, and haughty Turnus dead;
Eliza stretch'd upon the funeral pyre,
Æneas bending with his aged sire:
Troy flamed in burning gold, and o'er the throne
ARMS AND THE MAN in golden ciphers shone.
Four swans sustain a car of silver bright,[1]
With heads advanced, and pinions stretch'd for flight:
Here, like some furious prophet, Pindar rode,
And seem'd to labour with the inspiring god.
Across the harp a careless hand he flings,
And boldly sinks into the sounding strings.
The figured games of Greece the column grace,
Neptune and Jove survey the rapid race.
The youths hang o'er the chariots as they run;
The fiery steeds seem starting from the stone;
The champions in distorted postures threat;
And all appear'd irregularly great.

[1] Pindar, being seated in a chariot, alludes to the chariot-races he celebrated in the Grecian games. The swans are emblems of poetry, their soaring posture intimates the sublimity and activity of his genius. Neptune presided over the Isthmian, and Jupiter over the Olympian games.

Here happy Horace tuned the Ausonian lyre
To sweeter sounds, and temper'd Pindar's fire:
Pleased with Alcæus' manly rage to infuse
The softer spirit of the Sapphic muse.
The polish'd pillar different sculptures grace;
A work outlasting monumental brass.
Here smiling loves and bacchanals appear,
The Julian star, and great Augustus here.
The doves that round the infant poet spread
Myrtles and bays, hung hovering o'er his head.
Here in a shrine that cast a dazzling light,
Sate fix'd in thought the mighty Stagirite;
His sacred head a radiant zodiac crown'd,
And various animals his sides surround;
His piercing eyes, erect, appear to view
Superior worlds, and look all nature through.
With equal rays immortal Tully shone,
The Roman rostra deck'd the consul's throne:
Gathering his flowing robe, he seem'd to stand
In act to speak, and graceful stretch'd his hand.
Behind, Rome's genius waits with civic crowns,
And the great father of his country owns.
These massy columns in a circle rise,
O'er which a pompous dome invades the skies:
Scarce to the top I stretch'd my aching sight,
So large it spread, and swell'd to such a height.
Full in the midst proud Fame's imperial seat
With jewels blazed, magnificently great;
The vivid emeralds there revive the eye,
The flaming rubies show their sanguine dye,
Bright azure rays from lively sapphires stream,
And lucid amber casts a golden gleam.
With various-colour'd light the pavement shone,
And all on fire appear'd the glowing throne,
The dome's high arch reflects the mingled blaze,
And forms a rainbow of alternate rays.
When on the goddess first I cast my sight,
Scarce seem'd her stature of a cubit's height;
But swell'd to larger size, the more I gazed,
Till to the roof her towering front she raised.
With her, the temple every moment grew,
And ampler vistas open'd to my view:
Upward the columns shoot, the roofs ascend,
And arches widen, and long aisles extend.

Such was her form as ancient bards have told,
Wings raise her arms, and wings her feet infold;
A thousand busy tongues the goddess bears,
And thousand open eyes, and thousand listening ears.
Beneath, in order ranged, the tuneful nine
(Her virgin handmaids) still attend the shrine:
With eyes on Fame for ever fix'd, they sing;
For fame they raise the voice, and tune the string;
With time's first birth began the heavenly lays,
And last, eternal, through the length of days.
Around these wonders as I cast a look,
The trumpet sounded, and the Temple shook,
And all the nations, summon'd at the call,
From different quarters fill the crowded hall:
Of various tongues the mingled sounds were heard,
In various garbs promiscuous throngs appear'd;
Thick as the bees, that with the spring renew
Their flowery toils, and sip the fragrant dew,
When the wing'd colonies first tempt the sky,
O'er dusky fields and shaded waters fly,
Or settling, seize the sweets the blossoms yield,
And a low murmur runs along the field.
Millions of suppliant crowds the shrine attend,
And all degrees before the goddess bend;
The poor, the rich, the valiant, and the sage,
And boasting youth, and narrative old age.
Their pleas were different, their request the same:
For good and bad alike are fond of fame.
Some she disgraced, and some with honours crown'd;
Unlike successes equal merits found.
Thus her blind sister, fickle Fortune, reigns,
And, undiscerning, scatters crowns and chains.
First at the shrine the learned world appear,
And to the goddess thus prefer their prayer.
Long have we sought to instruct and please mankind,
With studies pale, with midnight vigils blind;
But thank'd by few, rewarded yet by none,
We here appeal to thy superior throne:
On wit and learning the just prize bestow,
For fame is all we must expect below.
The goddess heard, and bade the muses raise
The golden trumpet of eternal praise:
From pole to pole the winds diffuse the sound,
That fills the circuit of the world around:

Not all at once, as thunder breaks the cloud;
The notes at first were rather sweet than loud:
By just degrees they every moment rise,
Fill the wide earth, and gain upon the skies.
At every breath were balmy odours shed,
Which still grew sweeter as they wider spread;
Less fragrant scents the unfolding rose exhales,
Or spices breathing in Arabian gales.
  Next these the good and just, an awful train,
Thus on their knees address the sacred fane.
Since living virtue is with envy cursed,
And the best men are treated like the worst,
Do thou, just goddess, call our merits forth,
And give each deed the exact intrinsic worth.
Not with bare justice shall your act be crown'd,
(Said Fame,) but high above desert renown'd:
Let fuller notes the applauding world amaze,
And the loud clarion labour in your praise.
  This band dismiss'd, behold another crowd
Preferr'd the same request, and lowly bow'd;
The constant tenour of whose well-spent days
No less deserved a just return of praise.
But straight the direful trump of slander sounds;
Through the big dome the doubling thunder bounds;
Loud as the burst of cannon rends the skies,
The dire report through every region flies.
In every ear incessant rumours rung,
And gathering scandals grew on every tongue:
From the black trumpet's rusty concave broke
Sulphureous flames, and clouds of rolling smoke:
The poisonous vapour blots the purple skies,
And withers all before it as it flies.
  A troop came next, who crowns and armour wore,
And proud defiance in their looks they bore:
For thee, (they cried) amidst alarms and strife,
We sail'd in tempests down the stream of life;
For thee whole nations fill'd with flames and blood,
And swam to empire through the purple flood.
Those ills we dared, thy inspiration own,
What virtue seem'd, was done for thee alone.
Ambitious fools! (the queen replied, and frown'd,)
Be all your acts in dark oblivion drown'd;
There sleep forgot, with mighty tyrants gone,
Your statues moulder'd, and your names unknown!

A sudden cloud straight snatch'd them from my sight,
And each majestic phantom sunk in night.
  Then came the smallest tribe I yet had seen;
Plain was their dress, and modest was their mien.
Great idol of mankind! we neither claim
The praise of merit, nor aspire to fame!
But safe in deserts from the applause of men,
Would die unheard of, as we lived unseen.
'Tis all we beg thee, to conceal from sight
Those acts of goodness, which themselves requite.
Oh let us still the secret joy partake,
To follow virtue e'en for virtue's sake.
  And live there men, who slight immortal Fame?
Who then with incense shall adore our name?
But mortals! know, 'tis still our greatest pride
To blaze those virtues, which the good would hide.
Rise! muses, rise! add all your tuneful breath,
These must not sleep in darkness and in death.
She said: in air the trembling music floats,
And on the winds triumphant swell the notes:
So soft, though high, so loud, and yet so clear,
E'en listening angels lean'd from heaven to hear:
To farthest shores the ambrosial spirit flies,
Sweet to the world, and grateful to the skies.
  Next these a youthful train their vows express'd,
With feathers crown'd, with gay embroidery dress'd;
Hither (they cried) direct your eyes, and see
The men of pleasure, dress, and gallantry;
Ours is the place at banquets, balls, and plays,
Sprightly our nights, polite are all our days;
Courts we frequent, where 'tis our pleasing care
To pay due visits, and address the fair:
In fact, 'tis true, no nymph we could persuade,
But still in fancy vanquish'd every maid!
Of unknown duchesses lewd tales we tell,
Yet, would the world believe us, all were well.
The joy let others have, and we the name,
And what we want in pleasure, grant in fame.
  The Queen assents, the trumpet rends the skies,
And at each blast a lady's honour dies. [press'd
  Pleased with the strange success, vast numbers
Around the shrine, and made the same request:
What! you (she cried) unlearn'd in arts to please,
Slaves to yourselves, and even fatigued with ease,

Who lose a length of undeserving days,
Would you usurp the lover's dear-bought praise?
To just contempt, ye vain pretenders, fall,
The people's fable, and the scorn of all.
Straight the black clarion sends a horrid sound,
Loud laughs burst out, and bitter scoffs fly round,
Whispers are heard, with taunts reviling loud,
And scornful hisses run through all the crowd.
Last, those who boast of mighty mischiefs done,
Enslave their country, or usurp a throne;
Or who their glory's dire foundation laid
On sovereigns ruin'd, or on friends betray'd;
Calm, thinking villains, whom no faith could fix,
Of crooked counsels and dark politics;
Of these a gloomy tribe surround the throne,
And beg to make the immortal treasons known.
The trumpet roars, long flaky flames expire,
With sparks, that seem'd to set the world on fire.
At the dread sound, pale mortals stood aghast,
And startled nature trembled with the blast.
This having heard and seen, some power unknown
Straight changed the scene, and snatch'd me from the throne.
Before my view appear'd a structure fair,
Its site uncertain, if in earth or air;
With rapid motion turn'd the mansion round;
With ceaseless noise the ringing walls resound;
Not less in number were the spacious doors,
Than leaves on trees, or sands upon the shores;
Which still unfolded stand, by night, by day,
Pervious to winds, and open every way.
As flames by nature to the skies ascend,
As weighty bodies to the centre tend,
As to the sea returning rivers roll,
And the touch'd needle trembles to the pole;
Hither, as to their proper place, arise
All various sounds from earth, and seas, and skies,
Or spoke aloud, or whisper'd in the ear;
Nor ever silence, rest, or peace, is here.
As on the smooth expanse of crystal lakes
The sinking stone at first a circle makes;
The trembling surface by the motion stirr'd,
Spreads in a second circle, then a third;
Wide, and more wide, the floating rings advance,
Fill all the watery plain, and to the margin dance:

Thus every voice and sound, when first they break,
On neighbouring air a soft impression make;
Another ambient circle then they move;
That, in its turn, impels the next above;
Through undulating air the sounds are sent,
And spread o'er all the fluid element.
There various news I heard of love and strife,
Of peace and war, health, sickness, death, and life,
Of loss and gain, of famine and of store,
Of storms at sea, and travels on the shore,
Of prodigies, and portents seen in air,
Of fires and plagues, and stars with blazing hair,
Of turns of fortune, changes in the state,
The fall of favourites, projects of the great,
Of old mismanagements, taxations new:
All neither wholly false, nor wholly true.
Above, below, without, within, around,
Confused, unnumber'd multitudes are found,
Who pass, repass, advance, and glide away;
Hosts raised by fear, and phantoms of a day:
Astrologers, that future fates foreshow,
Projectors, quacks, and lawyers not a few;
And priests, and party-zealots, numerous bands
With home-born lies, or tales from foreign lands;
Each talk'd aloud, or in some secret place,
And wild impatience stared in every face.
The flying rumours gather'd as they roll'd,
Scarce any tale was sooner heard than told;
And all who told it added something new,
And all who heard it made enlargements too;
In every ear it spread, on every tongue it grew.
Thus flying east and west, and north and south,
News travell'd with increase from mouth to mouth.
So from a spark, that kindled first by chance,
With gathering force the quickening flames advance;
Till to the clouds their curling heads aspire,
And towers and temples sink in floods of fire.
When thus ripe, lies are to perfection sprung,
Full grown, and fit to grace a mortal tongue,
Through thousand vents, impatient, forth they flow,
And rush in millions on the world below.
Fame sits aloft, and points them out their course,
Their date determines, and prescribes their force:

Some to remain, and some to perish soon;
Or wane and wax alternate like the moon.
Around, a thousand winged wonders fly,
Borne by the trumpet's blast, and scatter'd through the [sky.
  There, at one passage, oft you might survey,
A lie and truth contending for the way;
And long 'twas doubtful, both so closely pent,
Which first should issue through the narrow vent:
At last agreed, together out they fly,
Inseparable now, the truth and lie;
The strict companions are for ever join'd,
And this or that unmix'd, no mortal e'er shall find.
  While thus I stood, intent to see and hear,
One came, methought, and whisper'd in my ear:
What could thus high thy rash ambition raise?
Art thou, fond youth, a candidate for praise?
  'Tis true, said I, not void of hopes I came,
For who so fond as youthful bards of Fame?
But few, alas! the casual blessing boast,
So hard to gain, so easy to be lost.
How vain that second life in others' breath,
The estate which wits inherit after death!
Ease, health, and life, for this they must resign,
(Unsure the tenure, but how vast the fine!)
The great man's curse, without the gains, endure,
Be envied, wretched; and be flatter'd, poor;
All luckless wits their enemies profess'd,
And all successful, jealous friends at best.
Nor Fame I slight, nor for her favours call;
She comes unlook'd for, if she comes at all.
But if the purchase costs so dear a price,
As soothing folly, or exalting vice:
Oh! if the muse must flatter lawless sway,
And follow still where fortune leads the way;
Or if no basis bear my rising name,
But the fallen ruins of another's fame;
Then teach me, Heaven! to scorn the guilty bays,
Drive from my breast that wretched lust of praise;
Unblemish'd let me live, or die unknown;
Oh! grant an honest fame, or grant me none!

JANUARY AND MAY;

OR,

The Merchant's Tale.

FROM CHAUCER.

There lived in Lombardy, as authors write,
In days of old, a wise and worthy knight;
Of gentle manners, as of generous race,
Blest with much sense, more riches, and some grace.
Yet led astray by Venus' soft delights,
He scarce could rule some idle appetites:
For long ago, let priests say what they could,
Weak sinful laymen were but flesh and blood.
  But in due time, when sixty years were o'er,
He vow'd to lead this vicious life no more;
Whether pure holiness inspired his mind,
Or dotage turn'd his brain, is hard to find;
But his high courage prick'd him forth to wed,
And try the pleasures of a lawful bed.
This was his nightly dream, his daily care,
And to the heavenly powers his constant prayer,
Once, ere he died, to taste the blissful life
Of a kind husband and a loving wife.
  These thoughts he fortified with reasons still,
(For none want reasons to confirm their will.)
Grave authors say, and witty poets sing,
That honest wedlock is a glorious thing:
But depth of judgment most in him appears,
Who wisely weds in his maturer years,
Then let him choose a damsel young and fair,
To bless his age, and bring a worthy heir;
To soothe his cares, and free from noise and strife,
Conduct him gently to the verge of life.
Let sinful bachelors their woes deplore,
Full well they merit all they feel, and more;
Unawed by precepts human or divine,
Like birds and beasts, promiscuously they join:
Nor know to make the present blessing last,
To hope the future, or esteem the past:
But vainly boast the joys they never tried,
And find divulged the secrets they would hide.

The married man may bear his yoke with ease,
Secure at once himself and Heaven to please;
And pass his inoffensive hours away,
In bliss all night, and innocence all day:
Though fortune change, his constant spouse remains,
Augments his joys, or mitigates his pains.
But what so pure, which envious tongues will spare?
Some wicked wits have libell'd all the fair.
With matchless impudence they style a wife
The dear-bought curse, and lawful plague of life;
A bosom-serpent, a domestic evil,
A night invasion, and a mid-day devil.
Let not the wise these slanderous words regard,
But curse the bones of every lying bard;
All other goods by fortune's hand are given,
A wife is the peculiar gift of Heaven.
Vain fortune's favours, never at a stay,
Like empty shadows, pass, and glide away;
One solid comfort, our eternal wife,
Abundantly supplies us all our life:
This blessing lasts (if those who try, say true)
As long as heart can wish—and longer too.
Our grandsire Adam, ere of Eve possess'd,
Alone, and even in Paradise unbless'd,
With mournful looks the blissful scenes survey'd,
And wander'd in the solitary shade:
The Maker saw, took pity, and bestow'd
Woman, the last, the best reserved of God,
A wife! ah gentle deities, can he
That has a wife e'er feel adversity?
Would men but follow what the sex advise,
All things would prosper, all the world grow wise.
'Twas by Rebecca's aid that Jacob won
His father's blessing from an elder son:
Abusive Nabal owed his forfeit life
To the wise conduct of a prudent wife:
Heroic Judith, as old Hebrews show,
Preserved the Jews, and slew the Assyrian foe:
At Hester's suit, the persecuting sword
Was sheathed, and Israel lived to bless the Lord.
These weighty motives, January the sage
Maturely pondered in his riper age;
And charm'd with virtuous joys, and sober life,
Would try that christian comfort, call'd a wife.

His friends were summon'd on a point so nice,
To pass their judgment, and to give advice;
But fix'd before, and well resolved was he;
(As men that ask advice are wont to be.)
My friends, he cried (and cast a mournful look
Around the room, and sigh'd before he spoke),
Beneath the weight of threescore years I bend,
And, worn with cares, am hastening to my end;
How have I lived, alas! you know too well,
In worldly follies, which I blush to tell;
But gracious Heaven has ope'd my eyes at last,
With due regret I view my vices past
And, as the precept of the Church decrees,
Will take a wife, and live in holy ease.
But since by counsel all things should be done,
And many heads are wiser still than one;
Choose you for me, who best shall be content
When my desire's approved by your consent.
One caution yet is needful to be told,
To guide your choice; this wife must not be old:
There goes a saying, and 'twas shrewdly said,
Old fish at table, but young flesh in bed.
My soul abhors the tasteless, dry embrace
Of a stale virgin with a winter face:
In that cold season Love but treats his guest
With bean-straw and tough forage at the best.
No crafty widows shall approach my bed;
Those are too wise for bachelors to wed.
As subtle clerks by many schools are made,
Twice-married dames are mistresses o' th' trade:
But young and tender virgins, ruled with ease,
We form like wax, and mould them as we please.
Conceive me, Sirs, nor take my sense amiss;
'Tis what concerns my soul's eternal bliss;
Since if I found no pleasure in my spouse,
As flesh is frail, and who (God help me) knows?
Then should I live in lewd adultery,
And sink downright to Satan when I die.
Or were I cursed with an unfruitful bed,
The righteous end were lost for which I wed;
To raise up seed to bless the powers above,
And not for pleasure only, or for love.
Think not I dote; 'tis time to take a wife,
When vigorous blood forbids a chaster life;

Those that are blest with store of grace divine,
May live like saints by Heaven's consent, and mine.
And since I speak of wedlock, let me say,
(As, thank my stars, in modest truth I may)
My limbs are active, still I'm sound at heart,
And a new vigour springs in every part.
Think not my virtue lost, tho' time has shed
These reverend honours on my hoary head:
Thus trees are crown'd with blossoms white as snow,
The vital sap then rising from below,
Old as I am, my lusty limbs appear
Like winter greens, that flourish all the year.
Now, Sirs, you know to what I stand inclined,
Let every friend with freedom speak his mind.
He said; the rest in different parts divide;
The knotty point was urged on either side:
Marriage, the theme on which they all declaim'd;
Some praised with wit, and some with reason blamed.
Till, what with proofs, objections, and replies,
Each wondrous positive, and wondrous wise,
There fell between his brothers a debate,
Placebo this was called, and Justin that.
First to the Knight Placebo thus begun
(Mild were his looks, and pleasing was his tone):
Such prudence, Sir, in all your words appears,
As plainly proves, experience dwells with years!
Yet you pursue sage Solomon's advice,
To work by counsel when affairs are nice:
But, with the wise man's leave, I must protest,
So may my soul arrive at ease and rest,
As still I hold your own advice the best.
Sir, I have lived a courtier all my days,
And studied men, their manners, and their ways;
And have observed this useful maxim still,
To let my betters always have their will.
Nay, if my lord affirm'd that black was white,
My word was this, "Your honour's in the right."
The assuming wit, who deems himself so wise
As his mistaken patron to advise,
Let him not dare to vent his dangerous thought,
A noble fool was never in a fault.
This, Sir, affects not you, whose every word
Is weigh'd with judgment, and befits a lord:

Your will is mine; and is (I will maintain)
Pleasing to God, and should be so to man;
At least your courage all the world must praise,
Who dare to wed in your declining days.
Indulge the vigour of your mounting blood,
And let grey fools be indolently good,
Who, past all pleasure, damn the joys of sense,
With reverend dulness and grave impotence.
Justin, who silent sate, and heard the man,
Thus, with a philosophic frown, began:
A heathen author, of the first degree
(Who, tho' not faith, had sense as well as we),
Bids us be certain our concerns to trust
To those of generous principles, and just.
The venture's greater, I'll presume to say,
To give your person, than your goods away:
And therefore, Sir, as you regard your rest,
First learn your lady's qualities at least;
Whether she's chaste or rampant, proud or civil;
Meek as a saint, or haughty as the devil;
Whether an easy, fond, familiar fool,
Or such a wit as no man e'er can rule.
'Tis true, perfection none must hope to find
In all this world, much less in woman-kind;
But if her virtues prove the larger share,
Bless the kind fates, and think your fortune rare.
Ah, gentle Sir, take warning of a friend,
Who knows too well the state you thus commend;
And spite of all his praises must declare,
All he can find is bondage, cost, and care.
Heaven knows, I shed full many a private tear,
And sigh in silence, lest the world should hear;
While all my friends applaud my blissful life,
And swear no mortal's happier in a wife;
Demure and chaste as any vestal nun,
The meekest creature that beholds the sun!
But, by the immortal powers, I feel the pain,
And he that smarts has reason to complain.
Do what you list, for me; you must be sage,
And cautious sure; for wisdom is in age:
But at these years to venture on the fair!
By him who made the ocean, earth, and air,
To please a wife, when her occasions call,
Would busy the most vigorous of us all.

And trust me, Sir, the chastest you can choose
Will ask observance, and exact her dues.
If what I speak my noble lord offend,
My tedious sermon here is at an end.
'Tis well, 'tis wondrous well, the Knight replies,
Most worthy kinsmen, faith you're mighty wise!
We, Sirs, are fools; and must resign the cause
To heathenish authors, proverbs, and old saws.
He spoke with scorn, and turn'd another way:—
What does my friend, my dear Placebo, say?
I say, quoth he, by Heaven the man's to blame,
To slander wives, and wedlock's holy name.
At this the council rose, without delay;
Each, in his own opinion, went his way;
With full consent, that, all disputes appeased;
The Knight should marry, when and where he pleased.

Who now but January exults with joy?
The charms of wedlock all his soul employ:
Each nymph by turns his wavering mind possest,
And reign'd the short-lived tyrant of his breast;
Whilst fancy pictured every lively part,
And each bright image wander'd o'er his heart.
Thus, in some public forum fix'd on high,
A mirror shows the figures moving by;
Still one by one, in swift succession, pass
The gliding shadows o'er the polish'd glass.
This lady's charms the nicest could not blame,
But vile suspicions had aspersed her fame;
That was with sense, but not with virtue blest:
And one had grace, that wanted all the rest.
Thus doubting long what nymph he should obey,
He fixed at last upon the youthful May.
Her faults he knew not, Love is always blind,
But every charm revolved within his mind:
Her tender age, her form divinely fair,
Her easy motion, her attractive air,
Her sweet behaviour, her enchanting face,
Her moving softness, and majestic grace.
Much in his prudence did our Knight rejoice,
And thought no mortal could dispute his choice:
Once more in haste he summon'd ev'ry friend,
And told them all, their pains were at an end.

Heaven, that (said he) inspired me first to wed,
Provides a consort worthy of my bed:
Let none oppose the election, since on this
Depends my quiet, and my future bliss.
A dame there is, the darling of my eyes,
Young, beauteous, artless, innocent, and wise;
Chaste, tho' not rich; and tho' not nobly born,
Of honest parents, and may serve my turn.
Her will I wed, if gracious Heaven so please;
To pass my age in sanctity and ease;
And thank the powers, I may possess alone
The lovely prize, and share my bliss with none!
If you, my friends, this virgin can procure,
My joys are full, my happiness is sure.
One only doubt remains: full oft, I've heard,
By casuists grave, and deep divines averr'd;
That 'tis too much for human race to know
The bliss of heaven above, and earth below.
Now should the nuptial pleasures prove so great,
To match the blessings of the future state,
Those endless joys were ill-exchanged for these;
Then clear this doubt, and set my mind at ease.
This Justin heard, nor could his spleen control,
Touch'd to the quick, and tickled at the soul.
Sir Knight, he cried, if this be all you dread,
Heaven put it past a doubt, whene'er you wed;
And to my fervent prayers so far consent,
That ere the rites are o'er, you may repent!
Good heaven, no doubt, the nuptial state approves
Since it chastises still what best it loves.
Then be not, Sir, abandon'd to despair;
Seek, and perhaps you'll find among the fair,
One, that may do your business to a hair;
Not e'en in wish, your happiness delay,
But prove the scourge to lash you on your way:
Then to the skies your mounting soul shall go,
Swift as an arrow soaring from the bow!
Provided still, you moderate your joy,
Nor in your pleasures all your might employ,
Let reason's rule your strong desires abate,
Nor please too lavishly your gentle mate.
Old wives there are, of judgment most acute,
Who solve these questions beyond all dispute;

Consult with those, and be of better cheer;
Marry, do penance, and dismiss your fear.
So said, they rose, nor more the work delay'd;
The match was offer'd, the proposals made.
The parents, you may think, would soon comply;
The old have interest ever in their eye.
Nor was it hard to move the lady's mind;
When fortune favours, still the fair are kind.
I pass each previous settlement and deed,
Too long for me to write, or you to read;
Nor will with quaint impertinence display
The pomp, the pageantry, the proud array.
The time approach'd; to church the parties went,
At once with carnal and devout intent:
Forth came the priest, and bade the obedient wife
Like Sarah or Rebecca lead her life:
Then pray'd the powers the fruitful bed to bless,
And made all sure enough with holiness.
And now the palace-gates are open'd wide,
The guests appear in order, side by side,
And placed in state, the bridegroom and the bride.
The breathing flute's soft notes are heard around,
And the shrill trumpets mix their silver sound;
The vaulted roofs with echoing music ring, [string.
These touch the vocal stops, and those the trembling
Not thus Amphion tuned the warbling lyre,
Nor Joab the sounding clarion could inspire,
Nor fierce Theodamas, whose sprightly strain
Could swell the soul to rage, and fire the martial train.
Bacchus himself, the nuptial feast to grace,
(So Poets sing) was present on the place:
And lovely Venus, goddess of delight,
Shook high her flaming torch in open sight,
And danced around, and smiled on every knight:
Pleased her best servant would his courage try,
No less in wedlock, than in liberty.
Full many an age old Hymen had not spied
So kind a bridegroom, or so bright a bride.
Ye bards! renown'd among the tuneful throng
For gentle lays, and joyous nuptial song;
Think not your softest numbers can display
The matchless glories of this blissful day;
The joys are such, as far transcend your rage,
When tender youth has wedded stooping age.

p. 124.

JANUARY AND MAY.

The guests appear in order, side by side,
And, placed in state, the bridegroom and the bride.

The beauteous dame sat smiling at the board,
And darted amorous glances at her lord.
Not Esther's self, whose charms the Hebrews sing,
E'er look'd so lovely on her Persian king:
Bright as the rising sun, in summer's day,
And fresh and blooming as the month of May!
The joyful knight survey'd her by his side,
Nor envied Paris with the Spartan bride;
Still as his mind revolved with vast delight
The entrancing raptures of the approaching night,
Restless he sate, invoking every power
To speed his bliss, and haste the happy hour.
Meantime the vigorous dancers beat the ground,
And songs were sung, and flowing bowls went round.
With odorous spices they perfumed the place,
And mirth and pleasure shone in every face.
Damian alone, of all the menial train,
Sad in the midst of triumphs, sigh'd for pain;
Damian alone, the knight's obsequious squire,
Consumed at heart, and fed a secret fire.
His lovely mistress all his soul possess'd;
He look'd, he languish'd, and could take no rest
His task perform'd, he sadly went his way,
Fell on his bed, and loathed the light of day.
There let him lie; till his relenting dame
Weep in her turn, and waste in equal flame.
The weary sun, as learned poets write,
Forsook the horizon, and roll'd down the light;
While glittering stars his absent beams supply,
And night's dark mantle overspread the sky.
Then rose the guests: and, as the time required,
Each paid his thanks, and decently retired.
The foe once gone, our Knight prepared to undress,
So keen he was, and eager to possess:
But first thought fit the assistance to receive,
Which grave physicians scruple not to give;
Satyrion near, with hot eringos stood,
Cantharides, to fire the lazy blood,
Whose use old bards describe in luscious rhymes,
And critics learn'd explain to modern times.
By this the sheets were spread, the bride undress'd,
The room was sprinkled, and the bed was bless'd.
What next ensued beseems not me to say;
'Tis sung, he laboured till the dawning day,

Then briskly sprung from bed, with heart so light,
As all were nothing he had done by night;
And sipp'd his cordial as he sat upright.
He kiss'd his balmy spouse with wanton play,
And feebly sung a lusty roundelay:
Then on the couch his weary limbs he cast;
For every labour must have rest at last.
But anxious cares the pensive squire oppress'd,
Sleep fled his eyes, and peace forsook his breast;
The raging flames that in his bosom dwell,
He wanted art to hide, and means to tell.
Yet hoping time the occasion might betray,
Composed a sonnet to the lovely May;
Which, writ and folded with the nicest art,
He wrapp'd in silk, and laid upon his heart.
When now the fourth revolving day was run,
('Twas June—and Cancer had received the sun)
Forth from her chamber came the beauteous bride,
The good old knight moved slowly by her side.
High mass was sung; they feasted in the hall;
The servants round stood ready at their call.
The squire alone was absent from the board,
And much his sickness grieved his worthy lord,
Who pray'd his spouse, attended with her train,
To visit Damian, and divert his pain.
The obliging dames obey'd with one consent;
They left the hall, and to his lodging went.
The female tribe surround him as he lay,
And close beside him sat the gentle May:
Where, as she tried his pulse, he softly drew
A heaving sigh, and cast a mournful view!
Then gave his bill, and bribed the powers divine,
With secret vows to favour his design.
Who studies now but discontented May?
On her soft couch uneasily she lay:
The lumpish husband snored away the night,
Till coughs awaked him near the morning light.
What then he did, I'll not presume to tell,
Nor if she thought herself in heaven or hell:
Honest and dull in nuptial bed they lay,
Till the bell toll'd, and all arose to pray.
Were it by forceful destiny decreed,
Or did from chance, or nature's power proceed;

Or that some star, with aspect kind to love
Shed its selectest influence from above;
Whatever was the cause, the tender dame
Felt the first motions of an infant flame;
Received the impressions of the love-sick squire,
And wasted in the soft infectious fire.
Ye fair, draw near, let May's example move
Your gentle minds to pity those who love!
Had some fierce tyrant in her stead been found,
The poor adorer sure had hang'd, or drown'd:
But she, your sex's mirror, free from pride,
Was much too meek to prove a homicide.
  But to my tale: Some sages have defined
Pleasure the sovereign bliss of human-kind:
Our Knight (who studied much, we may suppose)
Derived his high philosophy from those;
For, like a prince, he bore the vast expense
Of lavish pomp, and proud magnificence:
His house was stately, his retinue gay,
Large was his train, and gorgeous his array.
His spacious garden, made to yield to none,
Was compass'd round with walls of solid stone;
Priapus could not half describe the grace
(Though god of gardens) of this charming place:
A place to tire the rambling wits of France
In long descriptions, and exceed romance:
Enough to shame the gentlest bard that sings
Of painted meadows, and of purling springs.
  Full in the centre of the flowery ground,
A crystal fountain spread its streams around,
The fruitful banks with verdant laurels crown'd:
About this spring (if ancient fame say true)
The dapper elves their moonlight sports pursue:
Their pigmy king, and little fairy queen,
In circling dances gamboll'd on the green,
While tuneful sprites a merry concert made,
And airy music warbled through the shade.
  Hither the noble Knight would oft repair
(His scene of pleasure, and peculiar care)
For this he held it dear, and always bore
The silver key that lock'd the garden door.
To this sweet place in summer's sultry heat,
He used from noise and business to retreat:

And here in dalliance spend the live-long day,
Solus cum sola, with his sprightly May.
For whate'er work was undischarged a-bed,
The duteous Knight in this fair garden sped.
  But ah! what mortal lives of bliss secure,
How short a space our worldly joys endure!
O Fortune, fair, like all thy treacherous kind,
But faithless still, and wavering as the wind!
O painted monster, form'd mankind to cheat,
With pleasing poison, and with soft deceit!
This rich, this amorous, venerable knight,
Amidst his ease, his solace, and delight,
Struck blind by thee, resigns his days to grief,
And calls on death, the wretch's last relief.
  The rage of jealousy then seized his mind,
For much he fear'd the faith of woman-kind.
His wife not suffer'd from his side to stay,
Was captive kept, he watch'd her night and day,
Abridged her pleasures, and confined her sway.
Full oft in tears did hapless May complain,
And sigh'd full oft; but sigh'd and wept in vain;
She look'd on Damian with a lover's eye;
For oh, 'twas fix'd; she must possess or die!
Nor less impatience vex'd her amorous squire,
Wild with delay, and burning with desire.
Watch'd as she was, yet could he not refrain
By secret writing to disclose his pain;
The dame by signs reveal'd her kind intent,
Till both were conscious what each other meant.
  Ah, gentle Knight, what would thy eyes avail,
Tho' they could see as far as ships can sail?
'Tis better, sure, when blind, deceived to be,
Than be deluded when a man can see!
  Argus himself, so cautious and so wise,
Was over-watch'd, for all his hundred eyes:
So many an honest husband may, 'tis known,
Who, wisely, never thinks the case his own.
  The dame at last, by diligence and care,
Procured the key her Knight was wont to bear;
She took the wards in wax before the fire,
And gave the impression to the trusty squire.
By means of this, some wonder shall appear,
Which, in due place and season, you may hear.

Well sung sweet Ovid, in the days of yore,
What slight is that, which love will not explore?
And Pyramus and Thisbe plainly show
The feats true lovers, when they list, can do:
Though watch'd and captive, yet in spite of all,
They found the art of kissing through a wall.
But now no longer from our tale to stray;
It happ'd that once upon a summer's day,
Our reverend Knight was urged to amorous play:
He raised his spouse ere matin-bell was rung,
And thus his morning canticle he sung.
Awake, my love, disclose thy radiant eyes,
Arise, my wife, my beauteous lady, rise!
Hear how the doves with pensive notes complain,
And in soft murmurs tell the trees their pain:
The winter's past; the clouds and tempests fly;
The sun adorns the fields, and brightens all the sky
Fair without spot, whose every charming part
My bosom wounds, and captivates my heart;
Come, and in mutual pleasures let's engage,
Joy of my life, and comfort of my age.
This heard, to Damian straight a sign she made,
To haste before; the gentle squire obey'd:
Secret and undescried he took his way,
And ambush'd close behind an arbour lay.
It was not long ere January came,
And hand in hand with him his lovely dame;
Blind as he was, not doubting all was sure,
He turn'd the key, and made the gate secure.
Here let us walk, he said, observed by none,
Conscious of pleasures to the world unknown:
So may my soul have joy, as thou my wife
Art far the dearest solace of my life;
And rather would I choose, by Heaven above,
To die this instant, than to lose thy love.
Reflect what truth was in my passion shown,
When, unendow'd, I took thee for my own,
And sought no treasure but thy heart alone.
Old as I am, and now deprived of sight,
Whilst thou art faithful to thy own true Knight,
Nor age, nor blindness, robs me of delight.
Each other loss with patience I can bear,
The loss of thee is what I only fear.

Consider then, my lady and my wife,
The solid comforts of a virtuous life.
As first, the love of Christ himself you gain;
Next, your own honour undefiled maintain;
And lastly, that which sure your mind must move,
My whole estate shall gratify your love:
Make your own terms, and ere to-morrow's sun
Displays his light, by Heaven it shall be done.
I seal the contract with a holy kiss,
And will perform, by this—my dear, and this—
Have comfort, spouse, nor think thy lord unkind;
'Tis love, not jealousy, that fires my mind.
For when thy charms my sober thoughts engage,
And join'd to them my own unequal age,
From thy dear side I have no power to part,
Such secret transports warm my melting heart.
For who that once possess'd those heavenly charms
Could live one moment absent from thy arms?
He ceased, and May with modest grace replied;
(Weak was her voice, as while she spoke she cried;)
Heaven knows (with that a tender sigh she drew)
I have a soul to save as well as you;
And, what no less you to my charge commend,
My dearest honour, will to death defend.
To you in holy Church I gave my hand,
And join'd my heart in wedlock's sacred band:
Yet, after this, if you distrust my care,
Then hear, my lord, and witness what I swear:
First may the yawning earth her bosom rend,
And let me hence to hell alive descend;
Or die the death I dread no less than hell,
Sewed in a sack, and plunged into a well:
Ere I my fame by one lewd act disgrace,
Or once renounce the honour of my race.
For know, Sir Knight, of gentle blood I came,
I loathe a whore, and startle at the name.
But jealous men on their own crimes reflect,
And learn from thence their ladies to suspect:
Else why these needless cautions, Sir, to me?
These doubts and fears of female constancy!
This chime still rings in every lady's ear,
The only strain a wife must hope to hear.
Thus while she spoke a sidelong glance she cast
Where Damian kneeling, worshipp'd as she past:

She saw him watch the motions of her eye,
And singled out a pear-tree planted nigh:
'Twas charged with fruit which made a goodly show,
And hung with dangling pears was every bough.
Thither the obsequious squire address'd his pace,
And climbing, in the summit took his place;
The Knight and Lady walk'd beneath in view,
Where let us leave them, and our tale pursue.
'Twas now the season when the glorious sun
His heavenly progress through the Twins had run;
And Jove, exalted, his mild influence yields,
To glad the glebe, and paint the flowery fields:
Clear was the day, and Phœbus rising bright,
Had streak'd the azure firmament with light;
He pierced the glittering clouds with golden streams,
And warmed the womb of earth with genial beams.
It so befel, in that fair morning tide,
The Fairies sported on the garden side,
And in the midst their monarch and his bride.
So featly tripp'd the light-foot ladies round,
The knights so nimbly o'er the green-sward bound,
That scarce they bent the flowers or touch'd the ground.
The dances ended, all the fairy train
For pinks and daisies search'd the flowery plain;
While on the bank reclined of rising green,
Thus, with a frown, the king bespoke his queen.
'Tis too apparent, argue what you can,
The treachery you women use to man:
A thousand authors have this truth made out,
And sad experience leaves no room for doubt.
Heaven rest thy spirit, noble Solomon,
A wiser monarch never saw the sun:
All wealth, all honours, the supreme degree
Of earthly bliss, was well bestow'd on thee!
For sagely hast thou said: Of all mankind,
One only just and righteous, hope to find:
But should'st thou search the spacious world around,
Yet one good woman is not to be found.
Thus says the king who knew your wickedness;
The son of Sirach testifies no less.
So may some wildfire on your bodies fall,
Or some devouring flame consume you all;
As well you view the lecher in the tree,
And well this honourable Knight you see:

But since he's blind and old (a helpless case),
His squire shall cuckold him before your face.
Now by my own dread majesty I swear,
And by this awful sceptre which I bear,
No impious wretch shall 'scape unpunish'd long,
That in my presence offers such a wrong.
I will this instant undeceive the Knight,
And, in the very act, restore his sight:
And set the strumpet here in open view
A warning to the ladies, and to you,
And all the faithless sex, for ever to be true.
And will you so, replied the Queen, indeed!
Now, by my mother's soul it is decreed,
She shall not want an answer at her need.
For her, and for her daughters, I'll engage,
And all the sex in each succeeding age;
Art shall be theirs to varnish an offence,
And fortify their crimes with confidence.
Nay, were they taken in a strict embrace,
Seen with both eyes, and pinion'd on the place;
All they shall need is to protest and swear,
Breathe a soft sigh, and drop a tender tear;
Till their wise husbands, gull'd by arts like these
Grow gentle, tractable, and tame as geese.
What tho' this sland'rous Jew, this Solomon,
Called women fools, and knew full many a one;
The wiser wits of later times declare,
How constant, chaste, and virtuous women are:
Witness the martyrs, who resigned their breath,
Serene in torments, unconcerned in death;
And witness next what Roman authors tell,
How Arria, Portia, and Lucretia fell.
But since the sacred leaves to all are free,
And men interpret texts, why should not we?
By this no more was meant, than to have shown,
That sovereign goodness dwells in him alone
Who only is, and is but only one.
But grant the worst; shall women then be weighed
By every word that Solomon has said?
What tho' this King (as ancient story boasts)
Built a fair temple to the Lord of hosts;
He ceased at last his Maker to adore,
And did as much for idol gods, or more.
Beware what lavish praises you confer
On a rank lecher and idolater;

Whose reign indulgent God, says Holy Writ,
Did but for David's righteous sake permit;
David, the monarch after Heaven's own mind,
Who loved our sex, and honoured all our kind.
Well, I'm a woman, and as such must speak;
Silence would swell me, and my heart would break.
Know then, I scorn your dull authorities,
Your idle wits, and all their learned lies.
By Heaven, those authors are our sex's foes,
Whom, in our right, I must and will oppose.
Nay (quoth the King), dear Madam, be not wroth:
I yield it up; but since I gave my oath,
That this much injured Knight again should see,
It must be done—I am a king, said he,
And one, whose faith has ever sacred been—
And so has mine (she said)—I am a queen:
Her answer she shall have, I undertake;
And thus an end of all dispute I make.
Try when you list; and you shall find, my lord,
It is not in our sex to break our word.
We leave them here in this heroic strain,
And to the Knight our story turns again;
Who in the garden, with his lovely May,
Sung merrier than the cuckoo or the jay:
This was his song; "Oh kind and constant be,
Constant and kind I'll ever prove to thee."
Thus singing as he went, at last he drew
By easy steps, to where the pear-tree grew:
The longing dame look'd up, and spied her love,
Full fairly perch'd among the boughs above.
She stopp'd, and sighing—Oh! good gods, she cried,
What pangs, what sudden shoots distend my side!
O for that tempting fruit, so fresh, so green;
Help, for the love of heaven's immortal queen;
Help, dearest lord, and save at once the life
Of thy poor infant, and thy longing wife!
Sore sigh'd the Knight to hear his Lady's cry,
But could not climb, and had no servant nigh:
Old as he was, and void of eyesight too,
What could, alas! a helpless husband do?
And must I languish then, she said, and die
Yet view the lovely fruit before my eye?
At least, kind Sir, for charity's sweet sake,
Vouchsafe the trunk between your arms to take:

Then from your back I might ascend the tree
Do you but stoop, and leave the rest to me.
 With all my soul, he thus replied again,
I'd spend my dearest blood to ease thy pain.
With that, his back against the trunk he bent,
She seized a twig, and up the tree she went.
 Now prove your patience, gentle ladies all!
Nor let on me your heavy anger fall:
'Tis truth I tell, tho' not in phrase refined:
Tho' blunt my tale, yet honest is my mind.
What feats the lady in the tree might do,
I pass, as gambols never known to you;
But sure it was a merrier fit she swore,
Than in her life she ever felt before.
 In that nice moment, lo! the wondering Knight
Look'd out, and stood restored to sudden sight.
Straight on the tree his eager eyes he bent,
As one whose thoughts were on his spouse intent;
But when he saw his bosom-wife so dress'd,
His rage was such as cannot be express'd:
Not frantic mothers when their infants die,
With louder clamours rend the vaulted sky:
He cried, he roar'd, he storm'd, he tore his hair;
Death! hell! and furies! what dost thou do there!
 What ails my lord? the trembling dame replied;
I thought your patience had been better tried;
Is this your love, ungrateful and unkind,
This my reward for having cured the blind?
Why was I taught to make my husband see,
By struggling with a man upon a tree?
Did I for this the power of magic prove?
Unhappy wife, whose crime was too much love!
 If this be struggling, by this holy light
'Tis struggling with a vengeance! (quoth the Knight)
So Heaven preserve the sight it has restored,
As with these eyes I plainly saw thee whored;
Whored by my slave—perfidious wretch! may hell
As surely seize thee, as I saw too well.
 Guard me, good angels! cried the gentle May,
Pray Heaven this magic work the proper way!
Alas, my love! 'tis certain, could you see,
You ne'er had used these killing words to me;
So help me, fates, as 'tis no perfect sight,
But some faint glimmering of a doubtful light.

What I have said (quoth he) I must maintain,
For by the immortal pow'rs it *seemed* too plain—
By all those powers some frenzy seized your mind,
(Replied the dame) are these the thanks I find?
Wretch that I am, that e'er I was so kind!
She said; a rising sigh express'd her woe,
The ready tears apace began to flow,
And as they fell she wiped from either eye
The drops (for women, when they list, can cry).
The Knight was touch'd; and in his looks appeared
Signs of remorse, while thus his spouse he cheered:
Madam, 'tis past, and my short anger o'er!
Come down, and vex your tender heart no more;
Excuse me, dear, if aught amiss was said,
For, on my soul, amends shall soon be made:
Let my repentance your forgiveness draw,
By Heav'n, I swore but what I *thought* I saw.
Ah, my loved lord! 'twas much unkind (she cried)
On bare suspicion thus to treat your bride.
But till your sight's establish'd for a while,
Imperfect objects may your sense beguile.
Thus when from sleep we first our eyes display,
The balls are wounded with the piercing ray,
And dusky vapours rise, and intercept the day:
So just recovering from the shades of night,
Your swimming eyes are drunk with sudden light,
Strange phantoms dance around, and skim before your sight.
Then, Sir, be cautious, nor too rashly deem;
Heaven knows how seldom things are what they seem!
Consult your reason, and you soon shall find
'Twas you were jealous, not your wife unkind:
Jove ne'er spoke oracle more true than this,
None judge so wrong as those who think amiss.
With that she leap'd into her lord's embrace
With well-dissembled virtue in her face.
He hugg'd her close, and kiss'd her o'er and o'er,
Disturb'd with doubts and jealousies no more:
Both, pleased and bless'd, renew'd their mutual vows,
A fruitful wife and a believing spouse.
Thus ends our tale, whose moral next to make;
Let all wise husbands hence example take;
And pray, to crown the pleasure of their lives,
To be so well deluded by their wives.

THE WIFE OF BATH.

HER PROLOGUE.

FROM CHAUCER.

BEHOLD the woes of matrimonial life,
And hear with reverence an experienced wife!
To dear-bought wisdom give the credit due,
And think, for once, a woman tells you true.
In all these trials I have borne a part,
I was myself the scourge that caused the smart;
For, since fifteen, in triumph have I led
Five captive husbands from the church to bed.
  Christ saw a wedding once, the Scripture says,
And saw but one, 'tis thought, in all his days;
Whence some infer, whose conscience is too nice,
No pious Christian ought to marry twice.
  But let them read, and solve me, if they can,
The words address'd to the Samaritan:
Five times in lawful wedlock she was joined;
And sure the certain stint was ne'er defined.
  "Increase and multiply," was Heaven's command,
And that's a text I clearly understand.
This too, "Let men their sires and mothers leave,
And to their dearer wives for ever cleave."
More wives than one by Solomon were tried,
Or else the wisest of mankind's belied.
I've had myself full many a merry fit;
And trust in Heaven I may have many yet.
For when my transitory spouse, unkind,
Shall die, and leave his woeful wife behind,
I'll take the next good Christian I can find.
  Paul, knowing one could never serve our turn,
Declared 'twas better far to wed than burn.
There's danger in assembling fire and tow;
I grant 'em that, and what it means you know.
The same Apostle too has elsewhere own'd,
No precept for virginity he found:
'Tis but a counsel—and we women still
Take which we like, the counsel, or our will.

I envy not their bliss, if he or she
Think fit to live in perfect chastity;
Pure let them be, and free from taint or vice:
I, for a few slight spots, am not so nice.
Heaven calls us different ways, on these bestows
One proper gift, another grants to those:
Not every man's obliged to sell his store,
And give up all his substance to the poor;
Such as are perfect, may, I can't deny;
But, by your leaves, divines, so am not I.
Full many a saint, since first the world began,
Lived an unspotted maid, in spite of man:
Let such (a God's name) with fine wheat be fed,
And let us honest wives eat barley-bread.
For me, I'll keep the post assigned by Heaven,
And use the copious talent it has given:
Let my good spouse pay tribute, do me right,
And keep an equal reckoning every night:
His proper body is not his, but mine;
For so said Paul, and Paul's a sound divine.
Know then, of those five husbands I have had,
Three were just tolerable, two were bad.
The three were old, but rich and fond beside,
And toiled most piteously to please their bride:
But since their wealth (the best they had) was mine,
The rest, without much loss, I could resign.
Sure to be loved, I took no pains to please,
Yet had more pleasure far than they had ease.
Presents flowed in apace: with showers of gold,
They made their court, like Jupiter of old.
If I but smiled, a sudden youth they found,
And a new palsy seized them when I frown'd.
Ye sovereign wives! give ear, and understand,
Thus shall ye speak, and exercise command.
For never was it given to mortal man,
To lie so boldly as we women can:
Forswear the fact, though seen with both his eyes,
And call your maids to witness how he lies.
Hark, old Sir Paul! ('twas thus I used to say)
Whence is our neighbour's wife so rich and gay?
Treated, caress'd, where'er she's pleased to roam—
I sit in tatters, and immured at home.
Why to her house dost thou so oft repair?
Art thou so amorous? and is she so fair?

If I but see a cousin or a friend,
Lord! how you swell, and rage like any fiend!
But you reel home, a drunken beastly bear,
Then preach till midnight in your easy chair;
Cry, wives are false, and every woman evil,
And give up all that's female to the devil.
If poor (you say) she drains her husband's purse;
If rich, she keeps her priest, or something worse;
If highly born, intolerably vain,
Vapours and pride by turns possess her brain,
Now gaily mad, now sourly splenetic,
Freakish when well, and fretful when she's sick.
If fair, then chaste she cannot long abide,
By pressing youth attack'd on every side:
If foul, her wealth the lusty lover lures,
Or else her wit some fool-gallant procures,
Or else she dances with becoming grace,
Or shape excuses the defects of face.
There swims no goose so grey, but soon or late,
She finds some honest gander for her mate.
Horses (thou sayst) and asses men may try,
And ring suspected vessels ere they buy:
But wives, a random choice, untried they take,
They dream in courtship, but in wedlock wake;
Then, not till then, the veil's removed away,
And all the woman glares in open day.
You tell me, to preserve your wife's good grace,
Your eyes must always languish on my face,
Your tongue with constant flatteries feed my ear,
And tag each sentence with, My life! my dear!
If by strange chance, a modest blush be raised,
Be sure my fine complexion must be praised.
My garments always must be new and gay,
And feasts still kept upon my wedding-day.
Then must my nurse be pleased, and favourite maid;
And endless treats, and endless visits paid,
To a long train of kindred, friends, allies;
All this thou say'st, and all thou say'st are lies.
On Jenkin, too, thou cast a squinting eye:
What! can your 'prentice raise your jealousy?
Fresh are his ruddy cheeks, his forehead fair,
And like the burnish'd gold his curling hair.
But clear thy wrinkled brow, and quit thy sorrow,
I'd scorn your 'prentice, should you die to-morrow.

Why are thy chests all lock'd ? on what design ?
Are not thy worldly goods and treasure mine ?
Sir, I'm no fool; nor shall you, by St. John,
Have goods and body to yourself alone.
One you shall quit, in spite of both your eyes—
I heed not, I, the bolts, the locks, the spies.
If you had wit, you'd say, "Go where you will,
Dear spouse, I credit not the tales they tell:
Take all the freedoms of a married life;
I know thee for a virtuous faithful wife."
Lord! when you have enough, what need you care
How merrily soever others fare ?
Though all the day I give and take delight,
Doubt not, sufficient will be left at night.
'Tis but a just and rational desire,
To light a taper at a neighbour's fire.
There's danger too, you think, in rich array,
And none can long be modest that are gay:
The cat, if you but singe her tabby skin,
The chimney keeps, and sits content within;
But once grown sleek, will from her corner run,
Sport with her tail, and wanton in the sun;
She licks her fair round face, and frisks abroad,
To show her fur, and to be caterwau'd.
Lo thus, my friends, I wrought to my desires
These three right ancient venerable sires.
I told 'em Thus you say, and thus you do,
And told 'em false, but Jenkin swore 'twas true.
I, like a dog, could bite as well as whine,
And first complain'd, whene'er the guilt was mine.
I tax'd them oft with wenching and amours,
When their weak legs scarce dragg'd 'em out of doors;
And swore the rambles that I took by night,
Were all to spy what damsels they bedight.
That colour brought me many hours of mirth;
For all this wit is given us from our birth.
Heaven gave to woman the peculiar grace
To spin, to weep, and cully human race.
By this nice conduct, and this prudent course,
By murmuring, wheedling, stratagem, and force,
I still prevailed, and would be in the right,
Or curtain-lectures made a restless night.
If once my husband's arm was o'er my side,
What! so familiar with your spouse ? I cried:

I levied first a tax upon his need;
Then let him—'twas a nicety indeed!
Let all mankind this certain maxim hold,
Marry who will, our sex is to be sold.
With empty hands no tarsels you can lure,
But fulsome love for gain we can endure;
For gold we love the impotent and old,
And heave, and pant, and kiss, and cling, for gold.
Yet with embraces, curses oft I mixt,
Then kiss'd again, and chid and railed betwixt.
Well, I may make my will in peace, and die,
For not one word in man's arrears am I.
To drop a dear dispute I was unable,
Even though the pope himself had sat at table.
But when my point was gained, then thus I spoke,
"Billy, my dear, how sheepishly you look!
Approach, my spouse, and let me kiss thy cheek;
Thou should'st be always thus, resigned and meek!
Of Job's great patience since so oft you preach,
Well should you practise, who so well can teach.
'Tis difficult to do, I must allow,
But I, my dearest, will instruct you how.
Great is the blessing of a prudent wife,
Who puts a period to domestic strife.
One of us two must rule, and one obey;
And since in man right reason bears the sway,
Let that frail thing, weak woman, have her way.
The wives of all my family have ruled
Their tender husbands, and their passions cooled.
Fie, 'tis unmanly thus to sigh and groan;
What! would you have me to yourself alone?
Why take me, love! take all and every part!
Here's your revenge! you love it at your heart.
Would I vouchsafe to sell what nature gave,
You little think what custom I could have.
But see! I'm all your own—nay hold—for shame!
What means my dear—indeed—you are to blame."
  Thus with my first three lords I pass'd my life;
A very woman, and a very wife.
What sums from these old spouses I could raise,
Procured young husbands in my riper days.
Though past my bloom, not yet decayed was I,
Wanton and wild, and chattered like a pie.

In country dances still I bore the bell,
And sung as sweet as evening Philomel.
To clear my quail-pipe, and refresh my soul,
Full oft I drained the spicy nut-brown bowl;
Rich luscious wines, that youthful blood improve,
And warm the swelling veins to feats of love:
For 'tis as sure as cold engenders hail,
A liquorish mouth must have a lecherous tail;
Wine lets no lover unrewarded go,
As all true gamesters by experience know.
  But oh, good gods! whene'er a thought I cast
On all the joys of youth and beauty past,
To find in pleasures I have had my part,
Still warms me to the bottom of my heart.
This wicked world was once my dear delight;
Now all my conquests, all my charms, good night
The flour consumed, the best that now I can,
Is even to make my market of the bran.
  My fourth dear spouse was not exceeding true;
He kept, 'twas thought, a private miss or two:
But all that score I paid—as how? you'll say.
Not with my body, in a filthy way:
But I so dress'd, and danced, and drank, and dined;
And view'd a friend, with eyes so very kind,
As stung his heart, and made his marrow fry,
With burning rage, and frantic jealousy.
His soul, I hope, enjoys eternal glory,
For here on earth I was his purgatory.
Oft, when his shoe the most severely wrung,
He put on careless airs, and sat and sung.
How sore I gall'd him, only Heaven could know,
And he that felt, and I that caused the woe.
He died, when last from pilgrimage I came,
With other gossips from Jerusalem;
And now lies buried underneath a rood,
Fair to be seen, and reared of honest wood.
A tomb, indeed, with fewer sculptures graced
Than that Mausolus' pious widow placed,
Or where enshrined the great Darius lay;
But cost on graves is merely thrown away.
The pit fill'd up, with turf we covered o'er;
So bless the good man's soul, I say no more.
  Now for my fifth loved lord, the last and best;
(Kind Heaven afford him everlasting rest;)

Full hearty was his love, and I can shew
The tokens on my ribs in black and blue;
Yet, with a knack, my heart he could have won,
While yet the smart was shooting in the bone.
How quaint an appetite in woman reigns!
Free gifts we scorn, and love what costs us pains:
Let men avoid us, and on them we leap;
A glutted market makes provision cheap.
In pure good will I took this jovial spark,
Of Oxford he, a most egregious clerk.
He boarded with a widow in the town,
A trusty gossip, one dame Alison:
Full well the secrets of my soul she knew,
Better than e'er our parish priest could do.
To her I told whatever could befall:
Had but my husband piss'd against a wall,
Or done a thing that might have cost his life,
She—and my niece—and one more worthy wife,
Had known it all: what most he would conceal,
To these I made no scruple to reveal.
Oft has he blush'd from ear to ear for shame,
That e'er he told a secret to his dame.
It so befell, in holy time of Lent,
That oft a day I to this gossip went;
(My husband, thank my stars, was out of town;)
From house to house we rambled up and down,
This clerk, myself, and my good neighbour Alse,
To see, be seen, to tell, and gather tales.
Visits to every church we daily paid,
And march'd in every holy masquerade,
The stations duly and the vigils kept;
Not much we fasted, but scarce ever slept.
At sermons too I shone in scarlet gay,
The wasting moth ne'er spoil'd my best array;
The cause was this, I wore it every day.
'Twas when fresh May her early blossoms yields,
This clerk and I were walking in the fields.
We grew so intimate, I can't tell how,
I pawn'd my honour, and engaged my vow,
If e'er I laid my husband in his urn,
That he, and only he, should serve my turn.
We straight struck hands, the bargain was agreed;
I still have shifts against a time of need:

The mouse that always trusts to one poor hole,
Can never be a mouse of any soul.
I vow'd, I scarce could sleep since first I knew him,
And durst be sworn he had bewitch'd me to him,
If e'er I slept, I dreamed of him alone,
And dreams foretell, as learned men have shown:
All this I said; but dreams, Sirs, I had none:
I followed but my crafty crony's lore,
Who bid me tell this lie—and twenty more.
Thus day by day and month by month we pass'd:
It pleased the Lord to take my spouse at last.
I tore my gown, I soiled my locks with dust,
And beat my breasts, as wretched widows—must.
Before my face my handkerchief I spread,
To hide the flood of tears I did—not shed.
The good man's coffin to the church was borne;
Around, the neighbours, and my clerk, to mourn.
But as he march'd, good gods! he show'd a pair
Of legs and feet, so clean, so strong, so fair!
Of twenty winters' age he seem'd to be;
I (to say truth) was twenty more than he;
But vigorous still, a lively buxom dame;
And had a wondrous gift to quench a flame.
A conjuror once, that deeply could divine,
Assured me, Mars in Taurus was my sign.
As the stars order'd, such my life has been:
Alas, alas, that ever love was sin!
Fair Venus gave me fire, and sprightly grace,
And Mars assurance, and a dauntless face.
By virtue of this powerful constellation,
I followed always my own inclination.
But to my tale: A month scarce pass'd away,
With dance and song we kept the nuptial day.
All I possess'd I gave to his command,
My goods and chattels, money, house, and land:
But oft repented, and repent it still;
He proved a rebel to my sovereign will:
Nay once by Heaven he struck me on the face;
Hear but the fact, and judge yourselves the case.
Stubborn as any lioness was I;
And knew full well to raise my voice on high;
As true a rambler as I was before,
And would be so, in spite of all he swore.

He, against this right sagely would advise,
And old examples set before my eyes;
Tell how the Roman matrons led their life,
Of Gracchus' mother, and Duilius' wife;
And close the sermon, as beseemed his wit,
With some grave sentence out of Holy Writ.
Oft would he say, who builds his house on sands,
Pricks his blind horse across the fallow lands,
Or lets his wife abroad with pilgrims roam,
Deserves a fool's-cap and long ears at home.
All this availed not; for whoe'er he be
That tells my faults, I hate him mortally:
And so do numbers more, I'll boldly say,
Men, women, clergy, regular and lay.
My spouse (who was, you know, to learning bred)
A certain treatise oft at evening read,
Where divers authors (whom the devil confound
For all their lies) were in one volume bound.
Valerius, whole; and of St. Jerome, part;
Chrysippus and Tertullian, Ovid's Art,
Solomon's Proverbs, Eloïsa's loves;
And many more than sure the Church approves.
More legends were there here, of wicked wives,
Than good, in all the Bible and saints' lives.
Who drew the lion vanquish'd? 'Twas a man!
But could we women write as scholars can,
Men should stand mark'd with far more wickedness
Than all the sons of Adam could redress.
Love seldom haunts the breast where learning lies,
And Venus sets ere Mercury can rise.
Those play the scholars who can't play the men,
And use that weapon which they have, their pen;
When old, and past the relish of delight,
Then down they sit, and in their dotage write,
That not one woman keeps her mariage-vow.
(This by the way, but to my purpose now.)
It chanced my husband, on a winter's night,
Read in this book, aloud, with strange delight,
How the first female (as the Scriptures show)
Brought her own spouse and all his race to woe.
How Samson fell; and he whom Dejanire
Wrapp'd in the envenom'd shirt, and set on fire
How cursed Eryphile her lord betray'd,
And the dire ambush Clytemnestra laid.

But what most pleased him was the Cretan dame,
And husband-bull—oh monstrous! fie for shame!
He had by heart, the whole detail of woe
Xantippe made her good man undergo;
How oft she scolded in a day, he knew,
How many jordens on the sage she threw;
Who took it patiently, and wiped his head;
"Rain follows thunder:" that was all he said.
He read, how Arius to his friend complain'd,
A fatal tree was growing in his land,
On which three wives successively had twined
A sliding noose, and wavered in the wind.
Where grows this plant (replied the friend), oh where?
For better fruit did never orchard bear.
Give me some slip of this most blissful tree,
And in my garden planted shall it be.
Then how two wives their lords' destruction prove,
Through hatred one, and one through too much love;
That for her husband mix'd a poisonous draught,
And this for lust an amorous philtre bought:
The nimble juice soon seized his giddy head,
Frantic at night, and in the morning dead.
How some with swords their sleeping lords have slain,
And some have hammer'd nails into their brain,
And some have drench'd them with a deadly potion;
All this he read, and read with great devotion.
Long time I heard, and swell'd, and blush'd, and frown'd;
But when no end of these vile tales I found,
When still he read, and laugh'd, and read again,
And half the night was thus consumed in vain;
Provoked to vengeance, three large leaves I tore,
And with one buffet fell'd him on the floor.
With that my husband in a fury rose,
And down he settled me with hearty blows.
I groan'd, and lay extended on my side;
Oh! thou hast slain me for my wealth (I cried);
Yet I forgive thee—take my last embrace—
He wept, kind soul! and stoop'd to kiss my face;
I took him such a box as turn'd him blue,
Then sigh'd and cried, Adieu, my dear, adieu!
But after many a hearty struggle past,
I condescended to be pleased at last.
Soon as he said, My mistress and my wife,
Do what you list, the term of all your life:

I took to heart the merits of the cause,
And stood content to rule by wholesome laws;
Received the reins of absolute command,
With all the government of house and land,
And empire o'er his tongue, and o'er his hand.
As for the volume that reviled the dames,
'Twas torn to fragments, and condemn'd to flames.
Now Heaven, on all my husbands gone, bestow
Pleasures above, for tortures felt below:
That rest they wish'd for, grant them in the grave,
And bless those souls my conduct help'd to save!

THE FIRST BOOK OF STATIUS'S THEBAIS.

TRANSLATED IN THE YEAR MDCCIII.

ARGUMENT.

Œdipus, king of Thebes, having by mistake slain his father Laius, and married his mother Jocasta, put out his own eyes, and resigned his realm to his sons, Eteocles and Polynices. Being neglected by them, he makes his prayer to the fury Tisiphone, to sow debate betwixt the brothers. They agree at last to reign singly, each a year by turns, and the first lot is obtained by Eteocles. Jupiter, in a council of the gods, declares his resolution of punishing the Thebans, and Argives also, by means of a marriage betwixt Polynices and one of the daughters of Adrastus king of Argos. Juno opposes, but to no effect; and Mercury is sent on a message to the Shades, to the ghost of Laius, who is to appear to Eteocles, and provoke him to break the agreement. Polynices in the meantime departs from Thebes by night, is overtaken by a storm, and arrives at Argos; where he meets with Tydeus, who had fled from Calydon, having killed his brother. Adrastus entertains them, having received an oracle from Apollo that his daughters should be married to a boar and a lion, which he understands to be meant of these strangers, by whom the hides of those beasts were worn, and who arrived at the time when he kept an annual feast in honour of that god. The rise of this solemnity he relates to his guests, the loves of Phœbus and Psamathe, and the story of Chorœbus. He inquires, and is made acquainted with their descent and quality: The sacrifice is renewed, and the book concludes with a hymn to Apollo.

The translator hopes he need not apologise for his choice of this piece, which was made almost in his childhood. But finding the version better than he expected, he gave it some correction a few years afterwards.

FRATERNAL rage, the guilty Thebes' alarms,
The alternate reign destroy'd by impious arms,
Demand our song; a sacred fury fires
My ravish'd breast, and all the muse inspires.
O goddess, say, shall I deduce my rhymes
From the dire nation in its early times,
Europa's rape, Agenor's stern decree,
And Cadmus searching round the spacious sea?
How with the serpent's teeth he sow'd the soil,
And reap'd an iron harvest of his toil?
Or how from joining stones the city sprung,
While to his harp divine Amphion sung?
Or shall I Juno's hate to Thebes resound,
Whose fatal rage the unhappy monarch found?
The sire against the son his arrows drew,
O'er the wide fields the furious mother flew,
And while her arms a second hope contain,
Sprung from the rocks and plunged into the main.
  But waive whate'er to Cadmus may belong,
And fix, O Muse! the barrier of thy song.
At Œdipus—from his disasters trace
The long confusions of his guilty race:
Nor yet attempt to stretch thy bolder wing,
And mighty Cæsar's conquering eagles sing;
How twice he tamed proud Ister's rapid flood,
While Dacian mountains stream'd with barbarous blood;
Twice taught the Rhine beneath his laws to roll,
And stretch'd his empire to the frozen pole,
Or long before, with early valour strove,
In youthful arms to assert the cause of Jove.
And thou, great heir of all thy father's fame,
Increase of glory to the Latian name,
Oh! bless thy Rome with an eternal reign,
Nor let desiring worlds entreat in vain.
What though the stars contract their heavenly space,
And crowd their shining ranks to yield thee place;
Though all the skies, ambitious of thy sway,
Conspire to court thee from our world away;
Though Phœbus long to mix his rays with thine,
And in thy glories more serenely shine;
Though Jove himself no less content would be
To part his throne and share his heaven with thee;
Yet stay, great Cæsar! and vouchsafe to reign
O'er the wide earth, and o'er the watery main;

Resign to Jove his empire of the skies,
And people heaven with Roman deities.
The time will come, when a diviner flame
Shall warm my breast to sing of Cæsar's fame:
Meanwhile permit, that my preluding muse
In Theban wars an humbler theme may chuse:
Of furious hate surviving death, she sings,
A fatal throne to two contending kings,
And funeral flames, that, parting wide in air,
Express the discords of the souls they bear:
Of towns dispeopled, and the wandering ghosts
Of kings unburied in the wasted coasts;
When Dirce's fountain blush'd with Grecian blood,
And Thetis, near Ismenos' swelling flood,
With dread beheld the rolling surges sweep,
In heaps, his slaughter'd sons into the deep.
What Hero, Clio! wilt thou first relate?
The rage of Tydeus, or the Prophet's fate?
Or how, with hills of slain on every side,
Hippomedon repell'd the hostile tide?
Or how the youth with every grace adorn'd,
Untimely fell, to be for ever mourn'd?
Then to fierce Capaneus thy verse extend,
And sing with horror his prodigious end.
Now wretched Œdipus, deprived of sight,
Led a long death in everlasting night;
But while he dwells where not a cheerful ray
Can pierce the darkness, and abhors the day:
The clear reflecting mind presents his sin
In frightful views, and makes it day within;
Returning thoughts in endless circles roll,
And thousand furies haunt his guilty soul.
The wretch then lifted to the unpitying skies
Those empty orbs from whence he tore his eyes,
Whose wounds, yet fresh, with bloody hands he strook,
While from his breast these dreadful accents broke.
Ye gods! that o'er the gloomy regions reign,
Where guilty spirits feel eternal pain;
Thou, sable Styx! whose livid streams are roll'd
Through dreary coasts, which I tho' blind behold:
Tisiphone, that oft hast heard my prayer,
Assist, if Œdipus deserve thy care!
If you received me from Jocasta's womb,
And nursed the hope of mischiefs yet to come:

If, leaving Polybus, I took my way,
To Cyrrha's temple on that fatal day,
When by the son the trembling father died,
Where the three roads the Phocian fields divide:
If I the Sphynx's riddles durst explain,
Taught by thyself to win the promised reign:
If wretched I, by baleful furies led,
With monstrous mixture stain'd my mother's bed,
For hell and thee begot an impious brood,
And with full lust those horrid joys renew'd;
Then, self-condemn'd to shades of endless night,
Forced from these orbs the bleeding balls of sight;
Oh hear! and aid the vengeance I require,
If worthy thee, and what thou might'st inspire.
My sons their old, unhappy sire despise,
Spoil'd of his kingdom, and deprived of eyes;
Guideless I wander, unregarded mourn,
While these exalt their sceptres o'er my urn;
These sons, ye gods! who with flagitious pride
Insult my darkness, and my groans deride.
Art thou a father, unregarding Jove!
And sleeps thy thunder in the realms above?
Thou fury, then, some lasting curse entail,
Which o'er their children's children shall prevail:
Place on their heads that crown distain'd with gore,
Which these dire hands from my slain father tore;
Go! and a parent's heavy curses bear;
Break all the bonds of nature, and prepare
Their kindred souls to mutual hate and war.
Give them to dare, what I might wish to see,
Blind as I am, some glorious villany!
Soon shalt thou find, if thou but arm their hands,
Their ready guilt preventing thy commands:
Could'st thou some great, proportion'd mischief frame,
They'd prove the father from whose loins they came.
The fury heard, while on Cocytus' brink,
Her snakes untied, sulphureous waters drink;
But at the summons roll'd her eyes around,
And snatch'd the starting serpents from the ground.
Not half so swiftly shoots along the air
The gliding lightning, or descending star.
Through crowds of airy shades she wing'd her flight,
And dark dominions of the silent night;

Swift as she pass'd the flitting ghosts withdrew,
And the pale spectres trembled at her view:
To the iron gates of Tænarus she flies,
There spreads her dusky pinions to the skies.
The day beheld, and sickening at the sight,
Veil'd her fair glories in the shades of night.
Affrighted Atlas, on the distant shore,
Trembled, and shook the heavens and gods he bore.
Now from beneath Malea's airy height
Aloft she sprung, and steer'd to Thebes her flight;
With eager speed the well-known journey took,
Nor here regrets the hell she late forsook.
A hundred snakes her gloomy visage shade,
A hundred serpents guard her horrid head,
In her sunk eyeballs dreadful meteors glow:
Such rays from Phœbe's bloody circle flow,
When, labouring with strong charms, she shoots from high
A fiery gleam, and reddens all the sky.
Blood stain'd her cheeks, and from her mouth there came
Blue steaming poisons, and a length of flame;
From every blast of her contagious breath
Famine and drought proceed, and plagues, and death.
A robe obscene was o'er her shoulders thrown,
A dress by fates and furies worn alone.
She toss'd her meagre arms; her better hand
In waving circles whirl'd a funeral brand:
A serpent from her left was seen to rear
His flaming crest, and lash the yielding air.
But when the fury took her stand on high,
Where vast Cithæron's top salutes the sky,
A hiss from all the snaky tire went round:
The dreadful signal all the rocks rebound,
And through the Achaian cities send the sound.
Œta, with high Parnassus, heard the voice;
Eurotas' banks remurmur'd to the noise;
Again Leucothoë shook at these alarms,
And press'd Palæmon closer in her arms.
Headlong from thence the glowing fury springs,
And o'er the Theban palace spreads her wings,
Once more invades the guilty dome, and shrouds
Its bright pavilions in a veil of clouds.
Straight with the rage of all their race possess'd,
Stung to the soul, the brothers start from rest,
And all their furies wake within their breast.

Their tortured minds repining envy tears,
And hate, engender'd by suspicious fears;
And sacred thirst of sway, and all the ties
Of nature broke, and royal perjuries:
And impotent desire to reign alone,
That scorns the dull reversion of a throne:
Each would the sweets of sovereign rule devour,
While discord waits upon divided power.
As stubborn steers by brawny ploughmen broke,
And join'd reluctant to the galling yoke,
Alike disdain with servile necks to bear
The unwonted weight, or drag the crooked share,
But rend the reins, and bound a different way,
And all the furrows in confusion lay;
Such was the discord of the royal pair,
Whom fury drove precipitate to war.
In vain the chiefs contrived a specious way
To govern Thebes by their alternate sway:
Unjust decree! while this enjoys the state,
That mourns in exile his unequal fate,
And the short monarch of a hasty year
Foresees with anguish his returning heir.
Thus did the league their impious arms restrain,
But scarce subsisted to the second reign.
Yet then, no proud aspiring piles were raised,
No fretted roofs with polish'd metals blazed;
No labour'd columns in long order placed,
No Grecian stone the pompous arches graced;
No nightly bands in glittering armour wait
Before the sleepless tyrant's guarded gate;
No chargers then were wrought in burnish'd gold,
Nor silver vases took the forming mould;
Nor gems on bowls emboss'd were seen to shine,
Blaze on the brims, and sparkle in the wine—
Say, wretched rivals! what provokes your rage?
Say, to what end your impious arms engage?
Not all bright Phœbus views in early morn,
Or when his evening beams the west adorn,
When the south glows with his meridian ray,
And the cold north receives a fainter day;
For crimes like these, not all those realms suffice,
Were all those realms the guilty victor's prize!
But fortune now (the lots of empire thrown)
Decrees to proud Eteocles the crown:

What joys, oh tyrant! swell'd thy soul that day,
When all were slaves thou couldst around survey,
Pleased to behold unbounded power thy own,
And singly fill a fear'd and envied throne!
But the vile vulgar, ever discontent,
Their growing fears in secret murmurs vent;
Still prone to change, though still the slaves of state,
And sure the monarch whom they have, to hate;
New lords they madly make, then tamely bear,
And softly curse the tyrants whom they fear.
And one of those who groan beneath the sway
Of kings imposed, and grudgingly obey,
(Whom envy to the great, and vulgar spite
With scandal arm'd, the ignoble mind's delight,)
Exclaim'd—O Thebes! for thee what fates remain,
What woes attend this inauspicious reign?
Must we, alas! our doubtful necks prepare,
Each haughty master's yoke by turns to bear,
And still to change whom changed we still must fear?
These now control a wretched people's fate,
These can divide, and these reverse the state:
E'en Fortune rules no more!—O servile land,
Where exiled tyrants still by turns command!
Thou sire of gods and men, imperial Jove!
Is this the eternal doom decreed above?
On thy own offspring hast thou fix'd this fate,
From the first birth of our unhappy state;
When banish'd Cadmus, wandering o'er the main,
For lost Europa search'd the world in vain,
And fated in Bœotian fields to found
A rising empire on a foreign ground,
First raised our walls on that ill-omen'd plain,
Where earth-born brothers were by brothers slain?
What lofty looks the unrivall'd monarch bears!
How all the tyrant in his face appears!
What sullen fury clouds his scornful brow!
Gods! how his eyes with threatening ardour glow!
Can this imperious lord forget to reign,
Quit all his state, descend, and serve again?
Yet who, before, more popularly bow'd?
Who more propitious to the suppliant crowd?
Patient of right, familiar in the throne?
What wonder then? he was not then alone.

O wretched we, a vile, submissive train,
Fortune's tame fools, and slaves in every reign!
As when two winds with rival force contend,
This way and that, the wavering sails they bend,
While freezing Boreas and black Eurus blow,
Now here, now there, the reeling vessel throw:
Thus on each side, alas! our tottering state
Feels all the fury of resistless fate,
And doubtful still, and still distracted stands,
While that prince threatens, and while this commands.
And now the almighty father of the gods
Convenes a council in the blest abodes:
Far in the bright recesses of the skies,
High o'er the rolling heavens, a mansion lies,
Whence, far below, the gods at once survey
The realms of rising and declining day,
And all the extended space of earth, and air, and sea.
Full in the midst, and on a starry throne,
The majesty of heaven superior shone;
Serene he look'd, and gave an awful nod,
And all the trembling spheres confess'd the god.
At Jove's assent the deities around
In solemn state the consistory crown'd.
Next a long order of inferior powers
Ascend from hills, and plains, and shady bowers;
Those from whose urns the rolling rivers flow;
And those that give the wandering winds to blow:
Here all their rage, and even their murmurs cease,
And sacred silence reigns, and universal peace.
A shining synod of majestic gods
Gilds with new lustre the divine abodes;
Heaven seems improved with a superior ray,
And the bright arch reflects a double day.
The monarch then his solemn silence broke,
The still creation listen'd while he spoke,
Each sacred accent bears eternal weight,
And each irrevocable word is fate.
How long shall man the wrath of heaven defy,
And force unwilling vengeance from the sky!
O race confederate into crimes, that prove
Triumphant o'er the eluded rage of Jove!
This wearied arm can scarce the bolt sustain,
And unregarded thunder rolls in vain:

The o'erlabour'd Cyclops from his task retires;
The Æolian forge exhausted of its fires.
For this I suffer'd Phœbus' steeds to stray,
And the mad ruler to misguide the day;
When the wide earth to heaps of ashes turn'd,
And heaven itself the wand'ring chariot burn'd.
For this, my brother of the watery reign
Released the impetuous sluices of the main:
But flames consumed, and billows raged in vain.
Two races now, allied to Jove, offend;
To punish these, see Jove himself descend.
The Theban kings their line from Cadmus trace,
From godlike Perseus those of Argive race.
Unhappy Cadmus' fate who does not know,
And the long series of succeeding woe?
How oft the furies, from the deeps of night,
Arose, and mix'd with men in mortal fight:
The exulting mother, stain'd with filial blood;
The savage hunter and the haunted wood?
The direful banquet why should I proclaim,
And crimes that grieve the trembling gods to name?
Ere I recount the sins of these profane,
The sun would sink into the western main,
And rising gild the radiant east again.
Have we not seen (the blood of Laius shed)
The murdering son ascend his parent's bed,
Through violated nature force his way,
And stain the sacred womb where once he lay?
Yet now in darkness and despair he groans,
And for the crimes of guilty fate atones;
His sons with scorn their eyeless father view,
Insult his wounds, and make him bleed anew.
Thy curse, O Œdipus! just Heaven alarms,
And sets the avenging Thunderer in arms.
I from the root thy guilty race will tear,
And give the nations to the waste of war.
Adrastus soon, with gods averse, shall join
In dire alliance with the Theban line;
Hence strife shall rise, and mortal war succeed;
The guilty realms of Tantalus shall bleed,
Fix'd is their doom; this all-remembering breast
Yet harbours vengeance for the tyrant's feast.
He said; and thus the queen of heaven return'd
(With sudden grief her labouring bosom burn'd):

Must I, whose cares Phoroneus' towers defend,
Must I, O Jove! in bloody wars contend?
Thou know'st those regions my protection claim,
Glorious in arms, in riches, and in fame:
Though there the fair Egyptian heifer fed,
And there deluded Argus slept, and bled;
Though there the brazen tower was storm'd of old,
When Jove descended in almighty gold:
Yet I can pardon those obscurer rapes,
Those bashful crimes disguised in borrow'd shapes;
But Thebes, where, shining in celestial charms,
Thou camest triumphant to a mortal's arms,
When all thy glories o'er her limbs were spread,
And blazing lightnings danced around her bed;
Cursed Thebes the vengeance it deserves, may prove—
Ah why should Argos feel the rage of Jove?
Yet since thou wilt thy sister-queen control,
Since still the lust of discord fires thy soul,
Go, raze my Samos, let Mycene fall,
And level with the dust the Spartan wall;
No more let mortals Juno's power invoke,
Her fanes no more with eastern incense smoke,
Nor victims sink beneath the sacred stroke,
But to your Isis all my rites transfer,
Let altars blaze and temples smoke for her;
For her, through Egypt's fruitful clime renown'd,
Let weeping Nilus hear the timbrel sound.
But if thou must reform the stubborn times,
Avenging on the sons the father's crimes,
And from the long records of distant age
Derive incitements to renew thy rage;
Say, from what period then has Jove design'd
To date his vengeance; to what bounds confined
Begin from thence, where first Alpheus hides
His wandering stream, and through the briny tides
Unmix'd to his Sicilian river glides.
Thy own Arcadians there the thunder claim,
Whose impious rites disgrace thy mighty name;
Who raise thy temples where the chariot stood
Of fierce Œnomäus, defiled with blood;
Where once his steeds their savage banquet found,
And human bones yet whiten all the ground.
Say, can those honours please; and canst thou love
Presumptuous Crete, that boasts the tomb of Jove?

And shall not Tantalus's kingdoms share
Thy wife and sister's tutelary care?
Reverse, O Jove, thy too severe decree,
Nor doom to war a race derived from thee;
On impious realms and barbarous kings impose
Thy plagues, and curse them with such sons, as those.
Thus, in reproach and prayer, the queen express'd
The rage and grief contending in her breast.
Unmoved remain'd the ruler of the sky,
And from his throne return'd this stern reply:
'Twas thus I deem'd thy haughty soul would bear
The dire, though just, revenge which I prepare
Against a nation thy peculiar care:
No less Dione might for Thebes contend,
Nor Bacchus less his native town defend,
Yet these in silence see the fates fulfil
Their work, and reverence our superior will.
For by the black infernal Styx I swear,
(That dreadful oath which binds the Thunderer,)
'Tis fix'd; the irrevocable doom of Jove;
No force can bend me, no persuasion move.
Haste then, Cyllenius, through the liquid air;
Go, mount the winds, and to the shades repair;
Bid hell's black monarch my commands obey,
And give up Laius to the realms of day,
Whose ghost yet shivering on Cocytus' sand,
Expects its passage to the further strand:
Let the pale sire revisit Thebes, and bear
These pleasing orders to the tyrant's ear;
That from his exiled brother, swell'd with pride
Of foreign forces, and his Argive bride,
Almighty Jove commands him to detain
The promised empire, and alternate reign:
Be this the cause of more than mortal hate:
The rest, succeeding times shall ripen into fate.
The god obeys, and to his feet applies
Those golden wings that cut the yielding skies.
His ample hat his beamy locks o'erspread,
And veil'd the starry glories of his head.
He seized the wand that causes sleep to fly,
Or, in soft slumbers, seals the wakeful eye;
That drives the dead to dark Tartarean coasts,
Or back to life compels the wandering ghosts.

Thus, through the parting clouds, the son of May
Wings on the whistling winds his rapid way;
Now smoothly steers through air his equal flight,
Now springs aloft, and towers the ethereal height;
Then wheeling down the steep of heaven he flies,
And draws a radiant circle o'er the skies.
   Meantime the banish'd Polynices roves
(His Thebes abandon'd) through the Aonfan groves,
While future realms his wandering thoughts delight,
His daily vision and his dream by night;
Forbidden Thebes appears before his eye,
From whence he sees his absent brother fly,
With transport views the airy rule his own,
And swells on an imaginary throne.
Fain would he cast a tedious age away,
And live out all in one triumphant day.
He chides the lazy progress of the sun,
And bids the year with swifter motion run;
With anxious hopes his craving mind is toss'd,
And all his joys in length of wishes lost.
   The hero then resolves his course to bend
Where ancient Danaus' fruitful fields extend,
And famed Mycene's lofty towers ascend,
(Where late the sun did Atreus' crimes detest,
And disappear'd in horror of the feast.)
And now by chance, by fate, or furies led,
From Bacchus' consecrated caves he fled,
Where the shrill cries of frantic matrons sound,
And Pantheus' blood enrich'd the rising ground.
Then sees Cithæron towering o'er the plain,
And thence declining gently to the main.
Next to the bounds of Nisus' realm repairs,
Where treacherous Scylla cut the purple hairs:
The hanging cliffs of Scyron's rocks explores,
And hears the murmurs of the different shores:
Passes the strait that parts the foaming seas,
And stately Corinth's pleasing site surveys.
'Twas now the time when Phœbus yields to night,
And rising Cynthia sheds her silver light,
Wide o'er the world in solemn pomp she drew
Her airy chariot, hung with pearly dew;
All birds and beasts lie hush'd; sleep steals away
The wild desires of men, and toils of day,

And brings, descending through the silent air,
A sweet forgetfulness of human care.
Yet no red clouds, with golden borders gay,
Promise the skies the bright return of day;
No faint reflections of the distant light
Streak with long gleams the scattering shades of night:
From the damp earth impervious vapours rise,
Increase the darkness, and involve the skies.
At once the rushing winds, with roaring sound,
Burst from the Æolian caves, and rend the ground,
With equal rage their airy quarrel try,
And win by turns the kingdom of the sky:
But with a thicker night black Auster shrouds
The heavens, and drives on heaps the rolling clouds,
From whose dark womb a rattling tempest pours,
Which the cold north congeals to haily showers.
From pole to pole the thunder roars aloud,
And broken lightnings flash from every cloud.
Now smokes with showers the misty mountain-ground,
And floated fields lie undistinguish'd round.
The Inachian streams with headlong fury run,
And Erasinus rolls a deluge on:
The foaming Lerna swells above its bounds,
And spreads its ancient poisons o'er the grounds:
Where late was dust, now rapid torrents play,
Rush through the mounds, and bear the dams away:
Old limbs of trees, from crackling forests torn,
Are whirl'd in air, and on the winds are borne:
The storm the dark Lycæan groves display'd,
And first to light exposed the sacred shade.
The intrepid Theban hears the bursting sky,
Sees yawning rocks in massy fragments fly,
And views astonish'd, from the hills afar,
The floods descending, and the watery war,
That, driven by storms, and pouring o'er the plain,
Swept herds, and hinds, and houses to the main.
Through the brown horrors of the night he fled,
Nor knows, amazed, what dreadful path to tread;
His brother's image to his mind appears,
Inflames his heart with rage, and wings his feet with fears.
So fares a sailor on the stormy main,
When clouds conceal Boötes' golden wain,
When not a star its friendly lustre keeps,
Nor trembling Cynthia glimmers on the deeps;

He dreads the rocks, and shoals, and seas, and skies,
While thunder roars, and lightning round him flies.
  Thus strove the chief, on every side distress'd,
Thus still his courage with his toils increased;
With his broad shield opposed, he forced his way
Through thickest woods, and roused the beasts of prey,
Till he beheld, where from Larissa's height
The shelving walls reflect a glancing light:
Thither with haste the Theban hero flies;
On this side Lerna's poisonous water lies,
On that Prosymna's grove and temple rise:
He pass'd the gates which then unguarded lay,
And to the regal palace bent his way;
On the cold marble, spent with toil, he lies,
And waits till pleasing slumbers seal his eyes.
  Adrastus here his happy people sways,
Blest with calm peace in his declining days,
By both his parents of descent divine,
Great Jove and Phœbus graced his noble line:
Heaven had not crown'd his wishes with a son,
But two fair daughters heir'd his state and throne.
To him Apollo (wondrous to relate!
But who can pierce into the depths of fate?)
Had sung—"Expect thy sons on Argos' shore,
A yellow lion and a bristly boar."
This long revolved in his paternal breast,
Sate heavy on his heart, and broke his rest;
This, great Amphiaraus, lay hid from thee,
Though skill'd in fate, and dark futurity.
The father's care and prophet's art were vain,
For thus did the predicting god ordain.
  Lo, hapless Tydeus, whose ill-fated hand
Had slain his brother, leaves his native land,
And seized with horror, in the shades of night,
Through the thick deserts headlong urged his flight:
Now by the fury of the tempest driven,
He seeks a shelter from the inclement heaven,
Till, led by fate, the Theban's steps he treads,
And to fair Argos' open court succeeds.
  When thus the chiefs from different lands resort
To Adrastus' realms, and hospitable court;
The king surveys his guests with curious eyes,
And views their arms and habit with surprise.

A lion's yellow skin the Theban wears,
Horrid his mane, and rough with curling hairs;
Such once employ'd Alcides' youthful toils,
Ere yet adorn'd with Nemea's dreadful spoils.
A boar's stiff hide, of Calydonian breed,
Œnides' manly shoulders overspread.
Oblique his tusks, erect his bristles stood,
Alive, the pride and terror of the wood.
Struck with the sight, and fix'd in deep amaze,
The King the accomplish'd oracle surveys,
Reveres Apollo's vocal caves, and owns
The guiding godhead, and his future sons.
O'er all his bosom secret transports reign,
And a glad horror shoots through every vein.
To heaven he lifts his hands, erects his sight,
And thus invokes the silent queen of night.
Goddess of shades, beneath whose gloomy reign
Yon spangled arch glows with the starry train:
You who the cares of heaven and earth allay,
Till nature, quicken'd by the inspiring ray,
Wakes to new vigour with the rising day;
Oh thou, who freest me from my doubtful state,
Long lost and wilder'd in the maze of fate!
Be present still, oh goddess! in our aid;
Proceed, and 'firm those omens thou hast made.
We to thy name our annual rites will pay,
And on thy altars sacrifices lay;
The sable flock shall fall beneath the stroke,
And fill thy temples with a grateful smoke.
Hail, faithful Tripos! hail, ye dark abodes
Of awful Phœbus: I confess the gods!
Thus, seized with sacred fear, the monarch pray'd;
Then to his inner court the guests convey'd;
Where yet thin fumes from dying sparks arise,
And dust yet white upon each altar lies,
The relics of a former sacrifice.
The king once more the solemn rites requires,
And bids renew the feasts, and wake the fires.
His train obey, while all the courts around
With noisy care and various tumult sound.
Embroider'd purple clothes the golden beds;
This slave the floor, and that the table spreads;
A third dispels the darkness of the night,
And fills depending lamps with beams of light.

Here loaves in canisters are piled on high,
And there in flames the slaughtered victims fry.
Sublime in regal state Adrastus shone,
Stretch'd on rich carpets on his ivory throne;
A lofty couch receives each princely guest:
Around, at awful distance, wait the rest.
And now the king, his royal feast to grace,
Acestis calls, the guardian of his race,
Who first their youth in arts of virtue train'd,
And their ripe years in modest grace maintain'd.
Then softly whispered in her faithful ear,
And bade his daughters at the rites appear.
When from the close apartments of the night,
The royal nymphs approach divinely bright;
Such was Diana's, such Minerva's face;
Nor shine their beauties with superior grace,
But that in these a milder charm endears,
And less of terror in their looks appears,
As on the heroes first they cast their eyes,
O'er their fair cheeks the glowing blushes rise,
Their downcast looks a decent shame confess'd,
Then on their father's reverend features rest.
The banquet done, the monarch gives the sign
To fill the goblet high with sparkling wine,
Which Danaus used in sacred rites of old,
With sculpture graced, and rough with rising gold.
Here to the clouds victorious Perseus flies,
Medusa seems to move her languid eyes,
And, even in gold, turns paler as she dies.
There from the chase Jove's towering eagle bears,
On golden wings, the Phrygian to the stars:
Still as he rises in the ethereal height,
His native mountains lessen to his sight;
While all his sad companions upward gaze,
Fix'd on the glorious scene in wild amaze;
And the swift hounds, affrighted as he flies,
Run to the shade, and bark against the skies.
This golden bowl with generous juice was crown'd,
The first libations sprinkled on the ground,
By turns on each celestial power they call;
With Phœbus' name resounds the vaulted hall.
The courtly train, the strangers, and the rest,
Crown'd with chaste laurel, and with garlands dress'd

While rich with gums the fuming altars blaze,
Salute the god in numerous hymns of praise.
Then thus the king: Perhaps, my noble guests,
These honoured altars, and these annual feasts
To bright Apollo's awful name design'd,
Unknown, with wonder may perplex your mind.
Great was the cause; our old solemnities
From no blind zeal, or fond tradition rise;
But saved from death, our Argives yearly pay
These grateful honours to the god of day.
When by a thousand darts the Python slain
With orbs unroll'd lay covering all the plain,
(Transfix'd as o'er Castalia's streams he hung,
And suck'd new poisons with his triple tongue)
To Argos' realms the victor god resorts,
And enters old Crotopus' humble courts.
This rural prince one only daughter blest,
That all the charms of blooming youth possess'd;
Fair was her face, and spotless was her mind,
Where filial love with virgin sweetness join'd.
Happy! and happy still she might have proved,
Were she less beautiful, or less beloved!
But Phœbus loved, and on the flowery side
Of Nemea's stream, the yielding fair enjoy'd:
Now, ere ten moons their orb with light adorn,
The illustrious offspring of the god was born,
The nymph, her father's anger to evade,
Retires from Argos to the silvan shade;
To woods and wilds the pleasing burden bears,
And trusts her infant to a shepherd's cares.
How mean a fate, unhappy child, is thine!
Ah how unworthy those of race divine!
On flowery herbs in some green covert laid,
His bed the ground, his canopy the shade,
He mixes with the bleating lambs his cries,
While the rude swain his rural music tries
To call soft slumbers on his infant eyes.
Yet e'en in those obscure abodes to live,
Was more, alas! than cruel fate would give;
For on the grassy verdure as he lay,
And breathed the freshness of the early day,
Devouring dogs the helpless infant tore,
Fed on his trembling limbs, and lapp'd the gore.

The astonish'd mother, when the rumour came,
Forgets her father, and neglects her fame,
With loud complaints she fills the yielding air,
And beats her breast, and rends her flowing hair;
Then wild with anguish to her sire she flies,
Demands the sentence, and contented dies.
But touch'd with sorrow for the dead too late,
The raging god prepares to avenge her fate.
He sends a monster, horrible and fell,
Begot by furies in the depths of hell.
The pest a virgin's face and bosom bears;
High on a crown a rising snake appears,
Guards her black front, and hisses in her hairs:
About the realm she walks her dreadful round,
When night with sable wings o'erspreads the ground,
Devours young babes before their parents' eyes,
And feeds and thrives on public miseries.
But generous rage the bold Chorœbus warms,
Chorœbus! famed for virtue, as for arms;
Some few like him, inspired with martial flame,
Thought a short life well lost for endless fame.
These, where two ways in equal parts divide,
The direful monster from afar descried;
Two bleeding babes depending at her side;
Whose panting vitals, warm with life, she draws,
And in their hearts embrues her cruel claws.
The youths surround her with extended spears;
But brave Chorœbus in the front appears,
Deep in her breast he plunged his shining sword,
And hell's dire monster back to hell restored.
The Inachians view the slain with vast surprise,
Her twisting volumes and her rolling eyes,
Her spotted breast, and gaping womb imbued
With livid poison, and our children's blood.
The crowd in stupid wonder fix'd appear,
Pale e'en in joy, nor yet forget to fear.
Some with vast beams the squalid corpse engage,
And weary all the wild efforts of rage.
The birds obscene, that nightly flock'd to taste,
With hollow screeches fled the dire repast;
And ravenous dogs, allured by scented blood,
And starving wolves, ran howling to the wood.
But fired with rage, from cleft Parnassus' brow

Avenging Phœbus bent his deadly bow,
And hissing flew the feather'd fates below:
A night of sultry clouds involved around
The towers, the fields, and the devoted ground:
And now a thousand lives together fled,
Death with his scythe cut off the fatal thread,
And a whole province in his triumph led.
But Phœbus ask'd why noxious fires appear,
And raging Sirius blasts the sickly year;
Demands their lives by whom his monster fell,
And dooms a dreadful sacrifice to hell.
Blest be thy dust, and let eternal fame
Attend thy manes, and preserve thy name,
Undaunted hero! who divinely brave,
In such a cause disdain'd thy life to save;
But view'd the shrine with a superior look,
And its upbraided godhead thus bespoke:
With piety, the soul's securest guard,
And conscious virtue, still its own reward,
Willing I come, unknowing how to fear;
Nor shalt thou, Phœbus, find a suppliant here.
Thy monster's death to me was owed alone,
And 'tis a deed too glorious to disown.
Behold him here, for whom, so many days,
Impervious clouds concealed thy sullen rays;
For whom, as Man no longer claimed thy care,
Such numbers fell by pestilential air!
But if the abandoned race of human kind
From gods above no more compassion find;
If such inclemency in heaven can dwell,
Yet why must unoffending Argos feel
The vengeance due to this unlucky steel?
On me, on me, let all thy fury fall,
Nor err from me, since I deserve it all:
Unless our desert cities please thy sight,
Or funeral flames reflect a grateful light,
Discharge thy shafts, this ready bosom rend,
And to the shades a ghost triumphant send;
But for my country let my fate atone;
Be mine the vengeance, as the crime my own.
Merit distress'd, impartial Heaven relieves:
Unwelcome life relenting Phœbus gives;
For not the vengeful power, that glow'd with rage,
With such amazing virtue durst engage.

The clouds dispersed, Apollo's wrath expired,
And from the wondering god the unwilling youth
Thence we these altars in his temple raise, [retired.
And offer annual honours, feasts, and praise;
These solemn feasts propitious Phœbus please:
These honours, still renew'd, his ancient wrath appease.
But say, illustrious guest, (adjoined the King)
What name you bear, from what high race you spring?
The noble Tydeus stands confess'd, and known
Our neighbour prince, and heir of Calydon.
Relate your fortunes, while the friendly night
And silent hours to various talk invite.
The Theban bends on earth his gloomy eyes,
Confused, and sadly thus at length replies:
Before these altars how shall I proclaim
(O gen'rous prince) my nation, or my name,
Or through what veins our ancient blood has roll'd?
Let the sad tale for ever rest untold!
Yet if, propitious to a wretch unknown,
You seek to share in sorrows not your own;
Know then from Cadmus I derive my race,
Jocasta's son, and Thebes my native place.
To whom the king (who felt his generous breast
Touch'd with concern for his unhappy guest)
Replies:—Ah why forbears the son to name
His wretched father known too well by fame?
Fame, that delights around the world to stray,
Scorns not to take our Argos in her way;
E'en those who dwell where suns at distance roll,
In northern wilds, and freeze beneath the pole;
And those who tread the burning Libyan lands,
The faithless Syrtis and the moving sands;
Who view the western sea's extremest bounds,
Or drink of Ganges in their eastern grounds;
All these the woes of Œdipus have known,
Your fates, your furies, and your haunted town.
If on the sons the parents' crimes descend,
What prince from those his lineage can defend?
Be this thy comfort, that 'tis thine to efface
With virtuous acts thy ancestor's disgrace,
And be thyself the honour of thy race.
But see! the stars begin to steal away,
And shine more faintly at approaching day;

Now pour the wine; and in your tuneful lays
Once more resound the great Apollo's praise.
  Oh father Phœbus! whether Lycia's coast
And snowy mountain thy bright presence boast;
Whether to sweet Castalia thou repair,
And bathe in silver dews thy yellow hair;
Or pleased to find fair Delos float no more,
Delight in Cynthus and the shady shore;
Or choose thy seat in Ilion's proud abodes,
The shining structures raised by labouring gods
By thee the bow and mortal shafts are borne;
Eternal charms thy blooming youth adorn:
Skill'd in the laws of secret fate above,
And the dark counsels of almighty Jove,
'Tis thine the seeds of future war to know,
The change of sceptres, and impending woe;
When direful meteors spread through glowing air
Long trails of light, and shake their blazing hair.
Thy rage the Phrygian felt, who durst aspire
To excel the music of thy heavenly lyre;
Thy shafts avenged lewd Tityus' guilty flame,
The immortal victim of thy mother's fame;
Thy hand slew Python, and the dame who lost
Her numerous offspring for a fatal boast.
In Phlegyas' doom thy just revenge appears,
Condemn'd to furies and eternal fears;
He views his food, but dreads, with lifted eye,
The mouldering rock that trembles from on high.
  Propitious hear our prayer, O power divine!
And on thy hospitable Argos shine;
Whether the style of Titan please thee more,
Whose purple rays the Achæmenes adore;
Or great Osiris, who first taught the swain
In Pharian fields to sow the golden grain;
Or Mithras, to whose beams the Persian bows,
And pays, in hollow rocks, his awful vows;
Mithras, whose head the blaze of light adorns,
Who grasps the struggling heifer's lunar horns.

THE FABLE OF DRYOPE.

FROM THE NINTH BOOK OF OVID'S METAMORPHOSES.

Upon occasion of the death of Hercules, his mother Alcmena recounts her misfortunes to Iole, who answers with a relation of those of her own family, in particular the transformation of her sister Dryope, which is the subject of the ensuing fable.

Iole was a daughter of Eurytus, King of Œchalia. Her father promised her in marriage to Hercules, but refusing to perform his engagements, Iole was carried away by force. It was to extinguish the love of Hercules for Iole, that Dejanira sent him the poisoned tunic, which caused his death. After the death of Hercules, Iole married his son Hylius.

She said, and for her lost Galanthis sighs,
When the fair consort of her son replies:
Since you a servant's ravish'd form bemoan,
And kindly sigh for sorrows not your own,
Let me (if tears and grief permit) relate
A nearer woe, a sister's stranger fate.
No nymph of all Œchalia could compare
For beauteous form with Dryope the fair,
Her tender mother's only hope and pride,
(Myself the offspring of a second bride.)
This nymph compress'd by him who rules the day,
Whom Delphi and the Delian isle obey,
Andræmon loved; and, bless'd in all those charms
That pleased a god, succeeded to her arms.
  A lake there was, with shelving banks around,
Whose verdant summit fragrant myrtles crown'd:
These shades, unknowing of the fates, she sought,
And to the Naiads flowery garlands brought;
Her smiling babe (a pleasing charge) she prest
Within her arms, and nourish'd at her breast.
Not distant far a watery lotos grows,
The spring was new, and all the verdant boughs
Adorn'd with blossoms promised fruits that vie
In glowing colours with the Tyrian dye:

Of these she cropp'd, to please her infant son,
And I myself the same rash act had done:
But lo! I saw (as near her side I stood)
The violated blossoms drop with blood;
Upon the tree I cast a frightful look;
The trembling tree with sudden horror shook.
Lotis the nymph (if rural tales be true)
As from Priapus' lawless lust she flew,
Forsook her form; and fixing here became
A flowery plant, which still preserves her name.
 This change unknown, astonish'd at the sight,
My trembling sister strove to urge her flight:
And first the pardon of the nymphs implored,
And those offended silvan powers adored:
But when she backward would have fled, she found
Her stiffening feet were rooted in the ground:
In vain to free her fastened feet she strove,
And as she struggles, only moves above;
She feels the encroaching bark around her grow
By quick degrees, and cover all below:
Surprised at this, her trembling hand she heaves
To rend her hair; her hand is fill'd with leaves:
Where late was hair the shooting leaves are seen
To rise, and shade her with a sudden green.
The child Amphissus, to her bosom prest,
Perceived a colder and a harder breast,
And found the springs, that ne'er till then denied
Their milky moisture, on a sudden dried.
I saw, unhappy! what I now relate,
And stood the helpless witness of thy fate,
Embraced thy boughs, thy rising bark delay'd,
There wish'd to grow, and mingle shade with shade.
 Behold Andræmon and the unhappy sire
Appear, and for their Dryope inquire:
A springing tree for Dryope they find,
And print warm kisses on the panting rind.
Prostrate with tears their kindred plant bedew,
And close embrace as to the roots they grew.
The face was all that now remain'd of thee,
No more a woman, nor yet quite a tree;
Thy branches hung with humid pearls appear,
From every leaf distils a trickling tear,
And straight a voice, while yet a voice remains,
Thus through the trembling boughs in sighs complains.

If to the wretched any faith be given,
I swear, by all the unpitying powers of heaven,
No wilful crime this heavy vengeance bred;
In mutual innocence our lives we led:
If this be false, let these new greens decay,
Let sounding axes lop my limbs away,
And crackling flames on all my honours prey.
But from my branching arms this infant bear,
Let some kind nurse supply a mother's care:
And to his mother let him oft be led,
Sport in her shades, and in her shades be fed;
Teach him, when first his infant voice shall frame
Imperfect words, and lisp his mother's name,
To hail this tree, and say with weeping eyes,
" Within this plant my hapless parent lies:"
And when in youth he seeks the shady woods,
Oh! let him fly the crystal lakes and floods,
Nor touch the fatal flowers; but warn'd by me,
Believe a goddess shrined in every tree.
My sire, my sister, and my spouse, farewell!
If in your breasts or love or pity dwell,
Protect your plant, nor let my branches feel
The browzing cattle or the piercing steel.
Farewell! and since I cannot bend to join
My lips to yours, advance at least to mine.
My son, thy mother's parting kiss receive,
While yet thy mother has a kiss to give.
I can no more; the creeping rind invades
My closing lips, and hides my head in shades;
Remove your hands, the bark shall soon suffice
Without their aid to seal these dying eyes.
She ceased at once to speak, and ceased to be;
And all the nymph was lost within the tree;
Yet latent life through her new branches reign'd,
And long the plant a human heat retain'd.

VERTUMNUS AND POMONA.

FROM THE FOURTEENTH BOOK OF OVID'S METAMORPHOSES.

The fair Pomona flourish'd in his reign;
Of all the virgins of the silvan train,
None taught the trees a nobler race to bear,
Or more improved the vegetable care.
To her the shady grove, the flowery field,
The streams and fountains no delights could yield;
'Twas all her joy the ripening fruits to tend,
And see the boughs with happy burthens bend.
The hook she bore instead of Cynthia's spear,
To lop the growth of the luxuriant year,
To decent form the lawless shoots to bring,
And teach the obedient branches where to spring.
Now the cleft rind inserted grafts receives,
And yields an offspring more than nature gives;
Now sliding streams the thirsty plants renew,
And feed their fibres with reviving dew.
  These cares alone her virgin breast employ,
Averse from Venus and the nuptial joy.
Her private orchards, wall'd on every side,
To lawless silvans all access denied.
How oft the satyrs and the wanton fawns,
Who haunt the forests, or frequent the lawns,
The god whose ensign scares the birds of prey,
And old Silenus, youthful in decay
Employed their wiles, and unavailing care,
To pass the fences, and surprise the fair!
Like these, Vertumnus own'd his faithful flame,
Like these, rejected by the scornful dame.
To gain her sight a thousand forms he wears;
And first a reaper from the field appears.
Sweating he walks, while loads of golden grain
O'ercharge the shoulders of the seeming swain.
Oft o'er his back a crooked scythe is laid,
And wreaths of hay his sun-burnt temples shade;
Oft in his harden'd hand a goad he bears,
Like one who late unyoked the sweating steers.
Sometimes his pruning-hook corrects the vines,
And the loose stragglers to their ranks confines.

Now gathering what the bounteous year allows,
He pulls ripe apples from the bending boughs.
A soldier now, he with his sword appears;
A fisher next, his trembling angle bears;
Each shape he varies, and each art he tries,
On her bright charms to feast his longing eyes.
A female form at last Vertumnus wears,
With all the marks of reverend age appears,
His temples thinly spread with silver hairs;
Propp'd on his staff, and stooping as he goes,
A painted mitre shades his furrow'd brows.
The god in this decrepit form arrayed,
The gardens entered, and the fruit surveyed;
And "Happy you! (he thus address'd the maid)
Whose charms as far all other nymphs' outshine,
As other gardens are excell'd by thine!"
Then kiss'd the fair (his kisses warmer grow
Than such as women on their sex bestow).
Then, placed beside her on the flowery ground,
Beheld the trees with autumn's bounty crown'd.
An elm was near, to whose embraces led,
The curling vine her swelling clusters spread:
He view'd her twining branches with delight,
And praised the beauty of the pleasing sight.
Yet this tall elm, but for his vine (he said)
Had stood neglected, and a barren shade;
And this fair vine, but that her arms surround
Her married elm, had crept along the ground.
Ah! beauteous maid, let this example move
Your mind, averse from all the joys of love.
Deign to be loved, and every heart subdue!
What nymph could e'er attract such crowds as you?
Not she whose beauty urged the centaur's arms,
Ulysses' queen, nor Helen's fatal charms.
E'en now, when silent scorn is all they gain,
A thousand court you, though they court in vain;
A thousand silvans, demigods, and gods,
That haunt our mountains and our Alban woods.
But if you'll prosper, mark what I advise,
Whom age and long experience render wise,
And one whose tender care is far above
All that these lovers ever felt of love,
(Far more than e'er can by yourself be guess'd)
Fix on Vertumnus, and reject the rest.

For his firm faith I dare engage my own;
Scarce to himself himself is better known.
To distant lands Vertumnus never roves;
Like you, contented with his native groves;
Nor at first sight, like most, admires the fair;
For you he lives; and you alone shall share
His last affection as his early care.
Besides, he's lovely far above the rest,
With youth immortal, and with beauty blest.
Add, that he varies every shape with ease,
And tries all forms that may Pomona please.
But, what should most excite a mutual flame,
Your rural cares and pleasures are the same.
To him your orchard's early fruits are due;
(A pleasing offering when 'tis made by you)
He values these; but yet, alas! complains,
That still the best and dearest gift remains.
Not the fair fruit that on yon branches glows
With that ripe red the autumnal sun bestows;
Nor tasteful herbs that in these gardens rise,
Which the kind soil with milky sap supplies;
You, only you, can move the god's desire:
Oh crown so constant and so pure a fire!
Let soft compassion touch your gentle mind;
Think, 'tis Vertumnus begs you to be kind!
So may no frost, when early buds appear,
Destroy the promise of the youthful year;
Nor winds, when first your florid orchard blows,
Shake the light blossoms from their blasted boughs!
  This when the various god had urged in vain,
He straight assumed his native form again;
Such, and so bright an aspect now he bears,
As when through clouds the emerging sun appears,
And thence exerting his refulgent ray,
Dispels the darkness, and reveals the day.
Force he prepared, but check'd the rash design;
For when appearing in a form divine,
The nymph surveys him, and beholds the grace
Of charming features, and a youthful face,
In her soft breast consenting passions move,
And the warm maid confess'd a mutual love.

IMITATIONS OF ENGLISH POETS.

DONE BY THE AUTHOR IN HIS YOUTH.

I.

SPENSER.

THE ALLEY.

I.

In every town, where Thamis rolls his tyde,
A narrow pass there is, with houses low;
Where, ever and anon, the stream is eyed,
And many a boat soft sliding to and fro.
There oft are heard the notes of infant woe,
The short thick sob, loud scream, and shriller squall:
How can ye, mothers, vex your children so?
Some play, some eat, some cack against the wall,
And as they crouchen low, for bread and butter call.

II.

And on the broken pavement, here and there,
Doth many a stinking sprat and herring lie:
A brandy and tobacco shop is near,
And hens, and dogs, and hogs are feeding by;
And here a sailor's jacket hangs to dry.
At every door are sun-burnt matrons seen,
Mending old nets to catch the scaly fry;
Now singing shrill, and scolding eft between; [I ween.
Scolds answer foul-mouth'd scolds; bad neighbourhood

III.

The snappish cur (the passengers' annoy)
Close at my heel with yelping treble flies;
The whimpering girl, and hoarser-screaming boy
Join to the yelping treble, shrilling cries;

The scolding quean to louder notes doth rise,
And her full pipes those shrilling cries confound;
To her full pipes the grunting hog replies;
The grunting hogs alarm the neighbours round,
And curs, girls, boys, and scolds, in the deep bass are
drown'd.

IV.

Hard by a sty, beneath a roof of thatch,
Dwelt Obloquy, who in her early days
Baskets of fish at Billingsgate did watch,
Cod, whiting, oyster, mackerel, sprat, or plaice:
There learn'd she speech from tongues that never cease.
Slander beside her, like a magpie, chatters,
With Envy, (spitting cat) dread foe to peace;
Like a cursed cur, Malice before her clatters,
And vexing every wight, tears clothes and all to tatters.

V.

Her dugs were mark'd by every collier's hand,
Her mouth was black as bull-dog's at the stall:
She scratched, bit, and spared ne lace ne band,
And bitch and rogue her answer was to all;
Nay, even the parts of shame by name would call:
Yea, when she passes by or lane or nook,
Would greet the man who turn'd him to the wall,
And by his hand obscene the porter took
Nor ever did askance like modest virgin look.

VI.

Such place hath Deptford, navy-building town,
Woolwich and Wapping, smelling strong of pitch;
Such Lambeth, envy of each band and gown,
And Twickenham such, which fairer scenes enrich,
Grots, statues, urns, and Jo—n's dog and bitch,
Ne village is without, on either side,
All up the silver Thames, or all adown;
Ne Richmond's self, from whose tall front are eyed
Vales, spires, meandering streams, and Windsor's
towery pride.

II.

WALLER.

ON A LADY SINGING TO HER LUTE.

Fair charmer, cease, nor make your voice's prize
A heart resign'd the conquest of your eyes:
Well might, alas! that threaten'd vessel fail,
Which winds and lightning both at once assail.
We were too bless'd with these enchanting lays,
Which must be heavenly when an angel plays:
But killing charms your lover's death contrive,
Lest heavenly music should be heard alive.
Orpheus could charm the trees; but thus a tree,
Taught by your hand, can charm no less than he:
A poet made the silent wood pursue,
This vocal wood had drawn the poet too.

ON A FAN OF THE AUTHOR'S DESIGN,

ON WHICH WAS PAINTED THE STORY OF CEPHALUS AND PROCRIS, WITH THE MOTTO "AURA VENI."

Come, gentle air! the Æolian shepherd said,
While Procris panted in the secret shade;
Come, gentle air! the fairer Delia cries,
While at her feet her swain expiring lies.
Lo the glad gales o'er all her beauties stray,
Breathe on her lips, and in her bosom play!
In Delia's hand this toy is fatal found,
Nor could that fabled dart more surely wound:
Both gifts destructive to the givers prove;
Alike both lovers fall by those they love.
Yet guiltless too this bright destroyer lives,
At random wounds, nor knows the wound she gives;
She views the story with attentive eyes,
And pities Procris, while her lover dies.

III.

COWLEY.

THE GARDEN.

Fain would my muse the flowery treasures sing
And humble glories of the youthful spring;
Where opening roses breathing sweets diffuse,
And soft carnations shower their balmy dews;
Where lilies smile in virgin robes of white,
The thin undress of superficial light,
And varied tulips show so dazzling gay,
Blushing in bright diversities of day.
Each painted flow'ret in the lake below
Surveys its beauties, whence its beauties grow;
And pale Narcissus on the bank, in vain
Transformed, gazes on himself again.
Here aged trees cathedral walks compose,
And mount the hill in venerable rows:
There the green infants in their beds are laid,
The garden's hope, and its expected shade.
Here orange-trees with blooms and pendants shine,
And vernal honours to their autumn join,
Exceed their promise in the ripen'd store,
Yet in the rising blossom promise more.
There in bright drops the crystal fountains play,
By laurels shielded from the piercing day:
Where Daphne, now a tree as once a maid,
Still from Apollo vindicates her shade,
Still turns her beauties from the invading beam,
Nor seeks in vain for succour to the stream.
The stream at once preserves her virgin leaves,
At once a shelter from her boughs receives,
Where summer's beauty midst of winter stays,
And winter's coolness spite of summer's rays.

WEEPING.

WHILE Celia's tears make sorrow bright,
  Proud Grief sits swelling in her eyes;
The sun, next those the fairest light,
  Thus from the Ocean first did rise:
And thus through mists we see the sun,
Which else we durst not gaze upon.

These silver drops, like morning dew,
  Foretell the fervour of the day:
So from one cloud soft showers we view,
  And blasting lightnings burst away.
The stars that fall from Celia's eye,
Declare our doom in drawing nigh.

The baby in that sunny sphere
  So like a Phaëton appears,
That Heaven, the threaten'd world to spare,
  Thought fit to drown him in her tears;
Else might the ambitious nymph aspire,
To set, like him, heaven too on fire.

IV.

EARL OF ROCHESTER.

ON SILENCE.

I.

SILENCE! coeval with Eternity;
  Thou wert, ere Nature's self began to be,
'Twas one vast nothing, all, and all slept fast in thee.

II.

Thine was the sway, ere heaven was form'd, or earth
Ere fruitful thought conceived creation's birth,
Or midwife word gave aid, and spoke the infant forth.

III.

Then various elements, against thee join'd,
In one more various animal combined,
And framed the clamorous race of busy human kind.

IV.

The tongue moved gently first, and speech was low,
Till wrangling Science taught it noise and show,
And wicked Wit arose, thy most abusive foe.

V.

But rebel Wit deserts thee oft in vain;
Lost in the maze of words he turns again,
And seeks a surer state, and courts thy gentle reign.

VI.

Afflicted Sense thou kindly dost set free,
Oppress'd with argumental tyranny,
And routed Reason finds a safe retreat in thee.

VII.

With thee in private modest Dulness lies,
And in thy bosom lurks in Thought's disguise;
Thou varnisher of fools, and cheat of all the wise!

VIII.

Yet thy indulgence is by both confest;
Folly by thee lies sleeping in the breast,
And 'tis in thee at last that Wisdom seeks for rest.

IX.

Silence, the knave's repute, the whore's good name,
The only honour of the wishing dame;
The very want of tongue makes thee a kind of fame.

X.

But could'st thou seize some tongues that now are free,
How church and state should be obliged to thee!
At senate, and at bar, how welcome would'st thou be!

XI.

Yet speech even there, submissively withdraws,
From rights of subjects, and the poor man's cause:
Then pompous Silence reigns, and stills the noisy Laws.

XII.

Past services of friends, good deeds of foes,
What favourites gain, and what the nation owes,
Fly the forgetful world, and in thy arms repose.

XIII.

The country wit, religion of the town,
The courtier's learning, policy o' the gown,
Are best by thee express'd; and shine in thee alone.

XIV.

The parson's cant, the lawyer's sophistry,
Lord's quibble, critic's jest; all end in thee,
All rest in peace at last, and sleep eternally.

V.

EARL OF DORSET.

ARTEMISIA.

Though Artemisia talks by fits,
Of councils, classics, fathers, wits;
Reads Malebranche, Boyle, and Locke:
Yet in some things methinks she fails,
'Twere well if she would pare her nails,
And wear a cleaner smock.

Haughty and huge as High-Dutch bride,
Such nastiness, and so much pride,
Are oddly join'd by fate:
On her large squab you find her spread,
Like a fat corpse upon a bed,
That lies and stinks in state.

She wears no colours (sign of grace)
On any part except her face;
All white and black beside:
Dauntless her look, her gesture proud,
Her voice theatrically loud,
And masculine her stride.

So have I seen in black and white
A prating thing, a magpie hight,
Majestically stalk;
A stately worthless animal,
That plies the tongue, and wags the tail,
All flutter, pride, and talk.

PHRYNE.

PHRYNE had talents for mankind,
Open she was, and unconfined,
    Like some free port of trade:
Merchants unloaded here their freight,
And agents from each foreign state,
    Here first their entry made.

Her learning and good-breeding such,
Whether the Italian or the Dutch,
    Spaniards or French came to her:
To all obliging she'd appear.
'Twas *Si Signor*, 'twas *Yaw Mynheer*,
    'Twas *S'il vous plait, Monsieur*.

Obscure by birth, renown'd by crimes,
Still changing names, religions, climes,
    At length she turns a bride:
In diamonds, pearls, and rich brocades,
She shines the first of batter'd jades,
    And flutters in her pride.

So have I known those insects fair
(Which curious Germans hold so rare)
    Still vary shapes and dyes;
Still gain new titles with new forms;
First grubs obscene, then wriggling worms,
    Then painted butterflies.

VI.

DR. SWIFT.

THE HAPPY LIFE OF A COUNTRY PARSON.

PARSON, these things in thy possessing
Are better than the bishop's blessing.
A wife that makes conserves; a steed
That carries double when there's need;
October store, and best Virginia,
Tithe-pig, and mortuary guinea

Gazettes sent gratis down, and frank'd;
For which thy patron's weekly thank'd;
A large Concordance, bound long since;
Sermons to Charles the First, when Prince;
A Chronicle of ancient standing;
A Chrysostom to smooth thy band in:
The Polyglott—three parts,—my text:
Howbeit,—likewise—now to my next:
Lo here the Septuagint,—and Paul,
To sum the whole,—the close of all.

He that has these, may pass his life,
Drink with the 'squire, and kiss his wife;
On Sundays preach, and eat his fill;
And fast on Fridays—if he will;
Toast Church and Queen, explain the news,
Talk with church-wardens about pews,
Pray heartily for some new gift,
And shake his head at Dr. S—t.

MISCELLANIES.

EPISTLE TO ROBERT EARL OF OXFORD, AND EARL OF MORTIMER.

Sent to the Earl of Oxford with Dr. Parnell's Poems, published by our author, after the said Earl's imprisonment in the Tower, and retrea t into the country, in the year 1721.

SUCH were the notes thy once-loved poet sung,
Till death untimely stopp'd his tuneful tongue.
Oh just beheld, and lost! admired and mourn'd!
With softest manners, gentlest arts adorn'd!
Blest in each science, blest in every strain!
Dear to the Muse!—to HARLEY dear—in vain!
For him, thou oft hast bid the world attend,
Fond to forget the statesman in the friend;
For SWIFT and him, despised the farce of state,
The sober follies of the wise and great;
Dext'rous, the craving, fawning crowd to quit,
And pleased to 'scape from Flattery to Wit.
Absent or dead, still let a friend be dear,
(A sigh the absent claims, the dead a tear)
Recall those nights that closed thy toilsome days,
Still hear thy Parnell in his living lays,
Who, careless now of interest, fame, or fate,
Perhaps forgets that OXFORD e'er was great;
Or, deeming meanest what we greatest call,
Beholds thee glorious only in thy fall.
And sure, if aught below the seats divine
Can touch immortals, 'tis a soul like thine:
A soul supreme, in each hard instance tried,
Above all pain, all passion, and all pride,
The rage of power, the blast of public breath,
The lust of lucre, and the dread of death.
In vain to deserts thy retreat is made;
The Muse attends thee to thy silent shade:

'Tis hers, the brave man's latest steps to trace,
Rejudge his acts, and dignify disgrace.
When Interest calls off all her sneaking train,
And all the obliged desert, and all the vain;
She waits, or to the scaffold, or the cell,
When the last lingering friend has bid farewell.
Even now she shades thy evening-walk with bays,
(No hireling she, no prostitute to praise)
Even now, observant of the parting ray,
Eyes the calm sun-set of thy various day,
Through Fortune's cloud one truly great can see,
Nor fears to tell, that MORTIMER is he.

EPISTLE TO JAMES CRAGGS, ESQ.,

SECRETARY OF STATE.

A SOUL as full of worth, as void of pride,
Which nothing seeks to show, or needs to hide,
Which nor to guilt nor fear its caution owes,
And boasts a warmth that from no passion flows.
A face untaught to feign; a judging eye,
That darts severe upon a rising lie,
And strikes a blush through frontless flattery.
All this thou wert; and being this before,
Know, kings and fortune cannot make thee more.
Then scorn to gain a friend by servile ways,
Nor wish to lose a foe these virtues raise;
But candid, free, sincere, as you began,
Proceed—a minister, but still a man.
Be not (exalted to whate'er degree)
Ashamed of any friend, not even of me:
The patriot's plain, but untrod, path pursue;
If not, 'tis I must be ashamed of you.

EPISTLE TO MR. JERVAS,

WITH MR. DRYDEN'S TRANSLATION OF FRESNOY'S ART OF PAINTING.

THIS verse be thine, my friend, nor thou refuse
This, from no venal or ungrateful muse.
Whether thy hand strike out some free design,
Where life awakes, and dawns at every line;
Or blend in beauteous tints the colour'd mass,
And from the canvass call the mimic face:
Read these instructive leaves, in which conspire
Fresnoy's close art, and Dryden's native fire:
And reading, wish, like theirs, our fate and fame,
So mix'd our studies, and so join'd our name;
Like them to shine through long succeeding age,
So just thy skill, so regular my rage.
  Smit with the love of sister-arts we came,
And met congenial, mingling flame with flame;
Like friendly colours found them both unite,
And each from each contract new strength and light.
How oft in pleasing tasks we wear the day,
While summer-suns roll unperceived away!
How oft our slowly-growing works impart,
While images reflect from art to art!
How oft review; each finding like a friend
Something to blame, and something to commend.
  What flattering scenes our wandering fancy wrought,
Rome's pompous glories rising to our thought!
Together o'er the Alps methinks we fly,
Fired with ideas of fair Italy.
With thee, on Raphael's monument I mourn,
Or wait inspiring dreams at Maro's urn:
With thee repose, where Tully once was laid,
Or seek some ruin's formidable shade:
While fancy brings the vanish'd piles to view,
And builds imaginary Rome anew,
Here thy well-studied marbles fix our eye;
A fading fresco here demands a sigh;
Each heavenly piece unwearied we compare,
Match Raphael's grace with thy loved Guido's air,
Carracci's strength, Correggio's softer line,
Paulo's free stroke, and Titian's warmth divine.

How finish'd with illustrious toil appears
This small, well-polished gem, the work of years!
Yet still how faint by precept is express'd
The living image in the painter's breast!
Thence endless streams of fair ideas flow,
Strike in the sketch, or in the picture glow;
Thence beauty, waking all her forms, supplies
An angel's sweetness, or Bridgewater's eyes.
Muse! at that name thy sacred sorrows shed,
Those tears eternal, that embalm the dead:
Call round her tomb each object of desire,
Each purer frame inform'd with purer fire:
Bid her be all that cheers or softens life,
The tender sister, daughter, friend, and wife:
Bid her be all that makes mankind adore;
Then view this marble, and be vain no more!
Yet still her charms in breathing paint engage;
Her modest cheek shall warm a future age.
Beauty, frail flower! that every season fears,
Blooms in thy colours for a thousand years.
Thus Churchill's race shall other hearts surprise,
And other beauties envy Worsley's eyes;
Each pleasing Blount shall endless smiles bestow,
And soft Belinda's blush for ever glow.
Oh lasting as those colours may they shine,
Free as thy stroke, yet faultless as thy line;
New graces yearly like thy works display,
Soft without weakness, without glaring gay;
Led by some rule, that guides, but not constrains;
And finish'd more through happiness than pains.
The kindred arts shall in their praise conspire,
One dip the pencil, and one string the lyre.
Yet should the graces all thy figures place,
And breathe an air divine on every face;
Yet should the Muses bid my numbers roll
Strong as their charms, and gentle as their soul;
With Zeuxis' Helen thy Bridgewater vie,
And these be sung till Granville's Myra die:
Alas! how little from the grave we claim!
Thou but preserv'st a face, and I a name.

EPISTLE TO MRS. BLOUNT.

WITH THE WORKS OF VOITURE.

In these gay thoughts the loves and graces shine,
And all the writer lives in every line;
His easy art may happy nature seem,
Trifles themselves are elegant in him.
Sure to charm all was his peculiar fate,
Who without flattery pleased the fair and great;
Still with esteem no less conversed than read;
With wit well-natured, and with books well-bred:
His heart, his mistress and his friend did share,
His time, the muse, the witty, and the fair.
Thus wisely careless, innocently gay,
Cheerful he play'd the trifle, life, away;
Till fate scarce felt his gentle breath suprest,
As smiling infants sport themselves to rest.
Even rival wits did Voiture's death deplore,
And the gay mourn'd who never mourn'd before;
The truest hearts for Voiture heaved with sighs,
Voiture was wept by all the brightest eyes:
The smiles and loves had died in Voiture's death,
But that for ever in his lines they breathe.
Let the strict life of graver mortals be
A long, exact, and serious comedy;
In every scene some moral let it teach,
And, if it can, at once both please and preach.
Let mine an innocent gay farce appear,
And more diverting still than regular,
Have humour, wit, a native ease and grace,
Though not too strictly bound to time and place:
Critics in wit, or life, are hard to please,
Few write to those, and none can live to these.
Too much your sex is by their forms confined,
Severe to all, but most to womankind;
Custom, grown blind with age, must be your guide;
Your pleasure is a vice, but not your pride;
By nature yielding, stubborn but for fame;
Made slaves by honour, and made fools by shame.
Marriage may all those petty tyrants chase,
But sets up one, a greater in their place:

Well might you wish for change by those accurst,
But the last tyrant ever proves the worst.
Still in constraint your suffering sex remains,
Or bound in formal, or in real chains:
Whole years neglected, for some months adored,
The fawning servant turns a haughty lord.
Ah quit not the free innocence of life,
For the dull glory of a virtuous wife;
Nor let false shows nor empty titles please:
Aim not at joy, but rest content with ease.
The gods, to curse Pamela with her prayers
Gave the gilt coach and dappled Flanders mares,
The shining robes, rich jewels, beds of state,
And, to complete her bliss, a fool for mate.
She glares in balls, front boxes, and the ring,
A vain, unquiet, glittering, wretched thing!
Pride, pomp, and state, but reach her outward part,
She sighs, and is no duchess at her heart.
But, madam, if the fates withstand, and you
Are destined Hymen's willing victim too;
Trust not too much your now resistless charms,
Those, age or sickness, soon or late, disarms:
Good-humour only teaches charms to last,
Still makes new conquests, and maintains the past;
Love, raised on beauty, will like that decay,
Our hearts may bear its slender chain a day;
As flowery bands in wantonness are worn,
A morning's pleasure, and at evening torn;
This binds in ties more easy, yet more strong,
The willing heart, and only holds it long.
Thus Voiture's early care[1] still shone the same,
And Montausier was only changed in name:
By this, even now they live, even now they charm,
Their wit still sparkling, and their flames still warm.
Now crown'd with myrtle, on the Elysian coast,
Amid those lovers, joys his gentle ghost:
Pleased, while with smiles his happy lines you view,
And finds a fairer Rambouillet in you.
The brightest eyes of France inspired his Muse;
The brightest eyes of Britain now peruse;
And dead, as living, 'tis our author's pride
Still to charm those who charm the world beside.

[1] Mademoiselle Paulet.

EPISTLE TO THE SAME,

ON HER LEAVING THE TOWN AFTER THE CORONATION.[1]

As some fond virgin, whom her mother's care
Drags from the town to wholesome country air,
Just when she learns to roll a melting eye,
And hear a spark, yet think no danger nigh;
From the dear man unwilling she must sever,
Yet takes one kiss before she parts for ever:
Thus from the world fair Zephalinda flew,
Saw others happy, and with sighs withdrew;
Not that their pleasures caused her discontent,
She sigh'd not that they stay'd, but that she went.
She went, to plain-work, and to purling brooks,
Old-fashion'd halls, dull aunts, and croaking rooks:
She went from opera, park, assembly, play,
To morning-walks, and prayers three hours a day;
To part her time 'twixt reading and bohea,
To muse, and spill her solitary tea,
Or o'er cold coffee trifle with the spoon,
Count the slow clock, and dine exact at noon:
Divert her eyes with pictures in the fire,
Hum half a tune, tell stories to the squire;
Up to her godly garret after seven,
There starve and pray, for that's the way to heaven.
Some squire, perhaps, you take delight to rack;
Whose game is whist, whose treat a toast in sack;
Who visits with a gun, presents you birds,
Then gives a smacking buss, and cries,—No words!
Or with his hound comes hallooing from the stable;
Makes love with nods, and knees beneath a table;
Whose laughs are hearty, tho' his jests are coarse,
And loves you best of all things—but his horse.
In some fair evening, on your elbow laid,
You dream of triumphs in the rural shade;
In pensive thought recall the fancied scene,
See coronations rise on every green;
Before you pass the imaginary sights
Of lords, and earls, and dukes, and garter'd knights,
While the spread fan o'ershades your closing eyes;
Then give one flirt, and all the vision flies.

[1] Of King George I., 1715.

Thus vanish sceptres, coronets, and balls,
And leave your in lone woods, or empty walls!
So when you slave, at some dear idle time,
(Not plagued with head-aches, or the want of rhyme)
Stands in the streets, abstracted from the crew,
And while he seems to study, thinks of you;
Just when his fancy points your sprightly eyes,
Or sees the blush of soft Parthenia rise,
GAY pats my shoulder, and you vanish quite,
Streets, chairs, and coxcombs, rush upon my sight;
Vex'd to be still in town, I knit my brow,
Look sour, and hum a tune, as you may now.

THE BASSET-TABLE.

AN ECLOGUE.

CARDELIA. SMILINDA.

CARDELIA.

THE *basset-table* spread, the *tallier* come;
Why stays SMILINDA in the dressing-room?
Rise, pensive nymph, the tallier waits for you!

SMILINDA.

Ah, madam, since my SHARPER is untrue,
I joyless make my once adored *Alpeu*.
I saw him stand behind OMBRELIA'S chair,
And whisper with that soft, deluding air,
And those feign'd sighs which cheat the listening fair

CARDELIA.

Is this the cause of your romantic strains?
A mightier grief my heavy heart sustains.
As you by love, so I by fortune cross'd;
One, one bad *deal*, three *Septlevas* have lost.

SMILINDA.

Is that the grief, which you compare with mine?
With ease, the smiles of fortune I resign:
Would all my gold in one bad *deal* were gone!
Were lovely SHARPER mine, and mine alone.

CARDELIA.

A lover lost, is but a common care:
And prudent nymphs against that change prepare:
The KNAVE OF CLUBS thrice lost! Oh! who could guess
This fatal stroke, this unforeseen distress?

SMILINDA.

See BETTY LOVET! very *à-propos*,
She all the cares of *love* and *play* does know:
Dear BETTY shall the important point decide;
BETTY, who oft the pain of each has tried;
Impartial, she shall say who suffers most,
By *cards' ill usage*, or by *lovers lost.*

LOVET.

Tell, tell your griefs; attentive will I stay,
Though time is precious, and I want some tea.

CARDELIA.

Behold this *equipage*, by *Mather's* wrought,
With fifty guineas (a great pen'orth) bought.
See on the tooth-pick, Mars and Cupid strive;
And both the struggling figures seem alive.
Upon the bottom shines the queen's bright face;
A myrtle foliage round the thimble-case.
Jove, Jove himself, does on the scissors shine;
The metal, and the workmanship, divine!

SMILINDA.

This *snuff-box*,—once the pledge of SHARPER's love,
When rival beauties for the present strove;
At *Corticelli's* he the raffle won;
Then first his passion was in public shown:
HAZARDIA blush'd, and turn'd her head aside,
A rival's envy (all in vain) to hide.
This *snuff-box*—on the hinge see brilliants shine:
This *snuff-box* will I stake; the prize is mine.

CARDELIA.

Alas! far lesser losses than I bear,
Have made a soldier sigh, a lover swear.
And oh! what makes the disappointment hard,
'Twas my own lord that drew the *fatal card.*

In complaisance, I took the *queen* he gave;
Though my own secret wish was for the *knave*.
The *knave* won *Sonica*, which I had chose;
And the next *pull*, my *Septleva* I lose.

SMILINDA.

But ah! what aggravates the killing smart,
The cruel thought, that stabs me to the heart;
This cursed OMBRELIA, this undoing fair,
By whose vile arts this heavy grief I bear;
She, at whose name I shed these spiteful tears,
She owes to me the very charms she wears.
An awkward thing, when first she came to town;
Her shape unfashion'd, and her face unknown:
She was my friend: I taught her first to spread
Upon her sallow cheeks enlivening red:
I introduced her to the park and plays;
And by my interests, *Cozens* made her stays.
Ungrateful wretch, with mimic airs grown pert,
She dares to steal my fav'rite lover's heart.

CARDELIA.

Wretch that I was, how often have I swore,
When Winnall *tallied*, I would *punt* no more?
I knew the bite, yet to my ruin run;
And see the folly which I cannot shun.

SMILINDA.

How many maids have SHARPER'S vows deceived?
How many cursed the moment they believed?
Yet his known falsehoods could no warning prove:
Ah! what is warning to a maid in love?

CARDELIA.

But of what marble must that breast be form'd,
To gaze on *Basset*, and remain unwarm'd?
When *kings*, *queens*, *knaves*, are set in decent rank;
Exposed in glorious heaps the tempting bank,
Guineas, half-guineas, all the shining train,
The winner's pleasure, and the loser's pain:
In bright confusion open *rouleaus* lie,
They strike the soul, and glitter in the eye.

Fired by the sight, all reason I disdain;
My passions rise and will not bear the rein.
Look upon *Basset*, you who reason boast,
And see if reason must not there be lost.

SMILINDA.

What more than marble must that heart compose
Can hearken coldly to my SHARPER's vows?
Then, when he trembles! when his blushes rise!
When awful love seems melting in his eyes!
With eager beats his Mechlin cravat moves:
He loves,—I whisper to myself, *He loves!*
Such unfeign'd passion in his looks appears,
I lose all memory of my former fears;
My panting heart confesses all his charms,
I yield at once, and sink into his arms:
Think of that moment, you who prudence boast;
For such a moment, prudence well were lost.

CARDELIA.

At the *Groom-Porter's*, batter'd bullies play,
Some DUKES at *Mary-bone* bowl time away.
But who the bowl or rattling dice compares
To *Basset's* heavenly joys and pleasing cares?

SMILINDA.

Soft SIMPLICETTA doats upon a beau;
PRUDINA likes a man, and laughs at show.
Their several graces in my SHARPER meet;
Strong as the footman, as the master sweet.

LOVET.

Cease your contention, which has been too long;
I grow impatient, and the tea's too strong.
Attend and yield to what I now decide;
The *equipage* shall grace SMILINDA's side;
The *snuff-box* to CARDELIA I decree,
Now leave complaining, and begin your *tea*.

VERBATIM FROM BOILEAU.

Un jour, dit un auteur, etc.

Once (says an author, where I need not say)
Two travellers found an oyster in their way;
Both fierce, both hungry; the dispute grew strong;
While scale in hand dame *Justice* pass'd along.
Before her each with clamour pleads the laws,
Explain'd the matter, and would win the cause.
Dame *Justice* weighing long the doubtful right,
Takes, opens, swallows it, before their sight.
The cause of strife removed so rarely well,
There take (says *Justice*), take ye each a *shell.*
We thrive at *Westminster* on fools like you:
'Twas a fat oyster—Live in peace—Adieu.

ANSWER TO THE FOLLOWING QUESTION OF MRS. HOW.

What is prudery?
'Tis a beldam,
Seen with wit and beauty seldom.
'Tis a fear that starts at shadows;
'Tis (no 'tisn't) like Miss *Meadows.*
'Tis a virgin hard of feature,
Old, and void of all good-nature;
Lean and fretful, would seem wise;
Yet plays the fool before she dies.
'Tis an ugly envious shrew,
That rails at dear *Lepell* and you.

OCCASIONED BY SOME VERSES OF HIS GRACE THE DUKE OF BUCKINGHAM.

Muse, 'tis enough: at length thy labour ends,
And thou shalt live, for Buckingham commends.
Let crowds of critics now my verse assail,
Let Dennis write, and nameless numbers rail:
This more than pays whole years of thankless pain,
Time, health, and fortune, are not lost in vain.
Sheffield approves, consenting Phœbus bends,
And I and Malice from this hour are friends.

A PROLOGUE

TO A PLAY FOR MR. DENNIS'S BENEFIT IN 1733, WHEN HE WAS OLD, BLIND, AND IN GREAT DISTRESS, A LITTLE BEFORE HIS DEATH.

As when that hero, who in each campaign,
Had braved the *Goth*, and many a *Vandal* slain,
Lay fortune-struck, a spectacle of woe!
Wept by each friend, forgiven by every foe;
Was there a generous, a reflecting mind,
But pitied BELISARIUS old and blind?
Was there a chief but melted at the sight?
A common soldier, but who clubb'd his mite?
Such, such emotions should in *Britons* rise,
When press'd by want and weakness DENNIS lies;
Dennis, who long had warr'd with modern *Huns*,
Their quibbles routed, and defied their puns;
A desperate *bulwark*, sturdy, firm and fierce,
Against the *Gothic* sons of frozen verse:
How changed from him who made the boxes groan,
And shook the stage with thunders all his own!
Stood up to dash each vain PRETENDER's hope,
Maul the French tyrant or pull down the POPE!
If there's a *Briton* then, true bred and born,
Who holds dragoons and wooden shoes in scorn;
If there's a critic of distinguish'd rage;
If there's a senior, who contemns this age;
Let him to-night his just assistance lend,
And be the *critic's, Briton's, old man's* friend.

MACER:

A CHARACTER.

WHEN simple *Macer*, now of high renown,
First sought a poet's fortune in the town,
'Twas all the ambition his high soul could feel,
To wear red stockings, and to dine with *Steele*.
Some ends of verse his betters might afford,
And gave the harmless fellow a good word.
Set up with these, he ventured on the town,
And with a borrow'd play, outdid poor *Crown*.

There he stopp'd short, nor since has writ a tittle,
But has the wit to make the most of little:
Like stunted hide-bound trees, that just have got
Sufficient sap at once to bear and rot.
Now he begs verse, and what he gets commends,
Not of the wits his foes, but fools his friends.
  So some coarse country wench, almost decay'd,
Trudges to town, and first turns chambermaid;
Awkward and supple, each devoir to pay;
She flatters her good lady twice a day;
Thought wondrous honest, though of mean degree,
And strangely liked for her *simplicity:*
In a translated suit, then tries the town,
With borrow'd pins, and patches not her own:
But just endured the winter she began,
And in four months a batter'd harridan.
Now nothing left, but wither'd, pale, and shrunk,
To bawd for others, and go shares with Punk.

TO MR. JOHN MOORE,

INVENTOR OF THE CELEBRATED WORM-POWDER.

How much, egregious *Moore*, are we
  Deceived by shows and forms!
Whate'er we think, whate'er we see
  All humankind are worms.

Man is a very worm by birth,
  Vile, reptile, weak, and vain!
Awhile he crawls upon the earth,
  Then shrinks to earth again.

That woman is a worm, we find
  E'er since our grandame's evil;
She first conversed with her own kind,
  That ancient worm, the devil.

The learn'd themselves we book-worms name,
  The blockhead is a slow-worm;
The nymph whose tail is all on flame
  Is aptly term'd a glow-worm.

The fops are painted butterflies,
  That flutter for a day;
First from a worm they take their rise,
  And in a worm decay.

The flatterer an earwig grows:
  Thus worms suit all conditions;
Misers are muck-worms, silk-worms beaus,
  And death-watches physicians.

That statesmen have the worm, is seen
  By all their winding play;
Their conscience is a worm within,
  That gnaws them night and day.

Ah *Moore!* thy skill were well employ'd,
  And greater gain would rise,
If thou couldst make the courtier void
  The worm that never dies!

O learned friend of *Abchurch-lane*,
  Who sett'st our entrails free!
Vain is thy art, thy powder vain,
  Since worms shall eat even thee.

Our fate thou only canst adjourn
  Some few short years, no more!
Even *Button's* wits to worms shall turn,
  Who maggots were before.

SONG,

BY A PERSON OF QUALITY.

WRITTEN IN THE YEAR 1733.

FLUTTERING spread thy purple pinions,
  Gentle Cupid, o'er my heart,
I a slave in thy dominions;
  Nature must give way to art.

Mild *Arcadians*, ever blooming,
  Nightly nodding o'er your flocks,
See my weary days consuming,
  All beneath yon flowery rocks.

III.

Thus the *Cyprian* goddess weeping,
  Mourn'd *Adonis*, darling youth:
Him the boar, in silence creeping,
  Gored with unrelenting tooth.

Cynthia, tune harmonious numbers;
  Fair *Discretion*, string the lyre;
Soothe my ever-waking slumbers;
  Bright *Apollo*, lend thy choir.

Gloomy *Pluto*, king of terrors,
  Arm'd in adamantine chains,
Lead me to the crystal mirrors,
  Watering soft Elysian plains.

Mournful cypress, verdant willow,
  Gilding my *Aurelia's* brows,
Morpheus hovering o'er my pillow,
  Hear me pay my dying vows.

Melancholy smooth *Mæander*,
  Swiftly purling in a round,
On thy margin lovers wander,
  With thy flowery chaplets crown'd.

Thus when *Philomela*, drooping,
  Softly seeks her silent mate,
See the bird of *Juno* stooping;
  Melody resigns to fate.

ON A CERTAIN LADY AT COURT.

I KNOW the thing that's most uncommon;
  (Envy be silent, and attend!)
I know a reasonable woman,
  Handsome and witty, yet a friend.

Not warp'd by passion, awed by rumour,
  Not grave through pride, or gay through folly,
An equal mixture of good humour
  And sensible soft melancholy.

"Has she no faults then, (Envy says) Sir?"
Yes, she has one, I must aver;
When all the world conspires to praise her,
The woman's deaf, and does not hear.

ON HIS GROTTO AT TWICKENHAM,

COMPOSED OF MARBLES, SPARS, GEMS, ORES, AND MINERALS.

Thou who shalt stop, where *Thames'* translucent wave
Shines a broad mirror through the shadowy cave;
Where lingering drops from mineral roofs distil,
And pointed crystals break the sparkling rill,
Unpolish'd gems no ray on pride bestow,
And latent metals innocently glow:
Approach. Great Nature studiously behold!
And eye the mine without a wish for gold.
Approach: but awful! Lo! the Ægerian grot,
Where, nobly pensive, St. John sate and thought;
Where *British* sighs from dying Wyndham stole,
And the bright flame was shot through Marchmont's soul.
Let such, such only, tread this sacred floor,
Who dare to love their country, and be poor.

TO MR. GAY,

WHO CONGRATULATED HIM ON FINISHING HIS HOUSE AND GARDENS.

Ah, friend! 'tis true—this truth you lovers know—
In vain my structures rise, my gardens grow,
In vain fair Thames reflects the double scenes
Of hanging mountains, and of sloping greens:
Joy lives not here, to happier seats it flies,
And only dwells where Wortley casts her eyes.

What are the gay parterre, the checquer'd shade,
The morning bower, the evening colonnade,
But soft recesses of uneasy minds,
To sigh unheard in, to the passing winds?
So the struck deer in some sequester'd part
Lies down to die, the arrow at his heart,
He, stretch'd unseen in coverts hid from day,
Bleeds drop by drop, and pants his life away.

TO MRS. M. B.

ON HER BIRTH-DAY.

Oh be thou blest with all that Heaven can send,
Long health, long youth, long pleasure, and a friend:
Not with those toys the female world admire,
Riches that vex, and vanities that tire.
With added years, if life bring nothing new,
But like a sieve let every blessing through,
Some joys still lost, as each vain year runs o'er,
And all we gain, some sad reflection more;
Is that a birth-day? 'tis alas! too clear,
'Tis but the funeral of the former year.

Let joy or ease, let affluence or content,
And the gay conscience of a life well spent,
Calm every thought, inspirit every grace,
Glow in thy heart, and smile upon thy face.
Let day improve on day, and year on year,
Without a pain, a trouble, or a fear;
Till death unfelt that tender frame destroy,
In some soft dream, or ecstacy of joy,
Peaceful sleep out the sabbath of the tomb,
And wake to raptures in a life to come.

TO MR. THOMAS SOUTHERN,

ON HIS BIRTH-DAY, 1742.

Resigned to live, prepared to die,
With not one sin, but poetry,
This day Tom's fair account has run
(Without a blot) to eighty-one.
Kind Boyle, before his poet lays
A table, with a cloth of bays;
And Ireland, mother of sweet singers,
Presents her harp still to his fingers.
The feast, his towering genius marks
In yonder wild goose and the larks!
The mushrooms show his wit was sudden!
And for his judgment, lo a pudden!

Roast beef, though old, proclaims him stout,
And grace, although a bard, devout.
May TOM, whom Heaven sent down to raise
The price of prologues and of plays,
Be every birth-day more a winner,
Digest his thirty-thousandth dinner;
Walk to his grave without reproach,
And scorn a rascal in a coach.

ROXANA, OR THE DRAWING-ROOM.

AN ECLOGUE.

This Eclogue has by some been attributed to Lady Mary Wortley Montagu.

ROXANA from the court returning late,
Sigh'd her soft sorrow at St. James's gate:
Such heavy thoughts lay brooding in her breast;
Not her own chairmen with more weight oppress'd:
They curse the cruel weight they're doom'd to bear;
She in more gentle sounds express'd her care.

Was it for this, that I these roses wear?
For this, new-set the jewels for my hair?
Ah, princess! with what zeal have I pursued!
Almost forgot the duty of a prude.
This king, I never could attend too soon;
I miss'd my prayers, to get me dress'd by noon.
For thee, ah! what for thee did I resign?
My passions, pleasures, all that e'er was mine:
I've sacrificed both modesty and ease;
Left operas, and went to filthy plays:
Double-entendres shock'd my tender ear;
Yet even this, for thee, I choose to bear:
In glowing youth, when nature bids be gay,
And every joy of life before me lay;
By honour prompted, and by pride restrain'd,
The pleasures of the young my soul disdain'd:
Sermons I sought, and with a mien severe,
Censured my neighbours, and said daily prayer.

Alas, how changed! with this same sermon-mien,
The filthy what-d'ye-call it—I have seen.
Ah, royal princess! for whose sake I lost
The reputation, which so dear had cost;
I, who avoided every public place,
When bloom and beauty bid me show my face,
Now near thee, constant, I each night abide,
With never-failing duty by my side;
Myself and daughters standing in a row,
To all the foreigners a goodly show.
Oft had your drawing-room been sadly thin,
And merchants' wives close by your side had been;
Had I not amply fill'd the empty place,
And saved your highness from the dire disgrace:
Yet Cockatilla's artifice prevails,
When all my duty and my merit fails:
That Cockatilla, whose deluding airs
Corrupts our virgins, and our youth ensnares;
So sunk her character, and lost her fame,
Scarce visited, before your highness came;
Yet for the bed-chamber 'tis she you choose,
Whilst zeal, and fame, and virtue you refuse.
Ah worthy choice; not one of all your train,
Which censures blast not, or dishonours stain.
I know the court, with all its treacherous wiles,
The false caresses, and undoing smiles.
Ah, princess! learn'd in all the courtly arts,
To cheat our hopes, and yet to gain our hearts.

EXTEMPORANEOUS LINES,

ON THE PICTURE OF LADY MARY W. MONTAGU BY KNELLER.

The playful smiles around the dimpled mouth,
That happy air of majesty and truth;
So would I draw (but oh! 'tis vain to try,
My narrow genius does the power deny)
The equal lustre of the heavenly mind,
Where every grace with every virtue 's join'd;
Learning not vain, and wisdom not severe,
With greatness easy, and with wit sincere;
With just description show the work divine,
And the whole princess in my work should shine.

TO LADY MARY WORTLEY MONTAGU.

I.

In beauty, or wit,
No mortal as yet
To question your empire has dared;
But men of discerning
Have thought that in learning,
To yield to a lady was hard.

II.

Impertinent schools,
With musty dull rules,
Have reading to females denied;
So papists refuse
The Bible to use,
Lest flocks should be wise as their guide.

III.

'Twas a woman at first
(Indeed she was curst)
In knowledge that tasted delight,
And sages agree
The laws should decree
To the first possessor the right.

IV.

Then bravely, fair dame,
Resume the old claim,
Which to your whole sex does belong;
And let men receive,
From a second bright Eve,
The knowledge of right and of wrong.

V.

But if the first Eve
Hard doom did receive,
When only one apple had she,
What punishment new
Shall be found out for you,
Who tasting, have robb'd the whole tree?

THE LOOKING-GLASS.

ON MRS. PULTENEY.

WITH scornful mien, and various toss of air,
Fantastic, vain, and insolently fair,
Grandeur intoxicates her giddy brain,
She looks ambition, and she moves disdain.
Far other carriage graced her virgin life,
But charming Gumley's lost in Pulteney's wife.
Not greater arrogance in him we find,
And this conjunction swells at least her mind:
O could the sire, renowned in glass, produce
One faithful mirror for his daughter's use!
Wherein she might her haughty errors trace,
And by reflection learn to mend her face:
The wonted sweetness to her form restore,
Be what she was, and charm mankind once more!

A FAREWELL TO LONDON.

IN THE YEAR 1715.

DEAR, damn'd, distracting town, farewell!
Thy fools no more I'll tease:
This year in peace, ye critics, dwell,
Ye harlots, sleep at ease!

* * * * * * *

To drink and droll be Rowe allow'd
Till the third watchman's toll;
Let Jervas gratis paint, and Frowde
Save three-pence and his soul.

Farewell, Arbuthnot's raillery
On every learned sot;
And Garth, the best good Christian he,
Although he knows it not.

Lintot, farewell! thy bard must go;
Farewell, unhappy Tonson!
Heaven gives thee for thy loss of Rowe,
Lean Philips, and fat Johnson.

Why should I stay? Both parties rage;
My vixen mistress squalls;
The wits in envious feuds engage:
And Homer (damn him!) calls.

The love of arts lies cold and dead
In Halifax's urn;
And not one muse of all he fed
Has yet the grace to mourn.

My friends, by turns, my friends confound,
Betray, and are betray'd:
Poor Y——rs sold for fifty pounds,
And B——ll is a jade.

Why make I friendships with the great,
When I no favour seek?
* * * * * * *

Still idle, with a busy air,
Deep whimsies to contrive;
The gayest valetudinaire,
Most thinking rake alive.

Solicitous for other ends,
Though fond of dear repose;
Careless or drowsy with my friends,
And frolic with my foes.

Luxurious lobster-nights, farewell,
For sober, studious days!
And Burlington's delicious meal,
For salads, tarts, and pease!

Adieu to all but Gay alone,
Whose soul, sincere and free,
Loves all mankind, but flatters none,
And so may starve with me.

THE FOLLOWING LINES WERE SUNG BY DURASTANTI, WHEN SHE TOOK HER LEAVE OF THE ENGLISH STAGE.

THE WORDS WERE IN HASTE PUT TOGETHER BY MR. POPE, AT THE REQUEST OF THE EARL OF PETERBOROUGH.

Generous, gay, and gallant nation,
  Bold in arms, and bright in arts;
Land secure from all invasion,
  All but Cupid's gentle darts!
From your charms, oh who would run?
Who would leave you for the sun?

  Happy soil, adieu, adieu!
Let old charmers yield to new.
  In arms, in arts, be still more shining;
All your joys be still increasing;
  All your tastes be still refining;
All your jars for ever ceasing:
  But let old charmers yield to new:—
  Happy soil, adieu, adieu!

UPON THE DUKE OF MARLBOROUGH'S HOUSE AT WOODSTOCK.

Atria longa patent; sed nec cœnantibus usquam,
  Nec somno locus est: quàm bene non habitas!

Mart. Epig.

See, sir, here's the grand approach,
This way is for his Grace's coach;
There lies the bridge, and here's the clock,
Observe the lion and the cock,
The spacious court, the colonnade,
And mark how wide the hall is made!
The chimneys are so well design'd,
They never smoke in any wind.
This gallery's contrived for walking,
The windows to retire and talk in;
The council-chamber for debate,
And all the rest are rooms of state.

Thanks, sir, cried I, 'tis very fine,
But where d'ye sleep, or where d'ye dine
I find by all you have been telling,
That 'tis a house, but not a dwelling.

VERSES LEFT BY MR. POPE,

ON HIS LYING IN THE SAME BED WHICH WILMOT, THE CELEBRATED EARL OF ROCHESTER, SLEPT IN, AT ADDERBURY, THEN BELONGING TO THE DUKE OF ARGYLE, JULY 9, 1739.

With no poetic ardour fired
  I press the bed where Wilmot lay;
That here he loved, or here expired,
  Begets no numbers, grave or gay.

Beneath thy roof, Argyle, are bred
  Such thoughts as prompt the brave to lie
Stretch'd out in honour's nobler bed,
  Beneath a nobler roof—the sky.

Such flames as high in patriots burn
  Yet stoop to bless a child or wife;
And such as wicked kings may mourn,
  When freedom is more dear than life.

THE CHALLENGE.

A COURT BALLAD.

To the tune of "To all you ladies now at land," &c.

I.

To one fair lady out of court,
  And two fair ladies in,
Who think the Turk and Pope a sport,
  And wit and love no sin;
Come, these soft lines, with nothing stiff in,
To Bellenden, Lepell, and Griffin,
    With a fa, la, la.

II.

What passes in the dark third row,
  And what behind the scene,
Couches and crippled chairs I know,
  And garrets hung with green;
I know the swing of sinful hack,
Where many damsels cry alack.
        With a fa, la, la.

III.

Then why to courts should I repair,
  Where's such ado with Townshend?
To hear each mortal stamp and swear,
  And every speech with zounds end;
To hear 'em rail at honest Sunderland,
And rashly blame the realm of Blunderland.
        With a fa, la, la.

IV.

Alas! like Schutz I cannot pun,
  Like Grafton court the Germans;
Tell Pickenbourg how slim she's grown,
  Like Meadows run to sermons;
To court ambitious men may roam,
  But I and Marlbro' stay at home.
        With a fa, la, la.

V.

In truth, by what I can discern,
  Of courtiers 'twixt you three,
Some wit you have, and more may learn
  From court, than Gay or me:
Perhaps, in time, you'll leave high diet,
To sup with us on milk and quiet.
        With a fa, la, la.

VI.

At Leicester-Fields, a house full high,
  With door all painted green,
Where ribbons wave upon the tie,
  (A milliner I mean;)
There may you meet us three to three,
For Gay can well make two of me.
        With a fa, la, la.

VII.

But should you catch the prudish itch,
And each become a coward,
Bring sometimes with you Lady Rich,
And sometimes Mistress Howard;
For virgins, to keep chaste, must go
Abroad with such as are not so.
With a fa, la, la.

VIII.

And thus, fair maids, my ballad ends:
God send the king safe landing;
And make all honest ladies friends
To armies that are standing;
Preserve the limits of those nations,
And take off ladies' limitations.
With a fa, la, la.

THE THREE GENTLE SHEPHERDS.

Of gentle Philips will I ever sing,
With gentle Philips shall the valleys ring;
My numbers too for ever will I vary,
With gentle Budgell, and with gentle Carey.
Or if in ranging of the names I judge ill,
With gentle Carey and with gentle Budgell:
Oh! may all gentle bards together place ye,
Men of good hearts, and men of delicacy.
May satire ne'er befool ye, or beknave ye,
And from all wits that have a knack, God save ye.

VERSES TO DR. BOLTON,

IN THE NAME OF MRS. BUTLER'S SPIRIT, LATELY DECEASED.

Stripp'd to the naked soul, escaped from clay,
From doubts unfetter'd, and dissolved in day;
Unwarm'd by vanity, unreach'd by strife,
And all my hopes and fears thrown off with life;

Why am I charm'd by friendship's fond essays,
And though unbodied, conscious of thy praise?
Has pride a portion in the parted soul?
Does passion still the firmless mind control!
Can gratitude out-pant the silent breath!
Or a friend's sorrow pierce the gloom of death!
No—'tis a spirit's nobler task of bliss;
That feels the worth it left, in proofs like this;
That not its own applause, but thine approves,
Whose practice praises, and whose virtue loves;
Who livest to crown departed friends with fame;
Then dying, late, shalt all thou gavest reclaim.

EPITAPHS.

His saltem acumulem donis, et fungar inani
Munere! VIRG.

I.

ON CHARLES EARL OF DORSET,

IN THE CHURCH OF WITHYAM IN SUSSEX.

DORSET, the grace of courts, the Muses' pride,
Patron of arts, and judge of nature, died.
The scourge of pride, though sanctified or great,
Of fops in learning, and of knaves in state;
Yet soft his nature, though severe his lay,
His anger moral, and his wisdom gay.
Blest satirist! who touch'd the mean so true,
As showed vice had his hate and pity too.
Blest courtier! who could king and country please,
Yet sacred keep his friendships and his ease.
Blest peer! his great forefathers' every grace
Reflecting, and reflected in his race;
Where other BUCKHURSTS, other DORSETS shine,
And patriots still, or poets, deck the line.

II.

ON SIR WILLIAM TRUMBAL,

ONE OF THE PRINCIPAL SECRETARIES OF STATE TO KING WILLIAM III., WHO HAVING RESIGNED HIS PLACE, DIED IN HIS RETIREMENT AT EASTHAMSTED, IN BERKSHIRE, 1716.

A PLEASING form; a firm, yet cautious mind;
Sincere, though prudent; constant, yet resign'd:
Honour unchanged, a principle profest,
Fix'd to one side, but moderate to the rest:
An honest courtier, yet a patriot too;
Just to his prince, and to his country true:
Fill'd with the sense of age, the fire of youth,
A scorn of wrangling, yet a zeal for truth:
A generous faith, from superstition free;
A love to peace, and hate of tyranny:
Such this man was; who now, from earth removed,
At length enjoys that liberty he loved.

III.

ON GENERAL HENRY WITHERS,

IN WESTMINSTER-ABBEY, 1729.

HERE, WITHERS, rest! thou bravest, gentlest mind,
Thy country's friend, but more of human kind.
O born to arms! O worth in youth approved!
O soft humanity, in age beloved!
For thee the hardy veteran drops a tear,
And the gay courtier feels the sigh sincere.

WITHERS, adieu! yet not with thee remove
Thy martial spirit, or thy social love!
Amidst corruption, luxury, and rage,
Still leave some ancient virtues to our age:
Nor let us say (those English glories gone)
The last true Briton lies beneath this stone.

IV.

ON JAMES CRAGGS, Esq.

IN WESTMINSTER-ABBEY.

Statesman, yet friend to truth! of soul sincere,
In action faithful, and in honour clear!
Who broke no promise, served no private end,
Who gain'd no title, and who lost no friend;
Ennobled by himself, by all approved,
Praised, wept, and honour'd, by the muse he loved.

V.

INTENDED FOR MR. ROWE,

IN WESTMINSTER-ABBEY.

Thy reliques, Rowe, to this fair urn we trust,
And sacred, place by Dryden's awful dust:
Beneath a rude and nameless stone he lies,
To which thy tomb shall guide inquiring eyes.
Peace to thy gentle shade, and endless rest!
Blest in thy genius, in thy love too blest!
One grateful woman to thy fame supplies
What a whole thankless land to his denies.

VI.

ON MRS. CORBET,

WHO DIED OF A CANCER IN HER BREAST.

Here rests a woman, good without pretence,
Blest with plain reason, and with sober sense;
No conquest she, but o'er herself, desired,
No arts essay'd, but not to be admired.
Passion and pride were to her soul unknown,
Convinced that virtue only is our own.
So unaffected, so composed a mind;
So firm, yet soft; so strong, yet so refined;
Heaven, as its purest gold, by tortures tried!
The saint sustain'd it,—but the woman died.

VII.

ON THE MONUMENT OF THE HONOURABLE ROBERT DIGBY, AND OF HIS SISTER MARY,

ERECTED BY THEIR FATHER, THE LORD DIGBY, IN THE CHURCH OF SHERBORNE, IN DORSETSHIRE, 1727.

Go! fair example of untainted youth,
Of modest wisdom, and pacific truth:
Composed in sufferings, and in joy sedate,
Good without noise, without pretension great.
Just of thy word, in every thought sincere,
Who knew no wish but what the world might hear:
Of softest manners, unaffected mind,
Lover of peace, and friend of human kind:
Go live! for Heaven's eternal year is thine,
Go, and exalt thy mortal to divine.
And thou, blest maid! attendant on his doom,
Pensive hast follow'd to the silent tomb,
Steer'd the same course to the same quiet shore,
Not parted long, and now to part no more!
Go then, where only bliss sincere is known!
Go, where to love and to enjoy are one!
Yet take these tears, mortality's relief,
And till we share your joys, forgive our grief:
These little rites, a stone, a verse, receive;
'Tis all a father, all a friend can give!

VIII.

ON SIR GODFREY KNELLER,

IN WESTMINSTER-ABBEY, 1723.

KNELLER, by Heaven and not a master taught,
Whose art was nature, and whose pictures thought;
Now for two ages having snatch'd from fate
Whate'er was beauteous, or whate'er was great,
Lies crown'd with princes' honours, poets' lays,
Due to his merit, and brave thirst of praise.

Living, great Nature feared he might outvie
Her works; and, dying, fears herself may die.

IX.

ON THE HON. SIMON HARCOURT,

ONLY SON OF THE LORD CHANCELLOR HARCOURT; AT THE CHURCH OF STANTON-HARCOURT IN OXFORDSHIRE, 1720.

To this sad shrine, whoe'er thou art! draw near,
Here lies the friend most loved, the son most dear:
Who ne'er knew joy, but friendship might divide,
Or gave his father grief but when he died.

How vain is reason, eloquence how weak!
If *Pope* must tell what HARCOURT cannot speak.
Oh let thy once-loved friend inscribe thy stone,
And, with a father's sorrows, mix his own!

X.

ON EDMUND DUKE OF BUCKINGHAM,

WHO DIED IN THE NINETEENTH YEAR OF HIS AGE, 1735.

IF modest youth, with cool reflection crown'd,
And every opening virtue blooming round,
Could save a parent's justest pride from fate,
Or add one patriot to a sinking state;
This weeping marble had not ask'd thy tear,
Or sadly told, how many hopes lie here!
The living virtue now had shone approved,
The senate heard him, and his country loved.
Yet softer honours and less noisy fame
Attend the shade of gentle BUCKINGHAM:
In whom a race, for courage famed and art,
Ends in a milder merit of the heart;
And chiefs or sages long to Britain given,
Pays the last tribute of a saint to heaven.

XI.

FOR ONE WHO WOULD NOT BE BURIED IN WESTMINSTER-ABBEY.

HEROES and KINGS! your distance keep:
In peace let one poor poet sleep,
Who never flatter'd folks like you:
Let Horace blush, and Virgil too.

XII.

ON MR. ELIJAH FENTON,

AT EASTHAMSTED IN BERKS, 1730.

This modest stone, what few vain marbles can,
May truly say,—Here lies an honest man:
A poet, blest beyond the poet's fate,
Whom Heaven kept sacred from the proud and great:
Foe to loud praise, and friend to learned ease,
Content with science in the vale of peace.
Calmly he look'd on either life, and here
Saw nothing to regret, or there to fear;
From nature's temperate feast rose satisfied,
Thank'd Heaven that he had lived, and that he died.

XIII.

ON MR. GAY,

IN WESTMINSTER-ABBEY, 1732.

Of manners gentle, of affections mild;
In wit, a man; simplicity, a child:
With native humour tempering virtuous rage,
Form'd to delight at once and lash the age.
Above temptation, in a low estate,
And uncorrupted even among the great:
A safe companion, and an easy friend,
Unblamed through life, lamented in thy end.
These are thy honours! not that here thy bust
Is mix'd with heroes, or with kings thy dust;
But that the worthy and the good shall say,
Striking their pensive bosoms—*Here* lies Gay.

XIV.

INTENDED FOR SIR ISAAC NEWTON,

IN WESTMINSTER-ABBEY.

ISAACUS NEWTONUS:
Quem Immortalem
Testantur *Tempus, Natura, Cœlum:*
Mortalem
Hoc marmor fatetur.

Nature and Nature's laws lay hid in night:
God said, *Let Newton be!* and all was light.

XV.

ON DR. FRANCIS ATTERBURY,

BISHOP OF ROCHESTER,

WHO DIED IN EXILE AT PARIS, 1732, (HIS ONLY DAUGHTER HAVING EXPIRED IN HIS ARMS, IMMEDIATELY ATER SHE ARRIVED IN FRANCE TO SEE HIM.)

DIALOGUE.

SHE.

YES, we have lived—one pang, and then we part!
May Heaven, dear father! now have all thy heart.
Yet ah! how once we loved, remember still,
Till you are dust like me.

HE.

Dear shade! I will:
Then mix this dust with thine—O spotless ghost!
O more than fortune, friends, or country lost!
Is there on earth one care, one wish beside?
Yes—SAVE MY COUNTRY, HEAVEN,
—He said, and died.

XVI.

ON HIMSELF.

UNDER this marble, or under this sill,
Or under this turf, or e'en what they will;
Whatever an heir, or a friend in his stead,
Or any good creature shall lay o'er my head,
Lies one who ne'er cared, and still cares not a pin
What they said, or may say, of the mortal within:
But, who living and dying, serene still and free,
Trusts in GOD, that as well as he was, he shall be.

AN ESSAY ON MAN.

IN FOUR EPISTLES.

TO H. ST. JOHN, LORD BOLINGBROKE.

THE DESIGN.

HAVING proposed to write some pieces on Human Life and Manners, such as (to use my Lord Bacon's expression) *come home to men's business and bosoms*, I thought it more satisfactory to begin with considering *Man* in the abstract, his *nature* and his *state*; since, to prove any moral duty, to enforce any moral precept, or to examine the perfection or imperfection of any creature whatsoever, it is necessary first to know what *condition* and *relation* it is placed in, and what is the proper *end* and *purpose* of its *being*.

The science of human nature is, like all other sciences, reduced to a *few clear points*; there are not *many certain truths* in this world. It is therefore in the anatomy of the mind as in that of the body; more good will accrue to mankind, by attending to the large, open, and perceptible parts, than by studying too much such finer nerves and vessels, the conformations and uses of which will for ever escape our observation. The *disputes* are all upon these last, and, I will venture to say, they have less sharpened the *wits* than the *hearts* of men against each other, and have diminished the practice, more than advanced the theory, of morality. If I could flatter myself that this Essay has any merit, it is in steering betwixt the extremes of doctrines seemingly opposite, in passing over terms utterly unintelligible, and in forming a *temperate*, yet not *inconsistent*, and a *short*, yet not *imperfect*, system of ethics.

This I might have done in prose, but I chose verse, and even rhyme, for two reasons. The one will appear obvious; that principles, maxims, or precepts, so written, both strike the reader more strongly at first, and are more easily retained by him afterwards: the other may seem odd, but is true. I found I could express them more *shortly* this way than in prose itself; and nothing is more certain, than that much of the *force* as well as *grace* of arguments or instructions depends on their *conciseness*. I was unable to treat this part of my subject more in *detail*, without becoming dry and tedious; or more *poetically*, without sacrificing perspicuity to ornament, without wandering from the precision, or breaking the chain of reasoning: if any man can unite all these without diminution of any of them, I freely confess he will compass a thing above my capacity.

What is now published, is only to be considered as a *general map* of MAN, marking out no more than the *greater parts*, their *extent*, their *limits*, and their *connexion*, but leaving the particular to be more fully delineated in the charts which are now to follow. Consequently these Epistles in their progress (if I have health and leisure to make any progress) will be less dry, and more susceptible of poetical ornament. I am here only opening the *fountains*, and clearing the passage. To deduce the *rivers*, to follow them in their course, and to observe their effects, may be a task more agreeable.

EPISTLE I.

ARGUMENT.

OF THE NATURE AND STATE OF MAN, WITH RESPECT TO THE UNIVERSE.

Of *Man* in the abstract.—I. That we can judge only with regard to our *own system*, being ignorant of the *relations* of systems and things. II. That man is not to be deemed *imperfect*, but a being suited to his *place* and *rank* in the creation, agreeable to the *general order* of things, and conformable to *ends* and *relations* to him unknown. III. That it is partly upon his *ignorance* of *future* events, and partly upon the *hope* of a *future* state, that all his happiness in the present depends. IV. The *pride* of aiming at more knowledge, and pretending to more perfection, the cause of man's error and misery. The *impiety* of putting himself in the place of *God*, and judging of the fitness or unfitness, perfection or imperfection, justice or injustice, of his dispensations. V. The *absurdity* of conceiting himself the *final cause* of the creation, or expecting that perfection in the *moral* world, which is not in the *natural*. VI. The *unreasonableness* of his complaints against *Providence*, while on the one hand he demands the perfections of the angels, and on the other the bodily qualifications of the brutes; though to possess any of the *sensitive faculties* in a higher degree would render him miserable. VII. That, throughout the whole visible world, a universal *order* and *gradation* in the sensual and mental faculties is observed, which causes a *subordination* of creature to creature, and of all creatures to Man. The gradations of *sense, instinct, thought, reflection, reason;* that reason alone countervails all the other faculties. VIII. How much further this *order* and *subordination* of living creatures may extend, above and below us; were any part of which broken, not that part only, but the whole connected *creation* must be destroyed. IX. The *extravagance, madness*, and *pride* of such a desire. X. The consequence of all the *absolute submission* due to Providence, both as to our *present* and *future state*.

AWAKE, my ST. JOHN! leave all meaner things
To low ambition, and the pride of kings.
Let us (since life can little more supply
Than just to look about us and to die)
Expatiate free o'er all this scene of man;
A mighty maze! but not without a plan;
A wild, where weeds and flowers promiscuous shoot,
Or garden tempting with forbidden fruit.
Together let us beat this ample field,
Try what the open, what the covert yield;
The latent tracts, the giddy heights, explore
Of all who blindly creep, or sightless soar;
Eye nature's walks, shoot folly as it flies,
And catch the manners living as they rise;
Laugh where we must, be candid where we can;
But vindicate the ways of God to Man.
I. Say first, of God above, or man below,
What can we reason, but from what we know?
Of man, what see we but his station here,
From which to reason, or to which refer?
Thro' worlds unnumber'd tho' the God be known,
'Tis ours to trace him only in our own.
He, who through vast immensity can pierce,
See worlds on worlds compose one universe,
Observe how system into system runs,
What other planets circle other suns,
What varied Being peoples every star,
May tell why Heaven has made us as we are.
But of this frame, the bearings and the ties,
The strong connexions, nice dependencies,
Gradations just, has thy pervading soul
Look'd through? or can a part contain the whole?
Is the great chain, that draws all to agree,
And drawn supports, upheld by God, or thee?
II. Presumptuous Man! the reason wouldst thou find
Why form'd so weak, so little, and so blind?
First, if thou canst, the harder reason guess,
Why form'd no weaker, blinder, and no less?
Ask of thy mother Earth, why oaks are made
Taller or stronger than the weeds they shade?
Or ask of yonder argent fields above,
Why JOVE's satellites are less than JOVE?
Of systems possible, if 'tis confest
That Wisdom infinite must form the best,

Where all must full or not coherent be,
And all that rises, rise in due degree;
Then, in the scale of reasoning life, 'tis plain,
There must be, somewhere, such a rank as Man:
And all the question (wrangle e'er so long)
Is only this, if God has placed him wrong?
  Respecting Man, whatever wrong we call,
May, must be right, as relative to all.
In human works, though labcur'd on with pain,
A thousand movements scarce one purpose gain;
In God's, one single can its end produce;
Yet serves to second, too, some other use.
So Man, who here seems principal alone,
Perhaps acts second to some sphere unknown,
Touches some wheel, or verges to some goal;
'Tis but a part we see, and not a whole.
  When the proud steed shall know why Man restrains
His fiery course, or drives him o'er the plains;
When the dull ox, why now he breaks the clod,
Is now a victim, and now Egypt's god:
Then shall man's pride and dulness comprehend
His action's, passion's, being's, use and end;
Why doing, suffering; check'd, impell'd; and why
This hour a slave, the next a deity.
  Then say not Man's imperfect, Heaven in fault;
Say rather, Man's as perfect as he ought:
His knowledge measured to his state and place;
His time a moment, and a point his space.
If to be perfect in a certain sphere,
What matter, soon or late, or here or there?
The blest to-day is as completely so,
As who began a thousand years ago.
  III. Heaven from all creatures hides the book of fate
All but the page prescribed, their present state:
From brutes what men, from men what spirits know:
Or who could suffer being here below?
The lamb thy riot dooms to bleed to-day,
Had he thy reason, would he skip and play?
Pleased to the last, he crops the flowery food,
And licks the hand just raised to shed his blood.
Oh blindness to the future! kindly given,
That each may fill the circle mark'd by Heaven:
Who sees with equal eye, as God of all,
A hero perish, or a sparrow fall,

Atoms or systems into ruin hurl'd,
And now a bubble burst, and now a world.
Hope humbly then; with trembling pinions soar;
Wait the great teacher Death; and God adore.
What future bliss, he gives not thee to know,
But gives that hope to be thy blessing now.
Hope springs eternal in the human breast:
Man never is, but always to be blest.
The soul, uneasy and confined, from home,
Rests and expatiates in a life to come.
Lo, the poor Indian! whose untutor'd mind
Sees God in clouds, or hears him in the wind;
His soul, proud science never taught to stray
Far as the solar walk, or milky way;
Yet simple nature to his hope has given,
Behind the cloud-topp'd hill, an humbler heaven;
Some safer world, in depth of woods embraced,
Some happier island in the watery waste,
Where slaves once more their native land behold,
No fiends torment, no Christians thirst for gold:
To be, contents his natural desire,
He asks no angel's wing, no seraph's fire;
But thinks, admitted to that equal sky,
His faithful dog shall bear him company.
IV. Go, wiser thou! and, in thy scale of sense,
Weigh thy opinion against Providence;
Call imperfection what thou fanciest such,
Say, here he gives too little, there too much:
Destroy all creatures for thy sport or gust,
Yet cry, if Man's unhappy, God's unjust;
If Man alone engross not Heaven's high care,
Alone made perfect here, immortal there:
Snatch from his hand the balance and the rod,
Re-judge his justice, be the God of God.
In pride, in reasoning pride, our error lies;
All quit their sphere, and rush into the skies.
Pride still is aiming at the blest abodes,
Men would be angels, angels would be gods
Aspiring to be gods, if angels fell,
Aspiring to be angels, men rebel:
And who but wishes to invert the laws
Of Order, sins against the eternal Cause.
V. Ask for what end the heavenly bodies shine,
Earth for whose use? Pride answers, "'Tis for mine:

p. 220.

ESSAY ON MAN.

Lo, the poor Indian, whose untutored mind
Sees God in clouds, or hears him in the wind.

For me kind nature wakes her genial power,
Suckles each herb, and spreads out every flower;
Annual for me, the grape, the rose renew
The juice nectareous, and the balmy dew;
For me, the mine a thousand treasures brings;
For me health gushes from a thousand springs;
Seas roll to waft me, suns to light me rise;
My footstool earth, my canopy the skies."
  But errs not nature from this gracious end,
From burning suns when livid deaths descend,
When earthquakes swallow, or when tempests sweep
Towns to one grave, whole nations to the deep?
"No ('tis replied), the first almighty Cause
Acts not by partial, but by general laws;
The exceptions few; some change since all began:
And what created perfect?"—Why then Man?
If the great end be human happiness,
Then nature deviates; and can man do less?
As much that end a constant course requires
Of showers and sunshine, as of Man's desires;
As much eternal springs and cloudless skies,
As men for ever temperate, calm, and wise.
If plagues or earthquakes break not Heaven's design,
Why then a Borgia, or a Catiline?
Who knows but He, whose hand the lightning forms,
Who heaves old ocean, and who wings the storms:
Pours fierce ambition in a Cæsar's mind,
Or turns young Ammon loose to scourge mankind?
From pride, from pride, our very reasoning springs;
Account for moral, as for natural things:
Why charge we Heaven in those, in these acquit?
In both, to reason right, is to submit.
  Better for us, perhaps it might appear,
Were there all harmony, all virtue here:
That never air or ocean felt the wind;
That never passion discomposed the mind.
But ALL subsists by elemental strife;
And passions are the elements of life.
The general ORDER, since the whole began,
Is kept in Nature, and is kept in man.
  VI. What would this Man? Now upward will he soar
And little less than angels, would be more;
Now looking downwards, just as grieved appears
To want the strength of bulls, the fur of bears.

Made for his use all creatures if he call,
Say, what their use, had he the powers of all;
Nature to these, without profusion, kind,
The proper organs, proper powers assign'd;
Each seeming want compensated of course,
Here with degrees of swiftness, there of force;[1]
All in exact proportion to the state;
Nothing to add, and nothing to abate.
Each beast, each insect, happy in its own:
Is Heaven unkind to Man, and Man alone?
Shall he alone, whom rational we call,
Be pleased with nothing, if not blessed with all?
The bliss of Man (could pride that blessing find)
Is not to act or think beyond mankind;
No powers of body or of soul to share,
But what his nature and his state can bear.
Why has not man a microscopic eye?
For this plain reason, Man is not a fly
Say what the use, were finer optics given,
To inspect a mite, not comprehend the heaven?
Or touch, if tremblingly alive all o'er,
To smart and agonise at every pore?
Or quick effluvia darting through the brain,
Die of a rose in aromatic pain?
If nature thunder'd in his opening ears,
And stunn'd him with the music of the spheres,
How would he wish that Heaven had left him still,
The whispering zephyr, and the purling rill?
Who finds not Providence all good and wise,
Alike in what it gives, and what denies?
VII. Far as creation's ample range extends,
The scale of sensual, mental powers ascends:
Mark how it mounts, to Man's imperial race,
From the green myriads in the peopled grass:
What modes of sight betwixt each wide extreme,
The mole's dim curtain, and the lynx's beam
Of smell, the headlong lioness[2] between,
And hound sagacious on the tainted green:

[1] It is a certain axiom in the anatomy of creatures, that in proportion as they are formed for strength, their swiftness is lessened; or as they are formed for swiftness, their strength is abated.

[2] The manner of the lions hunting their prey in the deserts of Africa is this: At their first going out in the night-time, they set up a

Of hearing, from the life that fills the flood,
To that which warbles through the vernal wood?
The spider's touch, how exquisitely fine!
Feels at each thread, and lives along the line:
In the nice bee, what sense so subtly true
From poisonous herbs extracts the healing dew?
How instinct varies in the groveling swine,
Compared, half-reasoning elephant, with thine!
'Twixt that, and reason, what a nice barrier?
For ever separate, yet for ever near!
Remembrance and reflection, how allied;
What thin partitions sense from thought divide!
And middle natures, how they long to join,
Yet never pass the insuperable line!
Without this just gradation, could they be
Subjected, these to those, or all to thee?
The powers of all subdued by thee alone,
Is not thy reason all these powers in one? [earth,
VIII. See, through this air, this ocean, and this
All matter quick, and bursting into birth.
Above, how high, progressive life may go!
Around, how wide, how deep extend below!
Vast chain of being! which from God began
Natures ethereal, human, angel, man,
Beast, bird, fish, insect, what no eye can see,
No glass can reach; from Infinite to thee,
From thee to Nothing.—On superior powers,
Were we to press, inferior might on ours:
Or in the full creation leave a void,
Where, one step broken, the great scale's destroy'd:
From nature's chain whatever link you strike,
Tenth, or ten thousandth, breaks the chain alike.
And, if each system in gradation roll
Alike essential to the amazing whole,
The least confusion but in one, not all
That system only, but the whole must fall.
Let earth unbalanced from her orbit fly,
Planets and stars run lawless through the sky;
Let ruling angels from their sphere be hurl'd,
Being on being wreck'd, and world on world;

loud roar, and then listen to the noise made by the beasts in their flight, pursuing them by the ear, and not by the nostril. It is probable the story of the jackal's hunting for the lion, was occasioned by the observation of this defect of scent in that terrible animal.

Heaven's whole foundations to their centre nod,
And nature trembles to the throne of God.
All this dread ORDER break—for whom? for thee?
Vile worm!—oh madness! pride! impiety!
IX. What if the foot, ordain'd the dust to tread,
Or hand, to toil, aspired to be the head?
What if the head, the eye, or ear repined
To serve mere engines to the ruling mind?
Just as absurd for any part to claim
To be another, in this general frame:
Just as absurd, to mourn the tasks or pains,
The great directing MIND OF ALL ordains.
All are but parts of one stupendous whole,
Whose body nature is, and God the soul;
That, changed through all, and yet in all the same;
Great in the earth, as in the ethereal frame;
Warms in the sun, refreshes in the breeze,
Glows in the stars, and blossoms in the trees,
Lives through all life, extends through all extent,
Spreads undivided, operates unspent;
Breathes in our soul, informs our mortal part,
As full, as perfect, in a hair as heart;
As full, as perfect, in vile man that mourns,
As the rapt seraph, that adores and burns:
To Him no high, no low, no great, no small;
He fills, He bounds, connects, and equals all.
X. Cease then, nor ORDER imperfection name:
Our proper bliss depends on what we blame.
Know thy own point: This kind, this due degree
Of blindness, weakness, Heaven bestows on thee.
Submit.—In this, or any other sphere,
Secure to be as blest as thou canst bear:
Safe in the hand of one disposing Power,
Or in the natal, or the mortal hour.
All nature is but art, unknown to thee;
All chance, direction, which thou canst not see;
All discord, harmony not understood;
All partial evil, universal good:
And, spite of pride, in erring reason's spite,
One truth is clear, WHATEVER IS, IS RIGHT.

EPISTLE II.

ARGUMENT.

OF THE NATURE AND STATE OF MAN, WITH RESPECT TO HIMSELF AS AN INDIVIDUAL.

I. The business of man not to pry into *God*, but to study *himself*. His *middle nature;* his powers and frailties. The limits of his *capacity*. II. The two principles of man, *self-love* and *reason*, both necessary. *Self-love* the stronger, and why. Their end the same. III. The PASSIONS, and their use. The *predominant passion*, and its force. Its necessity, in directing men to different purposes. Its providential use, in fixing our principle, and ascertaining our virtue. IV. *Virtue* and *vice* joined in our mixed nature; the limits near, yet the things separate and evident: What is the office of *reason?* V. How odious *vice* in itself, and how we deceive ourselves in it. VI. That, however, the *ends* of *Providence* and *general good* are answered in our passions and imperfections. How usefully these are distributed to all *orders of men*. How useful they are to *society*. And to the *individuals*. In every *state*, and every *age* of life.

I. KNOW then thyself, presume not God to scan,
The proper study of mankind is Man.
Placed on this isthmus of a middle state,
A being darkly wise, and rudely great;
With too much knowledge for the sceptic side,
With too much weakness for the stoic's pride,
He hangs between; in doubt to act or rest;
In doubt to deem himself a god, or beast;
In doubt his mind or body to prefer;
Born but to die, and reasoning but to err;
Alike in ignorance, his reason such,
Whether he thinks too little, or too much:
Chaos of thought and passion, all confused;
Still by himself abused, or disabused;
Created half to rise, and half to fall;
Great lord of all things, yet a prey to all;
Sole judge of truth, in endless error hurl'd:
The glory, jest, and riddle of the world!
Go, wondrous creature! mount where science guides,
Go, measure earth, weigh air, and state the tides;
Instruct the planets in what orbs to run,
Correct old Time, and regulate the sun;
Go, soar with Plato, to the empyreal sphere,
To the first good, first perfect, and first fair!

Or tread the mazy round his followers trod,
And quitting sense call imitating God;
As Eastern priests in giddy circles run,
And turn their heads to imitate the sun.
Go, teach Eternal Wisdom how to rule—
Then drop into thyself, and be a fool!
  Superior beings, when of late they saw
A mortal man unfold all nature's law,
Admired such wisdom in an earthly shape,
And show'd a NEWTON as we show an ape.
  Could he, whose rules the rapid comet bind,
Describe or fix one movement of his mind?
Who saw its fires here rise, and there descend,
Explain his own beginning, or his end?
Alas, what wonder! Man's superior part
Uncheck'd may rise, and climb from art to art;
But when his own great work is but begun,
What reason weaves, by passion is undone.
  Trace science then, with modesty thy guide:
First strip off all her equipage of pride;
Deduct what is but vanity, or dress,
Or learning's luxury, or idleness;
Or tricks to show the stretch of human brain,
Mere curious pleasure, or ingenious pain;
Expunge the whole, or lop the excrescent parts
Of all our vices have created arts;
Then see how little the remaining sum,
Which served the past, and must the times to come!
  II. Two principles in human nature reign;
Self-love, to urge, and reason, to restrain;
Nor this a good, nor that a bad we call,
Each works its end, to move or govern all:
And to their proper operation still
Ascribe all good; to their improper, ill.
  Self-love, the spring of motion, acts the soul;
Reason's comparing balance rules the whole.
Man, but for that, no action could attend,
And but for this, were active to no end:
Fix'd like a plant on his peculiar spot,
To draw nutrition, propagate, and rot;
Or, meteor-like, flame lawless through the void,
Destroying others, by himself destroy'd.
  Most strength the moving principle requires:
Active its task, it prompts, impels, inspires.

Sedate and quiet, the comparing lies,
Form'd but to check, deliberate, and advise.
Self-love still stronger, as its objects nigh;
Reason's at distance, and in prospect lie:
That sees immediate good by present sense;
Reason, the future and the consequence.
Thicker than arguments, temptations throng,
At best more watchful this, but that more strong.
The action of the stronger to suspend
Reason still use, to reason still attend.
Attention, habit and experience gains;
Each strengthens reason, and self-love restrains.
  Let subtle schoolmen teach these friends to fight,
More studious to divide than to unite;
And grace and virtue, sense and reason split,
With all the rash dexterity of wit.
Wits, just like fools, at war about a name,
Have full as oft no meaning, or the same.
Self-love and reason to one end aspire,
Pain their aversion, pleasure their desire;
But greedy That, its object would devour,
This taste the honey, and not wound the flower:
Pleasure, or wrong or rightly understood,
Our greatest evil, or our greatest good.
  III. Modes of self-love the passions we may call;
'Tis real good, or seeming, moves them all:
But since not every good we can divide;
And reason bids us for our own provide:
Passions, though selfish, if their means be fair,
List under Reason, and deserve her care;
Those, that imparted, court a nobler aim,
Exalt their kind, and take some virtue's name.
  In lazy apathy let stoics boast
Their virtue fix'd; 'tis fix'd as in a frost;
Contracted all, retiring to the breast;
But strength of mind is exercise, not rest:
The rising tempest puts in act the soul,
Parts it may ravage, but preserves the whole.
On life's vast ocean diversely we sail,
Reason the card, but passion is the gale;
Nor God alone in the still calm we find,
He mounts the storm, and walks upon the wind.
  Passions, like elements, though born to fight,
Yet, mix'd and soften'd, in his work unite:

These, 'tis enough to temper and employ;
But what composes man, can man destroy.
Suffice that Reason keep to Nature's road,
Subject, compound them, follow her and God.
Love, hope, and joy, fair pleasure's smiling train,
Hate, fear, and grief, the family of pain,
These, mix'd with art, and to due bounds confined,
Make and maintain the balance of the mind:
The lights and shades, whose well-accorded strife
Gives all the strength and colour of our life.
Pleasures are ever in our hands or eyes;
And when in act they cease, in prospect rise:
Present to grasp, and future still to find,
The whole employ of body and of mind.
All spread their charms, but charm not all alike;
On different senses different objects strike;
Hence different passions more or less inflame,
As strong or weak, the organs of the frame;
And hence one MASTER PASSION in the breast,
Like Aaron's serpent, swallows up the rest.
  As man, perhaps, the moment of his breath,
Receives the lurking principle of death;
The young disease, that must subdue at length,
Grows with his growth, and strengthens with his strength;
So cast and mingled with his very frame,
The mind's disease, its RULING PASSION, came;
Each vital humour which should feed the whole,
Soon flows to this, in body and in soul:
Whatever warms the heart, or fills the head,
As the mind opens, and its functions spread,
Imagination plies her dangerous art,
And pours it all upon the peccant part.
Nature its mother, habit is its nurse;
Wit, spirit, faculties, but make it worse;
Reason itself but gives it edge and power;
As Heaven's blest beam turns vinegar more sour.
  We, wretched subjects, though to lawful sway,
In this weak queen, some favourite still obey;
Ah! if she lend not arms, as well as rules,
What can she more than tell us we are fools?
Teach us to mourn our nature, not to mend,
A sharp accuser, but a helpless friend!
Or from a judge turn pleader, to persuade
The choice we make, or justify it made;

Proud of an easy conquest all along,
She but removes weak passions for the strong:
So, when small humours gather to a gout,
The doctor fancies he has driven them out.
 Yes, nature's road must ever be preferr'd;
Reason is here no guide, but still a guard:
Tis hers to rectify, not overthrow,
And treat this passion more as friend than foe:
A mightier Power the strong direction sends,
And several men impels to several ends:
Like varying winds, by other passions toss'd,
This drives them constant to a certain coast.
Let power or knowledge, gold or glory, please;
Or (oft more strong than all) the love of ease;
Through life 'tis follow'd, e'en at life's expense;
The merchant's toil, the sage's indolence,
The monk's humility, the hero's pride,
All, all alike, find reason on their side.
 The Eternal Art educing good from ill,
Grafts on this passion our best principle:
'Tis thus the mercury of man is fix'd,
Strong grows the virtue with his nature mix'd;
The dross cements what else were too refined,
And in one interest body acts with mind.
 As fruits, ungrateful to the planter's care,
On savage stocks inserted, learn to bear;
The surest virtues thus from passions shoot,
Wild nature's vigour working at the root.
What crops of wit and honesty appear
From spleen, from obstinacy, hate, or fear!
See anger, zeal and fortitude supply;
Even avarice, prudence; sloth, philosophy;
Lust, through some certain strainers well refined,
Is gentle love, and charms all womankind;
Envy, to which the ignoble mind's a slave,
Is emulation in the learn'd or brave;
Nor virtue, male or female, can we name,
But what will grow on pride, or grow on shame.
 Thus nature gives us (let it check our pride)
The virtue nearest to our vice allied;
Reason the bias turns from good to ill,
And Nero reigns a Titus, if he will.
The fiery soul abhorr'd in Catiline,
In Decius charms, in Curtius is divine:

The same ambition can destroy or save,
And makes a patriot as it makes a knave.
IV. This light and darkness in our chaos join'd,
What shall divide? The God within the mind.
Extremes in nature equal ends produce,
In man they join to some mysterious use;
Though each by turns the other's bound invade,
As, in some well-wrought picture, light and shade,
And oft so mix, the difference is too nice
Where ends the virtue, or begins the vice.
Fools! who from hence into the notion fall,
That vice or virtue there is none at all.
If white and black blend, soften, and unite
A thousand ways, is there no black or white?
Ask your own heart, and nothing is so plain;
'Tis to mistake them costs the time and pain.
V. Vice is a monster of so frightful mien,
As, to be hated, needs but to be seen;
Yet seen too oft, familiar with her face,
We first endure, then pity, then embrace.
But where the extreme of vice, was ne'er agreed:
Ask where's the north? at York, 'tis on the Tweed;
In Scotland, at the Orcades; and there,
At Greenland, Zembla, or the Lord knows where.
No creature owns it in the first degree,
But thinks his neighbour farther gone than he;
Even those who dwell beneath its very zone,
Or never feel the rage, or never own;
What happier natures shrink at with affright,
The hard inhabitant contends is right.
Virtuous and vicious every man must be,
Few in the extreme, but all in the degree;
The rogue and fool by fits is fair and wise;
And even the best, by fits, what they despise.
'Tis but by parts we follow good or ill;
For, vice or virtue, self directs it still;
Each individual seeks a several goal;
But HEAVEN's great view is one, and that the whole.
VI. That counter-works each folly and caprice;
That disappoints the effect of every vice;
That, happy frailties to all ranks applied;
Shame to the virgin, to the matron pride,
Fear to the statesman, rashness to the chief,
To kings presumption, and to crowds belief:

That, virtue's ends from vanity can raise,
Which seeks no interest, no reward but praise;
And build on wants, and on defects of mind,
The joy, the peace, the glory of mankind.
  Heaven forming each on other to depend,
A master, or a servant, or a friend,
Bids each on other for assistance call,
Till one man's weakness grows the strength of all.
Wants, frailties, passions, closer still ally
The common interest, or endear the tie.
To these we owe true friendship, love sincere,
Each home-felt joy that life inherits here;
Yet from the same we learn, in its decline,
Those joys, those loves, those interests to resign;
Taught half by reason, half by mere decay,
To welcome death, and calmly pass away.
  Whate'er the passion, knowledge, fame, or pelf,
Not one will change his neighbour with himself.
The learn'd is happy nature to explore,
The fool is happy that he knows no more;
The rich is happy in the plenty given,
The poor contents him with the care of Heaven.
See the blind beggar dance, the cripple sing,
The sot a hero, lunatic a king;
The starving chemist in his golden views
Supremely blest, the poet in his muse.
  See some strange comfort every state attend,
And pride bestow'd on all, a common friend:
See some fit passion every age supply,
Hope travels through, nor quits us when we die.
  Behold the child, by nature's kindly law,
Pleased with a rattle, tickled with a straw:
Some livelier plaything gives his youth delight,
A little louder, but as empty quite:
Scarfs, garters, gold, amuse his riper stage,
And beads and prayer-books are the toys of age:
Pleased with this bauble still, as that before,
Till tired he sleeps, and life's poor play is o'er.
  Meanwhile opinion gilds with varying rays
Those painted clouds that beautify our days;
Each want of happiness by hope supplied,
And each vacuity of sense by pride:
These build as fast as knowledge can destroy;
In folly's cup still laughs the bubble, joy;

One prospect lost, another still we gain;
And not a vanity is given in vain;
Even mean self-love becomes, by force divine,
The scale to measure others' wants by thine.
See! and confess, one comfort still must rise;
'Tis this,—Though Man's a fool, yet GOD IS WISE.

EPISTLE III.

ARGUMENT.

OF THE NATURE AND STATE OF MAN WITH RESPECT TO SOCIETY.

I. The whole universe one system of society. Nothing made wholly for *itself*, nor yet wholly for *another*. The happiness of *animals* mutual. II. *Reason* or *instinct* operate alike to the good of each individual. *Reason* or *instinct* operate also to society, in all animals. III. How far *society* carried by instinct. How much farther by reason. IV. Of that which is called the *state of nature*. Reason instructed by instinct in the invention of *arts*, and in the forms of *society*. V. Origin of political societies. Origin of monarchy. Patriarchal government. VI. Origin of true religion and government, from the same principle, of love. Origin of superstition and tyranny, from the same principle, of fear. The influence of self-love operating to the *social* and *public* good. Restoration of true religion and government on their first principle. Mixed government. Various forms of each, and the true end of all.

HERE then we rest:—"The Universal Cause
Acts to one end, but acts by various laws."
In all the madness of superfluous health,
The trim of pride, the impudence of wealth,
Let this great truth be present night and day;
But most be present, if we preach or pray.
  Look round our world; behold the chain of love
Combining all below and all above.
See plastic nature working to this end,
The single atoms each to other tend,
Attract, attracted to, the next in place,
Form'd and impell'd its neighbour to embrace.
See matter next, with various life endued,
Press to one centre still, the general good.
See dying vegetables life sustain,
See life dissolving vegetate again:

All forms that perish other forms supply,
(By turns we catch the vital breath, and die)
Like bubbles on the sea of matter borne,
They rise, they break, and to that sea return.
Nothing is foreign; parts relate to whole;
One all-extending, all-preserving Soul
Connects each being, greatest with the least;
Made beast in aid of man, and man of beast;
All served, all serving: nothing stands alone;
The chain holds on, and where it ends, unknown.
  Has God, thou fool! work'd solely for thy good,
Thy joy, thy pastime, thy attire, thy food?
Who for thy table feeds the wanton fawn,
For him as kindly spread the flowery lawn:
Is it for thee the lark ascends and sings?
Joy tunes his voice, joy elevates his wings.
Is it for thee the linnet pours his throat?
Loves of his own and raptures swell the note.
The bounding steed you pompously bestride,
Shares with his lord the pleasure and the pride.
Is thine alone the seed that strews the plain?
The birds of heaven shall vindicate their grain.
Thine the full harvest of the golden year?
Part pays, and justly, the deserving steer:
The hog that ploughs not, nor obeys thy call,
Lives on the labours of this lord of all.
  Know, nature's children all divide her care;
The fur that warms a monarch, warm'd a bear.
While man exclaims, "See all things for my use!"
"See man for mine!" replies a pamper'd goose:
And just as short of reason he must fall,
Who thinks all made for one, not one for all.
  Grant that the powerful still the weak control;
Be man the wit and tyrant of the whole:
Nature that tyrant checks; he only knows,
And helps, another creature's wants and woes.
Say, will the falcon, stooping from above,
Smit with her varying plumage, spare the dove?
Admires the jay the insect's gilded wings?
Or hears the hawk when Philomela sings?
Man cares for all: to birds he gives his woods,
To beasts his pastures, and to fish his floods;
For some his interest prompts him to provide,
For more his pleasure, yet for more his pride:

All feed on one vain patron, and enjoy
The extensive blessing of his luxury.
That very life his learned hunger craves,
He saves from famine, from the savage saves;
Nay, feasts the animal he dooms his feast,
And, till he ends the being, makes it blest;
Which sees no more the stroke, or feels the pain,
Than favour'd man by touch ethereal slain.[1]
The creature had his feast of life before;
Thou too must perish, when thy feast is o'er!
To each unthinking being, Heaven a friend,
Gives not the useless knowledge of its end:
To man imparts it, but with such a view
As, while he dreads it, makes him hope it too:
The hour conceal'd, and so remote the fear,
Death still draws nearer, never seeming near.
Great standing miracle! that Heaven assign'd
Its only thinking thing this turn of mind.
II. Whether with reason or with instinct blest,
Know, all enjoy that power which suits them best;
To bliss alike by that direction tend,
And find the means proportion'd to their end.
Say, where full instinct is the unerring guide,
What pope or council can they need beside?
Reason, however able, cool at best,
Cares not for service, or but serves when prest,
Stays till we call, and then not often near;
But honest instinct comes a volunteer,
Sure never to o'ershoot, but just to hit;
While still too wide or short is human wit;
Sure by quick nature happiness to gain,
Which heavier reason labours at in vain.
This too serves always, reason never long;
One must go right, the other may go wrong.
See then the acting and comparing powers
One in their nature, which are two in ours;
And reason raise o'er instinct as you can,
In this 'tis God directs, in that 'tis man.
Who taught the nations of the field and wood
To shun their poison, and to choose their food?
Prescient, the tides or tempests to withstand,
Build on the wave, or arch beneath the sand?

[1] Several of the ancients, and many of the Orientals since, esteemed those who were struck by lightning as sacred persons, and the particular favourites of Heaven.

Who made the spider parallels design,
Sure as De Moivre, without rule or line?
Who bid the stork, Columbus-like, explore
Heavens not his own, and worlds unknown before?
Who calls the council, states the certain day,
Who forms the phalanx, and who points the way?
III. God, in the nature of each being, founds
Its proper bliss, and sets its proper bounds:
But as he framed the whole, the whole to bless,
On mutual wants built mutual happiness:
So from the first, eternal ORDER ran,
And creature link'd to creature, man to man.
Whate'er of life all-quickening ether keeps,
Or breathes through air, or shoots beneath the deeps,
Or pours profuse on earth, one nature feeds
The vital flame, and swells the genial seeds.
Not man alone, but all that roam the wood,
Or wing the sky, or roll along the flood,
Each loves itself, but not itself alone,
Each sex desires alike, till two are one.
Nor ends the pleasure with the fierce embrace;
They love themselves, a third time, in their race.
Thus beast and bird their common charge attend,
The mothers nurse it, and the sires defend;
The young dismiss'd to wander earth or air,
There stops the instinct, and there ends the care;
The link dissolves, each seeks a fresh embrace,
Another love succeeds, another race.
A longer care man's helpless kind demands;
That longer care contracts more lasting bands:
Reflection, reason, still the ties improve,
At once extend the interest, and the love;
With choice we fix, with sympathy we burn;
Each virtue in each passion takes its turn;
And still new needs, new helps, new habits rise,
That graft benevolence on charities.
Still as one brood, and as another rose,
These natural love maintain'd, habitual those:
The last, scarce ripen'd into perfect man,
Saw helpless him from whom their life began:
Memory and forecast just returns engage,
That pointed back to youth, this on to age;
While pleasure, gratitude, and hope, combined,
Still spread the interest, and preserved the kind.

IV. Nor think in NATURE'S STATE they blindly trod
The state of nature was the reign of God:
Self-love and social at her birth began,
Union the bond of all things, and of man.
Pride then was not; nor arts, that pride to aid;
Man walk'd with beast, joint-tenant of the shade;
The same his table, and the same his bed;
No murder clothed him, and no murder fed.
In the same temple, the resounding wood,
All vocal beings hymn'd their equal God:
The shrine with gore unstain'd, with gold undrest,
Unbribed, unbloody, stood the blameless priest:
Heaven's attribute was universal care,
And man's prerogative to rule, but spare.
Ah! how unlike the man of times to come!
Of half that live the butcher and the tomb!
Who, foe to nature, hears the general groan,
Murders their species, and betrays his own.
But just disease to luxury succeeds,
And every death its own avenger breeds;
The fury-passions from that blood began,
And turn'd on man a fiercer savage, man.
See him from nature rising slow to art!
To copy instinct then was reason's part;
Thus then to man the voice of nature spake—
"Go, from the creatures thy instructions take:
Learn from the birds what food the thickets yield;
Learn from the beasts the physic of the field;
Thy arts of building from the bee receive;
Learn of the mole to plough, the worm to weave;
Learn of the little nautilus to sail,
Spread the thin oar, and catch the driving gale.
Here too all forms of social union find,
And hence let reason, late, instruct mankind:
Here subterranean works and cities see;
There towns aërial on the waving tree.
Learn each small people's genius, policies,
The ants' republic, and the realm of bees;
How those in common all their wealth bestow,
And anarchy without confusion know;
And these for ever, though a monarch reign,
Their separate cells and properties maintain.
Mark what unvaried laws preserve each state,
Laws wise as nature, and as fix'd as fate.

In vain thy reason finer webs shall draw,
Entangle justice in her net of law,
And right, too rigid, harden into wrong,
Still for the strong too weak, the weak too strong.
Yet go! and thus o'er all the creatures sway,
Thus let the wiser make the rest obey;
And for those arts mere instinct could afford,
Be crown'd as monarchs, or as gods adored."
V. Great Nature spoke; observant men obey'd;
Cities were built, societies were made:
Here rose one little state; another near
Grew by like means, and join'd through love or fear.
Did here the trees with ruddier burthens bend,
And there the streams in purer rills descend?
What war could ravish, commerce could bestow,
And he return'd a friend, who came a foe.
Converse and love, mankind may strongly draw,
When love was liberty, and nature law.
Thus states were form'd; the name of king unknown,
Till common interest placed the sway in one.
'Twas VIRTUE ONLY (or in arts or arms,
Diffusing blessings, or averting harms)
The same which in a sire the sons obey'd,
A prince the father of a people made.
VI. Till then, by nature crown'd, each patriarch sate,
King, priest, and parent of his growing state;
On him, their second Providence, they hung,
Their law his eye, their oracle his tongue.
He from the wondering furrow call'd the food,
Taught to command the fire, control the flood,
Draw forth the monsters of the abyss profound,
Or fetch the aërial eagle to the ground.
Till drooping, sickening, dying, they began
Whom they revered as God to mourn as man:
Then, looking up from sire to sire, explored
One great first Father, and that first adored.
Or plain tradition that this *all* begun,
Convey'd unbroken faith from sire to son;
The worker from the work distinct was known,
And simple reason never sought but one:
Ere wit oblique had broke that steady light,
Man, like his Maker, saw that all was right;
To virtue, in the paths of pleasure trod,
And own'd a father when he own'd a God.

Love all the faith, and all the allegiance then;
For nature knew no right divine in men,
No ill could fear in God; and understood
A sovereign being but a sovereign good.
True faith, true policy, united ran,
That was but love of God, and this of man.
   Who first taught souls enslaved, and realms undone,
The enormous faith of many made for one;
That proud exception to all nature's laws,
To invert the work, and counterwork its cause?
Force first made conquest, and that conquest law;
Till superstition taught the tyrant awe,
Then shared the tyranny, then lent it aid,
And gods of conquerors, slaves of subjects made.
She 'midst the lightning's blaze, and thunder's sound,
When rock'd the mountains, and when groan'd the ground
She taught the weak to bend, the proud to pray,
To Power unseen, and mightier far than they:
She, from the rending earth and bursting skies,
Saw gods descend, and fiends infernal rise:
Here fix'd the dreadful, there the blest abodes:
Fear made her devils, and weak hope her gods;
Gods partial, changeful, passionate, unjust,
Whose attributes were rage, revenge, or lust;
Such as the souls of cowards might conceive,
And, form'd like tyrants, tyrants would believe.
Zeal then, not charity, became the guide;
And hell was built on spite, and heaven on pride.
Then sacred seem'd the ethereal vault no more;
Altars grew marble then, and reek'd with gore:
Then first the Flamen tasted living food;
Next his grim idol smear'd with human blood;
With heaven's own thunders shook the world below,
And play'd the god an engine on his foe.
   So drives self-love, through just and through unjust,
To one man's power, ambition, lucre, lust:
The same self-love in all, becomes the cause
Of what restrains him, government and laws.
For, what one likes if others like as well,
What serves one will, when many wills rebel?
How shall we keep, what, sleeping or awake,
A weaker may surprise, a stronger take?
His safety must his liberty restrain:
All join to guard what each desires to gain.

Forced into virtue thus by self-defence,
Even kings learn'd justice and benevolence:
Self-love forsook the path it first pursued,
And found the private in the public good.
'Twas then, the studious head, or generous mind,
Follower of God, or friend of human-kind,
Poet or Patriot, rose but to restore
The faith and moral, nature gave before;
Re-lumed her ancient light, not kindled new;
If not God's image, yet his shadow drew:
Taught power's due use to people and to kings,
Taught nor to slack nor strain its tender strings,
The less, or greater, set so justly true,
That touching one must strike the other too;
Till jarring interests, of themselves create
The according music of a well-mix'd state.
Such is the world's great harmony, that springs
From order, union, full consent of things:
Where small and great, where weak and mighty made
To serve, not suffer, strengthen, not invade;
More powerful each as needful to the rest,
And, in proportion as it blesses, blest;
Draw to one point, and to one centre bring
Beast, man, or angel, servant, lord, or king.
For forms of government let fools contest;
Whate'er is best administer'd is best:
For modes of faith let graceless zealots fight;
His can't be wrong whose life is in the right:
In faith and hope the world will disagree,
But all mankind's concern is charity:
All must be false that thwart this one great end;
And all of God, that bless mankind or mend.
Man, like the generous vine, supported lives;
The strength he gains is from the embrace he gives.
On their own axis as the planets run,
Yet make at once their circle round the sun;
So two consistent motions act the soul;
And one regards itself, and one the whole.
Thus God and Nature link'd the general frame,
And bade self-love and social be the same.

EPISTLE IV.

ARGUMENT.

OF THE NATURE AND STATE OF MAN, WITH RESPECT TO HAPPINESS.

I. False notions of happiness, philosophical and popular, answered. II. It is the end of all men, and attainable by all. God intends happiness to be *equal;* and to be so, it must be *social*, since all particular happiness depends on general, and since he governs by *general*, not *particular laws*. As it is necessary for *order*, and the peace and welfare of *society*, that *external goods* should be *unequal*, happiness is not made to consist in these. But, notwithstanding that inequality, the *balance* of happiness among mankind is kept even by Providence, by the two passions of *hope* and *fear*. III. What the happiness of *individuals* is, as far as is consistent with the constitution of this world; and that the *good man* has here the advantage. The error of imputing to *virtue* what are only the calamities of *nature*, or of *fortune*. IV. The folly of expecting that God should alter his general laws in favour of particulars. V. That we are not judges who are good; but that whoever they are, they must be happiest. VI. That *external goods* are not the proper rewards, but often inconsistent with, or destructive of, virtue. That even these can make no man happy without virtue:—instanced in *riches, honours, nobility, greatness, fame, superior talents*, with pictures of human infelicity in men possessed of them all. VII. That *virtue only* constitutes a happiness, whose object is *universal*, and whose prospect *eternal*. That the *perfection* of *virtue* and *happiness* consists in a *conformity* to the ORDER of PROVIDENCE here, and a *resignation* to it here and hereafter.

I. O HAPPINESS! our being's end and aim!
Good, pleasure, ease, content! whate'er thy name:
That something still which prompts the eternal sigh,
For which we bear to live, or dare to die,
Which still so near us, yet beyond us lies,
O'erlook'd, seen double, by the fool, and wise.
Plant of celestial seed! if dropp'd below,
Say, in what mortal soil thou deign'st to grow?
Fair opening to some court's propitious shrine,
Or deep with diamonds in the flaming mine?
Twined with the wreaths Parnassian laurels yield,
Or reap'd in iron harvests of the field?
Where grows?—where grows it not? If vain our toil,
We ought to blame the culture, not the soil:
Fix'd to no spot is happiness sincere,
'Tis no where to be found, or every where:

'Tis never to be bought, but always free,
And fled from monarchs, St. John! dwells with thee.
Ask of the learn'd the way? The learn'd are blind;
This bids to serve, and that to shun mankind;
Some place the bliss in action, some in ease,
Those call it pleasure, and contentment these;
Some sunk to beasts, find pleasure end in pain;
Some swell'd to gods, confess even virtue vain!
Or indolent, to each extreme they fall,
To trust in every thing, or doubt of all.
Who thus define it, say they more or less
Than this, that happiness is happiness?
Take nature's path, and mad opinion's leave;
All states can reach it, and all heads conceive;
Obvious her goods, in no extreme they dwell;
There needs but thinking right, and meaning well;
And mourn our various portions as we please,
Equal is common sense, and common ease.
II. Remember, man, "the Universal Cause
Acts not by partial, but by general laws:"
And makes what happiness we justly call
Subsist not in the good of one, but all.
There's not a blessing individuals find,
But some way leans and hearkens to the kind;
No bandit fierce, no tyrant mad with pride,
No cavern'd hermit, rests self-satisfied:
Who most to shun or hate mankind pretend,
Seek an admirer, or would fix a friend:
Abstract what others feel, what others think,
All pleasures sicken, and all glories sink:
Each has his share; and who would more obtain,
Shall find, the pleasure pays not half the pain.
Order is Heaven's first law; and this confest,
Some are, and must be, greater than the rest,
More rich, more wise; but who infers from hence
That such are happier, shocks all common sense.
Heaven to mankind impartial we confess,
If all are equal in their happiness:
But mutual wants this happiness increase;
All nature's difference keeps all nature's peace.
Condition, circumstance is not the thing;
Bliss is the same in subject or in king,
In who obtain defence, or who defend,
In him who is, or him who finds a friend:

Heaven breathes thro' every member of the whole
One common blessing, as one common soul.
But Fortune's gifts if each alike possest,
And each were equal, must not all contest?
If then to all men happiness was meant,
God in externals could not place content.
Fortune her gifts may variously dispose,
And these be happy call'd, unhappy those;
But Heaven's just balance equal will appear
While those are placed in hope, and these in fear:
Not present good or ill, the joy or curse,
But future views of better, or of worse.
Oh sons of earth! attempt ye still to rise,
By mountains piled on mountains, to the skies?
Heaven still with laughter the vain toil surveys,
And buries madmen in the heaps they raise.
III. Know, all the good that individuals find,
Or God and nature meant to mere mankind,
Reason's whole pleasure, all the joys of sense,
Lie in three words, health, peace, and competence.
But health consists with temperance alone;
And peace, O virtue! peace is all thy own.
The good or bad the gifts of fortune gain;
But these less taste them, as they worse obtain.
Say, in pursuit of profit or delight,
Who risk the most, that take wrong means, or right?
Of vice or virtue, whether blest or curst,
Which meets contempt, or which compassion first?
Count all the advantage prosperous vice attains,
'Tis but what virtue flies from and disdains:
And grant the bad what happiness they would,
One they must want, which is, to pass for good.
Oh blind to truth, and God's whole scheme below,
Who fancy bliss to vice, to virtue woe!
Who sees and follows that great scheme the best,
Best knows the blessing, and will most be blest.
But fools, the good alone unhappy call,
For ills or accidents that chance to all.
See FALKLAND dies, the virtuous and the just!
See godlike TURENNE prostrate on the dust!
See SIDNEY bleeds amid the martial strife!
Was this their virtue, or contempt of life?
Say, was it virtue, more though Heaven ne'er gave,
Lamented DIGBY! sunk thee to the grave?

Tell me, if virtue made the son expire,
Why, full of days and honour, lives the sire?
Why drew Marseilles' good bishop purer breath,
When nature sicken'd, and each gale was death?
Or why so long (in life if long can be)
Lent Heaven a parent to the poor and me?
  What makes all physical or moral ill?
There deviates nature, and here wanders will.
God sends not ill, if rightly understood;
Or partial ill is universal good,
Or change admits, or nature lets it fall!
Short, and but rare, till man improved it all.
We just as wisely might of Heaven complain
That righteous Abel was destroy'd by Cain,
As that the virtuous son is ill at ease
When his lewd father gave the dire disease. [Cause,
  IV. Think we, like some weak prince, the' Eternal
Prone for his favourites to reverse his laws?
  Shall burning Etna, if a sage requires,
Forget to thunder, and recal her fires?
On air or sea new motions be imprest,
O blameless Bethel, to relieve thy breast?
When the loose mountain trembles from on high,
Shall gravitation cease, if you go by?
Or some old temple, nodding to its fall,
For Chartres' head reserve the hanging wall?
  V. But still this world (so fitted for the knave)
Contents us not. A better shall we have?
A kingdom of the just then let it be:
But first consider how those just agree.
The good must merit God's peculiar care;
But who, but God, can tell us who they are?
One thinks on Calvin Heaven's own spirit fell;
Another deems him instrument of hell;
If Calvin feel Heaven's blessing, or its rod,
This cries, there is, and that, there is no God.
What shocks one part will edify the rest,
Nor with one system can they all be blest,
The very best will variously incline,
And what rewards your virtue, punish mine.
Whatever is, is right.—This world, 'tis true,
Was made for Cæsar—but for Titus too:
And which more blest? who chain'd his country? say
Or he whose virtue sigh'd to lose a day!

"But sometimes virtue starves, while vice is fed."
What then? Is the reward of virtue bread?
That, vice may merit, 'tis the price of toil;
The knave deserves it, when he tills the soil,
The knave deserves it, when he tempts the main,
Where folly fights for kings, or dives for gain.
The good man may be weak, be indolent;
Nor is his claim to plenty, but content.
But grant him riches, your demand is o'er?
"No—shall the good want health, the good want power?"
Add health, and power, and every earthly thing.
"Why bounded power? why private? why no king?"
Nay, why external for internal given?
Why is not man a god, and earth a heaven?
Who ask and reason thus, will scarce conceive
God gives enough, while he has more to give:
Immense the power, immense were the demand;
Say, at what part of nature will they stand?
VI. What nothing earthly gives, or can destroy,
The soul's calm sunshine, and the heartfelt joy,
Is virtue's prize: A better would you fix,
Then give Humility a coach and six,
Justice a conqueror's sword, or Truth a gown,
Or Public Spirit its great cure, a crown.
Weak, foolish man! will Heaven reward us there
With the same trash mad mortals wish for here?
The boy and man an individual makes,
Yet sigh'st thou now for apples and for cakes?
Go, like the Indian, in another life
Expect thy dog, thy bottle, and thy wife:
As well as dream such trifles are assign'd,
As toys and empires, for a godlike mind.
Rewards, that either would to virtue bring
No joy, or be destructive of the thing:
How oft by these at sixty are undone
The virtues of a saint at twenty-one!
To whom can riches give repute, or trust,
Content, or pleasure, but the good and just?
Judges and senates have been bought for gold,
Esteem and love were never to be sold.
Oh fool! to think God hates the worthy mind,
The lover and the love of human-kind,
Whose life is healthful, and whose conscience clear,
Because he wants a thousand pounds a year.

Honour and shame from no condition rise;
Act well your part, there all the honour lies.
Fortune in men has some small difference made,
One flaunts in rags, one flutters in brocade;
The cobbler apron'd, and the parson gown'd,
The friar hooded, and the monarch crown'd.
"What differ more (you cry) than crown and cowl?"
I'll tell you, friend! a wise man and a fool.
You'll find, if once the monarch acts the monk,
Or, cobbler-like, the parson will be drunk,
Worth makes the man, and want of it the fellow;
The rest is all but leather or prunella.
Stuck o'er with titles, and hung round with strings,
That thou may'st be by kings, or whores of kings,
Boast the pure blood of an illustrious race,
In quiet flow from Lucrece to Lucrece:
But by your fathers' worth if yours you rate,
Count me those only who were good and great.
Go! if your ancient, but ignoble blood
Has crept through scoundrels ever since the flood,
Go! and pretend your family is young;
Nor own, your fathers have been fools so long.
What can ennoble sots, or slaves, or cowards?
Alas! not all the blood of all the HOWARDS.
Look next on greatness! say where greatness lies?
"Where, but among the heroes and the wise?"
Heroes are much the same, the point's agreed,
From Macedonia's madman to the Swede;
The whole strange purpose of their lives, to find
Or make, an enemy of all mankind!
Not one looks backward, onward still he goes,
Yet ne'er looks forward further than his nose.
No less alike the politic and wise;
All sly slow things, with circumspective eyes:
Men in their loose unguarded hours they take,
Not that themselves are wise, but others weak.
But grant that those can conquer, these can cheat;
'Tis phrase absurd to call a villain great:
Who wickedly is wise, or madly brave,
Is but the more a fool, the more a knave.
Who noble ends by noble means obtains,
Or failing, smiles in exile or in chains,
Like good Aurelius let him reign, or bleed
Like Socrates that man is great indeed.

What's fame? a fancied life in others' breath,
A thing beyond us, e'en before our death.
Just what you hear, you have, and what's unknown
The same (my lord) if Tully's, or your own.
All that we feel of it begins and ends
In the small circle of our foes or friends;
To all beside as much an empty shade
A Eugene living, as a Cæsar dead;
Alike or when, or where, they shone, or shine,
Or on the Rubicon, or on the Rhine.
A wit's a feather, and a chief a rod;
An honest man's the noblest work of God.
Fame but from death a villain's name can save,
As justice tears his body from the grave;
When what to oblivion better were resign'd,
Is hung on high, to poison half mankind.
All fame is foreign, but of true desert;
Plays round the head, but comes not to the heart:
One self-approving hour whole years outweighs
Of stupid starers, and of loud huzzas;
And more true joy Marcellus exiled feels,
Than Cæsar with a senate at his heels.
In parts superior what advantage lies?
Tell (for you can) what is it to be wise?
'Tis but to know how little can be known;
To see all others' faults, and feel our own:
Condemn'd in business or in arts to drudge,
Without a second, or without a judge:
Truths would you teach, or save a sinking land?
All fear, none aid you, and few understand.
Painful pre-eminence! yourself to view
Above life's weakness, and its comforts too.
Bring then these blessings to a strict account:
Make fair deductions; see to what they mount;
How much of other each is sure to costs
How each for other oft is wholly lost,
How inconsistent greater goods with these;
How sometimes life is risk'd, and always ease:
Think, and if still the things thy envy call,
Say, would'st thou be the man to whom they fall
To sigh for ribands if thou art so silly,
Mark how they grace Lord Umbra, or Sir Billy.
Is yellow dirt the passion of thy life?
Look but on Gripus, or on Gripus' wife.

If parts allure thee, think how Bacon shined,
The wisest, brightest, meanest of mankind:
Or ravish'd with the whistling of a name,
See Cromwell, damn'd to everlasting fame!
If all, united, thy ambition call,
From ancient story learn to scorn them all.
There, in the rich, the honour'd, fam'd, and great,
See the false scale of happiness complete!
In hearts of kings, or arms of queens who lay
How happy! those to ruin, these betray.
Mark by what wretched steps their glory grows,
From dirt and sea-weed as proud Venice rose;
In each how guilt and greatness equal ran,
And all that raised the hero, sunk the man:
Now Europe's laurels on their brows behold,
But stain'd with blood, or ill exchanged for gold:
Then see them broke with toils, or sunk in ease,
Or infamous for plunder'd provinces.
O wealth ill-fated! which no act of fame
E'er taught to shine, or sanctified from shame!
What greater bliss attends their close of life?
Some greedy minion, or imperious wife,
The trophied arches, storied halls invade,
And haunt their slumbers in the pompous shade.
Alas! not dazzled with their noontide ray,
Compute the morn and evening to the day;
The whole amount of that enormous fame,
A tale, that blends their glory with their shame!
VII. Know then this truth (enough for man to know),
"Virtue alone is happiness below."
The only point where human bliss stands still,
And tastes the good without the fall to ill;
Where only merit constant pay receives,
Is blest in what it takes, and what it gives;
The joy unequall'd, if its end it gain,
And if it lose, attended with no pain:
Without satiety, though e'er so blest,
And but more relish'd as the more distress'd:
The broadest mirth unfeeling folly wears,
Less pleasing far than virtue's very tears:
Good, from each object, from each place acquired,
For ever exercised, yet never tired;
Never elated, while one man's oppress'd;
Never dejected, while another's bless'd;

And where no wants, no wishes can remain,
Since but to wish more virtue, is to gain.
See the sole bliss Heaven could on all bestow!
Which who but feels can taste, but thinks can know:
Yet poor with fortune, and with learning blind,
The bad must miss; the good, untaught, will find;
Slave to no sect, who takes no private road,
But looks through Nature up to Nature's God;
Pursues that chain which links the immense design,
Joins heaven and earth, and mortal and divine;
Sees, that no being any bliss can know,
But touches some above, and some below;
Learns from this union of the rising whole,
The first, last purpose of the human soul;
And knows where faith, law, morals, all began,
All end, in LOVE OF GOD, and LOVE OF MAN.
For him alone, Hope leads from goal to goal,
And opens still, and opens on his soul;
Till lengthen'd on to FAITH, and unconfined,
It pours the bliss that fills up all the mind.
He sees, why nature plants in man alone
Hope of known bliss, and faith in bliss unknown:
(Nature, whose dictates to no other kind
Are given in vain, but what they seek they find)
Wise is her present; she connects in this
His greatest virtue with his greatest bliss;
At once his own bright prospect to be blest,
And strongest motive to assist the rest.
Self-love thus push'd to social, to divine,
Gives thee to make thy neighbour's blessing thine.
Is this too little for the boundless heart?
Extend it, let thy enemies have part:
Grasp the whole world of reason, life, and sense,
In one close system of benevolence:
Happier as kinder, in whate'er degree,
And height of bliss but height of charity.
God loves from whole to parts: but human soul
Must rise from individual to the whole.
Self-love but serves the virtuous mind to wake,
As the small pebble stirs the peaceful lake;
The centre moved, a circle straight succeeds,
Another still, and still another spreads;
Friend, parent, neighbour, first it will embrace;
His country next, and next all human race;

Wide, and more wide, the' o'erflowings of the mind
Take every creature in, of every kind;
Earth smiles around, with boundless bounty blest,
And Heaven beholds its image in his breast.
  Come then, my friend! my genius! come along;
O master of the poet, and the song!
And while the muse now stoops, or now ascends,
To man's low passions, or their glorious ends,
Teach me, like thee, in various nature wise,
To fall with dignity, with temper rise;
Form'd by thy converse, happily to steer
From grave to gay, from lively to severe;
Correct with spirit, eloquent with ease,
Intent to reason, or polite to please.
Oh! while along the stream of time thy name
Expanded flies, and gathers all its fame;
Say, shall my little bark attendant sail,
Pursue the triumph, and partake the gale?
When statesmen, heroes, kings, in dust repose,
Whose sons shall blush their fathers were thy foes
Shall then this verse to future age pretend
Thou wert my guide, philosopher, and friend!
That urged by thee, I turn'd the tuneful art
From sounds to things, from fancy to the heart;
For wit's false mirror held up Nature's light;
Show'd erring pride, WHATEVER IS, IS RIGHT;
That REASON, PASSION, answer one great aim;
That true SELF-LOVE and SOCIAL are the same;
That VIRTUE only makes our bliss below;
And all our knowledge is, OURSELVES TO KNOW.

THE UNIVERSAL PRAYER.

FATHER of all! in every age,
  In every clime adored,
By saint, by savage, and by sage,
  Jehovah, Jove, or Lord!

Thou great First Cause, least understood,
  Who all my sense confined
To know but this, that Thou art good,
  And that myself am blind;

Yet gave me, in this dark estate,
  To see the good from ill;
And binding nature fast in fate,
  Left free the human will.

What conscience dictates to be done,
  Or warns me not to do,
This, teach me more than hell to shun,
  That, more than heaven pursue.

What blessings thy free bounty gives,
  Let me not cast away;
For God is paid when man receives,
  To enjoy is to obey.

Yet not to earth's contracted span
  Thy goodness let me bound,
Or think thee Lord alone of man,
  When thousand worlds are round:

Let not this weak, unknowing hand
  Presume thy bolts to throw,
And deal damnation round the land
  On each I judge thy foe.

If I am right, thy grace impart,
  Still in the right to stay;
If I am wrong, oh teach my heart
  To find that better way!

Save me alike from foolish pride,
  Or impious discontent,
At aught thy wisdom has denied,
  Or aught thy goodness lent.

Teach me to feel another's woe,
  To hide the fault I see;
That mercy I to others show,
  That mercy show to me.

Mean though I am, not wholly so,
  Since quicken'd by thy breath;
Oh lead me wheresoe'er I go,
  Through this day's life or death!

This day, be bread and peace my lot:
  All else beneath the sun,
Thou know'st if best bestow'd or not,
  And let Thy will be done.

To thee, whose temple is all space,
  Whose altar, earth, sea, skies!
One chorus let all Being raise!
  All Nature's incense rise!

MORAL ESSAYS,

IN

FOUR EPISTLES TO SEVERAL PERSONS.

Est brevitate opus, ut currat sententia, neu se
Impediat verbis lassis onerantibus aures:
Et sermone opus est modo tristi, sæpe jocoso,
Defendente vicem modo Rhetoris atque Poetæ
Interdum urbani, parcentis viribus, atque
Extenuantis eas consultò. HOR.

EPISTLE I.

TO SIR RICHARD TEMPLE, LORD COBHAM.

ARGUMENT.

OF THE KNOWLEDGE AND CHARACTERS OF MEN.

I. That it is not sufficient for this knowledge to consider man in the *abstract;* books will not serve the purpose, nor yet our own *experience* singly. General maxims, unless they be formed upon *both,* will be but notional. Some peculiarity in every man, characteristic to himself, yet varying from himself. Difficulties arising from our own passions, fancies, faculties, &c. The shortness of life, to observe in, and the uncertainty of the *principles of action* in men, to observe by. Our own principle of action often hid from ourselves. Some few characters plain, but in general confounded, dissembled, or inconsistent. The same man utterly different in different places and seasons. Unimaginable weaknesses in the greatest. Nothing constant and certain but *God* and *nature.* No judging of the *motives* from the actions; the same actions proceeding from contrary motives, and the same motives influencing contrary actions. II. Yet to form *characters,* we can only take the *strongest actions* of a man's life, and try to make them agree: the utter uncertainty of this, from *nature* itself, and from *policy. Characters* given according to the *rank* of men of the world. And some reason for it. Education alters the *nature,* or at least the *character,* of many. *Actions passions, opinions, manners, humours,* or *principles,* all subject to change. No judging by *nature.* III. It only remains to find (if we can) his RULING PASSION: that will certainly influence all the rest, and can

reconcile the seeming or real inconsistency of all his actions. Instanced in the extraordinary character of *Clodio*. A caution against mistaking *second qualities* for *first*, which will destroy all possibility of the knowledge of mankind. Examples of the strength of the *ruling passion*, and its continuation to the last breath.

I. YES, you despise the man to books confined,
Who from his study rails at human kind;
Tho' what he learns he speaks, and may advance
Some general maxims, or be right by chance.
The coxcomb bird, so talkative and grave,
That from his cage cries cuckold, whore, and knave,
Though many a passenger he rightly call,
You hold him no philosopher at all.
And yet the fate of all extremes is such,
Men may be read, as well as books, too much.
To observations which ourselves we make,
We grow more partial for the observer's sake;
To written wisdom, as another's, less:
Maxims are drawn from notions, those from guess.
There's some peculiar in each leaf and grain,
Some unmark'd fibre, or some varying vein:
Shall only man be taken in the gross?
Grant but as many sorts of mind as moss.
That each from other differs, first confess;
Next that he varies from himself no less:
Add nature's, custom's, reason's, passion's strife,
And all opinion's colours cast on life.
Our depths who fathoms, or our shallows finds,
Quick whirls, and shifting eddies, of our minds?
On human actions reason though you can,
It may be reason, but it is not man:
His principle of action once explore,
That instant 'tis his principle no more.
Like following life through creatures you dissect,
You lose it in the moment you detect.
Yet more; the difference is as great between
The optics seeing, as the objects seen.
All manners take a tincture from our own
Or come discolour'd through our passions shown.
Or fancy's beam enlarges, multiplies,
Contracts, inverts, and gives ten thousand dies.
Nor will life's stream for observation stay,
It hurries all too fast to mark their way:

In vain sedate reflections we would make,
When half our knowledge we must snatch, not take.
Oft, in the passions' wide rotation toss'd,
Our spring of action to ourselves is lost;
Tired, not determined, to the last we yield,
And what comes then is master of the field.
As the last image of the troubled heap,
When sense subsides, and fancy sports in sleep,
(Though past the recollection of the thought)
Becomes the stuff of which our dream is wrought:
Something as dim to our internal view,
Is thus, perhaps, the cause of most we do.
  True, some are open, and to all men known;
Others so very close, they're hid from none;
(So darkness strikes the sense no less than light)
Thus gracious CHANDOS is beloved at sight;
And every child hates Shylock, though his soul
Still sits at squat, and peeps not from its hole.
At half mankind when generous MANLY raves,
All know 'tis virtue, for he thinks them knaves:
When universal homage Umbra pays,
All see 'tis vice, and itch of vulgar praise.
When flattery glares, all hate it in a queen,
While one there is who charms us with his spleen.
  But these plain characters we rarely find;
Though strong the bent, yet quick the turns of mind:
Or puzzling contraries confound the whole;
Or affectations quite reverse the soul.
The dull, flat falsehood serves for policy;
And in the cunning, truth itself's a lie:
Unthought-of frailties cheat us in the wise;
The fool lies hid in inconsistencies.
  See the same man, in vigour, in the gout;
Alone, in company; in place, or out;
Early at business, and at hazard late;
Mad at a fox-chase, wise at a debate;
Drunk at a borough, civil at a ball;
Friendly at Hackney, faithless at Whitehall!
  Catius is ever moral, ever grave,
Thinks who endures a knave, is next a knave,
Save just at dinner—then prefers, no doubt,
A rogue with venison to a saint without.
  Who would not praise Patritio's high desert,
His hand unstain'd, his uncorrupted heart,

His comprehensive head! all interests weigh'd,
All Europe saved, yet Britain not betray'd?
He thanks you not, his pride is in piquet,
Newmarket fame, and judgment at a bet.
What made (say Montaigne, or more sage Charron!)
Otho a warrior, Cromwell a buffoon?
A perjured prince a leaden saint revere,[1]
A godless regent tremble at a star?[2]
The throne a bigot keep, a genius quit,[3]
Faithless through piety, and duped through wit?
Europe a woman, child, or dotard rule,
And just her wisest monarch made a fool?
Know, GOD and NATURE only are the same:
In man, the judgment shoots at flying game;
A bird of passage! gone as soon as found;
Now in the moon perhaps, now under ground.
II. In vain the sage, with retrospective eye,
Would from the apparent *what* conclude the *why*,
Infer the motive from the deed, and show,
That what we chanced was what we meant to do.
Behold! if fortune or a mistress frowns,
Some plunge in business, others shave their crowns:
To ease the soul of one oppressive weight,
This quits an empire, that embroils a state:
The same adust complexion has impell'd
Charles to the convent, Philip to the field.
Not always actions show the man: we find
Who does a kindness, is not therefore kind;
Perhaps prosperity becalm'd his breast;
Perhaps the wind just shifted from the east:
Not therefore humble he who seeks retreat,
Pride guides his steps, and bids him shun the great.
Who combats bravely, is not therefore brave,
He dreads a death-bed like the meanest slave;
Who reasons wisely, is not therefore wise,
His pride in reasoning, not in acting lies.

[1] Louis XI. of France wore in his hat a leaden image of the Virgin Mary, which, when he swore by, he feared to break his oath.

[2] Philip, duke of Orleans, regent in the minority of Louis XV., superstitious in judicial astrology, though an unbeliever in all religion

[3] Philip V. of Spain, who, after renouncing the throne for religion, resumed it to gratify his queen; and Victor Amadeus II., king of Sardinia, who resigned the crown, and trying to re-assume it, was imprisoned till his death.

But grant that actions best discover man;
Take the most strong, and sort them as you can.
The few that glare each character must mark,
You balance not the many in the dark.
What will you do with such as disagree?
Suppress them, or miscal them policy?
Must then at once (the character to save)
The plain-rough hero turn a crafty knave?
Alas! in truth the man but changed his mind,
Perhaps was sick, in love, or had not dined.
Ask why from Britain Cæsar would retreat?
Cæsar himself might whisper he was beat.
Why risk the world's great empire for a punk?
Cæsar perhaps might answer he was drunk.
But, sage historians! 'tis your task to prove
One action, conduct, one heroic love.
'Tis from high life high characters are drawn;
A saint in crape is twice a saint in lawn;
A judge is just, a chancellor juster still;
A gown-man learn'd; a bishop, what you will;
Wise, if a minister; but, if a king,
More wise, more learn'd, more just, more everything.
Court-virtues bear, like gems, the highest rate,
Born where Heaven's influence scarce can penetrate:
In life's low vale, the soil the virtues like,
They please as beauties, here as wonders strike.
Though the same sun with all-diffusive rays
Blush in the rose, and in the diamond blaze,
We prize the stronger effort of his power,
And justly set the gem above the flower.
'Tis education forms the common mind,
Just as the twig is bent, the tree's inclined.
Boastful and rough, your first son is a squire;
The next a tradesman, meek, and much a liar;
Tom struts a soldier, open, bold, and brave;
Will sneaks a scrivener, an exceeding knave:
Is he a churchman?—then he's fond of power:
A quaker?—sly: a presbyterian?—sour:
A smart freethinker?—all things in an hour.
Ask men's opinions: Scoto now shall tell
How trade increases, and the world goes well;
Strike off his pension, by the setting sun,
And Britain, if not Europe, is undone.

That gay freethinker, a fine talker once,
What turns him now a stupid silent dunce?
Some god, or spirit, he has lately found,
Or chancéd to meet a minister that frown'd.
Judge we by nature?—habit can efface,
Interest o'ercome, or policy take place:
By actions?—those uncertainty divides:
By passions?—those dissimulation hides:
Opinions?—they still take a wider range:
Find, if you can, in what you cannot change.
Manners with fortunes, humours turn with climes,
Tenets with books, and principles with times.
III. Search then the RULING PASSION: there, alone,
The wild are constant, and the cunning known;
The fool consistent, and the false sincere;
Priests, princes, women, no dissemblers here.
This clue once found, unravels all the rest,
The prospect clears, and WHARTON stands confest.
Wharton, the scorn and wonder of our days,
Whose ruling passion was the lust of praise:
Born with whate'er could win it from the wise,
Women and fools must like him, or he dies;
Though wondering senates hung on all he spoke,
The club must hail him master of the joke.
Shall parts so various aim at nothing new?
He'll shine a Tully and a Wilmot too.
Then turns repentant, and his God adores
With the same spirit that he drinks and whores;
Enough, if all around him but admire,
And now the punk applaud, and now the friar.
Thus with each gift of nature and of art,
And wanting nothing but an honest heart;
Grown all to all, from no one vice exempt;
And most contemptible to shun contempt;
His passion still, to covet general praise,
His life, to forfeit it a thousand ways;
A constant bounty which no friend has made;
An angel tongue, which no man can persuade!
A fool, with more of wit than half mankind,
Too rash for thought, for action too refined:
A tyrant to the wife his heart approves;
A rebel to the very king he loves;
He dies, sad outcast of each church and state,
And, harder still! flagitious, yet not great!

Ask you why Wharton broke through every rule?
'Twas all for fear the knaves should call him fool.
Nature well known, no prodigies remain,
Comets are regular, and WHARTON plain.
Yet, in this search, the wisest may mistake,
If second qualities for first they take.
When Catiline by rapine swell'd his store;
When Cæsar made a noble dame a whore;
In this the lust, in that the avarice
Were means, not ends; ambition was the vice.
That very Cæsar, born in Scipio's days,
Had aim'd, like him, by chastity at praise.
Lucullus, when frugality could charm,
Had roasted turnips in the Sabine farm.
In vain the observer eyes the builder's toil,
But quite mistakes the scaffold for the pile.
In this one passion man can strength enjoy,
As fits give vigour, just when they destroy.
Time, that on all things lays his lenient hand,
Yet tames not this; it sticks to our last sand.
Consistent in our follies and our sins,
Here honest nature ends as she begins.
Old politicians chew on wisdom past,
And totter on in business to the last;
As weak, as earnest; and as gravely out,
As sober Lanesb'row dancing in the gout.
Behold a reverend sire, whom want of grace
Has made the father of a nameless race,
Shoved from the wall perhaps, or rudely press'd
By his own son, that passes by unbless'd:
Still to his wench he crawls on knocking knees,
And envies every sparrow that he sees.
A salmon's belly, Helluo, was thy fate;
The doctor call'd, declares all help too late:
"Mercy!" cries Helluo, "mercy on my soul;
Is there no hope?—Alas!—then bring the jowl."
The frugal crone, whom praying priests attend,
Still tries to save the hallow'd taper's end,
Collects her breath, as ebbing life retires,
For one puff more, and in that puff expires.
"Odious! in woollen! 'twould a saint provoke,"
(Were the last words that poor Narcissa spoke;)
"No, let a charming chintz and Brussels lace
Wrap my cold limbs, and shade my lifeless face:

One would not, sure, be frightful when one's dead—
And—Betty—give this cheek a little red."
The courtier smooth, who forty years had shined
An humble servant to all human kind,
Just brought out this, when scarce his tongue could stir
"If—where I'm going—I could serve you, Sir?"
"I give and I devise" (old Euclio said,
And sigh'd) "my lands and tenements to Ned."
Your money, Sir? "My money, Sir! what all?
Why,—if I must—(then wept) I give it Paul."
The manor, Sir?—"The manor! hold," he cried,
"Not that,—I cannot part with that"—and died.
And you, brave COBHAM! to the latest breath,
Shall feel your ruling passion strong in death:
Such in those moments as in all the past;
"Oh, save my country, Heaven!" shall be your last.

EPISTLE II.

TO A LADY.

ARGUMENT.

OF THE CHARACTERS OF WOMEN.

That the particular characters of women are not so strongly marked as those of men, seldom so fixed, and still more inconsistent with themselves.—Instances of contrarieties given, even from such characters as are more strongly marked, and seemingly, therefore, most consistent: as, 1. In the affected.—2. In the soft-natured.—3. In the cunning and artful.—4. In the whimsical.—5. In the lewd and vicious.—6. In the witty and refined.—7. In the stupid and simple.—The former part having shown that the particular characters of women are more various than those of men, it is nevertheless observed that the general characteristic of the sex, as to the ruling passion, is more uniform.—This is occasioned partly by their nature, partly by their education, and in some degree by necessity.—What are the aims and the fate of this sex:—1. As to power.—2. As to pleasure.—Advice for their true interest.—The picture of an estimable woman, with the best kind of contrarieties.

NOTHING so true as what you once let fall,
"Most women have no characters at all."
Matter too soft a lasting mark to bear,
And best distinguish'd by black, brown, or fair.
How many pictures of one nymph we view,
All how unlike each other, all how true!

Arcadia's countess, here, in ermined pride,
Is there, Pastora by a fountain side.
Here Fannia, leering on her own good man,
And there, a naked Leda with a swan.
Let then the fair-one beautifully cry,
In Magdalen's loose hair and lifted eye
Or dress'd in smiles of sweet Cecilia shine,
With simpering angels, palms, and harps divine;
Whether the charmer sinner it, or saint it,
If folly grow romantic, I must paint it.
Come then, the colours and the ground prepare!
Dip in the rainbow, trick her off in air;
Choose a firm cloud, before it fall, and in it
Catch, ere she change, the Cynthia of this minute.
Rufa, whose eye quick-glancing o'er the park,
Attracts each light gay meteor of a spark,
Agrees as ill with Rufa studying Locke,
As Sappho's diamonds with her dirty smock;
Or Sappho at her toilet's greasy task,
With Sappho fragrant at an evening mask:
So morning insects that in muck begun,
Shine, buzz, and fly-blow in the setting sun.
How soft is Silia! fearful to offend;
The frail one's advocate, the weak one's friend.
To her, Calista proved her conduct nice;
And good Simplicius asks of her advice.
Sudden, she storms! she raves! You tip the wink,
But spare your censure; Silia does not drink.
All eyes may see from what the change arose,
All eyes may see——a pimple on her nose.
Papilia, wedded to her amorous spark,
Sighs for the shades!—"How charming is a park!"
A park is purchased, but the fair he sees
All bathed in tears—"Oh odious, odious trees!"
Ladies, like variegated tulips, show;
'Tis to their changes half their charms we owe;
Fine by defect, and delicately weak,
Their happy spots the nice admirer take.
'Twas thus Calypso once each heart alarm'd,
Awed without virtue, without beauty charm'd;
Her tongue bewitch'd as oddly as her eyes;
Less wit than mimic, more a wit than wise.
Strange graces still, and stranger flights she had,
Was just not ugly, and was just not mad;

Yet ne'er so sure our passion to create,
As when she touch'd the brink of all we hate.
  Narcissa's nature, tolerably mild,
To make a wash, would hardly stew a child;
Has even been proved to grant a lover's prayer,
And paid a tradesman once to make him stare;
Gave alms at Easter, in a Christian trim,
And made a widow happy, for a whim.
Why then declare good-nature is her scorn,
When 'tis by that alone she can be borne?
Why pique all mortals, yet affect a name?
A fool to pleasure, yet a slave to fame:
Now deep in Taylor and the Book of Martyrs,
Now drinking citron with his Grace and Chartres
Now conscience chills her, and now passion burns;
And atheism and religion take their turns;
A very heathen in the carnal part,
Yet still a sad, good Christian at her heart.
  See sin in state, majestically drunk;
Proud as a peeress, prouder as a punk;
Chaste to her husband, frank to all beside,
A teeming mistress, but a barren bride.
What then? let blood and body bear the fault.
Her head's untouch'd, that noble seat of thought:
Such this day's doctrine—in another fit
She sins with poets through pure love of wit.
What has not fired her bosom or her brain?
Cæsar and Tallboy, Charles and Charlemagne.
As Helluo, late dictator of the feast,
The nose of hautgout and the tip of taste,
Critiqued your wine, and analyzed your meat,
Yet on plain pudding deigned at home to eat:
So Philomedé, lecturing all mankind,
On the soft passion, and the taste refined,
The address, the delicacy—stoops at once,
And makes her hearty meal upon a dunce.
  Flavia's a wit, has too much sense to pray;
To toast our wants and wishes, is her way;
Nor asks of God, but of her stars, to give
The mighty blessing, "while we live, to live."
Then all for death, that opiate of the soul!
Lucretia's dagger, Rosamonda's bowl.
Say, what can cause such impotence of mind?
A spark too fickle, or a spouse too kind.

Wise wretch! with pleasures too refined to please;
With too much spirit to be e'er at ease:
With too much quickness ever to be taught;
With too much thinking to have common thought:
You purchase pain with all that joy can give,
And die of nothing but a rage to live.
  Turn then from wits! and look on Simo's mate,
No ass so meek, no ass so obstinate.
Or her, that owns her faults, but never mends,
Because she's honest, and the best of friends.
Or her, whose life the church and scandal share,
For ever in a passion, or a prayer.
Or her, who laughs at hell, but (like her grace)
Cries, "Ah! how charming if there's no such place!"
Or who in sweet vicissitude appears,
Of mirth and opium, ratifie and tears,
The daily anodyne, and nightly draught,
To kill those foes to fair ones, time and thought.
Woman and fool are two hard things to hit;
For true no-meaning puzzles more than wit.
  But what are these to great Atossa's mind?
Scarce once herself, by turns all womankind!
Who, with herself, or others, from her birth
Finds all her life one warfare upon earth:
Shines in exposing knaves, and painting fools,
Yet is, whate'er she hates and ridicules.
No thought advances, but her eddy brain
Whisks it about, and down it goes again.
Full sixty years the world has been her trade,
The wisest fool much time has ever made.
From loveless youth to unrespected age,
No passion gratified, except her rage.
So much the fury still outran the wit,
The pleasure miss'd her, and the scandal hit.
Who breaks with her, provokes revenge from hell,
But he's a bolder man who dares be well.
Her every turn with violence pursued,
No more a storm her hate than gratitude:
To that each passion turns, or soon or late;
Love, if it makes her yield, must make her hate;
Superiors? death! and equals?—what a curse!
But an inferior not dependent?—worse.
Offend her, and she knows not to forgive;
Oblige her, and she'll hate you while you live:

But die, and she'll adore you—Then the bust
And temple rise—then fall again to dust.
Last night, her lord was all that's good and great;
A knave this morning, and his will a cheat.
Strange! by the means defeated of the ends,
By spirit robb'd of power, by warmth of friends,
By wealth of followers! without one distress,
Sick of herself through very selfishness!
Atossa, cursed with every granted prayer,
Childless with all her children, wants an heir.
To heirs unknown, descends the unguarded store,
Or wanders, heaven-directed, to the poor.
 Pictures like these, dear madam, to design,
Asks no firm hand, and no unerring line;
Some wandering touches, some reflected light,
Some flying stroke alone can hit 'em right:
For how could equal colours do the knack?
Cameleons who can paint in white and black?
 "Yet Chloe sure was form'd without a spot."—
Nature in her then err'd not, but forgot.
"With every pleasing, every prudent part,
Say, what can Chloe want?"—She wants a heart.
She speaks, behaves, and acts just as she ought;
But never, never, reach'd one generous thought.
Virtue she finds too painful an endeavour,
Content to dwell in decencies for ever.
So very reasonable, so unmoved,
As never yet to love, or to be loved.
She, while her lover pants upon her breast,
Can mark the figures on an Indian chest:
And when she sees her friend in deep despair,
Observes how much a chintz exceeds mohair.
Forbid it, Heaven, a favour or a debt
She e'er should cancel!—but she may forget.
Safe is your secret still in Chloe's ear;
But none of Chloe's shall you ever hear.
Of all her dears she never slander'd one,
But cares not if a thousand are undone.
Would Chloe know if you're alive or dead?
She bids her footman put it in her head.
Chloe is prudent—Would you too be wise?
Then never break your heart when Chloe dies.
 One certain portrait may (I grant) be seen,
Which Heaven has varnish'd out and made a queen:

THE SAME FOR EVER! and described by all
With truth and goodness, as with crown and ball.
Poets heap virtues, painters gems at will,
And show their zeal, and hide their want of skill.
'Tis well—but, artists! who can paint or write,
To draw the naked is your true delight.
That robe of quality so struts and swells,
None see what parts of nature it conceals;
The exactest traits of body or of mind,
We owe to models of an humble kind.
If QUEENSBERRY to strip there's no compelling,
'Tis from a handmaid we must take a Helen.
From peer or bishop 'tis no easy thing
To draw the man who loves his God, or king:
Alas! I copy (or my draught would fail)
From honest Mahomet, or plain Parson Hale.
  But grant, in public, men sometimes are shown,
A woman's seen in private life alone:
Our bolder talents in full light display'd;
Your virtues open fairest in the shade.
Bred to disguise, in public 'tis you hide;
There, none distinguish 'twixt your shame or pride,
Weakness or delicacy; all so nice,
That each may seem a virtue, or a vice.
  In men, we various ruling passions find;
In women two almost divide the kind;
Those, only fix'd, they first or last obey,
The love of pleasure, and the love of sway.
  That, nature gives; and where the lesson taught
Is but to please, can pleasure seem a fault?
Experience, this; by man's oppression curst,
They seek the second not to lose the first.
  Men, some to business, some to pleasure take;
But every woman is at heart a rake:
Men, some to quiet, some to public strife;
But every lady would be queen for life.
  Yet mark the fate of a whole sex of queens!
Power all their end, but beauty all the means:
In youth they conquer, with so wild a rage,
As leaves them scarce a subject in their age:
For foreign glory, foreign joy, they roam;
No thought of peace or happiness at home.
But wisdom's triumph, is well-timed retreat,
As hard a science to the fair as great!

Beauties, like tyrants, old and friendless grown,
Yet hate repose, and dread to be alone,
Worn out in public, weary every eye,
Nor leave one sigh behind them when they die.
Pleasures the sex, as children birds, pursue,
Still out of reach, yet never out of view;
Sure, if they catch, to spoil the toy at most,
To covet flying, and regret when lost:
At last, to follies youth could scarce defend,
It grows their age's prudence to pretend;
Ashamed to own they gave delight before,
Reduced to feign it, when they give no more:
As hags hold sabbaths less for joy than spite,
So these their merry, miserable night:
Still round and round the ghosts of beauty glide
And haunt the places where their honour died.
See how the world its veterans rewards!
A youth of frolics, an old age of cards;
Fair to no purpose, artful to no end,
Young without lovers, old without a friend;
A fop their passion, but their prize a sot,
Alive, ridiculous; and dead, forgot!
Ah! friend! to dazzle let the vain design;
To raise the thought, and touch the heart, be thine!
That charm shall grow, while what fatigues the ring,
Flaunts and goes down, an unregarded thing:
So when the sun's broad beam has tired the sight,
All mild ascends the moon's more sober light,
Serene in virgin modesty she shines,
And unobserved the glaring orb declines.
Oh! blest with temper, whose unclouded ray
Can make to-morrow cheerful as to-day;
She who can love a sister's charms, or hear
Sighs for a daughter with unwounded ear;
She, who ne'er answers till a husband cools,
Or, if she rules him, never shows she rules;
Charms by accepting, by submitting sways,
Yet has her humour most, when she obeys;
Let fops or fortune fly which way they will;
Disdains all loss of tickets or codille;
Spleen, vapours, or small-pox, above them all,
And mistress of herself, though china fall.
And yet, believe me, good as well as ill,
Woman's at best a contradiction still.

Heaven, when it strives to polish all it can
Its last best work, but forms a softer man;
Picks from each sex, to make the favourite bless'd,
Your love of pleasure, our desire of rest:
Blends, in exception to all general rules,
Your taste of follies, with our scorn of fools:
Reserve with frankness, art with truth allied
Courage with softness, modesty with pride;
Fix'd principles, with fancy ever new;
Shakes all together, and produces——you.
  Be this a woman's fame: with this unbless'd,
Toasts live a scorn, and queens may die a jest.
This Phœbus promised (I forget the year)
When those blue eyes first open'd on the sphere;
Ascendant Phœbus watch'd that hour with care,
Averted half your parents' simple prayer;
And gave you beauty, but denied the pelf
That buys your sex a tyrant o'er itself.
The generous god, who wit and gold refines,
And ripens spirits as he ripens mines,
Kept dross for duchesses, the world shall know it,
To you gave sense, good-humour, and a poet.

EPISTLE III.

TO ALLEN LORD BATHURST.

This epistle was written after a violent outcry against our author, on suspicion that he had ridiculed a worthy nobleman merely for his wrong taste. He justified himself upon that article in a letter to the Earl of Burlington; at the end of which are these words: "I have learnt that there are some who would rather be wicked than ridiculous; and therefore it may be safer to attack vices than follies. I will therefore leave my betters in the quiet possession of their idols, their groves, and their high places, and change my subject from their pride to their meanness, from their vanities to their miseries; and as the only certain way to avoid misconstructions, to lessen offence, and not to multiply ill-natured applications, I may probably, in my next, make use of real names instead of fictitious ones."

ARGUMENT.

OF THE USE OF RICHES.

That it is known to few, most falling into one of the extremes, *avarice* or *profusion*. The point discussed whether the invention of money has been more commodious or pernicious to mankind. That riches, either to the *avaricious* or the *prodigal*, cannot afford happiness, scarcely necessaries. That avarice is an absolute frenzy, without an end or purpose. Conjectures about the motives of avaricious men.

That the conduct of men, with respect to riches, can only be accounted for by the ORDER OF PROVIDENCE, which works the general good out of extremes, and brings all to its great end by perpetual revolutions. How a *miser* acts upon principles which appear to him reasonable. How a *prodigal* does the same. The due medium and true use of riches. The Man of Ross. The fate of the *profuse* and the *covetous*, in two examples; both miserable in life and in death. The story of Sir Balaam.

P. WHO shall decide, when doctors disagree
And soundest casuists doubt, like you and me
You hold the word, from Jove to Momus given,
That man was made the standing jest of Heaven;
And gold but sent to keep the fools in play,
For some to heap, and some to throw away.
But I, who think more highly of our kind,
(And surely, Heaven and I are of a mind)
Opine, that Nature, as in duty bound,
Deep hid the shining mischief under ground.
But when by man's audacious labour won,
Flamed forth this rival to its sire, the sun,
Then careful Heaven supplied two sorts of men,
To squander these, and those to hide again.
Like doctors thus, when much dispute has past,
We find our tenets just the same at last.
Both fairly owning, riches, in effect,
No grace of Heaven, or token of the elect;
Given to the fool, the mad, the vain, the evil,
To Ward, to Waters, Chartres,[1] and the Devil.

[1] John Ward, of Hackney, Esq., Member of Parliament, being prosecuted by the Duchess of Buckingham, and convicted of forgery, was first expelled the House, and then stood on the pillory on the 17th of March, 1727. He was suspected of joining in a conveyance with Sir John Blunt, to secrete fifty thousand pounds of that Director's estate, forfeited to the South Sea Company by act of parliament. The Company recovered the fifty thousand pounds against Ward; but he set up prior conveyances of his real estate to his brother and son, and concealed all his personal, which was computed to be one hundred and fifty thousand pounds. These conveyances being also set aside by a bill in Chancery, Ward was imprisoned, and hazarded the forfeiture of his life by not giving in his effects till the last day, which was that of his examination. During his confinement, his amusement was to give poison to dogs and cats, and see them expire by slower or quicker torments. To sum up the *worth* of this gentleman, at the several eras of his life: at his standing in the pillory, he was *worth above two hundred thousand pounds;* at his commitment to prison, he was *worth one hundred and fifty thousand;* but has been since so far diminished in his reputation, as to be thought a *worse man* by *fifty or sixty thousand.*

Fr. Chartres, a man infamous for all manner of vices. When he was an ensign in the army, he was drummed out of the regiment for a

B. What nature wants, commodious gold bestows,
'Tis thus we eat the bread another sows.

cheat; he was next banished Brussels, and drummed out of Ghent, on the same account. After a hundred tricks at the gaming-tables, he took to lending of money at exorbitant interest and on great penalties, accumulating premium, interest, and capital, into a new capital, and seizing to a minute when the payments became due; in a word, by a constant attention to the vices, wants, and follies of mankind, he acquired an immense fortune. His house was a perpetual bawdy-house. He was twice condemned for rapes, and pardoned; but the last time not without imprisonment in Newgate, and large confiscations. He died in Scotland in 1731, aged 62. The populace at his funeral raised a great riot, almost tore the body out of the coffin, and cast dead dogs, &c. into the grave along with it. The followizg epitaph contains his character, very justly drawn by Dr. Arbuthnot:—

HERE continueth to rot
The body of FRANCIS CHARTRES,
Who, with an INFLEXIBLE CONSTANCY,
and
INIMITABLE UNIFORMITY of life,
PERSISTED,
In spite of AGE and INFIRMITIES,
In the practice of EVERY HUMAN VICE,
Excepting PRODIGALITY and HYPOCRISY:
His insatiable AVARICE exempted him from the first,
His matchless IMPUDENCE from the second.
Nor was he more singular
in the undeviating *pravity* of his *manners*,
Than successful
in *accumulating* WEALTH;
For, without TRADE or PROFESSION,
Without TRUST of PUBLIC MONEY,
And without BRIBE-WORTHY service,
He acquired, or more properly created,
A MINISTERIAL ESTATE.
He was the only person of his time
Who could CHEAT without the mask of HONESTY,
Retain his primeval MEANNESS
When possessed of TEN THOUSAND a year,
And having daily deserved the GIBBET for what he *did*,
Was at last condemned to it for what he *could* not *do*.
Oh, indignant reader!
Think not his life useless to mankind!
PROVIDENCE connived at his execrable designs,
To give to after ages
A conspicuous PROOF and EXAMPLE,
Of how small estimation is EXORBITANT WEALTH
In the sight of GOD,
By his bestowing it on the most UNWORTHY OF ALL
MORTALS.

This gentleman was *worth seven thousand pounds a year* estate in land, and about *one hundred thousand* in money.

Mr. Waters, the third of these worthies, was a man no way resem-

P. But how unequal it bestows, observe,
'Tis thus we riot, while, who sow it, starve:
What nature wants (a phrase I much distrust)
Extends to luxury, extends to lust:
Useful, I grant, it serves what life requires,
But dreadful too, the dark assassin hires.
B. Trade it may help, society extend.
P. But lures the pirate, and corrupts the friend.
B. It raises armies in a nation's aid.
P. But bribes a senate, and the land's betray'd.
In vain may heroes fight, and patriots rave;
If secret gold sap on from knave to knave.
Once, we confess, beneath the patriot's cloak,[1]
From the crack'd bag the dropping guinea spoke,
And jingling down the back-stairs, told the crew,
"Old Cato is as great a rogue as you."
Blest paper-credit! last and best supply!
That lends corruption lighter wings to fly!
Gold imp'd by thee, can compass hardest things,
Can pocket states, can fetch or carry kings;[2]
A single leaf shall waft an army o'er,
Or ship off senates to a distant shore:[3]
A leaf, like Sibyl's, scatter to and fro
Our fates and fortunes, as the winds shall blow:
Pregnant with thousands flits the scrap unseen,
And silent sells a king, or buys a queen.
Oh! that such bulky bribes as all might see,
Still, as of old, encumber'd villany!

bling the former in his military, but extremely so in his civil capacity; his great fortune having been raised by the like diligent attendance on the necessities of others. But this gentleman's history must be deferred till his death, when his *worth* may be known more certainly.

[1] This is a true story, which happened in the reign of William III. to an unsuspected old patriot, who coming out at the back-door from having been closeted by the king, where he had received a large bag of guineas, the bursting of the bag discovered his business there.

[2] In our author's time, many princes had been sent about the world, and great changes of kings projected in Europe. The partition treaty had disposed of Spain; France had set up a king for England, who was sent to Scotland, and back again; King Stanislaus was sent to Poland, and back again; the Duke of Anjou was sent to Spain, and Don Carlos to Italy.

[3] Alludes to several ministers, counsellors, and patriots, banished in our times to Siberia, and to that MORE GLORIOUS FATE of the PARLIAMENT of PARIS, banished to Pontoise in the year 1720.

Could France or Rome divert our brave designs,
With all their brandies or with all their wines?
What could they more than knights and squires confound,
Or water all the quorum ten miles round?
A statesman's slumbers how this speech would spoil!
"Sir, Spain has sent a thousand jars of oil;
Huge bales of British cloth blockade the door;
A hundred oxen at your levee roar."
Poor avarice one torment more would find;
Nor could profusion squander all in kind.
Astride his cheese Sir Morgan might we meet;
And Worldly crying coals from street to street;[1]
Whom with a wig so wild, and mien so mazed,
Pity mistakes for some poor tradesman crazed.
Had Colepepper's[2] whole wealth been hops and hogs,
Could he himself have sent it to the dogs?
His grace will game: to White's a bull be led,
With spurning heels and with a butting head.
To White's be carried, as to ancient games,
Fair coursers, vases, and alluring dames.
Shall then Uxorio, if the stakes he sweep,
Bear home six whores, and make his lady weep?
Or soft Adonis, so perfumed and fine,
Drive to St. James's a whole herd of swine?
O filthy check on all industrious skill,
To spoil the nation's last great trade, quadrille!
Since then, my lord, on such a world we fall,
What say you? B. Say? Why take it, gold and all.
P. What riches give us let us then inquire:
Meat, fire, and clothes. B. What more? P. Meat, clothes, and fire.

[1] Some misers of great wealth, proprietors of the coal mines, had entered at this time into an association to keep up coals to an extravagant price, whereby the poor were reduced almost to starve; till one of them, taking the advantage of underselling the rest, defeated the design. One of these misers was *worth ten thousand*, another *seven thousand* a year.

[2] Sir William Colepepper, Bart., a person of an ancient family and ample fortune, without one other quality of a gentleman, who, after ruining himself at the gaming-table, passed the rest of his days in sitting there to see the ruin of others; preferring to subsist upon borrowing and begging, rather than to enter into any reputable method of life, and refusing a post in the army, which was offered him.

Is this too little? would you more than live?
Alas! 'tis more than Turner[1] finds they give.
Alas! 'tis more than (all his visions past)
Unhappy Wharton,[2] waking, found at last!
What can they give? to dying Hopkins,[3] heirs
To Chartres, vigour; Japhet,[4] nose and ears?
Can they in gems bid pallid Hippia glow,
In Fulvia's buckle ease the throbs below:
Or heal, old Narses, thy obscener ail,
With all the embroidery plaster'd at thy tail?
They might (were Harpax not too wise to spend)
Give Harpax' self the blessing of a friend;
Or find some doctor that would save the life
Of wretched Shylock, spite of Shylock's wife:
But thousands die, without or this or that,
Die, and endow a college, or a cat.[5]
To some, indeed, Heaven grants the happier fate,
To enrich a bastard, or a son they hate.

[1] One who, being possessed of three hundred thousand pounds, laid down his coach, because interest was reduced from five to four *per cent.*, and then put seventy thousand into the charitable corporation for better interest; which sum having lost, he took it so much to heart, that he kept his chamber ever after. It is thought he would not have outlived it, but that he was heir to another considerable estate, which he daily expected, and that by this course of life he saved both clothes and all other expenses.

[2] A nobleman of great qualities, but as unfortunate in the application of them, as if they had been vices and follies. See his character in the first epistle.

[3] A citizen, whose rapacity obtained him the name of *Vulture Hopkins*. He lived worthless, but died *worth three hundred thousand pounds*, which he would give to no person living, but left it so as not to be inherited till after the second generation. His counsel representing to him how many years it must be before this could take effect, and that his money could only lie at interest all that time, he expressed great joy thereat, and said, "They would then be as long in spending, as he had been in getting it." But the chancery afterwards set aside the will and gave it to the heir-at-law.

[4] Japhet Crook, alias Sir *Peter Stranger*, was punished with the loss of those parts, for having forged a conveyance of an estate to himself, upon which he took up several thousand pounds. He was at the same time sued in chancery for having fraudulently obtained a will, by which he possessed another considerable estate, in wrong of the brother of the deceased. By these means he was *worth* a great sum, which (in reward for the small loss of his ears) he enjoyed in prison till his death, and quietly left to his executor.

[5] A certain duchess in her last will left considerable legacies and annuities to her cats.

Perhaps you think the poor might have their part?
Bond damns the poor,[1] and hates them from his heart:
The grave Sir Gilbert holds it for a rule
That every man in want is knave or fool:
"God cannot love (says Blunt, with tearless eyes)
The wretch he starves"—and piously denies:
But the good bishop, with a meeker air,
Admits, and leaves them, Providence's care.
Yet, to be just to these poor men of pelf,
Each does but hate his neighbour as himself:
Damn'd to the mines, an equal fate betides
The slave that digs it, and the slave that hides.
B. Who suffer thus, mere charity should own,
Must act on motives powerful, though unknown.
P. Some war, some plague, or famine, they foresee,
Some revelation hid from you and me.
Why Shylock wants a meal, the cause is found,
He thinks a loaf will rise to fifty pound.
What made directors cheat in South-Sea year?
To live on venison when it sold so dear.
Ask you why Phryne the whole auction buys?
Phryne foresees a general excise.[2]
Why she and Sappho raise that monstrous sum?
Alas! they fear a man will cost a plum.
Wise Peter[3] sees the world's respect for gold,
And therefore hopes this nation may be sold:

[1] This epistle was written in the year 1730, when a corporation was established to lend money to the poor upon pledges, by the name of the *Charitable Corporation*; but the whole was turned only to an iniquitous method of enriching particular people, to the ruin of such numbers, that it became a parliamentary-concern to endeavour the relief of those unhappy sufferers; and three of the managers, who were members of the House, were expelled. By the report of the Committee appointed to inquire into that iniquitous affair, it appears, that when it was objected to the intended removal of the office, that the poor, for whose use it was erected, would be hurt by it, Bond, one of the directors, replied, *Damn the poor!* That "God hates the poor," and, "that every man in want is either knave or fool," &c., were the genuine apophthegms of some of the persons here mentioned.

[2] Many people, about the year 1733, had a conceit that such a thing was intended, of which it is not improbable this lady might have some intimation.

[3] Peter Walter, a person not only eminent in the wisdom of his profession, as a dexterous attorney, but allowed to be a good, if not a safe, conveyancer; extremely respected by the nobility of this land, though free from all manner of luxury and ostentation: his wealth was never

Glorious ambition! Peter, swell thy store,
And be what Rome's great Didius[1] was before.
The crown of Poland,[2] venal twice an age,
To just three millions stinted modest Gage;
But nobler scenes Maria's dreams unfold,
Hereditary realms, and worlds of gold:
Congenial souls, whose life one avarice joins,
And one fate buries in the Asturian mines.
Much injured Blunt![3] why bears he Britain's hate?
A wizard told him in these words our fate:
"At length corruption, like a general flood,
(So long by watchful ministers withstood)
Shall deluge all; and avarice creeping on,
Spread like a low-born mist, and blot the sun;
Statesman and patriot ply alike the stocks,
Peeress and butler share alike the box,
And judges job, and bishops bite the town,
And mighty dukes pack cards for half-a-crown.
See Britain sunk in lucre's sordid charms,
And France revenged on ANNE's and EDWARD's arms!"
'Twas no court-badge, great scrivener! fired thy brain,
Nor lordly luxury, nor city gain:
No, 'twas thy righteous end, ashamed to see
Senates degenerate, patriots disagree,

seen, and his bounty never heard of, except to his own son, for whom he procured an employment of considerable profit, of which he gave him as much as was *necessary*. Therefore the taxing this gentleman with any ambition, is certainly a great wrong to him.

[1] A Roman lawyer, so rich as to purchase the empire when it was set to sale upon the death of Pertinax.

[2] The two persons here mentioned were of quality, each of whom in the Mississippi despised to realize above *three hundred thousand pounds;* the gentleman with a view to the purchase of the crown of Poland, the lady on a vision of the like royal nature. They afterwards retired into Spain, in search of gold in the mines of the Asturias.

[3] Sir John Blunt, originally a scrivener, was one of the first projectors of the South-Sea company, and afterwards one of the directors and chief managers of the famous scheme in 1720. He was also one of those who suffered most severely by the bill of pains and penalties on the said directors. He was a dissenter of a most religious deportment, and professed to be a great believer. Whether he did really credit the prophecy here mentioned is not certain, but it was constantly in this very style he declaimed against the corruption and luxury of the age, the partiality of parliaments, and the misery of party-spirit. He was particularly eloquent against *avarice* in great and noble persons, of which he had indeed lived to see many miserable examples. He died in the year 1732.

And nobly wishing party-rage to cease,
To buy both sides, and give thy country peace.
"All this is madness," cries a sober sage:
But who, my friend, has reason in his rage?
"The ruling passion, be it what it will,
The ruling passion conquers reason still."
Less mad the wildest whimsey we can frame,
Than even that passion, if it has no aim;
For though such motives folly you may call,
The folly's greater to have none at all.
Hear then the truth: "'Tis Heaven each passion sends,
And different men directs to different ends.
Extremes in nature equal good produce,
Extremes in man concur to general use."
Ask me what makes one keep, and one bestow?
That Power who bids the ocean ebb and flow,
Bids seed-time, harvest, equal course maintain,
Through reconciled extremes of drought and rain,
Builds life on death, on change duration founds,
And gives the eternal wheels to know their rounds.
Riches, like insects, when conceal'd they lie,
Wait but for wings, and in their season fly.
Who sees pale Mammon pine amidst his store,
Sees but a backward steward for the poor;
This year a reservoir, to keep and spare:
The next, a fountain, spouting through his heir,
In lavish streams to quench a country's thirst,
And men and dogs shall drink him till they burst.
Old Cotta shamed his fortune and his birth,
Yet was not Cotta void of wit or worth:
What though (the use of barbarous spits forgot)
His kitchen vied in coolness with his grot?
His court with nettles, moats with cresses stored,
With soups unbought and salads bless'd his board?
If Cotta lived on pulse, it was no more
Than Brahmins, saints, and sages, did before;
To cram the rich with prodigal expense,
And who would take the poor from Providence?
Like some lone Chartreux stands the good old hall,
Silence without, and fasts within the wall;
No rafter'd roofs with dance and tabor sound,
No noontide bell invites the country round:
Tenants with sighs the smokeless towers survey,
And turn the unwilling steeds another way:

Benighted wanderers, the forest o'er,
Curse the saved candle, and unopening door,
While the gaunt mastiff, growling at the gate,
Affrights the beggar whom he longs to eat.
Not so his son; he mark'd this oversight,
And then mistook reverse of wrong for right.
(For what to shun will no great knowledge need,
But what to follow, is a task indeed.)
Yet sure, of qualities deserving praise,
More go to ruin fortunes, than to raise.
What slaughter'd hecatombs, what floods of wine,
Fill the capacious 'squire, and deep divine!
Yet no mean motive this profusion draws,
His oxen perish in his country's cause;
'Tis George and Liberty that crowns the cup,
And zeal for that great house which eats him up.
The woods recede around the naked seat,
The silvans groan—no matter—for the fleet:
Next goes his wool—to clothe our valiant bands;
Last, for his country's love, he sells his lands.
To town he comes, completes the nation's hope,
And heads the bold train-bands, and burns a pope.
And shall not Britain now regard his toils,
Britain, that pays her patriots with her spoils?
In vain at court the bankrupt pleads his cause,
His thankless country leaves him to her laws.
The sense to value riches, with the art
To enjoy them, and the virtue to impart,
Not meanly, nor ambitiously pursued,
Not sunk by sloth, nor raised by servitude;
To balance fortune by a just expense,
Join with economy, magnificence;
With splendour, charity; with plenty, health;
Oh teach us, Bathurst! yet unspoil'd by wealth!
That secret rare, between the extremes to move
Of mad good-nature, and of mean self-love.
B. To worth or want well weigh'd be bounty given,
And ease, or emulate, the care of Heaven;
(Whose measure full o'erflows on human race;)
Mend fortune's fault, and justify her grace.
Wealth in the gross is death, but life diffused;
As poison heals, in just proportion used:
In heaps, like ambergrise, a stink it lies,
But well dispersed, is incense to the skies.

p. 275.

MORAL ESSAYS.

Is any sick? the Man of Ross relieves,
Prescribes, attends, the medicine makes and gives.

P. Who starves by nobles, or with nobles eats?
The wretch that trusts them, and the rogue that cheats.
Is there a lord, who knows a cheerful noon
Without a fiddler, flatterer, or buffoon?
Whose table, wit, or modest merit share,
Un-elbow'd by a gamester, pimp, or player?
Who copies yours, or OXFORD's better part,
To ease the oppress'd, and raise the sinking heart?
Where'er he shines, O Fortune! gild the scene,
And angels guard him in the golden mean!
There, English bounty yet awhile may stand,
And honour linger ere it leaves the land.
But all our praises why should lords engross?
Rise, honest muse! and sing the MAN of Ross:[1]
Pleased Vaga echoes through her winding bounds,
And rapid Severn hoarse applause resounds.
Who hung with woods yon mountain's sultry brow?
From the dry rock who bade the waters flow?
Not to the skies in useless columns toss'd,
Or in proud falls magnificently lost,
But clear and artless, pouring through the plain
Health to the sick, and solace to the swain.
Whose causeway parts the vale with shady rows?
Whose seats the weary traveller repose?
Who taught that heaven-directed spire to rise?
"The MAN of Ross!" each lisping babe replies.
Behold the market-place with poor o'erspread!
The MAN of Ross divides the weekly bread;
He feeds yon alms-house, neat, but void of state,
Where age and want sit smiling at the gate:
Him portion'd maids, apprenticed orphans bless'd,
The young who labour, and the old who rest.
Is any sick? the MAN of Ross relieves,
Prescribes, attends, the medicine makes, and gives.
Is there a variance? enter but his door,
Balk'd are the courts, and contest is no more.
Despairing quacks with curses fled the place,
And vile attorneys, now a useless race.

[1] The person here celebrated, who with a small estate actually performed all these good works, and whose true name was almost lost (partly by the title of *The Man of Ross*, given him by way of eminence, and partly by being buried without so much as an inscription), was called Mr. John Kyrle. He died in the year 1724, aged 90, and lies interred in the chancel of the church of Ross in Herefordshire.

B. Thrice happy man! enabled to pursue
What all so wish, but want the power to do!
Oh say, what sums that generous hand supply?
What mines, to swell that boundless charity?
P. Of debts, and taxes, wife and children clear,
This man possess'd——five hundred pounds a-year.
Blush, grandeur, blush; proud courts, withdraw your blaze!
Ye little stars! hide your diminish'd rays.
B. And what? no monument, inscription, stone?
His race, his form, his name almost unknown?
P. Who builds a church to God, and not to Fame,
Will never mark the marble with his name:
Go, search it there, where to be born and die,
Of rich and poor, makes all the history;
Enough, that virtue fill'd the space between;
Proved, by the ends of being, to have been.
When Hopkins dies, a thousand lights attend
The wretch, who living saved a candle's end:
Shouldering God's altar a vile image stands,
Belies his features, nay, extends his hands;
That live-long wig which Gorgon's self might own,
Eternal buckle takes in Parian stone.
Behold what blessings wealth to life can lend!
And see, what comfort it affords our end.
In the worst inn's worst room, with mat half-hung,
The floors of plaster, and the walls of dung,
On once a flock-bed, but repair'd with straw,
With tape-tied curtains, never meant to draw,
The George and Garter dangling from that bed
Where tawdry yellow strove with dirty red,
Great Villiers lies[1]—alas! how changed from him,
That life of pleasure, and that soul of whim!

[1] This duke, yet more famous for his vices than his misfortunes, having been possessed of about 50,000*l.* a-year, and passed through many of the highest posts in the kingdom, died in the year 1687.

[This picture of destitution is greatly exaggerated. The Duke of Buckingham had not reduced himself to beggary, nor did he breathe his last "in the worst inn's worst room." He had retired to his seat at Helmsley, in Yorkshire, and died at the house of a tenant, at Kirby Moorside, after a few days' fever, produced by sitting on the damp ground when heated by a fox-chase. Dryden, in the character of Zimri, in Absalom and Achitophel, has drawn the duke's portrait much more faithfully.]

Gallant and gay, in Cliefden's[1] proud alcove,
The bower of wanton Shrewsbury[2] and love;
Or just as gay, at council, in a ring
Of mimic statesmen, and their merry king.
No wit to flatter, left of all his store!
No fool to laugh at, which he valued more.
There, victor of his health, of fortune, friends,
And fame; this lord of useless thousands ends.
His Grace's fate sage Cutler could foresee,
And well (he thought) advised him, "Live like me."
As well his Grace replied, "Like you, Sir John?
That I can do, when all I have is gone."
Resolve me, Reason, which of these is worse,
Want with a full, or with an empty purse?
Thy life more wretched, Cutler, was confess'd,
Arise, and tell me, was thy death more bless'd?
Cutler saw tenants break, and houses fall,
For very want; he could not build a wall.
His only daughter in a stranger's power,
For very want; he could not pay a dower.
A few grey hairs his reverend temples crown'd,
'Twas very want that sold them for two pound.
What, e'en denied a cordial at his end,
Banish'd the doctor, and expell'd the friend?
What but a want, which you perhaps think mad,
Yet numbers feel, the want of what he had!
Cutler and Brutus, dying, both exclaim,
"Virtue! and wealth! what are ye but a name!"
Say, for such worth are other worlds prepared?
Or are they both, in this, their own reward?
A knotty point! to which we now proceed.
But you are tired—I'll tell a tale.—B. Agreed.
P. Where London's column,[3] pointing at the skies
Like a tall bully, lifts the head, and lies;
There dwelt a citizen of sober fame,
A plain good man, and Balaam was his name;

[1] A delightful palace, on the banks of the Thames, built by the Duke of Buckingham.

[2] The Countess of Shrewsbury, a woman abandoned to gallantries. The earl, her husband, was killed by the Duke of Buckingham in a duel; and it has been said, that during the combat she held the duke's horses in the habit of a page.

[3] The Monument, built in memory of the Great Fire of London, with an inscription importing that city to have been burnt by the papists. This inscription has since been erased.

Religious, punctual, frugal, and so forth;
His word would pass for more than he was worth.
One solid dish his week-day meal affords,
An added pudding solemnized the Lord's:
Constant at church, and 'Change; his gains were sure
His givings rare, save farthings to the poor.
The devil was piqued such saintship to behold,
And long'd to tempt him like good Job of old:
But Satan now is wiser than of yore,
And tempts by making rich, not making poor.
Roused by the prince of air, the whirlwinds sweep
The surge, and plunge his father in the deep;
Then full against his Cornish lands they roar,
And two rich shipwrecks bless the lucky shore.
Sir Balaam now, he lives like other folks,
He takes his chirping pint, and cracks his jokes:
"Live like yourself," was soon my lady's word;
And lo! two puddings smoked upon the board.
Asleep and naked as an Indian lay,
An honest factor stole a gem away:
He pledged it to the knight; the knight had wit,
So kept the diamond, and the rogue was bit.
Some scruple rose, but thus he eased his thought,
"I'll now give sixpence where I gave a groat;
Where once I went to church, I'll now go twice—
And am so clear too of all other vice."
The tempter saw his time; the work he plied;
Stocks and subscriptions pour on every side,
Till all the demon makes his full descent
In one abundant shower of cent. per cent.,
Sinks deep within him, and possesses whole,
Then dubs director, and secures his soul.
Behold Sir Balaam, now a man of spirit,
Ascribes his gettings to his parts and merit;
What late he call'd a blessing, now was wit,
And God's good providence a lucky hit.
Things change their titles as our manners turn:
His counting-house employ'd the Sunday morn;
Seldom at church ('twas such a busy life),
But duly sent his family and wife.
There (so the devil ordain'd) one Christmas-tide
My good old lady catch'd a cold, and died.
A nymph of quality admires our knight;
He marries, bows at court, and grows polite:

Leaves the dull cits, and joins (to please the fair)
The well-bred cuckolds in St. James's air:
First, for his son a gay commission buys,
Who drinks, whores, fights, and in a duel dies:
His daughter flaunts a viscount's tawdry wife;
She bears a coronet and pox for life.
In Britain's senate he a seat obtains,
And one more pensioner St. Stephen gains.
My lady falls to play; so bad her chance,
He must repair it; takes a bribe from France;
The House impeach him; Coningsby harangues;
The court forsake him, and Sir Balaam hangs:
Wife, son, and daughter, Satan! are thy own,
His wealth, yet dearer, forfeit to the crown:
The devil and the king divide the prize,
And sad Sir Balaam curses God and dies.

EPISTLE IV.

TO RICHARD BOYLE, EARL OF BURLINGTON.

ARGUMENT.

OF THE USE OF RICHES.

The vanity of expense in people of wealth and quality. The abuse of the word *taste*. That the first principle and foundation in this, as in everything else, is *good sense*. The chief proof of it is to *follow nature*, even in works of mere luxury and elegance. Instanced in *architecture* and *gardening*, where all must be adapted to the *genius* and *use* of the *place*, and the beauties not forced into it, but resulting from it. How men are disappointed in their most expensive undertakings, for want of this true foundation, without which nothing can please *long*, if *at all*; and the best *examples* and *rules* will be but perverted into something *burdensome* and *ridiculous*. A description of the *false taste* of *magnificence*; the first grand error of which is to imagine that *greatness* consists in the *size* and *dimension*, instead of the *proportion* and *harmony* of the *whole*, and the second, either in joining together *parts incoherent*, or too *minutely resembling*, or in the *repetition* of the *same* too frequently. A word or two of false taste in *books*, in *music*, in *painting*, even in *preaching* and *prayer*, and lastly in *entertainments*. Yet PROVIDENCE is justified in giving wealth to be squandered in this manner, since it is dispersed to the poor and laborious part of mankind (recurring to what is laid down in the first book, Ep. ii. and in the epistle preceding this). What are the *proper objects* of magnificence, and a proper field for the expense of *great* men, and finally, the great and public works which become a *prince*.

'Tis strange, the miser should his cares employ
To gain those riches he can ne'er enjoy:
Is it less strange, the prodigal should waste
His wealth, to purchase what he ne'er can taste?
Not for himself he sees, or hears, or eats;
Artists must choose his pictures, music, meats:
He buys for Topham,[1] drawings and designs,
For Pembroke, statues, dirty gods, and coins;
Rare monkish manuscripts for Hearne alone,
And books for Mead, and butterflies for Sloane.[2]
Think we all these are for himself? no more
Than his fine wife, alas! or finer whore.
  For what has Virro painted, built, and planted?
Only to show how many tastes he wanted.
What brought Sir Visto's ill-got wealth to waste?
Some demon whisper'd, "Visto! have a taste."
Heaven visits with a taste the wealthy fool,
And needs no rod but Ripley[3] with a rule.
See! sportive fate, to punish awkward pride,
Bids Bubo build, and sends him such a guide:
A standing sermon, at each year's expense,
That never coxcomb reach'd magnificence!
  You show us, Rome was glorious, not profuse,[4]
And pompous buildings once were things of use.
Yet shall (my lord) your just, your noble rules,
Fill half the land with imitating fools;
Who random drawings from your sheets shall take,
And of one beauty many blunders make;
Load some vain church with old theatric state,
Turn arcs of triumph to a garden-gate;
Reverse your ornaments; and hang them all
On some patch'd dog-hole eked with ends of wall;
Then clap four slices of pilaster on't,
That, laced with bits of rustic, makes a front:

1 A gentleman famous for a judicious collection of drawings.

2 Two eminent physicians: the one had an excellent library, the other the finest collection in Europe of natural curiosities; both men of great learning and humanity.

3 This man was a carpenter, employed by a first minister, who raised him to an architect, without any genius in the art; and after some wretched proofs of his insufficiency in public buildings, made him comptroller of the board of works.

4 The Earl of Burlington was then publishing the designs of Inigo Jones, and the antiquities of Rome by Palladio.

Shall call the winds through long arcades to roar,
Proud to catch cold at a Venetian door;
Conscious they act a true Palladian part,
And if they starve, they starve by rules of art.
Oft have you hinted to your brother peer,
A certain truth, which many buy too dear:
Something there is more needful than expense,
And something previous e'en to taste—'tis sense:
Good sense, which only is the gift of Heaven,
And though no science, fairly worth the seven:
A light, which in yourself you must perceive;
Jones and Le Nôtre have it not to give.
To build, to plant, whatever you intend,
To rear the column, or the arch to bend,
To swell the terrace, or to sink the grot;
In all, let nature never be forgot.
But treat the goddess like a modest fair,
Nor over-dress, nor leave her wholly bare;
Let not each beauty everywhere be spied,
Where half the skill is decently to hide.
He gains all points who pleasingly confounds,
Surprises, varies, and conceals the bounds.
Consult the genius of the place in all;
That tells the waters or to rise or fall;
Or helps the ambitious hill the heavens to scale,
Or scoops in circling theatres the vale:
Calls in the country, catches opening glades,
Joins willing woods, and varies shades from shades;
Now breaks, or now directs, the intending lines;
Paints as you plant, and, as you work, designs.
Still follow sense, of every art the soul,
Parts answering parts shall slide into a whole,
Spontaneous beauties all around advance,
Start even from difficulty, strike from chance;
Nature shall join you; Time shall make it grow
A work to wonder at—perhaps a STOWE.[1]
Without it, proud Versailles! thy glory falls;
And Nero's terraces desert their walls:
The vast parterres a thousand hands shall make,
Lo! COBHAM comes, and floats them with a lake:

[1] The seat and gardens of the Lord Viscount Cobham, in Buckinghamshire; now possessed by the Duke of Buckingham.

Or cut wide views through mountains to the plain,
You'll wish your hill or shelter'd seat again.[1]
Even in an ornament its place remark,
Nor in an hermitage set Dr. Clarke.[2]
Behold Villario's ten-years' toil complete;
His quincunx darkens, his espaliers meet;
The wood supports the plain, the parts unite,
And strength of shade contends with strength of light;
A waving glow the bloomy beds display,
Blushing in bright diversities of day,
With silver-quivering rills meander'd o'er-
Enjoy them, you! Villario can no more;
Tired of the scene parterres and fountains yield,
He finds, at last, he better likes a field.
Through his young woods how pleased Sabinus stray'd,
Or sat delighted in the thickening shade,
With annual joy the reddening shoots to greet,
Or see the stretching branches long to meet!
His son's fine taste an opening vista loves,
Foe to the dryads of his father's groves;
One boundless green, or flourish'd carpet views,
With all the mournful family of yews;
The thriving plants, ignoble broomsticks made,
Now sweep those alleys they were born to shade.
At Timon's villa let us pass a day,
Where all cry out, "What sums are thrown away!"
So proud, so grand; of that stupendous air,
Soft and agreeable come never there.
Greatness, with Timon, dwells in such a draught
As brings all Brobdignag before your thought.
To compass this, his building is a town,
His pond an ocean, his parterre a down:
Who but must laugh, the master when he sees,
A puny insect, shivering at a breeze!
Lo, what huge heaps of littleness around!
The whole, a labour'd quarry above ground.
Two cupids squirt before: a lake behind
Improves the keenness of the northern wind.

[1] This was done in Hertfordshire by a wealthy citizen, at the expense of above five thousand pounds, by which means (merely to overlook a dead plain) he let in the north wind upon his house and parterre, which were before adorned and defended by beautiful woods.

[2] Dr. S. Clarke's busto, placed by the queen in the hermitage, while the doctor duly frequented the court.

His gardens next your admiration call,
On every side you look, behold the wall!
No pleasing intricacies intervene,
No artful wildness to perplex the scene;
Grove nods at grove, each alley has a brother,
And half the platform just reflects the other.
The suffering eye inverted nature sees,
Trees cut to statues, statues thick as trees;
With here a fountain, never to be play'd;
And there a summer-house, that knows no shade;
Here Amphitrite sails through myrtle bowers;
There gladiators fight, or die in flowers;
Unwater'd see the drooping sea-horse mourn,
And swallows roost in Nilus' dusty urn.
  My Lord advances with majestic mien,
Smit with the mighty pleasure, to be seen:
But soft—by regular approach—not yet—
First through the length of yon hot terrace sweat;
And when up ten steep slopes you've dragg'd your thighs,
Just at his study-door he'll bless your eyes.
  His study! with what authors is it stored?
In books, not authors, curious is my lord;
To all their dated backs he turns you round;
These Aldus printed, those Du Suëil has bound!
Lo, some are vellum, and the rest as good
For all his lordship knows, but they are wood.
For Locke or Milton 'tis in vain to look,
These shelves admit not any modern book.
  And now the chapel's silver bell you hear,
That summons you to all the pride of pray'r:
Light quirks of music, broken and uneven,
Make the soul dance upon a jig to Heaven.
On painted ceilings you devoutly stare,
Where sprawl the saints of Verrio or Laguerre,[1]
On gilded clouds in fair expansion lie,
And bring all paradise before your eye.
To rest, the cushion and soft dean invite,
Who never mentions hell to ears polite.[2]

[1] Verrio (Antonio) painted many ceilings, &c., at Windsor, Hampton Court, &c., and Laguerre at Blenheim Castle, and other places.

[2] This is a fact. A reverend dean, preaching at court, threatened the sinner with punishment in "a place which he thought it not decent to name in so polite an assembly."

But hark! the chiming clocks to dinner call;
A hundred footsteps scrape the marble hall:
The rich buffet well-colour'd serpents grace,
And gaping Tritons spew to wash your face.
Is this a dinner? this a genial room;
No, 'tis a temple, and a hecatomb.
A solemn sacrifice, perform'd in state,
You drink by measure, and to minutes eat.
So quick retires each flying course, you'd swear
Sancho's dread doctor and his wand were there.
Between each act the trembling salvers ring,
From soup to sweet wine, and God bless the king.
In plenty starving, tantalized in state,
And complaisantly help'd to all I hate,
Treated, caress'd, and tired, I take my leave,
Sick of his civil pride from morn to eve;
I curse such lavish cost, and little skill,
And swear no day was ever pass'd so ill.
Yet hence the poor are clothed, the hungry fed;[1]
Health to himself, and to his infants bread
The labourer bears: what his hard heart denies,
His charitable vanity supplies.
Another age shall see the golden ear
Imbrown the slope, and nod on the parterre,
Deep harvests bury all his pride has plann'd,
And laughing Ceres re-assume the land.
Who then shall grace, or who improve the soil?
Who plants like BATHURST, or who builds like BOYLE.
'Tis use alone that sanctifies expense,
And splendour borrows all her rays from sense.
His father's acres who enjoys in peace,
Or makes his neighbours glad if he increase:
Whose cheerful tenants bless their yearly toil,
Yet to their lord owe more than to the soil;
Whose ample lawns are not ashamed to feed
The milky heifer, and deserving steed;
Whose rising forests, not for pride or show,
But future buildings, future navies grow:
Let his plantations stretch from down to down,
First shade a country, and then raise a town.

[1] This is the *moral* of the whole; where Providence is justified in giving riches to those who squander them in this manner. A bad taste employs more hands, and diffuses wealth more usefully than a good one.

You too proceed! make falling arts your care,
Erect new wonders, and the old repair;
Jones and Palladio to themselves restore,
And be whate'er Vitruvius was before:
Till kings call forth the ideas of your mind,
(Proud to accomplish what such hands design'd)
Bid harbours open, public ways extend,
Bid temples worthier of the God ascend,
Bid the broad arch the dangerous flood contain,
The mole projected break the roaring main;
Back to his bounds their subject sea command,
And roll obedient rivers through the land:
These honours, peace to happy BRITAIN brings,
These are imperial works, and worthy kings.

EPISTLE V.

TO MR. ADDISON.

OCCASIONED BY HIS DIALOGUES ON MEDALS.

This was originally written in the year 1715, when Mr. Addison intended to publish his book of medals; it was some time before he was Secretary of State; but not published till Mr. Tickell's edition of his works: at which time the verses on Mr. Craggs, which conclude the poem, were added, viz., in 1720.

SEE the wild waste of all-devouring years!
How Rome her own sad sepulchre appears!
With nodding arches, broken temples spread!
The very tombs now vanish'd like their dead!
Imperial wonders raised on nations spoil'd,
Where, mix'd with slaves, the groaning martyr toil'd:
Huge theatres, that now unpeopled woods,
Now drain'd a distant country of her floods:
Fanes, which admiring gods with pride survey
Statues of men, scarce less alive than they!
Some felt the silent stroke of mouldering age,
Some hostile fury, some religious rage.
Barbarian blindness, Christian zeal conspire,
And Papal piety, and Gothic fire.

Perhaps, by its own ruins saved from flame,
Some buried marble half preserves a name;
That name the learn'd with fierce disputes pursue,
And give to Titus old Vespasian's due.
Ambition sigh'd: she found it vain to trust
The faithless column, and the crumbling bust:
Huge moles, whose shadow stretch'd from shore to shore
Their ruins perish'd, and their place no more!
Convinced, she now contracts her vast design,
And all her triumphs shrink into a coin.
A narrow ORB each crowded conquest keeps,
Beneath her palm here sad Judea weeps.
Now scantier limits the proud arch confine,
And scarce are seen the prostrate Nile or Rhine;
A small Euphrates through the piece is roll'd,
And little eagles wave their wings in gold.
The medal, faithful to its charge of fame,
Through climes and ages bears each form and name:
In one short view, subjected to our eye,
Gods, emperors, heroes, sages, beauties, lie.
With sharpen'd sight, pale antiquaries pore,
The inscription value, but the rust adore.
This the blue varnish, that the green endears,
The sacred rust of twice ten hundred years!
To gain Pescennius one employs his schemes,
One grasps a Cecrops in ecstatic dreams.
Poor Vadius, long with learned spleen devour'd,
Can taste no pleasure since his shield was scour'd:
And Curio, restless by the fair one's side,
Sighs for an Otho, and neglects his bride.
Theirs is the vanity, the learning thine:
Touch'd by thy hand, again Rome's glories shine;
Her gods, and godlike heroes rise to view,
And all her faded garlands bloom anew.
Nor blush, these studies thy regard engage;
These pleased the fathers of poetic rage;
The verse and sculpture bore an equal part,
And art reflected images to art.
Oh when shall Britain, conscious of her claim,
Stand emulous of Greek and Roman fame?
In living medals see her wars enroll'd,
And vanquish'd realms supply recording gold?
Here, rising bold, the patriot's honest face;
There warriors frowning in historic brass:

Then future ages with delight shall see
How Plato's, Bacon's, Newton's looks agree;
Or in fair series laurell'd bards be shown,
A Virgil there, and here an Addison.
Then shall thy Craggs (and let me call him mine)
On the cast ore, another Pollio, shine;
With aspect open, shall erect his head,
And round the orb in lasting notes be read,
"Statesman, yet friend to truth! of soul sincere,
In action faithful, and in honour clear;
Who broke no promise, served no private end,
Who gain'd no title, and who lost no friend;
Ennobled by himself, by all approved,
And praised, unenvied, by the muse he loved."

EPISTLE TO DR. ARBUTHNOT,

BEING

THE PROLOGUE TO THE SATIRES.

ADVERTISEMENT.

This paper is a sort of bill of complaint, begun many years since, and drawn up by snatches, as the several occasions offered. I had no thoughts of publishing it, till it pleased some persons of rank and fortune (the authors of *Verses to the Imitator of Horace*, and of an *Epistle to a Doctor of Divinity from a Nobleman at Hampton-court*) to attack, in a very extraordinary manner, not only my writings (of which, being public, the public is judge), but my *person*, *morals*, and *family*, whereof, to those who know me not, a truer information may be requisite. Being divided between the necessity to say something of *myself*, and my own laziness to undertake so awkward a task, I thought it the shortest way to put the last hand to this epistle. If it have anything pleasing, it will be that by which I am most desirous to please, the *truth*, and the *sentiment*; and if anything offensive, it will be only to those I am least sorry to offend, *the vicious*, or *the ungenerous*.

Many will know their own pictures in it, there being not a circumstance but what is true; but I have for the most part spared their *names*, and they may escape being laughed at, if they please.

I would have some of them know, it was owing to the request of the learned and candid friend to whom it is inscribed, that I make not as free use of theirs, as they have done of mine. However, I shall have this advantage and honour on my side, that whereas, by their proceeding, any abuse may be directed at any man, no injury can possibly be done by mine, since a nameless character can never be found out, but by its *truth* and *li*[illegible].

P. SHUT, shut the door, good John! fatigued I said,
Tie up the knocker, say I'm sick, I'm dead.
The Dog-star rages! nay, 'tis past a doubt,
All Bedlam, or Parnassus, is let out:
Fire in each eye, and papers in each hand,
They rave, recite, and madden round the land.
What walls can guard me, or what shades can hide?
They pierce my thickets, through my grot they glide,
By land, by water, they renew the charge,
They stop the chariot, and they board the barge.
No place is sacred, not the church is free,
Even Sunday shines no Sabbath-day to me:
Then from the Mint walks forth the man of rhyme,
Happy! to catch me, just at dinner-time.
Is there a parson much be-mused in beer,
A maudlin poetess, a rhyming peer,
A clerk, foredoom'd his father's soul to cross,
Who pens a stanza, when he should engross?
Is there, who, lock'd from ink and paper, scrawls
With desperate charcoal round his darken'd walls?
All fly to TWIC'NAM, and in humble strain
Apply to me, to keep them mad or vain.
Arthur, whose giddy son neglects the laws,
Imputes to me and my damn'd works the cause:
Poor Cornus sees his frantic wife elope,
And curses wit, and poetry, and Pope.
Friend to my life! (which did not you prolong,
The world had wanted many an idle song)
What *drop* or *nostrum* can this plague remove?
Or which must end me, a fool's wrath or love?
A dire dilemma! either way I'm sped,
If foes, they write,—if friends, they read me dead.
Seized and tied down to judge, how wretched I!
Who can't be silent, and who will not lie:
To laugh, were want of goodness and of grace,
And to be grave, exceeds all power of face.
I sit with sad civility, I read
With honest anguish, and an aching head;
And drop at last, but in unwilling ears,
This saving counsel, "Keep your piece nine years."
Nine years! cries he, who high in Drury-lane,
Lull'd by soft zephyrs through the broken pane,
Rhymes ere he wakes, and prints before Term ends,
Obliged by hunger, and request of friends

"The piece, you think, is incorrect? why take it,
I'm all submission, what you'd have it, make it."
Three things another's modest wishes bound,
My friendship and a prologue, and ten pound.
Pitholeon sends to me: "You know his Grace,
I want a patron; ask him for a place."
Pitholeon libell'd me—"but here's a letter
Informs you, sir, 'twas when he knew no better.
Dare you refuse him? Curl invites to dine,
He'll write a *journal*, or he'll turn divine."
Bless me! a packet.—"'Tis a stranger sues,
A virgin tragedy, an orphan muse."
If I dislike it, "Furies, death, and rage!"
If I approve, "Commend it to the stage."
There (thank my stars) my whole commission ends,
The players and I are, luckily, no friends.
Fired that the house reject him, "'Sdeath, I'll print it,
And shame the fools—Your interest, sir, with Lintot."
Lintot, dull rogue! will think your price too much:
"Not, sir, if you revise it, and retouch."
All my demurs but double his attacks;
At last he whispers, "Do; and we go snacks."
Glad of a quarrel, straight I clap the door,
Sir, let me see your works and you no more.
'Tis sung, when Midas' ears began to spring,
(Midas, a sacred person and a king),
His very minister who spied them first
(Some say his queen) was forced to speak or burst.
And is not mine, my friend, a sorer case,
When every coxcomb perks them in my face?
A. Good friend, forbear! you deal in dang'rous things.
I'd never name queens, ministers, or kings;
Keep close to ears, and those let asses prick,
'Tis nothing—P. Nothing? if they bite and kick?
Out with it, DUNCIAD! let the secret pass,
That secret to each fool, that he's an ass;
The truth once told (and wherefore should we lie?)
The queen of Midas slept, and so may I.
You think this cruel? take it for a rule,
No creature smarts so little as a fool.
Let peals of laughter, Codrus! round thee break,
Thou unconcern'd canst hear the mighty crack:
Pit, box, and gallery in convulsions hurl'd,
Thou stand'st unshook amidst a bursting world.

Who shames a scribbler? break one cobweb through,
He spins the slight, self-pleasing thread anew:
Destroy his fib, or sophistry, in vain,
The creature's at his dirty work again,
Throned in the centre of his thin designs,
Proud of a vast extent of flimsy lines!
Whom have I hurt? has poet yet, or peer,
Lost the arch'd eyebrow, or Parnassian sneer?
And has not Colley still his lord, and whore?
His butchers Henley, his freemasons Moore?
Does not one table Bavius still admit?
Still to one bishop Philips seem a wit?
Still Sappho—A. Hold! for God's sake—you'll offend,
No names—be calm—learn prudence of a friend:
I too could write, and I am twice as tall;
But foes like these—P. One flatterer's worse than all.
Of all mad creatures, if the learn'd are right,
It is the slaver kills, and not the bite.
A fool quite angry is quite innocent,
Alas! 'tis ten times worse when they *repent.*
  One dedicates in high heroic prose,
And ridicules beyond a hundred foes:
One from all Grub-street will my fame defend,
And, more abusive, calls himself my friend.
This prints my *Letters*, that expects a bribe,
And others roar aloud, "Subscribe, subscribe."
  There are, who to my person pay their court:
I cough like *Horace*, and, though lean, am short;
Ammon's great son one shoulder had too high,
Such *Ovid's* nose, and "Sir! you have an eye."—
Go on, obliging creatures, make me see,
All that disgraced my betters, met in me.
Say for my comfort, languishing in bed,
"Just so immortal *Maro* held his head:"
And when I die, be sure you let me know
Great *Homer* died three thousand years ago.
  Why did I write? what sin to me unknown
Dipp'd me in ink, my parents', or my own?
As yet a child, nor yet a fool to fame,
I lisp'd in numbers, for the numbers came.
I left no calling for this idle trade,
No duty broke, no father disobey'd.
The muse but served to ease some friend, not wife,
To help me through this long disease, my life,

To second, ARBUTHNOT! thy art and care,
And teach, the being you preserved, to bear.
A. But why then publish? P. *Granville* the polite,
And knowing *Walsh*, would tell me I could write;
Well-natured *Garth* inflamed with early praise,
And *Congreve* loved, and *Swift* endured my lays;
The courtly *Talbot*, *Somers*, *Sheffield* read,
Even mitred *Rochester* would nod the head,
And *St. John's*[1] self (great *Dryden's* friends before)
With open arms received one poet more.
Happy my studies, when by these approved!
Happier their author, when by these beloved!
From these the world will judge of men and books
Not from the *Burnets*, *Oldmixons*, and *Cooks*.[2]
Soft were my numbers; who could take offence
While pure description held the place of sense?
Like gentle *Fanny's* was my flowery theme,
A painted mistress, or a purling stream.
Yet then did *Gildon* draw his venal quill;
I wish'd the man a dinner, and sate still.
Yet then did *Dennis* rave in furious fret;
I never answer'd, I was not in debt.
If want provoked, or madness made them print,
I waged no war with *Bedlam* or the *Mint*.
Did some more sober critic come abroad;
If wrong, I smiled; if right, I kiss'd the rod.
Pains, reading, study, are their just pretence,
And all they want is spirit, taste, and sense.
Commas and points they set exactly right,
And 'twere a sin to rob them of their mite.
Yet ne'er one sprig of laurel graced these ribalds,
From slashing *Bentley* down to piddling *Tibbalds:*
Each wight who reads not, and but scans and spells.
Each word-catcher that lives on syllables,
Even such small critics some regard may claim,
Preserved in *Milton's* or in *Shakspeare's* name.

1 All these were patrons or admirers of Mr. Dryden; though a scandalous libel against him, entitled *Dryden's Satire to his Muse*, has been printed in the name of the Lord Somers, of which he was wholly ignorant.

These are the persons to whose account the author charges the publication of his first pieces: persons with whom he was conversant (and he adds beloved) at sixteen or seventeen years of age; an early period for such acquaintance.

2 Authors of secret and scandalous history.

Pretty! in amber to observe the forms
Of hairs, or straws, or dirt, or grubs, or worms!
The things, we know, are neither rich nor rare.
But wonder how the devil they got there.
Were others angry: I excused them too;
Well might they rage, I gave them but their due.
A man's true merit 'tis not hard to find;
But each man's secret standard in his mind,
That casting-weight pride adds to emptiness,
This, who can gratify? for who can *guess?*
The bard whom pilfer'd pastorals renown,
Who turns a Persian tale[1] for half-a-crown,
Just writes to make his barrenness appear,
And strains, from hard-bound brains, eight lines a-year;
He, who still wanting, though he lives on theft,
Steals much, spends little, yet has nothing left:
And he, who now to sense, now nonsense leaning,
Means not, but blunders round about a meaning:
And he, whose fustian's so sublimely bad,
It is not poetry, but prose run mad:
All these, my modest satire bade translate,
And own'd that nine such Poets made a Tate.
How did they fume, and stamp, and roar, and chafe!
And swear not ADDISON himself was safe.
Peace to all such! but were there one whose fires
True genius kindles, and fair fame inspires;
Blest with each talent and each art to please,
And born to write, converse, and live with ease:
Should such a man, too fond to rule alone,
Bear, like the Turk, no brother near the throne,
View him with scornful, yet with jealous eyes,
And hate for arts that caused himself to rise;
Damn with faint praise, assent with civil leer,
And without sneering, teach the rest to sneer;
Willing to wound, and yet afraid to strike
Just hint a fault, and hesitate dislike;
Alike reserved to blame, or to commend,
A timorous foe, and a suspicious friend;
Dreading e'en fools, by flatterers besieged,
And so obliging, that he ne'er obliged;
Like *Cato*, give his little senate laws,
And sit attentive to his own applause;

[1] Amb. Philips translated a book called the *Persian Tales*, a book full of fancy and imagination.

While wits and templars every sentence raise,
And wonder with a foolish face of praise—
Who but must laugh, if such a man there be?
Who would not weep, if ATTICUS were he?
What though my name stood rubric on the walls,
Or plaster'd posts, with claps, in capitals?
Or smoking forth, a hundred hawkers' load,
On wings of winds came flying all abroad!
I sought no homage from the race that write;
I kept, like Asian monarchs, from their sight:
Poems I heeded (now be-rhymed so long)
No more than thou, great GEORGE! a birthday song.
I ne'er with wits or witlings pass'd my days,
To spread about the itch of verse and praise;
Nor like a puppy, daggled through the town,
To fetch and carry sing-song up and down;
Nor at rehearsals sweat, and mouth'd, and cried,
With handkerchief and orange at my side;
But sick of fops, and poetry, and prate,
To *Bufo* left the whole *Castalian* state.
Proud as *Apollo* on his forked hill,
Sat full-blown *Bufo*, puff'd by every quill;
Fed with soft dedication all day long,
Horace and he went hand and hand in song.
His library (where busts of poets dead
And a true *Pindar* stood without a head)
Received of wits an undistinguish'd race,
Who first his judgment ask'd, and then a place:
Much they extoll'd his pictures, much his seat,
And flatter'd every day, and some days eat:
Till grown more frugal in his riper days,
He paid some bards with port, and some with praise;
To some a dry rehearsal was assign'd,
And others (harder still) he paid in kind.
Dryden alone (what wonder?) came not nigh,
Dryden alone escaped this judging eye:
But still the *great* have kindness in reserve,
He help'd to bury whom he help'd to starve.
May some choice patron bless his grey goose-quill!
May every *Bavius* have his *Bufo* still!
So when a statesman wants a day's defence,
Or envy holds a whole week's war with sense,
Or simple pride for flattery makes demands,
May dunce by dunce be whistled off my hands!

Bless'd be the great, for those they take away,
And those they left me—for they left me GAY;
Left me to see neglected genius bloom,
Neglected die, and tell it on his tomb:
Of all thy blameless life, the sole return
My verse, and QUEENSBERRY weeping o'er thy urn!
Oh let me live my own, and die so too!
(To live and die is all I have to do)
Maintain a poet's dignity and ease,
And see what friends, and read what books I please:
Above a patron, though I condescend
Sometimes to call a minister my friend.
I was not born for courts or great affairs;
I pay my debts, believe, and say my prayers;
Can sleep without a poem in my head,
Nor know if *Dennis* be alive or dead.
  Why am I ask'd what next shall see the light?
Heavens! was I born for nothing but to write?
Has life no joys for me? or (to be grave)
Have I no friend to serve, no soul to save?
"I found him close with *Swift*—Indeed? no doubt
(Cries prating *Balbus*) something will come out."
'Tis all in vain, deny it as I will;
"No, such a genius never can lie still;"
And then for mine obligingly mistakes
The first lampoon Sir *Will.* or *Bubo* makes.
Poor guiltless I! and can I choose but smile,
When every coxcomb knows me by my style?
  Cursed be the verse, how well soe'er it flow,
That tends to make one worthy man my foe,
Give virtue scandal, innocence a fear,
Or from the soft-eyed virgin steal a tear!
But he who hurts a harmless neighbour's peace,
Insults fallen worth, or beauty in distress,
Who loves a lie, lame slander helps about,
Who writes a libel, or who copies out:
That fop whose pride affects a patron's name,
Yet absent wounds an author's honest fame:
Who can *your* merit *selfishly* approve,
And show the *sense* of it without the *love;*
Who has the vanity to call you friend,
Yet wants the honour, injured, to defend;
Who tells whate'er you think, whate'er you say,
And, if he lie not, must at least betray:

Who to the *Dean*, and *silver bell* can swear,
And sees at *Canons* what was never there;
Who reads but with a lust to misapply,
Make satire a lampoon, and fiction lie;
A lash like mine no honest man shall dread,
But all such babbling blockheads in his stead.
Let *Sporus* tremble—A. What? that thing of silk,
Sporus, that mere white curd of ass's milk?
Satire of sense, alas! can *Sporus* feel?
Who breaks a butterfly upon a wheel?
P. Yet let me flap this bug with gilded wings,
This painted child of dirt, that stinks and stings;
Whose buzz the witty and the fair annoys,
Yet wit ne'er tastes, and beauty ne'er enjoys:
So well-bred spaniels civilly delight
In mumbling of the game they dare not bite.
Eternal smiles his emptiness betray,
As shallow streams run dimpling all the way.
Whether in florid impotence he speaks,
And, as the prompter breathes, the puppet squeaks,
Or at the ear of Eve, familiar toad,
Half froth, half venom, spits himself abroad,
In puns, or politics, or tales, or lies,
Or spite, or smut, or rhymes, or blasphemies.
His wit all see-saw, between *that* and *this*.
Now high, now low, now master up, now miss,
And he himself one vile antithesis.
Amphibious thing! that acting either part,
The trifling head, or the corrupted heart,
Fop at the toilet, flatterer at the board,
Now trips a lady, and now struts a lord.
Eve's tempter thus the rabbins have express'd,
A cherub's face, a reptile all the rest,
Beauty that shocks you, parts that none will trust,
Wit that can creep, and pride that licks the dust.
Not fortune's worshipper, nor fashion's fool,
Not lucre's madman, nor ambition's tool,
Not proud, nor servile; be one poet's praise,
That, if he pleased, he pleased by manly ways:
That flattery, even to kings, he held a shame,
And thought a lie in verse or prose the same:
That not in fancy's maze he wander'd long,
But stoop'd to truth, and moralized his song:
That not for fame, but virtue's better end,
He stood the furious foe, the timid friend,

The damning critic, half-approving wit,
The coxcomb hit, or fearing to be hit;
Laugh'd at the loss of friends he never had,
The dull, the proud, the wicked, and the mad;
The distant threats of vengeance on his head,
The blow unfelt, the tear he never shed;
The tale revived, the lie so oft o'erthrown,[1]
The imputed trash, and dulness not his own;
The morals blacken'd when the writings 'scape,
The libell'd person, and the pictured shape;
Abuse on all he loved, or loved him, spread,[2]
A friend in exile, or a father dead;
The whisper, that to greatness still too near,
Perhaps, yet vibrates on his SOVEREIGN'S ear—
Welcome for thee, fair *virtue!* all the past:
For thee, fair virtue! welcome even the *last!*
A. But why insult the poor, affront the great?
P. A knave's a knave to me, in every state:
Alike my scorn, if he succeed or fail,
Sporus at court, or *Japhet* in a jail,
A hireling scribbler, or a hireling peer,
Knight of the post corrupt, or of the shire;
If on a pillory, or near a throne,
He gain his prince's ear, or lose his own.
Yet soft by nature, more a dupe than wit,
Sappho can tell you how this man was bit:
This dreaded satirist *Dennis* will confess
Foe to his pride, but friend to his distress:
So humble, he has knock'd at *Tibbald's* door,
Has drunk with *Cibber*, nay has rhymed for *Moore*.
Full ten years[3] slander'd, did he once reply?
Three thousand suns went down on *Welsted's* lie.[4]

1 As, that he received subscriptions for Shakspeare, that he set his name to Mr. Broome's verses, &c., which, though publicly disproved, were nevertheless shamelessly repeated in the Libels, and even in that called the *Nobleman's Epistle*.

2 Namely, on the Duke of Buckingham, the Earl of Burlington, Lord Bathurst, Lord Bolingbroke, Bishop Atterbury, Dr. Swift, Dr. Arbuthnot, Mr. Gay, his friends, his parents, and his very nurse, aspersed in printed papers, by James Moore, G. Duckett, L. Welsted, Tho. Bentley, and other obscure persons.

3 It was so long, after many libels, before the author of the Dunciad published that poem; till when, he never writ a word in answer to the many scurrilities and falsehoods concerning him.

4 This man had the impudence to tell, in print, that Mr. P. had occasioned a *lady's death*, and to name a person he never heard of. He also published that he libelled the Duke of Chandos; with whom (it was

To please his mistress, one aspersed his life;
He lash'd him not, but let her be his wife:
Let *Budgell*[1] charge low *Grub-street* on his quill,
And write whate'er he pleased, except his will;[2]
Let the two *Curlls* of town and court, abuse
His father, mother, body, soul, and muse.[3]
Yet why? that father held it for a rule,
It was a sin to call our neighbour fool:
That harmless mother thought no wife a whore:
Hear this, and spare his family, *James Moore!*
Unspotted names, and memorable long!
If there be force in virtue, or in song.

added) that he had lived in familiarity, and received from him a present of *five hundred pounds:* the falsehood of both which is known to his Grace. Mr. P. never received any present, farther than the subscription for Homer, from him, or from *any great man* whatsoever.

[1] Budgell, in a weekly pamphlet called *The Bee*, bestowed much abuse on him, in the imagination that he writ some things about the *last will* of Dr. Tindal, in the *Grub-street Journal;* a paper wherein he never had the least hand, direction, or supervisal, nor the least knowledge of its author.

[2] Alluding to Tindal's will: by which, and other indirect practices, Budgell, to the exclusion of the next heir, a nephew, got to himself almost the whole fortune of a man entirely unrelated to him.

[3] In some of Curll's and other pamphlets, Mr. Pope's father was said to be a mechanic, a hatter, a farmer, nay, a bankrupt. But, what is stranger, a *nobleman* (if such a reflection could be thought to come from a nobleman) had dropt an allusion to that pitiful untruth, in a paper called *An Epistle to a Doctor of Divinity;* and the following line,

"Hard as thy heart, and as thy birth obscure,"

had fallen from a like *courtly* pen, in certain verses *to the imitator of Horace.* Mr. Pope's father was of a gentleman's family in Oxfordshire, the head of which was the Earl of Downe, whose sole heiress married the Earl of Lindsay.—His mother was the daughter of William Turner, Esq., of York: she had three brothers, one of whom was killed, another died in the service of King Charles; the eldest following his fortunes, and becoming a general officer in Spain, left her what estate remained after the sequestrations and forfeitures of her family.—Mr. Pope died in 1717, aged 75; she in 1733, aged 93, a very few weeks after this poem was finished. The following inscription was placed by their son on their monument in the parish of Twickenham, in Middlesex:—

D. O. M.

ALEXANDRO. POPE. VIRO. INNOCVO. PROBO. PIO.
QUI. VIXIT. ANNOS. LXXV. OB. MDCCXVII.
ET. EDITHÆ. CONIVGI. INCVLPABILI.
PIENTISSIMÆ. QUÆ. VIXIT. ANNOS.
XCIII. OB. MDCCXXXIII.
PARENTIBVS. BENEMERENTIBVS. FILIVS. FECIT.
ET. SIBI.

Of gentle blood (part shed in honour's cause,
While yet in *Britain* honour had applause)
Each parent sprung—A. What fortune, pray?—
P. Their own;
And better got, than *Bestia's* from the throne.
Born to no pride, inheriting no strife,
Nor marrying discord in a noble wife,
Stranger to civil and religious rage,
The good man walk'd innoxious through his age.
No courts he saw, no suits would ever try,
Nor dared an oath, nor hazarded a lie.
Unlearn'd, he knew no schoolman's subtle art,
No language but the language of the heart.
By nature honest, by experience wise,
Healthy by temperance, and by exercise;
His life, though long, to sickness past unknown,
His death was instant, and without a groan.
O grant me thus to live, and thus to die!
Who sprung from kings shall know less joy than I.
O friend! may each domestic bliss be thine!
Be no unpleasing melancholy mine:
Me, let the tender office long engage,
To rock the cradle of reposing age,
With lenient arts extend a mother's breath,
Make languor smile, and smooth the bed of death,
Explore the thought, explain the asking eye,
And keep a while one parent from the sky!
On cares like these, if length of days attend,
May Heaven, to bless those days, preserve my friend,
Preserve him social, cheerful, and serene,
And just as rich as when he served a QUEEN.
A. Whether that blessing be denied or given,
Thus far was right, the rest belongs to Heaven.

SATIRES AND EPISTLES OF HORACE IMITATED.

Ludentis speciem dabit, et torquebitur.—HOR.

ADVERTISEMENT.

THE occasion of publishing these *Imitations* was the clamour raised on some of my *Epistles*. An answer from Horace was both more full, and of more dignity, than any I could have made in my own person; and the example of much greater freedom in so eminent a divine as Dr. Donne, seemed a proof with what indignation and contempt a Christian may treat vice or folly, in ever so low, or ever so high a station. Both these authors were acceptable to the *princes* and *ministers* under whom they lived. The Satires of Dr. Donne I versified at the desire of the Earl of Oxford, while he was lord treasurer, and of the Duke of Shrewsbury, who had been secretary of state; neither of whom looked upon a satire on vicious courts as any reflection on those they served in. And indeed there is not in the world a greater error than that which fools are so apt to fall into, and knaves with good reason to encourage,—the mistaking a *satirist* for a *libeller*, whereas to a *true satirist* nothing is so odious as a *libeller*, for the same reason as to a man *truly virtuous* nothing is so hateful as a *hypocrite*.

Uni æquus virtuti atque ejus amicis.

SATIRE I.

TO MR. FORTESCUE.

P. THERE are, (I scarce can think it, but am told)
There are, to whom my Satire seems too bold:
Scarce to wise Peter complaisant enough,
And something said of Chartres much too rough.
The lines are weak, another's pleased to say,
Lord Fanny spins a thousand such a day.
Timorous by nature, of the rich in awe,
I come to counsel learned in the law:
You'll give me, like a friend both sage and free,
Advice; and (as you use) without a fee.

F. I'd write no more.
P. Not write? but then I think,
And for my soul I cannot sleep a wink.
I nod in company, I wake at night,
Fools rush into my head, and so I write.
F. You could not do a worse thing for your life.
Why, if the nights seem tedious—take a wife:
Or rather truly, if your point be rest,
Lettuce and cowslip-wine; *probatum est.*
But talk with Celsus, Celsus will advise
Hartshorn, or something that shall close your eyes.
Or, if you needs must write, write CÆSAR's praise,
You'll gain at least a *knighthood*, or the *bays.*
P. What? like Sir Richard, rumbling, rough, and fierce,
With ARMS, and GEORGE, and BRUNSWICK, crowd the verse,
Rend with tremendous sound your ears asunder,
With gun, drum, trumpet, blunderbuss, and thunder?
Or nobly wild, with Budgell's fire and force,
Paint angels trembling round his falling horse?
F. Then all your muse's softer art display,
Let CAROLINA smooth the tuneful lay,
Lull with AMELIA's liquid name the nine,
And sweetly flow through all the royal line.
P. Alas! few verses touch their nicer ear;
They scarce can bear their *laureat* twice a year;
And justly CÆSAR scorns the poet's lays,
It is to *history* he trusts for praise.
F. Better be Cibber, I'll maintain it still,
Than ridicule all taste, blaspheme quadrille,
Abuse the city's best good men in metre,
And laugh at peers that put their trust in Peter.
E'en those you touch not hate you.
P. What should ail 'em?
F. A hundred smart in Timon and in Balaam:
The fewer still you name, you wound the more;
Bond is but one, but Harpax is a score.
P. Each mortal has his pleasure: none deny
Scarsdale his bottle, Darty his ham-pie;
Ridotta sips and dances, till she see
The doubling lustres dance as fast as she;
F—— loves the senate, Hockley-hole his brother,
Like in all else, as one egg to another.

I love to pour out all myself as plain
As downright SHIPPEN, or as old Montaigne:
In them as certain to be loved as seen,
The soul stood forth, nor kept a thought within;
In me what spots (for spots I have) appear,
Will prove at least the medium must be clear.
In this impartial glass, my muse intends
Fair to expose myself, my foes, my friends;
Publish the present age; but where my text
Is vice too high, reserve it for the next;
My foes shall wish my life a longer date,
And every friend the less lament my fate.
My head and heart thus flowing through my quill,
Verse-man or prose-man, term me which you will,
Papist or Protestant, or both between,
Like good Erasmus in an honest mean,
In moderation placing all my glory,
While tories call me whig, and whigs a tory.
  Satire's my weapon, but I'm too discreet
To run a muck, and tilt at all I meet;
I only wear it in a land of Hectors,
Thieves, supercargoes, sharpers, and directors.
Save but our *army!* and let Jove incrust
Swords, pikes, and guns, with everlasting rust!
Peace is my dear delight—not FLEURY's more:
But touch me, and no minister so sore.
Whoe'er offends, at some unlucky time
Slides into verse, and hitches in a rhyme,
Sacred to ridicule his whole life-long,
And the sad burthen of some merry song.
  Slander or poison dread from Delia's rage,
Hard words or hanging, if your judge be Page.
From furious Sappho scarce a milder fate,
Pox'd by her love, or libell'd by her hate.
Its proper power to hurt, each creature feels;
Bulls aim their horns, and asses lift their heels
'Tis a bear's talent not to kick, but hug;
And no man wonders he's not stung by pug.
So drink with Walters, or with Chartres eat,
They'll never poison you, they'll only cheat.
  Then, learned Sir! (to cut the matter short)
Whate'er my fate, or well or ill at court,
Whether old age, with faint but cheerful ray,
Attends to gild the evening of my day,

Or Death's black wing already be display'd,
To wrap me in the universal shade;
Whether the darken'd room to muse invite,
Or whiten'd wall provoke the skewer to write;
In durance, exile, Bedlam, or the Mint,
Like Lee or Budgell, I will rhyme and print.
F. Alas, young man! your days can ne'er be long!
In flower of age you perish for a song!
Plums and directors, Shylock and his wife,
Will club their testers, now, to take your life!
P. What? arm'd for virtue when I point the pen,
Brand the bold front of shameless guilty men;
Dash the proud gamester in his gilded car;
Bare the mean heart that lurks beneath a star;
Can there be wanting, to defend her cause,
Lights of the church, or guardians of the laws?
Could pension'd Boileau lash in honest strain
Flatterers and bigots e'en in Louis' reign?
Could laureate Dryden pimp and friar engage,
Yet neither Charles nor James be in a rage?
And I not strip the gilding off a knave,
Unplaced, unpension'd, no man's heir, or slave?
I will, or perish in the generous cause:
Hear this, and tremble! you who 'scape the laws.
Yes, while I live, no rich or noble knave
Shall walk the world, in credit, to his grave.
TO VIRTUE ONLY and HER FRIENDS A FRIEND,
The world beside may murmur, or commend.
Know, all the distant din that world can keep,
Rolls o'er my grotto, and but soothes my sleep.
There, my retreat the best companions grace,
Chiefs out of war, and statesmen out of place.
There ST. JOHN mingles with my friendly bowl
The feast of reason and the flow of soul:
And he, whose lightning pierced the Iberian lines,[1]
Now forms my quincunx, and now ranks my vines,
Or tames the genius of the stubborn plain
Almost as quickly as he conquer'd Spain.
Envy must own I live among the great,
No pimp of pleasure, and no spy of state,

[1] Charles Mordaunt, Earl of Peterborough, who in the year 1705 took Barcelona, and in the winter following, with only two hundred and eighty horse and nine hundred foot enterprised and accomplished the conquest of Valencia.

With eyes that pry not, tongue that ne'er repeats,
Fond to spread friendships, but to cover heats;
To help who want, to forward who excel;
This all who know me, know; who love me, tell;
And who unknown defame me, let them be
Scribblers or peers, alike are *mob* to me.
This is my plea, on this I rest my cause—
What saith my counsel, learned in the laws?
  F. Your plea is good; but still I say beware!
Laws are explain'd by men—so have a care.
It stands on record, that in Richard's times
A man was hang'd for very honest rhymes.
Consult the statute: *quart.* I think, it is,
Edwardi sext. or *prim. et quint. Eliz.*
See *Libels, Satires*—here you have it—read.
  P. *Libels* and *Satires!* lawless things indeed!
But grave *epistles*, bringing vice to light,
Such as a king might read, a bishop write,
Such as Sir Robert would approve—
F. Indeed!
The case is alter'd—you may then proceed;
In such a cause the plaintiff will be hiss'd,
My lords the judges laugh, and you're dismiss'd.

THE SECOND SATIRE

OF THE

SECOND BOOK OF HORACE.

TO MR. BETHEL.

What, and how great, the virtue and the art
To live on little with a cheerful heart;
(A doctrine sage, but truly none of mine)
Let's talk, my friends, but talk before we dine.
Not when a gilt buffet's reflected pride
Turns you from sound philosophy aside;
Not when from plate to plate your eyeballs roll,
And the brain dances to the mantling bowl.
  Hear Bethel's sermon, one not versed in schools,
But strong in sense, and wise without the rules.

Go work, hunt, exercise! (he thus began)
Then scorn a homely dinner, if you can.
Your wine lock'd up, your butler stroll'd abroad,
Or fish denied, (the river yet unthaw'd)
If then plain bread and milk will do the feat,
The pleasure lies in you, and not the meat.
Preach as I please, I doubt our curious men
Will choose a pheasant still before a hen;
Yet hens of Guinea full as good I hold,
Except you eat the feathers green and gold.
Of carps and mullets why prefer the great,
(Though cut in pieces ere my lord can eat)
Yet for small turbots such esteem profess?
Because God made these large, the other less.
Oldfield with more than harpy throat endued,
Cries "Send me, Gods! a whole hog barbecued!"[1]
Oh blast it, south winds! till a stench exhale
Rank as the ripeness of a rabbit's tail.
By what criterion do ye eat, d'ye think,
If this is prized for sweetness, that for stink?
When the tired glutton labours through a treat,
He finds no relish in the sweetest meat,
He calls for something bitter, something sour,
And the rich feast concludes extremely poor:
Cheap eggs, and herbs, and olives still we see;
Thus much is left of old simplicity;
The robin-redbreast till of late had rest,
And children sacred held a martin's nest,
Till becaficos sold so devilish dear
To one that was, or would have been, a peer.
Let me extol a cat, on oysters fed;
I'll have a party at the Bedford-head:[2]
Or e'en to crack live craw-fish recommend;
I'd never doubt at court to make a friend.
'Tis yet in vain, I own, to keep a pother
About one vice, and fall into the other;
Between excess and famine lies a mean;
Plain, but not sordid, though not splendid, clean.
Avidien or his wife, (no matter which,
For him you'll call a dog, and her a bitch)

[1] A West Indian term of gluttony; a hog roasted whole, stuffed with spice, and basted with Madeira wine.
[2] A famous eating-house in Maiden-lane.

p. 304.

IMITATIONS OF HORACE.

Sell their presented partridges, and fruits,
And humbly live on rabbits and on roots:
One half-pint bottle serves them both to dine,
And is at once their vinegar and wine.
But on some lucky day (as when they found
A lost bank-bill, or heard their son was drown'd)
At such a feast, old vinegar to spare,
Is what two souls so generous cannot bear:
Oil, though it stink, they drop by drop impart,
But souse the cabbage with a bounteous heart.
He knows to live, who keeps the middle state,
And neither leans on this side, nor on that;
Nor stops, for one bad cork, his butler's pay,
Swears, like Albutius, a good cook away;
Nor lets, like Nævius, every error pass,
The musty wine, foul cloth, or greasy glass.
Now hear what blessings temperance can bring:
(Thus said our friend, and what he said I sing)
First health: the stomach (cramm'd from every dish
A tomb of boil'd and roast, and flesh and fish,
Where bile, and wind, and phlegm, and acid jar,
And all the man is one intestine war)
Remembers oft the schoolboy's simple fare,
The temperate sleeps, and spirits light as air.
How pale, each worshipful and reverend guest
Rise from a clergy or a city feast!
What life in all that ample body say?
What heavenly particle inspires the clay?
The soul subsides, and wickedly inclines
To seem but mortal, e'en in sound divines.
On morning wings how active springs the mind
That leaves the load of yesterday behind?
How easy every labour it pursues?
How coming to the poet every muse?
Not but we may exceed, some holy time,
Or tired in search of truth, or search of rhyme;
Ill health some just indulgence may engage,
And more the sickness of long life, old age:
For fainting age what cordial drop remains,
If our intemperate youth the vessel drains?
Our fathers praised rank venison. You suppose,
Perhaps, young men, our fathers had no nose.
Not so: a buck was then a week's repast,
And 'twas their point, I ween, to make it last;

More pleased to keep it till their friends could come,
Than eat the sweetest by themselves at home.
Why had not I in those good times my birth,
Ere coxcomb-pies, or coxcombs were on earth?
  Unworthy he the voice of Fame to hear,
That sweetest music to an honest ear,
(For 'faith, Lord Fanny! you are in the wrong,
The world's good word is better than a song)
Who has not learn'd, fresh sturgeon and ham-pie
Are no rewards for want, and infamy!
When luxury has lick'd up all thy pelf,
Cursed by thy neighbours, thy trustees, thyself,
To friends, to fortune, to mankind a shame,
Think how posterity will treat thy name;
And buy a rope, that future times may tell
Thou hast at least bestow'd one penny well.
  "Right," cries his lordship, "for a rogue in need
To have a taste, is insolence indeed:
In me 'tis noble, suits my birth and state,
My wealth unwieldy, and my heap too great."—
Then, like the sun, let bounty spread her ray,
And shine that superfluity away.
O impudence of wealth! with all thy store,
How darest thou let one worthy man be poor?
Shall half the new-built churches round thee fall?
Make quays, build bridges, or repair Whitehall:
Or to thy country let that heap be lent,
As M * * o's was, but not at five per cent.
  Who thinks that Fortune cannot change her mind,
Prepares a dreadful jest for all mankind.
And who stands safest? tell me, is it he
That spreads and swells in puff'd prosperity,
Or blest with little, whose preventing care
In peace provides fit arms against a war?
  Thus BETHEL spoke, who always speaks his thought,
And always thinks the very thing he ought:
His equal mind I copy what I can,
And as I love, would imitate the man.
In South-sea days not happier, when surmised
The lord of thousands, than if now excised;
In forest planted by a father's hand,
Than in five acres now of rented land.
Content with little, I can piddle here
On brocoli and mutton round the year;

But ancient friends (though poor, or out of play)
That touch my bell, I cannot turn away.
'Tis true, no turbots dignify my boards,
But gudgeons, flounders, what my Thames affords:
To Hounslow-heath I point, and Banstead-down,
Thence comes your mutton, and these chicks my own:
From yon old walnut-tree a shower shall fall;
And grapes, long lingering on my only wall,
And figs from standard and espalier join;
The devil is in you if you cannot dine:
Then cheerful healths, (your mistress shall have place)
And, what's more rare, a poet shall say grace.
  Fortune not much of humbling me can boast;
Though double tax'd, how little have I lost?
My life's amusements have been just the same,
Before and after standing armies came.
My lands are sold, my father's house is gone;
I'll hire another's; is not that my own,
And yours, my friends? through whose free-opening gate
None comes too early, none departs too late;
(For I who hold sage Homer's rule the best,
Welcome the coming, speed the going guest.)
"Pray Heaven it last!" (cries Swift) "as you go on
I wish to God this house had been your own:
Pity! to build, without a son or wife:
Why, you'll enjoy it only all your life."
Well, if the use be mine, can it concern one,
Whether the name belong to Pope or Vernon?
What's *property?* dear Swift! you see it alter
From you to me, from me to Peter Walter;
Or, in a mortgage, prove a lawyer's share;
Or, in a jointure, vanish from the heir;
Or, in pure equity, (the case not clear)
The Chancery takes your rents for twenty year:
At best, it falls to some ungracious son,
Who cries, "My father's damn'd, and all's my own,"
Shades, that to Bacon could retreat afford,
Become the portion of a booby lord;
And Hemsley, once proud Buckingham's delight,[1]
Slides to a scrivener or a city knight.
Let lands and houses have what lords they will,
Let us be fix'd, and our own masters still.

[1] Villiers Duke of Buckingham.

THE FIRST EPISTLE

OF THE

FIRST BOOK OF HORACE.

TO LORD BOLINGBROKE.

St. John, whose love indulged my labours past,
Matures my present, and shall bound my last!
Why will you break the Sabbath of my days?
Now sick alike of envy and of praise.
Public too long, ah, let me hide my age!
See modest Cibber now has left the stage:
Our generals now, retired to their estates,
Hang their old trophies o'er the garden gates,
In life's cool evening satiate of applause,
Nor fond of bleeding, e'en in Brunswick's cause.
A voice there is, that whispers in my ear,
('Tis Reason's voice, which sometimes one can hear)
"Friend Pope! be prudent, let your muse take breath,
And never gallop Pegasus to death;
Lest stiff and stately, void of fire or force,
You limp, like Blackmore, on a lord mayor's horse."[1]
Farewell then verse, and love, and every toy,
The rhymes and rattles of the man or boy;
What right, what true, what fit we justly call,
Let this be all my care—for this is all:
To lay this harvest up, and hoard with haste
What every day will want, and most, the last.
But ask not to what doctors I apply;
Sworn to no master, of no sect am I:
As drives the storm, at any door I knock:
And house with Montaigne now, or now with Locke.
Sometimes a patriot, active in debate,
Mix with the world, and battle for the state,

[1] The fame of this heavy poet, however problematical elsewhere, was universally received in the city of London. His versification is here exactly described: stiff, and not strong; stately, and yet dull, like the sober and slow-paced animal generally employed to mount the lord mayor; and therefore here humorously opposed to Pegasus.

Free as young Lyttelton, her cause pursue,
Still true to virtue, and as warm as true:
Sometimes with Aristippus, or St. Paul,
Indulge my candour, and grow all to all;
Back to my native moderation slide,
And win my way by yielding to the tide.
  Long, as to him who works for debt the day,
Long as the night to her whose love's away,
Long as the year's dull circle seems to run,
When the brisk minor pants for twenty-one:
So slow the unprofitable moments roll,
That lock up all the functions of my soul;
That keep me from myself; and still delay
Life's instant business to a future day:
That task, which as we follow, or despise,
The eldest is a fool, the youngest wise,
Which done, the poorest can no wants endure;
And which not done, the richest must be poor.
  Late as it is, I put myself to school,
And feel some comfort not to be a fool.
Weak though I am of limb, and short of sight,
Far from a lynx, and not a giant quite;
I'll do what Mead and Cheselden advise,
To keep these limbs, and to preserve these eyes.
Not to go back, is somewhat to advance,
And men must walk at least before they dance.
  Say, does thy blood rebel, thy bosom move
With wretched avarice, or as wretched love?
Know, there are words, and spells, which can control
Between the fits this fever of the soul;
Know, there are rhymes which, fresh and fresh applied,
Will cure the arrant'st puppy of his pride.
Be furious, envious, slothful, mad, or drunk,
Slave to a wife, or vassal to a punk,
A Switz, a High-Dutch, or a Low-Dutch bear;
All that we ask is but a patient ear.
  'Tis the first virtue, vices to abhor;
And the first wisdom, to be fool no more.
But to the world no bugbear is so great,
As want of figure, and a small estate.
To either India see the merchant fly,
Scared at the spectre of pale poverty!
See him, with pains of body, pangs of soul,
Burn through the tropic, freeze beneath the pole!

Wilt thou do nothing for a nobler end,
Nothing to make philosophy thy friend?
To stop thy foolish views, thy long desires,
And ease thy heart of all that it admires?
Here, Wisdom calls: "Seek virtue first, be bold!
As gold to silver, virtue is to gold."
There, London's voice: "Get money, money still!
And then let Virtue follow, if she will."
This, this the saving doctrine, preach'd to all,
From low St. James's up to high St. Paul;
From him whose quills stand quiver'd at his ear,
To him who notches sticks at Westminster.
Barnard in spirit, sense, and truth abounds;
"Pray then, what wants he?" Fourscore thousand [pounds.
A pension, or such harness for a slave
As Bug now has, and Dorimant would have.
Barnard, thou art a cit, with all thy worth;
But Bug and D * l, their honours, and so forth.
Yet every child another song will sing,
"Virtue, brave boys! 'tis virtue makes a king."
True, conscious honour is to feel no sin,
He's arm'd without that's innocent within;
Be this thy screen, and this thy wall of brass;
Compared to this, a minister's an ass.
And say, to which shall our applause belong,
This new court jargon, or the good old song?
The modern language of corrupted peers,
Or what was spoke at Crecy and Poictiers?
Who counsels best? who whispers, "Be but great,
With praise or infamy leave that to fate;
Get place and wealth, if possible, with grace;
If not, by any means get wealth and place."
For what? to have a box where eunuchs sing,
And foremost in the circle eye a king.
Or he, who bids thee face with steady view
Proud Fortune, and look shallow Greatness through:
And, while he bids thee, sets the example too?
If such a doctrine, in St. James's air,
Should chance to make the well-drest rabble stare;
If honest Schutz take scandal at a spark,
That less admires the palace than the park:
Faith I shall give the answer reynard gave:
"I cannot like, dread sir, your royal cave:
Because I see, by all the tracks about,
Full many a beast goes in, but none come out."

Adieu to virtue, if you're once a slave:
Send her to court, you send her to her grave.
  Well, if a king's a lion, at the least
The people are a many-headed beast:
Can they direct what measures to pursue,
Who know themselves so little what to do?
Alike in nothing but one lust of gold,
Just half the land would buy, and half be sold:
Their country's wealth our mightier misers drain,
Or cross, to plunder provinces, the main;
The rest, some farm the poor-box, some the pews;
Some keep assemblies, and would keep the stews;
Some with fat bucks on childless dotards fawn;
Some win rich widows by their chine and brawn;
While with the silent growth of ten per cent.,
In dirt and darkness, hundreds stink content.
  Of all these ways, if each pursues his own,
Satire, be kind, and let the wretch alone:
But show me one who has it in his power
To act consistent with himself an hour.
Sir Job sail'd forth, the evening bright and still,
"No place on earth (he cried) like Greenwich-hill!"
Up starts a palace: lo! the obedient base
Slopes at its foot, the woods its sides embrace,
The silver Thames reflects its marble face.
Now let some whimsey, or that devil within
Which guides all those who know not what they mean,
But give the knight (or give his lady) spleen;
"Away, away! take all your scaffolds down,
For snug's the word: my dear! we'll live in town."
  At amorous Flavio is the stocking thrown?—
That very night he longs to lie alone.
The fool, whose wife elopes some thrice a quarter,
For matrimonial solace dies a martyr.
Did ever Proteus, Merlin, any witch,
Transform themselves so strangely as the rich!—
Well, but the poor—the poor have the same itch!
They change their weekly barber, weekly news,
Prefer a new japanner to their shoes,
Discharge their garrets, move their beds, and run
(They know not whither) in a chaise and one;
They hire their sculler, and when once aboard,
Grow sick—and damn the climate—like a lord.
  You laugh, half beau, half sloven if I stand,
My wig all powder, and all snuff my band;

You laugh, if coat and breeches strangely vary,
White gloves, and linen worthy Lady Mary!
But when no prelate's lawn, with hair-shirt lined,
Is half so incoherent as my mind,
When (each opinion with the next at strife,
One ebb and flow of follies all my life)
I plant, root up; I build, and then confound;
Turn round to square, and square again to round;
You never change one muscle of your face,
You think this madness but a common case;
Nor once to Chancery, nor to Hale apply;
Yet hang your lip, to see a seam awry!
Careless how ill I with myself agree,
Kind to my dress, my figure,—not to me.
Is this my guide, philosopher, and friend?
This he, who loves me, and who ought to mend?
Who ought to make me (what he can or none)
That man divine whom wisdom calls her own;
Great without title, without fortune bless'd;
Rich e'en when plunder'd, honour'd while oppress'd;
Loved without youth, and follow'd without power;
At home, though exiled; free, though in the Tower;
In short, that reasoning, high, immortal thing,
Just less than Jove, and much above a king,
Nay, half in heaven—except (what's mighty odd)
A fit of vapours clouds this demi-god.

THE SIXTH EPISTLE

OF THE

FIRST BOOK OF HORACE.

TO MR. MURRAY,

AFTERWARDS EARL OF MANSFIELD.

"Not to admire, is all the art I know,
To make men happy, and to keep them so."
(Plain truth, dear Murray, needs no flowers of speech,
So take it in the very words of Creech.)
This vault of air, this congregated ball,
Self-centred sun, and stars that rise and fall,

There are, my friend! whose philosophic eyes
Look through, and trust the ruler with his skies,
To him commit the hour, the day, the year,
And view this dreadful all—without a fear.
Admire we then what earth's low entrails hold,
Arabian shores, or Indian seas infold;
All the mad trade of fools and slaves for gold?
Or popularity? or stars and strings?
The mob's applauses, or the gifts of kings?
Say with what eyes we ought at courts to gaze,
And pay the great our homage of amaze?
If weak the pleasure that from these can spring,
The fear to want them is as weak a thing:
Whether we dread, or whether we desire,
In either case, believe me, we admire;
Whether we joy or grieve, the same the curse,
Surprised at better, or surprised at worse.
Thus good or bad, to one extreme betray
The unbalanced mind, and snatch the man away;
For virtue's self may too much zeal be had;
The worst of madmen is a saint run mad.
Go then, and if you can, admire the state
Of beaming diamonds, and reflected plate;
Procure a TASTE to double the surprise,
And gaze on Parian charms with learned eyes:
Be struck with bright brocade, or Tyrian dye,
Our birth-day nobles' splendid livery.
If not so pleased, at council-board rejoice,
To see their judgments hang upon thy voice;
From morn to night, at senate, rolls, and hall,
Plead much, read more, dine late, or not at all.
But wherefore all this labour, all this strife?
For fame, for riches, for a noble wife?
Shall one whom nature, learning, birth, conspired
To form, not to admire, but be admired,
Sigh, while his Chloe, blind to wit and worth,
Weds the rich dulness of some son of earth?
Yet time ennobles, or degrades each line;
It brighten'd CRAGGS's, and may darken thine:
And what is fame? the meanest have their day,
The greatest can but blaze, and pass away.
Graced as thou art, with all the power of words,
So known, so honour'd, at the house of lords:
Conspicuous scene! another yet is nigh,
(More silent far) where kings and poets lie;

Where MURRAY (long enough his country's pride)
Shall be no more than TULLY, or than HYDE!
  Rack'd with sciatics, martyr'd with the stone,
Will any mortal let himself alone?
See Ward by batter'd beaus invited over,
And desperate misery lays hold on Dover.
The case is easier in the mind's disease;
There all men may be cured, whene'er they please.
Would ye be blest? despise low joys, low gains;
Disdain whatever CORNBURY disdains;
Be virtuous, and be happy for your pains.
  But art thou one, whom new opinions sway,
One who believes as Tindal leads the way,
Who virtue and a church alike disowns,
Thinks that but words, and this but brick and stones?
Fly then, on all the wings of wild desire,
Admire whate'er the maddest can admire.
Is wealth thy passion? hence! from pole to pole,
Where winds can carry, or where waves can roll,
For Indian spices, for Peruvian gold,
Prevent the greedy, and outbid the bold:
Advance thy golden mountain to the skies;
On the broad base of fifty thousand rise,
Add one round hundred, and (if that's not fair)
Add fifty more, and bring it to a square.
For, mark the advantage; just so many score
Will gain a wife with half as many more,
Procure her beauty, make that beauty chaste,
And then such friends—as cannot fail to last.
A man of wealth is dubb'd a man of worth,
Venus shall give him form, and Anstis birth.
(Believe me, many a German prince is worse,
Who proud of pedigree, is poor of purse.)
His wealth brave Timon gloriously confounds;
Ask'd for a groat, he gives a hundred pounds;
Or if three ladies like a luckless play,
Takes the whole house upon the poet's day.
Now, in such exigencies not to need,
Upon my word you must be rich indeed;
A noble superfluity it craves,
Not for yourself, but for your fools and knaves;
Something, which for your honour they may cheat,
And which it much becomes you to forget.
If wealth alone then make and keep us blest,
Still, still be getting; never, never rest.

But if to power and place your passion lie,
If in the pomp of life consist the joy;
Then hire a slave, or (if you will) a lord,
To do the honours, and to give the word;
Tell at your levee, as the crowds approach,
To whom to nod, whom take into your coach,
Whom honour with your hand: to make remarks,
Who rules in Cornwall, or who rules in Berks:
"This may be troublesome, is near the chair;
That makes three members, this can choose a mayor."
Instructed thus, you bow, embrace, protest,
Adopt him son, or cousin at the least,
Then turn about, and laugh at your own jest.
Or if your life be one continued treat,
If to live well means nothing but to eat;
Up, up! cries Gluttony, 'tis break of day,
Go drive the deer, and drag the finny prey;
With hounds and horns go hunt an appetite—
So Russel did, but could not eat at night,
Call'd happy dog! the beggar at his door,
And envied thirst and hunger to the poor.
Or shall we every decency confound,
Through taverns, stews, and bagnios take our round?
Go dine with Chartres, in each vice outdo
K—l's lewd cargo, or Ty—y's crew,
From Latian syrens, French Circæan feasts,
Return well travell'd, and transform'd to beasts,
Or for a titled punk, or foreign flame,
Renounce our country, and degrade our name?
If, after all, we must with Wilmot own,
The cordial drop of life is love alone;
And SWIFT cry wisely, "Vive la bagatelle!"
The man that loves and laughs, must sure do well.
Adieu—if this advice appear the worst,
Even take the counsel which I gave you first:
Or better precepts if you can impart,
Why do; I'll follow them with all my heart.

THE FIRST EPISTLE

OF THE

SECOND BOOK OF HORACE.

ADVERTISEMENT.

THE reflections of Horace, and the judgments passed in his epistle to Augustus, seemed so seasonable to the present time, that I could not help applying them to the use of my own country. The author thought them considerable enough to address them to his prince, whom he paints with all the great and good qualities of a monarch upon whom the Romans depended for the increase of an *absolute empire*. But to make the poem entirely English, I was willing to add one or two of those which contribute to the happiness of a *free people*, and are more consistent with the welfare of our *neighbours*.

This epistle will show the learned world to have fallen into two mistakes: one, that *Augustus was a patron of poets in general:* whereas he not only prohibited all but the best writers to name him, but recommended that care even to the civil magistrate: *Admonebat prætores, ne paterentur nomen suum obsolefieri*, &c. The other, that this piece was only a *general discourse of poetry:* whereas it was an *apology for the poets*, in order to render Augustus more their patron. Horace here pleads the cause of his contemporaries, first, against the taste of the *town*, whose humour it was to magnify the authors of the preceding age; secondly, against the *court* and *nobility*, who encouraged only the writers for the theatre; and, lastly, against the *emperor* himself, who had conceived them of little use to the government. He shows (by a view of the progress of learning, and the change of taste among the Romans) that the introduction of the polite arts of Greece had given the writers of his time great advantages over their predecessors; that their *morals* were much improved, and the licence of those ancient poets restrained; that *satire* and *comedy* were become more just and useful; that whatever extravagancies were left on the stage were owing to the *ill taste* of the *nobility:* that poets, under due regulations, were in many respects useful to the *state:* and concludes that it was upon them the emperor himself must depend for his fame with posterity.

We may further learn from this epistle, that Horace made his court to this great prince by writing with a decent freedom toward him, with a just contempt of his low flatterers, and with a manly regard to his own character.

EPISTLE I.

TO AUGUSTUS.

WHILE you, great patron of mankind! sustain
The balanced world, and open all the main;
Your country, chief, in arms abroad defend,
At home, with morals, arts, and laws amend;
How shall the muse, from such a monarch, steal
An hour, and not defraud the public weal?
  Edward and Henry, now the boast of Fame,
And virtuous Alfred, a more sacred name,
After a life of generous toils endured,
The Gaul subdued, or property secured,
Ambition humbled, mighty cities storm'd,
Or laws establish'd, and the world reform'd;
Closed their long glories, with a sigh, to find
The unwilling gratitude of base mankind!
All human virtue, to its latest breath,
Finds Envy never conquer'd, but by Death.
The great Alcides, every labour past,
Had still this monster to subdue at last.
Sure fate of all, beneath whose rising ray
Each star of meaner merit fades away!
Oppress'd we feel the beam directly beat,
Those suns of glory please not till they set.
  To thee, the world its present homage pays,
The harvest early, but mature the praise:
Great friend of LIBERTY! in kings a name
Above all Greek, above all Roman fame:
Whose word is truth, as sacred and revered,
As Heaven's own oracles from altars heard.
Wonder of kings! like whom, to mortal eyes
None e'er has risen, and none e'er shall rise.
  Just in one instance, be it yet confess'd
Your people, Sir, are partial in the rest:
Foes to all living worth except your own,
And advocates for folly dead and gone.
Authors, like coins, grow dear as they grow old;
It is the rust we value, not the gold.
Chaucer's worst ribaldry is learned by rote,
And beastly Skelton[1] heads of houses quote:

[1] Skelton, poet laureat to Henry VIII., a volume of whose verses had been reprinted, consisting almost wholly of ribaldry, and obscenity.

One likes no language but the Faery Queene;
A Scot will fight for Christ's Kirk o' the Green;[1]
And each true Briton is to Ben so civil,
He swears the Muses met him at the Devil.[2]
 Though justly Greece her eldest sons admires,
Why should not we be wiser than our sires?
In every public virtue we excel;
We build, we paint, we sing, we dance as well,
And learned Athens to our art must stoop,
Could she behold us tumbling through a hoop.
 If time improve our wit as well as wine,
Say at what age a poet grows divine?
Shall we, or shall we not, account him so,
Who died, perhaps, a hundred years ago?
End all dispute; and fix the year precise
When British bards began to immortalise?
 "Who lasts a century can have no flaw,
I hold that wit a classic, good in law."
 Suppose he wants a year, will you compound?
And shall we deem him ancient, right, and sound,
Or damn to all eternity at once,
At ninety-nine, a modern and a dunce?
 "We shall not quarrel for a year or two:
By courtesy of England, he may do."
 Then, by the rule that made the horse-tail bare,
I pluck out year by year, as hair by hair,
And melt down ancients like a heap of snow:
While you, to measure merits, look in Stowe,
And estimating authors by the year,
Bestow a garland only on a bier.
 Shakspeare, (whom you and every playhouse bill
Style the divine, the matchless, what you will)
For gain, not glory, wing'd his roving flight,
And grew immortal in his own despite.
Ben, old and poor, as little seem'd to heed
The life to come, in every poet's creed.
Who now reads Cowley? if he pleases yet,
His moral pleases, not his pointed wit:
Forgot his epic, nay Pindaric art,
But still I love the language of his heart.
 "Yet surely, surely, these were famous men!
What boy but hears the sayings of old Ben?

[1] A poem by James I., king of Scotland.
[2] The Devil Tavern, where Ben Jonson held his Poetical Club.

In all debates where critics bear a part,
Not one but nods, and talks of Jonson's art,
Of Shakspeare's nature, and of Cowley's wit;
How Beaumont's judgment check'd what Fletcher writ.
How Shadwell hasty, Wycherley was slow;
But, for the passions, Southern, sure, and Rowe.
These, only these, support the crowded stage,
From eldest Heywood down to Cibber's age."
All this may be; the people's voice is odd,
It is, and it is not, the voice of God.
To Gammer Gurton[1] if it give the bays,
And yet deny the Careless Husband praise,
Or say our fathers never broke a rule;
Why then, I say, the public is a fool.
But let them own, that greater faults than we
They had, and greater virtues, I'll agree.
Spenser himself affects the obsolete,
And Sidney's verse halts ill on Roman feet:
Milton's strong pinion now not heaven can bound,
Now serpent-like, in prose he sweeps the ground,
In quibbles, angel and archangel join,
And God the Father turns a school-divine.
Not that I'd lop the beauties from his book,
Like slashing Bentley with his desperate hook,
Or damn all Shakspeare, like the affected fool
At court, who hates whate'er he read at school.
But for the wits of either Charles's days,
The mob of gentlemen who wrote with ease;
Sprat, Carew, Sedley, and a hundred more,
(Like twinkling stars the miscellanies o'er)
One simile, that solitary shines
In the dry desert of a thousand lines,
Or lengthen'd thought that gleams through many a page,
Has sanctified whole poems for an age.
I lose my patience, and I own it too,
When works are censured, not as bad but new;
While if our elders break all reason's laws,
These fools demand not pardon, but applause.
On Avon's bank, where flowers eternal blow,
If I but ask, if any weed can grow?
One tragic sentence if I dare deride
Which Betterton's grave action dignified,

[1] A piece of very low humour; one of the first printed plays in English, and therefore much valued by some antiquaries.

Or well-mouth'd Booth with emphasis proclaims,
(Though but, perhaps, a muster-roll of names)
How will our fathers rise up in a rage,
And swear all shame is lost in George's age!
You'd think no fools disgraced the former reign,
Did not some grave examples yet remain,
Who scorn a lad should teach his father skill,
And, having once been wrong, will be so still.
He, who to seem more deep than you or I,
Extols old bards, or Merlin's prophecy,
Mistake him not; he envies, not admires,
And to debase the sons, exalts the sires.
Had ancient times conspired to disallow
What then was new, what had been ancient now?
Or what remain'd, so worthy to be read
By learned critics, of the mighty dead?
In days of ease, when now the weary sword
Was sheathed, and luxury with Charles restored;
In every taste of foreign courts improved,
"All, by the king's example, lived and loved."
Then peers grew proud in horsemanship to excel,[1]
Newmarket's glory rose, as Britain's fell;
The soldier breathed the gallantries of France,
And every flowery courtier writ romance.
Then marble, soften'd into life, grew warm,
And yielding metal flow'd to human form:
Lely on animated canvas stole
The sleepy eye, that spoke the melting soul.
No wonder then, when all was love and sport,
The willing muses were debauch'd at court:
On each enervate string they taught the note[2]
To pant, or tremble through a eunuch's throat.
But Britain, changeful as a child at play,
Now calls in princes, and now turns away.
Now Whig, now Tory, what we loved we hate;
Now all for pleasure, now for church and state;
Now for prerogative, and now for laws;
Effects unhappy! from a noble cause.

[1] The Duke of Newcastle's book of Horsemanship; the romance of *Parthenissa*, by the Earl of Orrery; and most of the French romances translated by *persons of quality*.

[2] The siege of Rhodes, by Sir William Davenant, the first opera sung in England.

Time was, a sober Englishman would knock
His servants up, and rise by five o'clock
Instruct his family in every rule,
And send his wife to church, his son to school.
To worship like his fathers, was his care;
To teach their frugal virtues to his heir;
To prove, that luxury could never hold;
And place, on good security, his gold.
Now times are changed, and one poetic itch
Has seized the court and city, poor and rich:
Sons, sires, and grandsires, all will wear the bays,
Our wives read Milton, and our daughters plays,
To theatres, and to rehearsals throng,
And all our grace at table is a song.
I, who so oft renounce the Muses' lie,
Not ——'s self e'er tells more *fibs* than I;
When sick of Muse, or follies we deplore,
And promise our best friends to rhyme no more;
We wake next morning in a raging fit,
And call for pen and ink to show our wit.
He served a 'prenticeship, who sets up shop;
Ward[1] tried on puppies, and the poor, his drop;
E'en Radcliffe's doctors travel first to France,
Nor dare to practise till they've learn'd to dance.
Who builds a bridge, that never drove a pile?
(Should Ripley venture, all the world would smile)
But those who cannot write, and those who can,
All rhyme, and scrawl, and scribble, to a man.
Yet, sir, reflect: the mischief is not great;
These madmen never hurt the church or state:
Sometimes the folly benefits mankind:
And rarely avarice taints the tuneful mind.
Allow him but his plaything of a pen,
He ne'er rebels, or plots, like other men:
Flight of cashiers, or mobs, he'll never mind;
And knows no losses while the Muse is kind.
To cheat a friend, or ward, he leaves to Peter;
The good man heaps up nothing but mere metre,
Enjoys his garden and his book in quiet;
And then—a perfect hermit in his diet.

[1] A famous empiric, whose pill and drop had several surprising effects, and were one of the principal subjects of writing and conversation at this time.

Of little use the man you may suppose,
Who says in verse what others say in prose;
Yet let me show, a poet's of some weight,
And (though no soldier) useful to the state.
What will a child learn sooner than a song?
What better teach a foreigner the tongue?
What's long or short, each accent where to place,
And speak in public with some sort of grace,
I scarce can think him such a worthless thing,
Unless he praise some monster of a king;
Or virtue, or religion turn to sport,
To please a lewd, or unbelieving court.
Unhappy Dryden!——In all Charles's days,
Roscommon only boasts unspotted bays;
And in our own (excuse some courtly stains)
No whiter page than Addison's remains.
He, from the taste obscene reclaims our youth,
And sets the passions on the side of truth;
Forms the soft bosom with the gentlest art,
And pours each human virtue in the heart.
Let Ireland tell, how wit upheld her cause,
Her trade supported, and supplied her laws;
And leave on SWIFT this grateful verse engraved,
"The rights a court attack'd, a poet saved."
Behold the hand that wrought a nation's cure,
Stretch'd to relieve the idiot and the poor,[1]
Proud vice to brand, or injured worth adorn,
And stretch the ray to ages yet unborn.
Not but there are, who merit other palms;
Hopkins and Sternhold glad the heart with psalms:
The boys and girls whom charity maintains,
Implore your help in these pathetic strains:
How could devotion touch the country pews,
Unless the gods bestow'd a proper muse?
Verse cheers their leisure, verse assists their work,
Verse prays for peace, or sings down Pope and Turk.
The silenced preacher yields to potent strain,
And feels that grace his prayer besought in vain;
The blessing thrills through all the labouring throng,
And Heaven is won by violence of song.
Our rural ancestors, with little blest,
Patient of labour when the end was rest,

[1] A foundation for the maintenance of idiots, and a fund for assisting the poor, by lending small sums of money on demand.

Indulged the day that housed their annual grain,
With feasts, and offerings, and a thankful strain:
The joy their wives, their sons, and servants share,
Ease of their toil, and partners of their care:
The laugh, the jest, attendants on the bowl,
Smoothed every brow, and open'd every soul:
With growing years the pleasing licence grew,
And taunts alternate innocently flew.
But times corrupt, and Nature, ill-inclined,
Produced the point that left a sting behind;
Till friend with friend, and families at strife,
Triumphant malice raged through private life.
Who felt the wrong, or fear'd it, took the alarm,
Appeal'd to law, and justice lent her arm.
At length, by wholesome dread of statutes bound,
The poets learn'd to please, and not to wound:
Most warp'd to flattery's side; but some, more nice,
Preserved the freedom, and forbore the vice.
Hence satire rose, that just the medium hit,
And heals with morals what it hurts with wit.
We conquer'd France, but felt our captive's charms;
Her arts victorious triumph'd o'er our arms;
Britain to soft refinements less a foe,
Wit grew polite, and numbers learn'd to flow.
Waller was smooth;[1] but Dryden taught to join
The varying verse, the full resounding line,
The long majestic march, and energy divine.
Though still some traces of our rustic vein,
And splay-foot verse, remain'd, and will remain.
Late, very late, correctness grew our care,
When the tired nation breathed from civil war.
Exact Racine, and Corneille's noble fire,
Show'd us that France had something to admire.
Not but the tragic spirit was our own,
And full in Shakspeare, fair in Otway shone:
But Otway fail'd to polish or refine,
And fluent Shakspeare scarce effaced a line.
Even copious Dryden wanted, or forgot,
The last and greatest art, the art to blot.
Some doubt, if equal pains, or equal fire
The humble muse of comedy require.

[1] Mr. Waller, about this time, with the Earl of Dorset, Mr. Godolphin, and others, translated the Pompey of Corneille, and the more correct French poets began to be in reputation.

But in known images of life, I guess
The labour greater, as the indulgence less.
Observe how seldom even the best succeed:
Tell me if Congreve's fools are fools indeed?
What pert, low dialogue has Farquhar writ!
How Van[1] wants grace, who never wanted wit!
The stage how loosely does Astrea[2] tread,
Who fairly puts all characters to bed!
And idle Cibber, how he breaks the laws,
To make poor Pinky eat with vast applause!
But fill their purse, our poets' work is done,
Alike to them, by pathos or by pun.
O you! whom vanity's light bark conveys
On Fame's mad voyage by the wind of praise,
With what a shifting gale your course you ply,
For ever sunk too low, or borne too high!
Who pants for glory finds but short repose,
A breath revives him, or a breath o'erthrows.
Farewell the stage! if just as thrives the play,
The silly bard grows fat, or falls away.
There still remains, to mortify a wit,
The many-headed monster of the pit
A senseless, worthless, and unhonour'd crowd;
Who, to disturb their betters mighty proud,
Clattering their sticks before ten lines are spoke,
Call for the farce, the Bear, or the Black-joke.
What dear delight to Britons farce affords!
Ever the taste of mobs, but now of lords:
(Taste, that eternal wanderer, which flies
From heads to ears, and now from ears to eyes.)
The play stands still; damn action and discourse;
Back fly the scenes, and enter foot and horse;
Pageants on pageants, in long order drawn,
Peers, heralds, bishops, ermine, gold, and lawn;
The champion too! and, to complete the jest,
Old Edward's armour beams on Cibber's breast.[3]
With laughter sure Democritus had died,
Had he beheld an audience gape so wide.

[1] Sir John Vanbrugh.

[2] A name taken by Mrs. Behn, authoress of several obscene plays.

[3] The coronation of Henry VIII. and Queen Anne Boleyn, in which the playhouses vied with each other to represent all the pomp of a coronation. In this noble contention the armour of one of the kings of England was borrowed from the Tower, to dress the champion.

Let bear or elephant be e'er so white,
The people, sure, the people are the sight!
Ah luckless poet! stretch thy lungs and roar,
That bear or elephant shall heed thee more;
While all its throats the gallery extends,
And all the thunder of the pit ascends!
Loud as the wolves, on Orcas' stormy steep,[1]
Howl to the roarings of the northern deep;
Such is the shout, the long-applauding note,
At Quin's high plume, or Oldfield's petticoat;
Or when from court a birth-day suit bestow'd,
Sinks the lost actor in the tawdry load.
Booth enters,—hark! the universal peal!
"But has he spoken?"—Not a syllable.
"What shook the stage, and made the people stare?"
Cato's long wig, flower'd gown, and lacquer'd chair.
  Yet, lest you think I rally more than teach,
Or praise malignly arts I cannot reach,
Let me for once presume to instruct the times,
To know the poet from the man of rhymes:
'Tis he, who gives my breast a thousand pains,
Can make me feel each passion that he feigns;
Enrage, compose, with more than magic art;
With pity, and with terror, tear my heart;
And snatch me, o'er the earth, or through the air,
To Thebes, to Athens, when he will, and where.
  But not this part of the poetic state,
Alone, deserves the favour of the great.
Think of those authors, sir, who would rely
More on a reader's sense than gazer's eye.
Or who shall wander where the Muses sing?
Who climb their mountain, or who taste their spring?
How shall we fill a library[2] with wit,
When Merlin's Cave[3] is half-unfinish'd yet!
  My liege! why writers little claim your thought.
I guess, and, with their leave, will tell the fault!
We poets are (upon a poet's word)
Of all mankind, the creatures most absurd:

[1] The farthest northern promontory of Scotland, opposite to the Orcades.

[2] The Palatine Library, then building by Augustus.

[3] A building in the Royal Gardens of Richmond, where was a small but choice collection of books.

The season, when to come; and when to go,
To sing, or cease to sing, we never know;
And if we will recite nine hours in ten,
You lose your patience, just like other men.
Then too we hurt ourselves, when to defend
A single verse, we quarrel with a friend;
Repeat unask'd; lament, the wit's too fine
For vulgar eyes, and point out every line.
But most, when straining with too weak a wing,
We needs will write epistles to the king;
And from the moment we oblige the town,
Expect a place, or pension from the crown;
Or dubb'd historians by express command,
To enrol your triumphs o'er the seas and land,
Be call'd to court to plan some work divine,
As once for Louis, Boileau and Racine.
Yet think, great sir! (so many virtues shown)
Ah think, what poet best may make them known?
Or choose at least some minister of grace,
Fit to bestow the laureat's weighty place.
Charles, to late times to be transmitted fair,
Assign'd his figure to Bernini's care;
And great Nassau to Kneller's hand decreed
To fix him graceful on the bounding steed;
So well in paint and stone they judged of merit:
But kings in wit may want discerning spirit.
The hero William, and the martyr Charles,
One knighted Blackmore, and one pension'd Quarles;
Which made old Ben and surly Dennis swear
"No lord's anointed, but a Russian bear."
Not with such majesty, such bold relief,
The forms august, of king, or conquering chief,
E'er swell'd on marble; as in verse have shined
(In polish'd verse) the manners and the mind.
Oh! could I mount on the Mæonian wing,
Your arms, your actions, your repose to sing!
What seas you traversed, and what fields you fought!
Your country's peace, how oft, how dearly bought!
How barbarous rage subsided at your word,
And nations wonder'd while they dropp'd the sword!
How, when you nodded, o'er the land and deep,
Peace stole her wing, and wrapt the world in sleep;
Till earth's extremes your mediation own,
And Asia's tyrants tremble at your throne—

But verse, alas! your majesty disdains;
And I'm not used to panegyric strains:
The zeal of fools offends at any time,
But most of all, the zeal of fools in rhyme.
Besides, a fate attends on all I write,
That when I aim at praise, they say I bite.
A vile encomium doubly ridicules:
There's nothing blackens like the ink of fools.
If true, a woful likeness; and if lies,
"Praise undeserved is scandal in disguise:"
Well may he blush, who gives it, or receives;
And when I flatter, let my dirty leaves
(Like journals, odes, and such forgotten things
As Eusden, Philips, Settle, writ of kings)
Clothe spice, line trunks, or fluttering in a row,
Befringe the rails of Bedlam and Soho.

THE SECOND EPISTLE

OF THE

SECOND BOOK OF HORACE.

DEAR Colonel, COBHAM'S and your country's friend!
You love a verse, take such as I can send.
A Frenchman comes, presents you with his boy,
Bows and begins—"This lad, sir, is of Blois:[1]
Observe his shape how clean! his locks how curl'd!
My only son, I'd have him see the world:
His French is pure; his voice too—you shall hear.
Sir, he's your slave, for twenty pound a-year.
Mere wax as yet, you fashion him with ease,
Your barber, cook, upholsterer, what you please:
A perfect genius at an opera song—
To say too much, might do my honour wrong.
Take him with all his virtues, on my word;
His whole ambition was to serve a lord;
But, sir, to you, with what would I not part?
Tho' faith, I fear, 'twill break his mother's heart.

[1] A town in Beauce, where the French tongue is spoken in great purity.

Once (and but once) I caught him in a lie,
And then, unwhipp'd, he had the grace to cry:
The fault he has I fairly shall reveal,
(Could you o'erlook but that) it is, to steal."
 If, after this, you took the graceless lad,
Could you complain, my friend, he proved so bad?
Faith, in such case, if you should prosecute,
I think Sir Godfrey[1] should decide the suit;
Who sent the thief that stole the cash away,
And punish'd him that put it in his way.
 Consider then, and judge me in this light;
I told you when I went, I could not write;
You said the same; and are you discontent
With laws to which you gave your own assent?
Nay, worse, to ask for verse at such a time!
D'ye think me good for nothing but to rhyme?
 In ANNA'S wars, a soldier poor and old,
Had dearly earned a little purse of gold:
Tired with a tedious march, one luckless night,
He slept, poor dog! and lost it, to a doit.
This put the man in such a desperate mind,
Between revenge, and grief, and hunger, join'd,
Against the foe, himself, and all mankind,
He leap'd the trenches, scaled a castle wall,
Tore down a standard, took the fort and all.
"Prodigious well:" his great commander cried,
Gave him much praise, and some reward beside.
Next pleased his excellence a town to batter;
(Its name I know not, and 'tis no great matter)
"Go on, my friend, (he cried) see yonder walls!
Advance and conquer! go where glory calls!
More honours, more rewards, attend the brave."
Don't you remember what reply he gave?
"D'ye think me, noble general, such a sot?
Let him take castles who has ne'er a groat."
 Bred up at home, full early I begun
To read in Greek the wrath of Peleus' son.
Besides, my father taught me from a lad,
The better art to know the good from bad:
(And little sure imported to remove,
To hunt for truth in Maudlin's learned grove.)

[1] An eminent justice of peace, who decided much in the manner of Sancho Pancha.

But knottier points we knew not half so well,
Deprived us soon of our paternal cell;
And certain laws, by sufferers thought unjust,
Denied all posts of profit or of trust:
Hopes after hopes of pious papists fail'd,
While mighty WILLIAM's thundering arm prevail'd.
For right hereditary tax'd and fined,
He stuck to poverty with peace of mind;
And me, the muses help'd to undergo it;
Convict a papist he, and I a poet.
But, (thanks to Homer) since I live and thrive,
Indebted to no prince or peer alive,
Sure I should want the care of ten Monroes,
If I would scribble, rather than repose.
Years following years, steal something every day,
At last they steal us from ourselves away;
In one our frolics, one amusements end,
In one a mistress drops, in one a friend:
This subtle thief of life, this paltry time,
What will it leave me, if it snatch my rhyme?
If every wheel of that unwearied mill,
That turn'd ten thousand verses, now stands still?
But after all, what would you have me do?
When out of twenty I can please not two;
When this heroics only deigns to praise,
Sharp satire that, and that Pindaric lays?
One likes the pheasant's wing, and one the leg;
The vulgar boil, the learned roast an egg;
Hard task! to hit the palate of such guests,
When Oldfield loves, what Dartineuf detests.
But grant I may relapse, for want of grace,
Again to rhyme; can London be the place!
Who there his muse, or self, or soul attends,
In crowds, in courts, law, business, feasts, and friends?
My counsel sends to execute a deed:
A poet begs me I will hear him read:
In Palace-yard, at nine you'll find me there—
At ten for certain, sir, in Bloomsbury-square—
Before the lords, at twelve, my cause comes on—
There's a rehearsal, sir, exact at one.—
"Oh but a wit can study in the streets,
And raise his mind above the mob he meets."
Not quite so well, however, as one ought;
A hackney-coach may chance to spoil a thought;

And then a nodding beam, or pig of lead,
God knows, may hurt the very ablest head.
Have you not seen, at Guildhall's narrow pass,
Two aldermen dispute it with an ass?
And peers give way, exalted as they are,
Even to their own sir-reverence in a car?
Go, lofty poet! and in such a crowd,
Sing thy sonorous verse—but not aloud.
Alas! to grottoes and to groves we run,
To ease and silence, every Muse's son:
Blackmore himself, for any grand effort,
Would drink and doze at Tooting or Earl's-court.
How shall I rhyme in this eternal roar?
How match the bards whom none e'er match'd before?
The man, who stretch'd in Isis' calm retreat,
To books and study gives seven years complete,
See! strew'd with learned dust, his nightcap on,
He walks, an object new beneath the sun!
The boys flock round him, and the people stare:
So stiff, so mute! some statue you would swear,
Stept from its pedestal to take the air!
And here, while town, and court, and city roars,
With mobs, and duns, and soldiers, at their doors;
Shall I, in London, act this idle part?
Composing songs for fools to get by heart?
The Temple late two brother serjeants saw,
Who deem'd each other oracles of law;
With equal talents, these congenial souls,
One lull'd the Exchequer, and one stunn'd the Rolls
Each had a gravity would make you split,
And shook his head at MURRAY, as a wit.
'Twas, "Sir, your law,"—and "Sir, your eloquence,"
"Yours Cowper's manner,"—and "Yours Talbot's sense."
Thus we dispose of all poetic merit,
Yours Milton's genius, and mine Homer's spirit.
Call Tibbald Shakspeare, and he'll swear the Nine,
Dear Cibber! never match'd one ode of thine.
Lord! how we strut through Merlin's Cave, to see
No poets there, but Stephen, you, and me.
Walk with respect behind, while we at ease
Weave laurel crowns, and take what names we please.
"My dear Tibullus!" (if that will not do,)
"Let me be Horace, and be Ovid you:

Or, I'm content, allow me Dryden's strains,
And you shall rise up Otway for your pains."
Much do I suffer, much to keep in peace
This jealous, waspish, wrong-head, rhyming race;
And much must flatter, if the whim should bite,
To court applause by printing what I write:
But let the fit pass o'er, I'm wise enough
To stop my ears to their confounded stuff.
In vain bad rhymers all mankind reject,
They treat themselves with most profound respect;
'Tis to small purpose that you hold your tongue,
Each praised within, is happy all day long;
But how severely with themselves proceed
The men, who write such verse as we can read?
Their own strict judges, not a word they spare
That wants or force, or light, or weight, or care,
Howe'er unwillingly it quits its place,
Nay, though at court (perhaps) it may find grace:
Such they'll degrade; and sometimes, in its stead,
In downright charity revive the dead;
Mark where a bold expressive phrase appears,
Bright through the rubbish of some hundred years;
Command old words that long have slept, to wake,
Words, that wise Bacon or brave Raleigh spake;
Or bid the new be English, ages hence,
(For use will father what's begot by sense)
Pour the full tide of eloquence along,
Serenely pure, and yet divinely strong,
Rich with the treasures of each foreign tongue;
Prune the luxuriant, the uncouth refine,
But show no mercy to an empty line:
Then polish all, with so much life and ease,
You think 'tis nature, and a knack to please:
"But ease in writing flows from art, not chance;
As those move easiest who have learn'd to dance."
If such the plague and pains to write by rule,
Better (say I) be pleased, and play the fool;
Call, if you will, bad rhyming a disease,
It gives men happiness, or leaves them ease.
There lived *in primo Georgii* (they record)
A worthy member, no small fool, a lord;
Who, though the house was up, delighted sate,
Heard, noted, answered, as in full debate:

In all but this, a man of sober life,
Fond of his friend, and civil to his wife;
Not quite a madman, though a pasty fell,
And much too wise to walk into a well.
Him, the damn'd doctors and his friends immured,
They bled, they cupp'd, they purged; in short, they
Whereat the gentleman began to stare— [cured:
My friends! he cried, pox take you for your care!
That from a patriot of distinguish'd note,
Have bled and purged me to a simple vote.
Well, on the whole, plain prose must be my fate:
Wisdom (curse on it) will come soon or late.
There is a time when poets will grow dull:
I'll e'en leave verses to the boys at school:
To rules of poetry no more confined,
I'll learn to smooth and harmonize my mind,
Teach every thought within its bounds to roll,
And keep the equal measure of the soul.
Soon as I enter at my country-door,
My mind resumes the thread it dropt before;
Thoughts, which at Hyde-park corner I forgot,
Meet and rejoin me, in the pensive grot.
There all alone, and compliments apart,
I ask these sober questions of my heart;
If, when the more you drink, the more you crave,
You tell the doctor; when the more you have
The more you want, why not with equal ease
Confess as well your folly as disease?
The heart resolves this matter in a trice,
"Men only feel the smart, but not the vice."
When golden angels cease to cure the evil,
You give all royal witchcraft to the devil:
When servile chaplains cry, that birth and place
Indue a peer with honour, truth, and grace,
Look in that breast, most dirty D—! be fair,
Say, can you find out one such lodger there?
Yet still, not heeding what your heart can teach,
You go to church to hear these flatterers preach.
Indeed, could wealth bestow or wit or merit,
A grain of courage, or a spark of spirit,
The wisest man might blush, I must agree
If D*** loved sixpence, more than he.
If there be truth in law, and use can give
A property, that's yours on which you live.

Delightful Abs-court, if its fields afford
Their fruits to you, confesses you its lord:
All Worldly's hens, nay partridge, sold to town,
His venison too, a guinea makes your own;
He bought at thousands, what with better wit
You purchase as you want, and bit by bit;
Now, or long since, what difference will be found!
You pay a penny, and he paid a pound.
 Heathcote himself, and such large-acred men,
Lords of fat E'sham, or of Lincoln fen,
Buy every stick of wood, that lends them heat,
Buy every pullet they afford to eat.
Yet these are wights, who fondly call their own
Half that the devil o'erlooks from Lincoln town.
The laws of God, as well as of the land,
Abhor a perpetuity should stand:
Estates have wings, and hang in fortune's power,
Loose on the point of every wavering hour;
Ready by force, or of your own accord,
By sale, at least by death, to change their lord.
Man? and *for ever?* wretch! what would'st thou have?
Heir urges heir, like wave impelling wave.
All vast possessions, (just the same the case
Whether you call them villa, park, or chase),
Alas, my BATHURST! what will they avail?
Join Cotswold hills to Saperton's fair dale,
Let rising granaries and temples here,
There mingled farms and pyramids appear,
Link towns to towns with avenues of oak,
Enclose whole downs in walls, 'tis all a joke!
Inexorable death shall level all,
And trees, and stones, and farms, and farmer, fall.
 Gold, silver, ivory, vases sculptured high,
Paint, marble, gems, and robes of Persian dye,
There are who have not,—and thank Heaven there are,
Who, if they have not, think not worth their care.
 Talk what you will of taste, my friend, you'll find
Two of a face, as soon as of a mind.
Why, of two brothers, rich and restless one
Ploughs, burns, manures, and toils from sun to sun;
The other slights, for women, sports, and wines,
All Townshend's turnips, and all Grosvenor's mines:
Why one like Bu— with pay and scorn content,
Bows and votes on, in court and Parliament;

One driven by strong benevolence of soul,
Shall fly like Oglethorpe, from pole to pole:
Is known alone to that directing power,
Who forms the genius in the natal hour;
That God of Nature, who, within us still,
Inclines our action, not constrains our will;
Various of temper, as of face or frame,
Each individual: His great end the same.
Yes, sir, how small soever be my heap,
A part I will enjoy, as well as keep.
My heir may sigh, and think it want of grace
A man so poor would live without a place:
But sure no statute in his favour says,
How free, or frugal, I shall pass my days:
I, who at some times spend, at others spare,
Divided between carelessness and care.
'Tis one thing madly to disperse my store;
Another, not to heed to treasure more;
Glad, like a boy, to snatch the first good day,
And pleased, if sordid want be far away.
What is't to me, (a passenger, God wot)
Whether my vessel be first rate or not?
The ship itself may make a better figure,
But I that sail, am neither less nor bigger.
I neither strut with every favouring breath,
Nor strive with all the tempest in my teeth.
In power, wit, figure, virtue, fortune, placed
Behind the foremost, and before the last.
"But why all this of avarice? I have none."
I wish you joy, sir, of a tyrant gone;
But does no other lord it at this hour,
As wild and mad? the avarice of power?
Does neither rage inflame, nor fear appal?
Not the black fear of death that saddens all?
With terrors round, can Reason hold her throne,
Despise the known, nor tremble at the unknown?
Survey both worlds, intrepid and entire,
In spite of witches, devils, dreams, and fire?
Pleased to look forward, pleased to look behind,
And count each birth-day with a grateful mind?
Has life no sourness, drawn so near its end!
Canst thou endure a foe, forgive a friend?
Has age but melted the rough parts away,
As winter-fruits grow mild ere they decay?

Or will you think, my friend, your business done,
When, of a hundred thorns, you pull out one?
   Learn to live well, or fairly make your will;
You've play'd, and loved, and eat and drank your fill
Walk sober off, before a sprightlier age
Comes tittering on, and shoves you from the stage:
Leave such to trifle with more grace and ease,
Whom folly pleases, and whose follies please.

EPISTLE VII.

IMITATED IN THE MANNER OF DR. SWIFT.

'Tis true, my lord, I gave my word,
I would be with you June the third;
Changed it to August, and in short,
Have kept it—as you do at court.
You humour me when I am sick,
Why not when I am splenetic?
In town, what objects could I meet?
The shops shut up in every street,
And funerals blackening all the doors,
And yet more melancholy whores:
And what a dust in every place!
And a thin court that wants your face,
And fevers raging up and down,
And W* and H** both in town!
   "The dog-days are no more the case."
'Tis true, but winter comes apace:
Then southward let your bard retire,
Hold out some months 'twixt sun and fire,
And you shall see, the first warm weather,
Me and the butterflies together.
   My lord, your favours well I know;
'Tis with distinction you bestow;
And not to every one that comes,
Just as a Scotsman does his plums:
"Pray take them, sir—enough's a feast
Eat some, and pocket up the rest."—
What, rob your boys? those pretty rogues!
"No, sir, you'll leave them to the hogs."

Thus fools, with compliments besiege ye,
Contriving never to oblige ye.
Scatter your favours on a fop,
Ingratitude's the certain crop
And 'tis but just, I'll tell ye wherefore,
You give the things you never care for.
A wise man always is, or should
Be mighty ready to do good:
But makes a difference in his thought
Betwixt a guinea and a groat.
  Now this I'll say, you'll find in me
A safe companion, and a free;
But if you'd have me always near—
A word, pray, in your honour's ear.
I hope it is your resolution
To give me back my constitution!
The sprightly wit, the lively eye,
The engaging smile, the gaiety
That laugh'd down many a summer sun,
And kept you up so oft till one;
And all that voluntary vein,
As when Belinda raised my strain.
  A weasel once made shift to slink
In at a corn-loft through a chink,
But having amply stuff'd his skin,
Could not get out as he got in;
Which one belonging to the house
('Twas not a man, it was a mouse)
Observing, cried, "You 'scape not so!
Lean as you came, sir, you must go."
  Sir, you may spare your application!
I'm no such beast, nor his relation;
Nor one that temperance advance,
Cramm'd to the throat with ortolans:
Extremely ready to resign
All that may make me none of mine.
South-sea subscriptions take who please,
Leave me but liberty and ease.
'Twas what I said to Craggs and Child,
Who praised my modesty and smiled.
Give me, I cried, (enough for me)
My bread, and independency!
So bought an annual rent or two,
And lived—just as you see I do;

Near fifty, and without a wife,
I trust that sinking fund, my life.
Can I retrench? Yes, mighty well,
Shrink back to my paternal cell,
A little house, with trees a-row,
And, like its master, very low.
There died my father, no man's debtor,
And there I'll die, nor worse nor better.
  To set this matter full before ye,
Our old friend Swift will tell his story.
  "Harley, the nation's great support,"—
But you may read it, I stop short.

BOOK II.—SATIRE VI.

THE FIRST PART IMITATED IN THE YEAR 1714, BY DR. SWIFT, THE LATTER PART ADDED AFTERWARDS.

I'VE often wish'd that I had clear
For life, six hundred pounds a year,
A handsome house to lodge a friend,
A river at my garden's end,
A terrace-walk, and half a rood
Of land, set out to plant a wood.
  Well, now I have all this and more,
I ask not to increase my store;
But here a grievance seems to lie,
All this is mine but till I die;
I can't but think 'twould sound more clever
To me and to my heirs for ever.
  If I ne'er got or lost a groat,
By any trick, or any fault;
And if I pray by Reason's rules,
And not like forty other fools:
As thus, 'Vouchsafe, O gracious Maker!
To grant me this and t'other acre:
Or, if it be thy will and pleasure,
Direct my plough to find a treasure:
But only what my station fits,
And to be kept in my right wits,
Preserve, Almighty Providence!
Just what you gave me, competence:

And let me in these shades compose
Something in verse as true as prose,
Removed from all the ambitious scene.
Nor puff'd by pride, nor sunk by spleen.
In short, I'm perfectly content,
Let me but live on this side Trent;
Nor cross the channel twice a year,
To spend six months with statesmen here.
I must, by all means, come to town,
'Tis for the service of the crown.
"Lewis, the Dean will be of use,
Send for him up, take no excuse."
The toil, the danger of the seas,
Great ministers ne'er think of these;
Or let it cost five hundred pound,
No matter where the money's found.
It is but so much more in debt,
And *that* they ne'er consider'd yet.
"Good Mr. Dean, go change your gown,
Let my lord know you're come to town."
I hurry me in haste away,
Not thinking it is levee-day;
And find his honour in a pound,
Hemm'd by a triple circle round,
Chequer'd with ribbons blue and green:
How should I thrust myself between?
Some wag observes me thus perplex'd
And smiling, whispers to the next,
"I thought the Dean had been too proud,
To justle here among a crowd."
Another, in a surly fit,
Tells me I have more zeal than wit:
"So eager to express your love,
You ne'er consider whom you shove,
But rudely press before a duke."
I own, I'm pleased with this rebuke,
And take it kindly meant to show
What I desire the world should know.
I get a whisper, and withdraw:
When twenty fools I never saw
Come with petitions fairly penn'd,
Desiring I would stand their friend.
This humbly offers me his case—
That, begs my interest for a place—

A hundred other men's affairs,
Like bees, are humming in my ears.
"To-morrow my appeal comes on,
Without your help the cause is gone"—
The duke expects my lord and you,
About some great affair, at two—
"Put my Lord Bolingbroke in mind,
To get my warrant quickly sign'd:
Consider 'tis my first request."—
Be satisfied, I'll do my best:—
Then presently he falls to tease,
"You may for certain if you please;
I doubt not, if his lordship knew—
And Mr. Dean, one word from you"—
'Tis (let me see) three years and more,
(October next it will be four)
Since Harley bid me first attend,
And chose me for an humble friend;
Would take me in his coach to chat,
And question me of this and that;
As, "What's-o-clock?" And, "How's the wind?"
"Whose chariot's that we left behind?"
Or gravely try to read the lines
Writ underneath the country signs;
Or, "Have you nothing new to-day
From Pope, from Parnell, or from Gay?"
Such tattle often entertains
My lord and me as far as Staines,
As once a week we travel down
To Windsor, and again to town;
Where all that passes, *inter nos*,
Might be proclaim'd at Charing-cross.
Yet some, I know, with envy swell,
Because they see me used so well:
"How think you of our friend the Dean?
I wonder what some people mean;
My lord and he are grown so great,
Always together, *tête-à-tête*.
What, they admire him for his jokes—
See but the fortune of some folks!"
There flies about a strange report
Of some express arrived at court;
I'm stopp'd by all the fools I meet,
And catechised in every street.

"You, Mr. Dean, frequent the great;
Inform us, will the emperor treat?
Or do the prints and papers lie?"
"Faith, sir, you know as much as I."
"Ah, Doctor, how you love to jest!
'Tis now no secret"—I protest
'Tis one to me—"Then tell us, pray,
When are the troops to have their pay?"
And though I solemnly declare
I know no more than my Lord Mayor,
They stand amazed, and think me grown
The closest mortal ever known.
Thus in a sea of folly toss'd,
My choicest hours of life are lost;
Yet always wishing to retreat,
Oh, could I see my country seat!
There leaning near a gentle brook,
Sleep, or peruse some ancient book,
And there in sweet oblivion drown
Those cares that haunt the court and town.
O charming noons! and nights divine!
Or when I sup, or when I dine,
My friends above, my folks below,
Chatting and laughing, all-a-row,
The beans and bacon set before 'em,
The grace-cup served with all decorum:
Each willing to be pleased, and please,
And even the very dogs at ease!
Here no man prates of idle things;
How this or that Italian sings,
A neighbour's madness, or his spouse's,
Or what's in either of the houses:
But something much more our concern,
And quite a scandal not to learn:
Which is the happier, or the wiser,
A man of merit, or a miser?
Whether we ought to choose our friends,
For their own worth, or our own ends?
What good, or better, we may call,
And what, the very best of all?
Our friend Dan Prior told, (you know,)
A tale extremely *à propos:*
Name a town life, and in a trice,
He had a story of two mice.

Once on a time (so runs the fable)
A country mouse, right hospitable,
Received a town mouse at his board,
Just as a farmer might a lord.
A frugal mouse upon the whole,
Yet loved his friend, and had a soul;
Knew what was handsome, and would do't,
On just occasion, *coûte qui coûte.*
He brought him bacon, (nothing lean)
Pudding, that might have pleased a dean;
Cheese, such as men in Suffolk make,
But wish'd it Stilton for his sake;
Yet, to his guest though no way sparing,
He eat himself the rind and paring.
Our courtier scarce could touch a bit,
But show'd his breeding and his wit;
He did his best to seem to eat,
And cried, "I vow you're mighty neat.
But Lord, my friend, this savage scene!
For God's sake, come, and live with men:
Consider, mice, like men, must die,
Both small and great, both you and I:
Then spend your life in joy and sport.
(This doctrine, friend, I learn'd at court.)"
The veriest hermit in the nation
May yield, God knows, to strong temptation.
Away they come, through thick and thin,
To a tall house near Lincoln's Inn;
('Twas on the night of a debate,
When all their lordships had sat late.)
Behold the place, where if a poet
Shined in description, he might show it;
Tell how the moon-beam trembling falls,
And tips with silver all the walls;
Palladian walls, Venetian doors,
Grotesco roofs, and stucco floors;
But let it, in a word, be said,
The moon was up, and men a-bed,
The napkins white, the carpet red;
The guests withdrawn had left the treat,
And down the mice sat, *tête-à-tête.*
Our courtier walks from dish to dish,
Tastes for his friend of fowl and fish:

Tells all their names, lays down the law,
"*Que ça est bon! Ah goûtez ça!*
That jelly's rich, this malmsey healing,
Pray, dip your whiskers and your tail in."
Was ever such a happy swain?
He stuffs and swills, and stuffs again.
"I'm quite ashamed—'tis mighty rude
To eat so much—but all's so good.
I have a thousand thanks to give—
My lord alone knows how to live."
No sooner said, but from the hall
Rush chaplain, butler, dogs, and all:
"A rat! a rat! clap to the door"—
The cat comes bouncing on the floor.
O for the heart of Homer's mice,
Or gods to save them in a trice!
(It was by Providence they think,
For your damn'd stucco has no chink.)
"An't please your honour," quoth the peasant:
"This same dessert is not so pleasant:
Give me again my hollow tree,
A crust of bread, and liberty!"

BOOK IV.—ODE I.

TO VENUS.

Again! new tumults in my breast?
Ah spare me, Venus! let me, let me rest!
I am not now, alas! the man
As in the gentle reign of my queen Anne.
Ah sound no more thy soft alarms,
Nor circle sober fifty with thy charms.
Mother too fierce of dear desires!
Turn, turn to willing hearts your wanton fires.
To *number five* direct your doves,
There spread round Murray all your blooming loves
Noble and young, who strikes the heart
With every sprightly, every decent part;
Equal, the injured to defend,
To charm the mistress, or to fix the friend.
He with a hundred arts refined,
Shall stretch thy conquests over half the kind:

To him each rival shall submit,
Make but his riches equal to his wit.
Then shall thy form the marble grace,
(Thy Grecian form) and Chlöe lend the face:
His house embosom'd in the grove,
Sacred to social life and social love,
Shall glitter o'er the pendent green,
Where Thames reflects the visionary scene:
Thither, the silver-sounding lyres
Shall call the smiling Loves, and young Desires;
There every Grace and Muse shall throng,
Exalt the dance, or animate the song;
There youths and nymphs, in consort gay,
Shall hail the rising, close the parting day
With me, alas! those joys are o'er;
For me, the vernal garlands bloom no more.
Adieu! fond hope of mutual fire,
The still-believing, still-renew'd desire;
Adieu! the heart-expanding bowl,
And all the kind deceivers of the soul!
But why? ah tell me, ah too dear!
Steals down my cheek, the involuntary tear?
Why words so flowing, thoughts so free,
Stop, or turn nonsense, at one glance of thee!
Thee, drest in fancy's airy beam,
Absent I follow through the extended dream
Now, now I seize, I clasp thy charms,
And now you burst (ah cruel!) from my arms
And swiftly shoot along the Mall,
Or softly glide by the canal,
Now shown by Cynthia's silver ray,
And now, on rolling waters snatch'd away.

PART OF THE NINTH ODE

OF THE FOURTH BOOK.

A FRAGMENT.

Lest you should think that verse shall die,
  Which sounds the silver Thames along,
Taught on the wings of truth to fly
  Above the reach of vulgar song;

Though daring Milton sits sublime,
  In Spenser native muses play;
Nor yet shall Waller yield to time,
  Nor pensive Cowley's moral lay—

Sages and chiefs long since had birth
  Ere Cæsar was, or Newton named;
Those raised new empires o'er the earth,
  And these, new heavens and systems framed.

Vain was the chief's, the sage's pride!
They had no poet, and they died.
In vain they schemed, in vain they bled!
They had no poet, and are dead.

THE SATIRES OF DR. JOHN DONNE,

DEAN OF ST. PAUL'S,

VERSIFIED.

Quid vetat et nosmet *Lucili* scripta legentes
Quærere num illius, num rerum dura negârit
Versiculos natura magis factos, et euntes
Mollius? HOR.

SATIRE II.

YES; thank my stars! as early as I knew
This town, I had the sense to hate it too:
Yet here, as even in hell, there must be still
One giant-vice so excellently ill,
That all beside, one pities, not abhors;
As who knows Sappho, smiles at other whores.
  I grant that poetry's a crying sin;
It brought (no doubt) the *excise* and *army* in:
Catch'd like the plague, or love, the Lord knows how,
But that the cure is starving, all allow.
Yet like the papist's, is the poet's state,
Poor and disarm'd and hardly worth your hate!

Here a lean bard, whose wit could never give
Himself a dinner, makes an actor live:
The thief condemn'd in law already dead,
So prompts, and saves a rogue who cannot read.
Thus as the pipes of some carved organ move,
The gilded puppets dance and mount above.
Heaved by the breath, the inspiring bellows blow:
The inspiring bellows lie and pant below.
One sings the fair; but songs no longer move;
No rat is rhymed to death, nor maid to love:
In love's, in nature's spite, the siege they hold,
And scorn the flesh, the devil, and all but gold.
These write to lords, some mean reward to get,
As needy beggars sing at doors for meat.
Those write because all write, and so have still
Excuse for writing, and for writing ill.
Wretched indeed! but far more wretched yet
Is he who makes his meal on others' wit:
'Tis changed, no doubt, from what it was before;
His rank digestion makes it wit no more:
Sense, pass'd through him, no longer is the same;
For food digested takes another name.
I pass o'er all those confessors and martyrs
Who live like Sutton, or who die like Chartres,
Out-cant old Esdras, or out-drink his heir,
Out-usure Jews, or Irishmen out-swear;
Wicked as pages, who in early years
Act sins which Prisca's confessor scarce hears.
Even those I pardon, for whose sinful sake
Schoolmen new tenements in hell must make;
Of whose strange crimes no canonist can tell
In what commandment's large contents they dwell.
One, one man only breeds my just offence;
Whom crimes gave wealth, and wealth gave impudence:
Time, that at last matures a clap to pox,
Whose gentle progress makes a calf an ox,
And brings all natural events to pass,
Hath made him an attorney of an ass.
No young divine, new beneficed, can be
More pert, more proud, more positive than he.
What further could I wish the fop to do,
But turn a wit, and scribble verses too;
Pierce the soft labyrinth of a lady's ear
With rhymes of this *per cent.* and that *per year*?

Or court a wife, spread out his wily parts,
Like nets, or lime-twigs, for rich widows' hearts;
Call himself barrister to every wench,
And woo in language of the Pleas and Bench?
Language, which Boreas might to Auster hold,
More rough than forty Germans when they scold.
  Cursed be the wretch, so venal and so vain:
Paltry and proud, as drabs in Drury-lane.
'Tis such a bounty as was never known,
If PETER deigns to help you to your *own:*
What thanks, what praise, if *Peter* but supplies!
And what a solemn face, if he denies!
Grave, as when prisoners shake the head and swear
'Twas only suretyship that brought them there.
His *office* keeps your parchment fates entire,
He starves with cold to save them from the fire;
For you he walks the streets through rain or dust,
For not in chariots *Peter* put his trust;
For you he sweats and labours at the laws,
Takes God to witness he affects your cause,
And lies to every lord, in every thing,
Like a king's favourite—or like a king.
These are the talents that adorn them all,
From wicked Waters even to godly * *;
Not more of simony beneath black gowns,
Nor more of bastardy in heirs to crowns.
In shillings and in pence at first they deal;
And steal so little, few perceive they steal;
Till, like the sea, they compass all the land,
From *Scots* to *Wight*, from *Mount* to *Dover* strand:
And when rank widows purchase luscious nights,
Or when a duke to *Jansen* punts at White's,
Or city-heir in mortgage melts away;
Satan himself feels far less joy than they.
Piecemeal they win this acre first, then that,
Glean on, and gather up the whole estate.
Then strongly fencing ill-got wealth by law,
Indenture, covenants, articles they draw,
Large as the fields themselves, and larger far
Than civil codes, with all their glosses, are;
So vast, our new divines, we must confess,
Are fathers of the church for writing less.
But let them write for you, each rogue impairs
The deeds, and dextrously omits, *ses heires:*

No commentator can more slily pass
O'er a learn'd unintelligible place;
Or, in quotation, shrewd divines leave out
Those words, that would against them clear the doubt.
So Luther thought the paternoster long,
When doom'd to say his beads and even-song;
But having cast his cowl, and left those laws,
Adds to Christ's prayer, the *power and glory* clause.
The lands are bought; but where are to be found
Those ancient woods that shaded all the ground?
We see no new-built palaces aspire,
No kitchens emulate the vestal fire.
Where are those troops of poor, that throng'd of yore
The good old landlord's hospitable door?
Well, I could wish, that still in lordly domes
Some beasts were kill'd, though not whole hecatombs;
That both extremes were banish'd from their walls,
Carthusian fasts, and fulsome bacchanals;
And all mankind might that just mean observe,
In which none e'er could surfeit, none could starve.
These as good works, 'tis true, we all allow,
But oh! these works are not in fashion now:
Like rich old wardrobes, things extremely rare,
Extremely fine, but what no man will wear.
Thus much I've said, I trust, without offence;
Let no court sycophant pervert my sense,
Nor sly informer watch these words to draw
Within the reach of treason, or the law.

SATIRE IV

Well, if it be my time to quit the stage,
Adieu to all the follies of the age!
I die in charity with fool and knave,
Secure of peace at least beyond the grave.
I've had my purgatory here betimes,
And paid for all my satires, all my rhymes.
The poet's hell, its tortures, fiends, and flames,
To this were trifles, toys, and empty names.
With foolish pride my heart was never fired,
Nor the vain itch to admire, or be admired;

I hoped for no commission from his grace;
I bought no benefice, I begg'd no place;
Had no new verses, nor new suit to show;
Yet went to court!—the devil would have it so.
But, as the fool that in reforming days
Would go to mass in jest (as story says)
Could not but think, to pay his fine was odd,
Since 'twas no form'd design of serving God;
So was I punish'd, as if full as proud
As prone to ill, as negligent of good,
As deep in debt, without a thought to pay,
As vain, as idle, and as false, as they
Who live at court, for going once that way!
Scarce was I enter'd, when, behold! there came
A thing which Adam had been posed to name;
Noah had refused it lodging in his ark,
Where all the race of reptiles might embark:
A verier monster, than on Afric's shore
The sun e'er got, or slimy Nilus bore,
Or Sloane or Woodward's wondrous shelves contain,
Nay, all that lying travellers can feign.
The watch would hardly let him pass at noon,
At night would swear him dropt out of the moon.
One, whom the mob, when next we find or make
A popish plot, shall for a Jesuit take,
And the wise justice, starting from his chair,
Cry, By your priesthood tell me what you are?
Such was the wight: The apparel on his back,
Though coarse, was reverend, and though bare, was black:
The suit, if by the fashion one might guess,
Was velvet in the youth of good Queen *Bess*,
But mere tuff-taffety what now remain'd;
So Time, that changes all things, had ordain'd!
Our sons shall see it leisurely decay,
First turn plain rash, then vanish quite away.
 This thing has travell'd, speaks each language too,
And knows what's fit for every state to do;
Of whose best phrase and courtly accent join'd,
He forms one tongue, exotic and refined.
Talkers I've learn'd to bear; Motteux I knew,
Henley himself I've heard, and Budgell too.
The Doctor's wormwood style, the hash of tongues
A pedant makes, the storm of Gonson's lungs,

The whole artillery of the terms of war,
And (all those plagues in one) the bawling bar:
These I could bear; but not a rogue so civil,
Whose tongue will compliment you to the devil:
A tongue, that can cheat widows, cancel scores,
Make Scots speak treason, cozen subtlest whores,
With royal favourites in flattery vie,
And Oldmixon and Burnet both outlie.
  He spies me out; I whisper, gracious God!
What sin of mine could merit such a rod?
That all the shot of dulness now must be
From this thy blunderbuss discharged on me!
Permit (he cries) no stranger to your fame
To crave your sentiment, if ——'s your name.
What *speech* esteem you most? "The *king's*," said I.
But the best *words?*—"O, Sir, the *dictionary*."
You miss my aim; I mean the most acute,
And perfect *speaker?*—"Onslow, past dispute."
But, Sir, of writers? "Swift for closer style,
But Hoadly for a period of a mile."
Why yes, 'tis granted, these indeed may pass:
Good common linguists, and so Panurge was;
Nay troth the apostles (though perhaps too rough)
Had once a pretty *gift of tongues* enough:
Yet these were all poor gentlemen! I dare
Affirm, 'twas travel made them what they were.
  Thus other talents having nicely shown,
He came by sure transition to his own:
Till I cried out, You prove yourself so able,
Pity! you was not dragoman at Babel;
For had they found a linguist half so good,
I make no question but the tower had stood.
  "Obliging Sir! for courts you sure were made:
Why then for ever buried in the shade?
Spirits like you, should see and should be seen,
The king would smile on you—at least the queen."
"Ah, gentle Sir! you courtiers so cajole us—
But Tully has it, *Nunquam minus solus:*
And as for courts, forgive me, if I say
No lessons now are taught the Spartan way:
Though in his pictures lust be full display'd,
Few are the converts Aretine has made:
And though the court show vice exceeding clear,
None should, by my advice, learn virtue there."

At this entranced, he lifts his hands and eyes,
Squeaks like a high-stretch'd lutestring, and replies;
"Oh, 'tis the sweetest of all earthly things
To gaze on princes, and to talk of kings!"
Then, happy man who shows the tombs! said I,
He dwells amidst the royal family;
He every day, from king to king can walk,
Of all our Harries, all our Edwards talk,
And get by speaking truth of monarchs dead,
What few can of the living, ease and bread.
"Lord, Sir, a mere mechanic! strangely low,
And coarse of phrase,—your English all are so.
How elegant your Frenchmen?" Mine, d'ye mean?
I have but one, I hope the fellow's clean.
"Oh! Sir, politely so! nay, let me die,
Your only wearing is your paduasoy."
Not, Sir, my only, I have better still,
And this you see is but my dishabille.—
Wild to get loose, his patience I provoke,
Mistake, confound, object at all he spoke:
But as coarse iron, sharpen'd, mangles more,
And itch most hurts when anger'd to a sore;
So when you plague a fool, 'tis still the curse,
You only make the matter worse and worse.
He pass'd it o'er; affects an easy smile
At all my peevishness, and turns his style.
He asks, "What news?" I tell him of new plays,
New eunuchs, harlequins, and operas.
He hears, and as a still with simples in it,
Between each drop it gives, stays half a minute,
Loth to enrich me with too quick replies,
By little, and by little, drops his lies.
Mere household trash! of birth-nights, balls, and shows,
More than ten Hollinsheds, or Halls, or Stowes.
When the queen frown'd, or smiled, he knows; and what
A subtle minister may make of that:
Who sins with whom: who got his pension rug,
Or quicken'd a reversion by a drug:
Whose place is quarter'd out, three parts in four,
And whether to a bishop, or a whore:
Who, having lost his credit, pawn'd his rent,
Is therefore fit to have a government:
Who in the secret, deals in stocks secure,
And cheats the unknowing widow and the poor

Who makes a trust of charity a job,
And gets an act of parliament to rob:
Why turnpikes rise, and now no cit nor clown
Can gratis see the country, or the town:
Shortly no lad shall chuck, or lady vole,
But some excising courtier will have toll.
He tells what strumpet places sells for life,
What squire his lands, what citizen his wife;
And last (which proves him wiser still than all)
What lady's face is not a whited wall.
 As one of Woodward's patients, sick, and sore,
I puke, I nauseate,—yet he thrusts in more:
Trims Europe's balance, tops the statesman's part,
And talks Gazettes and Post-boys o'er by heart.
Like a big wife at sight of loathsome meat
Ready to cast, I yawn, I sigh, and sweat.
Then as a licensed spy, whom nothing can
Silence or hurt, he libels the great man;
Swears every place entail'd for years to come,
In sure succession to the day of doom:
He names the price for every office paid,
And says our wars thrive ill, because delay'd:
Nay, hints, 'tis by connivance of the court,
That Spain robs on, and Dunkirk's still a port.
Not more amazement seized on Circe's guests,
To see themselves fall endlong into beasts,
Than mine, to find a subject staid and wise
Already half turn'd traitor by surprise.
I felt the infection slide from him to me,
As in the pox, some give it to get free;
And quick to swallow me, methought I saw
One of our giant statues ope its jaw.
 In that nice moment, as another lie
Stood just a-tilt, the minister came by.
To him he flies, and bows, and bows again,
Then, close as Umbra, joins the dirty train.
Not Fannius' self more impudently near,
When half his nose is in his Prince's ear.
I quaked at heart; and still afraid, to see
All the court fill'd with stranger things than he,
Ran out as fast as one, that pays his bail
And dreads more actions, hurries from a gaol.
 Bear me, some god! oh quickly bear me hence
To wholesome solitude, the nurse of sense:

Where Contemplation prunes her ruffled wings,
And the free soul looks down to pity kings!
There sober thought pursued the amusing theme
Till fancy colour'd it, and form'd a dream.
A vision hermits can to hell transport,
And forced even me to see the damn'd at court.
Not Dante dreaming all the infernal state
Beheld such scenes of envy, sin, and hate.
Base fear becomes the guilty, not the free;
Suits tyrants, plunderers, but suits not me:
Shall I, the terror of this sinful town,
Care, if a liveried lord or smile or frown?
Who cannot flatter, and detest who can,
Tremble before a noble serving-man?
O my fair mistress, Truth! shall I quit thee
For huffing, braggart, puff'd nobility?
Thou, who since yesterday hast roll'd o'er all
The busy, idle blockheads of the ball,
Hast thou, O Sun! beheld an emptier sort,
Than such as swell this bladder of a court?
Now pox on those who show a *court in wax!*[1]
It ought to bring all courtiers on their backs:
Such painted puppets! such a varnish'd race
Of hollow gew-gaws, only dress and face!
Such waxen noses, stately staring things—
No wonder some folks bow, and think them kings.
See! where the British youth, engaged no more
At Fig's, at White's,[2] with felons, or a whore,
Pay their last duty to the court, and come
All fresh and fragrant to the drawing room;
In hues as gay, and odours as divine,
As the fair fields they sold to look so fine.
"That's velvet for a king!" the flatterer swears;
'Tis true, for ten days hence 'twill be king Lear's.
Our court may justly to our stage give rules,
That helps it both to fools-coats and to fools.
And why not players strut in courtiers' clothes?
For these are actors too, as well as those:

[1] A famous show of the court of France, in wax-work.

[2] White's was a noted gaming-house: Fig's, a prize-fighter's academy where the young nobility received instruction in those days: it was also customary for the nobility and gentry to visit the condemned criminals in Newgate.

Wants reach all states; they beg but better drest,
And all is splendid poverty at best.
Painted for sight, and essenced for the smell,
Like frigates fraught with spice and cochine'l,
Sail in the ladies. how each pirate eyes
So weak a vessel, and so rich a prize!
Top-gallant he, and she in all her trim,
He boarding her, she striking sail to him:
"Dear countess! you have charms all hearts to hit!"
And "Sweet Sir Fopling! you have so much wit!"
Such wits and beauties are not praised for nought,
For both the beauty and the wit are bought.
'Twould burst even Heraclitus with the spleen,
To see those antics, Fopling and Courtin:
The presence seems, with things so richly odd,
The mosque of Mahound, or some queer pagod.
See them survey their limbs by Durer's rules,
Of all beau-kind the best proportion'd fools!
Adjust their clothes, and to confession draw
Those venial sins, an atom, or a straw;
But oh! what terrors must distract the soul
Convicted of that mortal crime, a hole;
Or should one pound of powder less bespread
Those monkey-tails that wag behind their head.
Thus finish'd, and corrected to a hair,
They march, to prate their hour before the fair.
So first to preach a white-gloved chaplain goes,
With band of lily, and with cheek of rose,
Sweeter than Sharon, in immaculate trim,
Neatness itself impertinent in him.
Let but the ladies smile, and they are blest:
Prodigious! how the things *protest, protest:*
Peace, fools, or Gonson will for papists seize you,
If once he catch you at your *Jesu! Jesu!*
Nature made every fop to plague his brother,
Just as one beauty mortifies another.
But here's the captain that will plague them both,
Whose air cries arm! whose very look's an oath:
The captain's honest, sirs, and that's enough,
Though his soul's bullet, and his body buff.
He spits fore-right; his haughty chest before,
Like batt'ring rams, beats open every door:
And with a face as red, and as awry,
As Herod's hang-dogs in old tapestry,

Scarecrow to boys, the breeding woman's curse,
Has yet a strange ambition to look worse;
Confounds the civil, keeps the rude in awe,
Jests like a licensed fool, commands like law.
  Frighted, I quit the room, but leave it so
As men from gaols to execution go;
For, hung with deadly sins,[1] I see the wall,
And lined with giants deadlier than them all:
Each man an *Ascapart*,[2] of strength to toss
For quoits, both Temple-bar and Charing-cross.
Scared at the grizly forms, I sweat, I fly,
And shake all o'er, like a discover'd spy.
  Courts are too much for wits so weak as mine:
Charge them with Heaven's artillery, bold divine!
From such alone the great rebukes endure,
Whose satire's sacred, and whose rage secure:
'Tis mine to wash a few light stains, but theirs
To deluge sin, and drown a court in tears.
Howe'er what's now *Apocrypha*, my wit,
In time to come, may pass for Holy Writ.

EPILOGUE TO THE SATIRES.

IN TWO DIALOGUES.

WRITTEN IN 1738.

DIALOGUE I.

FR. Not twice a twelvemonth you appear in print,
And when it comes, the court see nothing in't.
You grow correct that once with rapture writ,
And are, besides, too moral for a wit.
Decay of parts, alas! we all must feel—
Why now, this moment, don't I see you steal?
'Tis all from Horace; Horace long before ye
Said, "Tories call'd him whig, and whigs a tory;"
And taught his Romans, in much better metre,
"To laugh at fools who put their trust in Peter."

[1] The room hung with old tapestry, representing the seven deadly sins.

[2] A giant famous in romances.

But Horace, Sir, was delicate, was nice
Bubo observes,[1] he lash'd no sort of *vice:*
Horace would say, Sir Billy *served the crown,*
Blunt could *do business,* H—ggins[2] *knew the town;*
In Sappho touch the *failings of the sex,*
In reverend bishops note some *small neglects,*
And own, the Spaniard did a *waggish thing,*
Who cropt our ears,[3] and sent them to the king.
His sly, polite, insinuating style
Could please at court, and make AUGUSTUS smile:
An artful manager, that crept between
His friend and shame, and was a kind of *screen.*
But 'faith your very friends will soon be sore;
Patriots there are, who wish you'd jest no more—
And where's the glory? 'twill be only thought
The Great man never offer'd you a groat.
Go see SIR ROBERT—
P. See SIR ROBERT!—hum!
And never laugh—for all my life to come?
Seen him I have, but in his happier hour
Of social pleasure, ill exchanged for power;
Seen him, uncumber'd with the venal tribe,
Smile without art, and win without a bribe.
Would he oblige me? let me only find,
He does not think me what he thinks mankind.
Come, come, at all I laugh he laughs, no doubt;
The only difference is, I dare laugh out.
F. Why, yes: with *Scripture* still you may be free;
A horse-laugh, if you please, at *Honesty;*
A joke on JEKYL,[4] or some odd *Old Whig*
Who never changed his principle, or wig:
A patriot is a fool in every age,
Whom all Lord Chamberlains allow the stage:
These nothing hurts; they keep their fashion still,
And wear their strange old virtue, as they will.

[1] Some guilty person, very fond of making such an observation.

[2] Formerly gaoler of the Fleet prison, enriched himself by many exactions, for which he was tried and expelled.

[3] Said to be executed by the captain of a Spanish ship on one Jenkins, a captain of an English one. He cut off his ears, and bid him carry them to the king his master

[4] Sir Joseph Jekyl, Master of the Rolls, a true Whig in his principles, and a man of the utmost probity. He sometimes voted against the Court, which drew upon him the laugh here described of ONE who bestowed it equally upon religion and honesty.

If any ask you, "Who's the man so near
His prince, that writes in verse, and has his ear?"
Why, answer LYTTELTON,[1] and I'll engage
The worthy youth shall ne'er be in a rage:
But were his verses vile, his whisper base,
You'd quickly find him in Lord *Fanny's* case.
Sejanus, Wolsey,[2] hurt not honest FLEURY,[3]
But well may put some statesmen in a fury.
Laugh then at any, but at fools or foes;
These you but anger, and you mend not those.
Laugh at your friends, and, if your friends are sore,
So much the better, you may laugh the more.
To vice and folly to confine the jest,
Sets half the world, God knows, against the rest;
Did not the sneer of more impartial men
At sense and virtue balance all again.
Judicious wits spread wide the ridicule,
And charitably comfort knave and fool.
P. Dear sir, forgive the prejudice of youth:
Adieu distinction, satire, warmth, and truth!
Come, harmless characters that no one hit;
Come Henley's oratory, Osborn's wit!
The honey dropping from Favonio's tongue,
The flowers of Bubo, and the flow of Young!
The gracious dew[4] of pulpit eloquence,
And all the well-whipt cream of courtly sense,
That first was H—vy's, F—'s next, and then
The S—te's, and then H—vy's once again.
O come, that easy, Ciceronian style,
So Latin, yet so English all the while,
As, though the pride of Middleton and Bland,
All boys may read, and girls may understand!
Then might I sing, without the least offence,
And all I sung should be the *nation's sense;*

1 George Lyttelton, Secretary to the Prince of Wales, distinguished both for his writings and speeches in the spirit of liberty.

2 The one the wicked minister of Tiberius; the other of Henry VIII. The writers against the Court usually bestowed these and other odious names on the Minister, without distinction.

3 Cardinal; and Minister to Louis XV. It was a patriot-fashion, at that time, to cry up his wisdom and honesty.

4 Alludes to some Court sermons, and florid panegyrical speeches particularly one very full of puerilities and flatteries.

Or teach the melancholy muse to mourn,
Hang the sad verse on CAROLINA's[1] urn,
And hail her passage to the realms of rest,
All parts perform'd, and *all* her children blest!
So—Satire is no more—I feel it die—
No *Gazetteer* more innocent than I—
And let, a God's-name, every fool and knave
Be graced through life, and flatter'd in his grave.
F. Why so? if Satire knows its time and place
You still may lash the greatest—in disgrace:
For merit will by turns forsake them all;
Would you know when? exactly when they fall.
But let all satire in all changes spare
Immortal S—k, and grave D——re.[2]
Silent and soft, as saints remove to heaven,
All ties dissolved, and every sin forgiven,
These may some gentle ministerial wing
Receive, and place for ever near a king!
There, where no passion, pride, or shame transport,
Lull'd with the sweet Nepenthe of a court;
There, where no father's, brother's, friend's disgrace
Once break their rest, or stir them from their place:
But past the sense of human miseries,
All tears are wiped for ever from all eyes;
No cheek is known to blush, no heart to throb,
Save when they lose a question, or a job.
P. Good heaven forbid that I should blast their glory,
Who know how like Whig Ministers to Tory,
And when three sovereigns died, could scarce be vext,
Considering what a *gracious prince* was next.
Have I, in silent wonder, seen such things
As pride in slaves, and avarice in kings;
And at a peer, or peeress, shall I fret,
Who starves a sister, or forswears a debt?
Virtue, I grant you, is an empty boast;
But shall the dignity of *Vice* be lost?
Ye gods! shall Cibber's son,[3] without rebuke,
Swear like a lord, or Rich[3] outwhore a duke?

[1] Queen consort to King George II. She died in 1737. Her death gave occasion, as is observed above, to many indiscreet and mean performances unworthy of her memory.

[2] A title given to that lord by King James II. He was of the Bedchamber to King William; he was so to King George I.; he was so to King George II. His lordship was very skilful in all the forms of the House, which he discharged with great gravity.

[3] Two players.

A Favourite's porter with his master vie,
Be bribed as often, and as often lie?
Shall Ward draw contracts with a statesman's skill?
Or Japhet pocket, like his Grace, a will?
Is it for Bond or Peter (paltry things)
To pay their debts, or keep their faith, like kings?
If Blount[1] dispatch'd himself, he play'd the man,
And so may'st thou, illustrious Passeran!
But shall a printer,[2] weary of his life,
Learn from their books, to hang himself and wife?
This, this, my friend, I cannot, must not bear;
Vice, thus abused, demands a nation's care:
This calls the church to deprecate our sin,
And hurls the thunder of the laws on *gin*.[3]
  Let modest FOSTER, if he will, excel
Ten metropolitans in preaching well;
A simple quaker, or a quaker's wife,
Outdo Llandaff in doctrine,—yea in life:
Let humble ALLEN, with an awkward shame,
Do good by stealth, and blush to find it fame.
Virtue may choose the high or low degree,
'Tis just alike to Virtue, and to me;
Dwell in a monk, or light upon a king,
She's still the same, beloved, contented thing.
Vice is undone, if she forgets her birth,
And stoops from angels to the dregs of earth:
But 'tis the *fall* degrades her to a whore;
Let *Greatness* OWN HER, and she's mean no more:
Her birth, her beauty, crowds and courts confess,
Chaste matrons praise her, and grave bishops bless;
In golden chains the willing world she draws,
And hers the gospel is, and hers the laws;
Mounts the tribunal, lifts her scarlet head,
And sees pale Virtue carted in her stead.
Lo! at the wheels of her triumphal car,
Old England's genius, rough with many a scar,

1 Author of an impious foolish book called *The Oracles of Reason*, who being in love with a near kinswoman, and rejected, gave himself a stab in the arm, as pretending to kill himself, of the consequence of which he really died.

2 A fact that happened in London a few years previous. The unhappy man left behind him a paper justifying his action by the reasonings of some of these authors.

3 The exorbitant use of this spirit had created such great mischief to the lowest rank of the people, that the sale of it was restrained by an act of parliament in 1736.

Dragg'd in the dust! his arms hang idly round,
His flag inverted trails along the ground!
Our youth, all liveried o'er with foreign gold,
Before her dance: behind her, crawl the old!
See thronging millions to the pagod run,
And offer country, parent, wife, or son!
Hear her black trumpet through the land proclaim
That NOT TO BE CORRUPTED IS THE SHAME.
In soldier, churchman, patriot, man in power,
'Tis avarice all, ambition is no more!
See all our nobles begging to be slaves!
See all our fools aspiring to be knaves!
The wit of cheats, the courage of a whore,
Are what ten thousand envy and adore:
All, all look up, with reverential awe,
At crimes that 'scape, or triumph o'er the law:
While truth, worth, wisdom, daily they decry—
"Nothing is sacred now but villany."
Yet may this verse (if such a verse remain)
Show there was one who held it in disdain.

DIALOGUE II.

FR. 'Tis all a libel—Paxton (Sir) will say.
P. Not yet, my friend! to-morrow 'faith it may;
And for that very cause I print to-day.
How should I fret to mangle every line,
In reverence to the sins of *Thirty-nine?*
Vice with such giant strides comes on amain,
Invention strives to be before in vain;
Feign what I will, and paint it e'er so strong,
Some rising genius sins up to my song.
F. Yet none but you by name the guilty lash;
Even Guthry[1] saves half Newgate by a dash.
Spare then the person, and expose the vice.
P. How, Sir! not damn the sharper, but the dice?
Come on, then, Satire! general, unconfined,
Spread thy broad wing, and souse on all the kind.
Ye statesmen, priests, of one religion all!
Ye tradesmen vile, in army, court, or hall!

[1] The Ordinary of Newgate, who at that time published the memoirs of the malefactors, and was prevailed upon to be so tender of their reputation, as to set down no more than the initials of their name.

Ye reverend atheists.—F. Scandal! name them. Who?
P. Why that's the thing you bid me not to do.
Who starved a sister, who forswore a debt,
I never named; the town's inquiring yet. [do.
The poisoning dame—F. You mean—P. I don't—F. You
P. See, now I keep the secret, and not you!
The bribing statesman—F. Hold, too high you go.
P. The bribed elector—F. There you stoop too low.
P. I fain would please you, if I knew with what;
Tell me which knave is lawful game, which not.
Must great offenders, once escaped the crown,
Like royal harts, be never more run down?
Admit your law to spare the knight requires,
As beasts of nature, may we hunt the squires?
Suppose I censure—you know what I mean—
To save a Bishop, may I name a Dean?
F. A Dean, Sir? No: his fortune is not made,
You hurt a man that's rising in the trade.
P. If not the tradesman who set up to-day,
Much less the 'prentice who to-morrow may.
Down, down, proud Satire! though a realm be spoil'd,
Arraign no mightier thief than wretched *Wild*;[1]
Or, if a court or country's made a job,
Go drench a pickpocket, and join the mob.
But, Sir, I beg you, (for the love of vice!)
The matter's weighty, pray consider twice;
Have you less pity for the needy cheat,
The poor and friendless villain, than the great?
Alas! the small discredit of a bribe
Scarce hurts the lawyer, but undoes the scribe.
Then better sure it charity becomes
To tax Directors, who (thank God) have plums;
Still better, Ministers; or if the thing
May pinch even there—why lay it on a king.
F. Stop! stop!
P. Must Satire, then, not rise nor fall?
Speak out, and bid me blame no rogues at all.
F. Yes, strike that *Wild*, I'll justify the blow.
P. Strike! why the man was hang'd ten years ago:
Who now that obsolete example fears?
Even Peter trembles only for his ears.[2]

[1] Jonathan Wild, a famous thief and informer, who was at last caught in his own toils, and hanged.

[2] Peter had, the year before this, narrowly escaped the pillory for forgery; and got off with a severe rebuke only from the bench.

F. What, always *Peter?* Peter thinks you mad,
You make men desperate if they once are bad:
Else might he take to virtue some years hence—
P. As S—k, if he lives, will love the PRINCE.
F. Strange spleen to S—k!
P. Do I wrong the man?
God knows, I praise a courtier where I can.
When I confess, there is who feels for fame,
And melts to goodness, need I SCARBOROUGH name![1]
Pleased let me own, in *Esher's* peaceful grove,[2]
(Where *Kent* and nature vie for PELHAM'S love,)
The scene, the master, opening to my view,
I sit and dream I see my CRAGGS anew!
Even in a bishop I can spy desert;
Secker is decent, *Rundel* has a heart:
Manners with candour are to *Benson* given,
To *Berkeley*, every virtue under heaven.
But does the court a worthy man remove?
That instant, I declare, he has my love:
I shun his zenith, court his mild decline;
Thus SOMERS[3] once, and HALIFAX,[4] were mine.
Oft, in the clear, still mirror of retreat,
I studied SHREWSBURY,[5] the wise and great:
CARLETON'S[6] calm sense, and STANHOPE'S[7] noble flame,
Compared, and knew their gen'rous end the same:
How pleasing ATTERBURY'S softer hour!
How shined the soul, unconquer'd in the Tower!
How can I PULTENEY, CHESTERFIELD forget,
While Roman spirit charms, and Attic wit?

[1] Earl of, whose personal attachment to the king appeared from his steady adherence to the royal interest, and his known honour and virtue made him esteemed by all parties.

[2] The house and gardens of Esher, in Surrey, belonging to the Honourable Mr. Pelham, brother of the Duke of Newcastle.

[3] John Lord Somers died in 1716. A faithful, able, and incorrupt Minister, who, to qualities of a consummate statesman, added those of a man of learning and politeness.

[4] A peer no less distinguished by his love of letters than his abilities in parliament.

[5] Charles Talbot, Duke of Shrewsbury. He several times quitted his employments, and was often recalled. He died in 1718.

[6] Hen. Boyle, Lord Carleton, President of the Council under Queen Anne.

[7] James, Earl of Stanhope. A nobleman of equal courage, spirit, and learning.

ARGYLL, the state's whole thunder born to wield,
And shake alike the senate and the field?
Or WYNDHAM,[1] just to freedom and the throne,
The master of our passions, and his own?
Names, which I long have loved, nor loved in vain,
Rank'd with their friends, not number'd with their train
And if yet higher the proud list should end,
Still let me say! No follower, but a friend.
Yet think not friendship only prompts my lays;
I follow *Virtue:* where she shines, I praise:
Point she to Priest or Elder, Whig or Tory,
Or round a Quaker's beaver cast a glory.
I never (to my sorrow I declare)
Dined with the MAN of ROSS, or my LORD MAYOR.
Some, in their choice of friends (nay, look not grave)
Have still a secret bias to a knave:
To find an honest man I beat about,
And love him, court him, praise him, in or out.
F. Then why so few commended?
P. Not so fierce;
Find you the virtue, and I'll find the verse.
But random praise—the task can ne'er be done;
Each mother asks it for her booby son,
Each widow asks it for *the best of men,*
For him she weeps, for him she weds again.
Praise cannot stoop, like Satire, to the ground;
The number may be hang'd, but not be crown'd.
Enough for half the greatest of these days,
To 'scape my censure, not expect my praise.
Are they not rich? what more can they pretend?
Dare they to hope a poet for their friend?
What RICHELIEU wanted, LOUIS scarce could gain,
And what young AMMON wish'd, but wish'd in vain.
No power the muse's friendship can command;
No power when virtue claims it, can withstand:
To *Cato, Virgil* paid one honest line:
O let my country's friends illumine mine!
—What are you thinking? F. Faith, the thought's no sin,
I think your friends are out, and would be in.

[1] Sir William Wyndham, Chancellor of the Exchequer under Queen Anne, made early a considerable figure; but afterwards a much greater both by his ability and eloquence, joined with the utmost judgment and temper.

P. If merely to come in, sir, they go out,
The way they take is strangely roundabout.
F. They too may be corrupted, you'll allow?
P. I only call those knaves who are so now.
Is that too little? Come, then, I'll comply—
Spirit of ARNALL! aid me while I lie.
COBHAM'S a coward, POLWARTH[1] is a slave,
And LYTTELTON a dark designing knave;
ST. JOHN has ever been a wealthy fool—
But let me add, SIR ROBERT'S mighty dull,
Has never made a friend in private life,
And was, besides, a tyrant to his wife.
But pray, when others praise him, do I blame?
Call Verres, Wolsey, any odious name?
Why rail they then, if but a wreath of mine,
O all-accomplish'd ST. JOHN! deck thy shrine?
What! shall each spur-gall'd hackney of the day,
When Paxton gives him double pots and pay,
Or each new-pension'd sycophant, pretend
To break my windows if I treat a friend;
Then wisely plead, to me they meant no hurt,
But 'twas my guest at whom they threw the dirt?
Sure, if I spare the Minister, no rules
Of honour bind me, not to maul his tools;
Sure, if they cannot cut, it may be said
His saws are toothless, and his hatchet's lead.
It anger'd TURENNE, once upon a day,
To see a footman kick'd that took his pay:
But when he heard the affront the fellow gave,
Knew one a man of honour, one a knave;
The prudent general turn'd it to a jest,
And begg'd he'd take the pains to kick the rest:
Which not at present having time to do—— [you?
F. Hold, Sir! for God's sake, where's the affront to
Against your worship when had Sherlock writ?
Or Page pour'd forth the torrent of his wit?
Or grant the bard, whose distich all commend,
[*In power a servant, out of power a friend,*]
To Walpole guilty of some venial sin;
What's that to you, who ne'er was out nor in?

1 The Hon. Hugh Hume, son of Alexander, Earl of Marchmont, distinguished in the cause of liberty.

The priest whose flattery be-dropp'd the crown,
How hurt he you? he only stain'd the gown.
And how did, pray, the florid youth offend,
Whose speech you took, and gave it to a friend?
P. Faith, it imports not much from whom it came;
Whoever borrow'd could not be to blame,
Since the whole House did afterwards the same.
Let courtly wits to wits afford supply,
As hog to hog in huts of Westphaly;
If one, through Nature's bounty or his lord's,
Has what the frugal dirty soil affords,
From him the next receives it, thick or thin,
As pure a mess almost as it came in;
The blessed benefit, not there confined,
Drops to the third, who nuzzles close behind;
From tail to mouth they feed and they carouse:
The last full fairly gives it to the *House.*
F. This filthy simile, this beastly line,
Quite turns my stomach——
P. So does flattery mine;
And all your courtly civet-cats can vent,
Perfume to you, to me is excrement.
But hear me further—Japhet, 'tis agreed,
Writ not, and Chartres scarce could write or read;
In all the courts of Pindus guiltless quite;
But pens can forge, my friend, that cannot write;
And must no egg in Japhet's face be thrown,
Because the deed he forged was not my own?
Must never patriot, then, declaim at gin,
Unless, good man! he has been fairly in?
No zealous pastor blame a failing spouse,
Without a staring reason on his brows?
And each blasphemer quite escape the rod,
Because the insult's not on man, but God?
Ask you what provocation I have had?
The strong antipathy of good to bad.
When truth or virtue an affront endures,
The affront is mine, my friend, and should be yours.
Mine, as a foe profess'd to false pretence,
Who think a coxcomb's honour like his sense;
Mine, as a friend to every worthy mind;
And mine as man, who feel for all mankind.
F. You're strangely proud.

P. So proud, I am no slave:
So impudent, I own myself no knave:
So odd, my country's ruin makes me grave.
Yes, I am proud; I must be proud to see
Men, not afraid of God, afraid of me:
Safe from the bar, the pulpit, and the throne,
Yet touched and shamed by ridicule alone.
O sacred weapon! left for truth's defence,
Sole dread of folly, vice, and insolence!
To all but Heaven-directed hands denied,
The muse may give thee, but the gods must guide:
Reverent I touch thee! but with honest zeal;
To rouse the watchman of the public weal,
To virtue's work provoke the tardy hall,
And goad the prelate slumbering in his stall.
Ye tinsel insects! whom a court maintains,
That counts your beauties only by your stains,
Spin all your cobwebs o'er the eye of day!
The MUSE's wing shall brush you all away:
All his grace preaches, all his lordship sings,
All that makes saints of queens, and gods of kings;
All, all but truth, drops dead-born from the press,
Like the last gazette, or the last address.
When black ambition stains a public cause,
A monarch's sword when mad vain-glory draws,
Not Waller's wreath can hide the nation's scar,
Nor Boileau turn the feather to a star.
Not so, when diadem'd with rays divine,
Touch'd with the flame that breaks from Virtue's shrine,
Her priestess Muse forbids the good to die,
And opes the temple of Eternity.
There, other trophies deck the truly brave,
Than such as ANSTIS[1] casts into the grave;
Far other stars than * and ** wear,
And may descend to Mordington from STAIR;[2]
(Such as on HOUGH'S[3] unsullied mitre shine,
Or beam, good DIGBY, from a heart like thine;)

[1] The chief herald at arms. It is the custom, at the funeral of great men, to cast into the grave the broken staves and ensigns of honour.

[2] John Dalrymple, Earl of Stair, served in all the wars under the Duke of Marlborough.

[3] Dr. John Hough, Bishop of Worcester, and the Lord Digby: the one an assertor of the church of England, in opposition to the false

Let *Envy* howl, while heaven's whole chorus sings,
And bark at honour not conferr'd by kings;
Let *Flattery* sickening see the incense rise,
Sweet to the world, and grateful to the skies:
Truth guards the poet, sanctifies the line,
And makes immortal, verse as mean as mine.
Yes, the last pen for freedom let me draw,
When Truth stands trembling on the edge of law;
Here, last of Britons! let your names be read;
Are none, none living? let me praise the dead,
And for that cause which made your fathers shine,
Fall by the votes of their degenerate line.
F. Alas! alas! pray end what you began,
And write next winter more *Essays on Man*.[1]

LINES ON RECEIVING FROM THE

RT. HON. THE LADY FRANCES SHIRLEY

A STANDISH AND TWO PENS.

Yes, I beheld the Athenian queen
Descend in all her sober charms;
"And take" (she said, and smiled serene)
"Take at this hand celestial arms:

"Secure the radiant weapons wield;
This golden lance shall guard desert,
And if a vice dares keep the field,
This steel shall stab it to the heart."

measures of King James II.; the other as firmly attached to the cause of that king; both acting out of principle, and equally men of honour and virtue.

[1] This was the last poem of the kind printed by our author, with a resolution to publish no more, but to enter thus, in the most plain and solemn manner he could, a sort of PROTEST against that insuperable corruption and depravity of manners which he had been so unhappy as to live to see. Could he have hoped to have amended any, he had continued those attacks; but bad men were grown so shameless and so powerful, that ridicule was become as unsafe as it was ineffectual. The poem raised him, as he knew it would, some enemies: but he had reason to be satisfied with the approbation of good men, and the testimony of his own conscience.

Awed, on my bended knees I fell,
  Received the weapons of the sky;
And dipt them in the sable well,
  The fount of fame or infamy.

"What *well?* what *weapon?*" (Flavia cries)
  "A standish, steel and golden pen!
It came from Bertrand's, not the skies;
  I gave it you to write again.

"But, friend, take heed whom you attack;
  You'll bring a house (I mean of peers)
Red, blue, and green, nay white and black,
  L—— and all about your ears.

"You'd write as smooth again on glass,
  And run, on ivory, so glib,
As not to stick at fool or ass,
  Nor stop at flattery or fib.

"*Athenian queen! and sober charms!*
  I tell ye, fool, there's nothing in't:
'Tis Venus, Venus gives these arms;
  In Dryden's Virgil see the print.

"Come, if you'll be a quiet soul,
  That dares tell neither truth nor lies,
I'll list you in the harmless roll
  Of those that sing of these poor eyes."

TO

THE AUTHOR OF A POEM ENTITLED "SUCCESSIO,"

[ELKANAH SETTLE.]

Begone, ye critics! and restrain your spite,
Codrus writes on, and will for ever write:
The heaviest muse the swiftest course has gone,
As clocks run fastest when most lead is on.
What though no bees around your cradle flew,
Nor on your lips distill'd their golden dew?
Yet have we oft discover'd in their stead
A swarm of drones that buzz'd about your head.

When you, like Orpheus, strike the warbling lyre,
Attentive blocks stand round you and admire.
Wit pass'd through thee no longer is the same,
As meat digested takes a different name;
But sense must sure thy safest plunder be,
Since no reprisals can be made on thee.
Thus thou may'st rise, and in thy daring flight
(Tho' ne'er so weighty) reach a wondrous height:
So forced from engines, lead itself can fly,
And ponderous slugs move nimbly through the sky.
Sure Bavius copied Mævius to the full,
And Chœrilus taught Codrus to be dull;
Therefore, dear friend, at my advice give o'er
This needless labour; and contend no more
To prove a *dull succession* to be true,
Since 'tis enough we find it so in you.

1740.

A FRAGMENT OF A POEM.

O WRETCHED B——! jealous now of all,
What God, what mortal, shall prevent thy fall?
Turn, turn thy eyes from wicked men in place,
And see what succour from the patriot race.
C——, his own proud dupe, thinks monarchs things
Made just for him, as other fools for kings;
Controls, decides, insults thee every hour,
And antedates the hatred due to power.
Thro' clouds of passion P——'s views are clear,
He foams a patriot to subside a peer;
Impatient sees his country bought and sold,
And damns the market where he takes no gold.
Grave, righteous S—— jogs on, till, past belief,
He finds himself companion with a thief.
To purge and let thee blood, with fire and sword,
Is all the help stern S—— would afford.
That those who bind and rob thee, would not kill,
Good C—— hopes, and candidly sits still.
Of Ch—s W—— who speaks at all,
No more than of Sir Harry or Sir Paul?
Whose names once up, they thought it was not wrong
To lie in bed, but sure they lay too long.

G——r, C——m, B——t, pay thee due regards,
Unless the ladies bid them mind their cards.
with wit that must
And C———d, who speaks so well and writes,
Whom (saving W.) every S. *harper bites.*
must needs
Whose wit and equally provoke one,
Finds thee, at best, the butt to crack his joke on.
As for the rest, each winter up they run,
And all are clear, that something must be done.
Then urged by C——t, or by C——t stopp'd,
Inflamed by P——, and by P—— dropp'd;
They follow reverently each wondrous wight,
Amazed that one can read, that one can write:
So geese to gander prone obedience keep,
Hiss if he hiss, and if he slumber, sleep.
Till having done whate'er was fit or fine,
Utter'd a speech, and ask'd their friends to dine;
Each hurries back to his paternal ground,
Content but for five shillings in the pound;
Yearly defeated, yearly hopes they give,
And all agree, Sir Robert cannot live.
Rise, rise, great W——, fated to appear,
Spite of thyself, a glorious minister!
Speak the loud language princes . . . .
And treat with half the . . . .
At length to B—— kind, as to thy . . . .
Espouse the nation, you . . . .
What can thy H . . . .
Dress in Dutch . . . .
Though still he travels on no bad pretence,
To show . . . .
Or those foul copies of thy face and tongue,
Veracious W——— and frontless Young;
Sagacious Bub, so late a friend, and there
So late a foe, yet more sagacious H——?
Hervey and Hervey's school, F—, H——y, H——n,
Yea, moral Ebor, or religious Winton.
How! what can O——w, what can D——,
The wisdom of the one and other chair,
N—— laugh, or D——'s sager,
Or thy dread truncheon, M.'s mighty peer?
What help from J——'s opiates canst thou draw,
Or H——k's quibbles voted into law?

C., that Roman in his nose alone,
Who hears all causes, B——, but thy own,
Or those proud fools whom nature, rank, and fate
Made fit companions for the sword of state.
Can the light packhorse, or the heavy steer,
The sowzing prelate, or the sweating peer,
Drag out with all its dirt and all its weight,
The lumbering carriage of thy broken state?
Alas! the people curse, the carman swears,
The drivers quarrel, and the master stares.
The plague is on thee, Britain, and who tries
To save thee in the infectious office *dies*.
The first firm P——y soon resign'd his breath,
Brave S——w loved thee, and was lied to death.
Good M—m—t's fate tore P——th from thy side,
And thy last sigh was heard when W——m died.
Thy nobles sl—s, thy se—s bought with gold,
Thy clergy perjured, thy whole people sold.
An atheist ⌣ a ⊕''''s ad . . . . . .
Blotch thee all o'er, and sink . . .
Alas! on one alone our all relies,
Let him be honest, and he must be wise;
Let him no trifler from his school,
Nor like his . . . . still a . . . .
Be but a man! unminister'd, alone,
And free at once the senate and the throne;
Esteem the public love his best supply,
A ⊙'s true glory his integrity;
Rich *with* his . . . . *in* his . . . strong,
Affect no conquest, but endure no wrong.
Whatever his religion or his blood,
His public virtue makes his title good.
Europe's just balance and our own may stand,
And one man's honesty redeem the land.

THE DUNCIAD,[1]

IN FOUR BOOKS.

PRINTED ACCORDING TO THE COMPLETE COPY FOUND IN THE YEAR 1742; WITH THE PROLEGOMENA OF SCRIBLERUS, AND NOTES.

Tandem *Phœbus* adest, morsusque inferre parantem
Congelat, et patulos, ut erant, indurat hiatus.—OVID.

ADVERTISEMENT TO THE READER

I HAVE long had a design of giving some sort of notes on the works of this poet. Before I had the happiness of his acquaintance, I had written a commentary on his *Essay on Man*, and have since finished another on the *Essay on Criticism*. There was one already on the *Dunciad*, which had met with general approbation: but I still thought some additions were wanting (of a more serious kind) to the humorous notes of *Scriblerus*, and even to those written by *Mr. Cleland, Dr. Arbuthnot*, and others. I had lately the pleasure to pass some months with the author in the country, where I prevailed upon him to do what I had long desired, and favour me with his explanation of several passages in his works. It happened, that just at that juncture was published a ridiculous book against him, full of personal reflections, which furnished him with a lucky opportunity of improving *this poem*, by giving it the only thing it wanted, a *more considerable hero*. He was always sensible of its defect in that particular, and owned he had let it pass with the hero it had, purely for want of a better; not entertaining the least expectation that such an one was reserved for this post, as has since obtained the *laurel*: but since that had happened, he could no longer deny this justice either to *him* or the *Dunciad*.

And yet I will venture to say, there was another motive which had still more weight with our author: this person was one, who from every folly (not to say vice) of which another would be ashamed, has constantly derived a *vanity*: and therefore was the *man in the world who would least be hurt by it*.

W. W.

[1] The Dunciad is here reprinted from the last and the only complete edition issued during the life of the author, and approved by him; with the sole addition of the variations in the poem noticed by Warburton in his edition published after the death of Pope.

BY AUTHORITY.

BY VIRTUE OF THE AUTHORITY IN US VESTED BY THE ACT FOR SUBJECTING POETS TO THE POWER OF A LICENSER, WE HAVE REVISED THIS PIECE; WHERE, FINDING THE STYLE AND APPELLATION OF KING TO HAVE BEEN GIVEN TO A CERTAIN PRETENDER, PSEUDO-POET, OR PHANTOM, OF THE NAME OF TIBBALD; AND APPREHENDING THE SAME MAY BE DEEMED IN SOME SORT A REFLECTION ON MAJESTY, OR AT LEAST AN INSULT ON THAT LEGAL AUTHORITY WHICH HAS BESTOWED ON ANOTHER PERSON THE CROWN OF POESY: WE HAVE ORDERED THE SAID PRETENDER, PSEUDO-POET, OR PHANTOM, UTTERLY TO VANISH AND EVAPORATE OUT OF THIS WORK: AND DO DECLARE THE SAID THRONE OF POESY FROM HENCEFORTH TO BE ABDICATED AND VACANT, UNLESS DULY AND LAWFULLY SUPPLIED BY THE LAUREATE HIMSELF, AND IT IS HEREBY ENACTED, THAT NO OTHER PERSON DO PRESUME TO FILL THE SAME.

OC. CH.

MARTINUS SCRIBLERUS

HIS PROLEGOMENA AND ILLUSTRATIONS TO THE DUNCIAD: WITH THE HYPER-CRITICS OF ARISTARCHUS.

A LETTER TO THE PUBLISHER,

OCCASIONED BY THE FIRST CORRECT EDITION OF THE DUNCIAD.

It is with pleasure I hear, that you have procured a correct copy of the Dunciad, which the many surreptitious ones have rendered so necessary: and it is yet with more, that I am informed it will be attended with a Commentary: a work so requisite, that I cannot think the author himself would have omitted it, had he approved of the first appearance of this poem.

Such *notes* as have occurred to me I herewith send you: you will oblige me by inserting them amongst those which are, or will be, transmitted to you by others; since not only the author's friends, but even strangers appear engaged by humanity, to take some care of an orphan of so much genius and spirit, which its parent seems to have abandoned from the very beginning, and suffered to step into the world naked, unguarded, and unattended.

It was upon reading some of the abusive papers lately published, that my great regard to a person, whose friendship I esteem as one of the chief honours of my life, and a much greater respect to truth, than to him or any man living, engaged me in inquiries, of which the inclosed *notes* are the fruit.

I perceived, that most of these authors had been (doubtless very wisely) the first aggressors. They had tried, 'till they were weary, what was to be got by railing at each other: nobody was either concerned or surprised, if this or that scribbler was proved a dunce. But every one was curious to read what could be said to prove Mr. POPE one, and was ready to pay something for such a discovery: a stratagem, which would they fairly own, it might not only reconcile them to me, but screen them from the resentment of their lawful superiors, whom they daily abuse, only (as I charitably hope) to get that *by* them, which they cannot get *from* them.

I found this was not all: ill success in that had transported them to personal abuse, either of himself, or (what I think he could less forgive) of his friends. They had called men of virtue and honour bad men, long before he had either leisure or inclination to call them bad writers: and some had been such old offenders, that he had quite forgotten their persons as well as their slanders, till they were pleased to revive them.

Now what had Mr. POPE done before, to incense them? He had published those works which are in the hands of every body, in which not the least mention is made of any of them. And what has he done since? He has laughed, and written the DUNCIAD. What has that said of them? A very serious truth, which the public had said before, that they were dull: and what it had no sooner said, but they themselves were at great pains to procure or even purchase room in the prints, to testify under their hands to the truth of it.

I should still have been silent, if either I had seen any inclination in my friend to be serious with such accusers, or if they had only meddled with his writings; since whoever publishes, puts himself on his trial by his country. But when his moral character was attacked, and in a manner from which neither truth nor virtue can secure the most innocent, in a manner, which, though it annihilates the credit of the accusation with the just and impartial, yet aggravates very much the guilt of the accusers; I mean by authors *without names:* then I thought, since the danger was common to all, the concern ought to be so; and that it was an act of justice to detect the authors, not only on this account, but as many of them are the same who for several years past have made free with the greatest names in church and state, exposed to the world the private misfortunes of families, abused all, even to women, and whose prostituted papers (for one or other party, in the unhappy divisions of their country) have insulted the fallen, the friendless, the exiled, and the dead.

Besides this, which I take to be a public concern, I have already confessed I had a private one. I am one of that number who have long loved and esteemed Mr. Pope; and had often declared it was not his capacity or writings (which we ever thought the least valuable part of his character) but the honest, open, and beneficent man, that we most esteemed, and loved in him. Now, if what these people say were believed, I must appear to all my friends either a fool, or a knave; either imposed on myself, or imposing on them; so that I am as much interested in the confutation of these calumnies, as he is himself.

I am no author, and consequently not to be suspected either of jealousy or resentment against any of the men, of whom scarce one is known to me by sight; and as for their writings, I have sought them (on this one occasion) in vain, in the closets and libraries of all my acquaintance. I had still been in the dark, if a gentleman had not procured me (I suppose from some of themselves, for they are generally much more dangerous friends than enemies) the passages I send you. I solemnly protest I have added nothing to the malice or absurdity of them; which it behoves me to declare, since the vouchers themselves will be so soon and so irrecoverably lost. You may in some measure prevent it, by preserving at least their titles, and discovering (as far as you can depend on the truth of your information) the names of the concealed authors.

The first objection I have heard made to the poem is, that the persons are too *obscure* for satire. The persons themselves, rather than allow the objection, would forgive the satire; and if one could be tempted to afford it a serious answer, were not all assassinates, popular insurrections, the insolence of the rabble without doors, and of domestics within, most wrongfully chastised, if the meanness of offenders indemnified them from punishment? On the contrary, obscurity renders them more dangerous, as less thought of: law can pronounce judgment only on open facts; morality alone can pass censure on intentions of mischief; so that for secret calumny, or the arrow flying in the dark, there is no public punishment left, but what a good writer inflicts.

The next objection is, that these sort of authors are *poor*. That might be pleaded as an excuse at the Old Bailey, for lesser crimes than defamation, (for 'tis the case of almost all who are tried there,) but sure it can be none: for who will pretend that the robbing another of his reputation supplies the want of it in himself? I question not but such authors are poor, and heartily wish the objection were removed by any honest livelihood. But poverty is here the accident, not the subject: he who describes malice and villany to be pale and meagre, expresses not the least anger against paleness or leanness, but against malice and villany. The apothecary in Romeo and Juliet is poor; but is he therefore justified in vending poison? Not but poverty itself becomes a just subject of satire, when it is the consequence of vice, prodigality, or neglect of one's lawful calling; for then it increases the public burden, fills the streets and highways with robbers, and the garrets with clippers, coiners, and weekly journalists.

But admitting that two or three of these offend less in their morals, than in their writings; must poverty make nonsense sacred? If so, the fame of bad authors would be much better consulted than that of all the good ones in the world; and not one of an hundred had ever been called by his right name.

They mistake the whole matter: It is not charity to encourage them in the way they follow, but to get them out of it; for men are not bunglers because they are poor, but they are poor because they are bunglers.

Is it not pleasant enough, to hear our authors crying out on the one hand, as if their persons and characters were too sacred for satire; and the public objecting, on the other, that they are too mean even for ridicule? But whether bread or fame be their end, it must be allowed, our author, by and in this poem, has mercifully given them a little of both.

There are two or three, who by their rank and fortune have no benefit from the former objections, supposing them good, and these I was sorry to see in such company. But if, without any provocation, two or three gentlemen will fall upon one, in an affair wherein his interest and reputation are equally embarked, they cannot certainly, after they have been content to print themselves his enemies, complain of being put into the number of them.

Others, I am told, pretend to have been once his friends. Surely they are their enemies who say so, since nothing can be more odious than to treat a friend as they have done. But of this I cannot persuade myself, when I consider the constant and eternal aversion of all bad writers to a good one.

Such as claim a merit from being his admirers I would gladly ask, if it lays him under a personal obligation? At that rate, he would be the most obliged humble servant in the world. I dare swear for these in particular, he never desired them to be his admirers, nor promised in return, to be theirs: that had truly been a sign he was of their acquaintance; but would not the malicious world have suspected such an approbation of some motive worse than ignorance, in the author of the "Essay on Criticism?" Be it as it will, the reasons of their admiration and of his contempt are equally subsisting, for his works and theirs are the very same that they were.

One, therefore, of their assertions I believe may be true, "That he has a contempt for their writings." And there is another, which would probably be sooner allowed by himself than by any good judge beside, "That his own have found too much success with the public." But as it cannot consist with his modesty to claim this as a justice, it lies not on him, but entirely on the public, to defend its own judgment.

There remains what in my opinion might seem a better plea for these people, than any they have made use of. If obscurity or poverty were to exempt a man from satire, much more should folly or dulness, which are still more involuntary; nay, as much so as personal deformity. But even this will not help them: deformity becomes an object of ridicule when a man sets up for being handsome; and so must dulness when he sets up for a wit. They are not ridiculed because ridicule in itself is, or ought to be, a pleasure; but because it is just to undeceive and vindicate the honest and unpretending part of mankind from imposition, because particular interest ought to yield to general, and a great number who are not naturally fools, ought never to be made so, in complaisance to a few who are. Accordingly we find that in all ages, all vain pretenders, were they ever so poor or ever so dull, have been constantly the topics of the most candid satirists, from the Codrus of JUVENAL to the Damon of BOILEAU.

Having mentioned BOILEAU, the greatest poet and most judicious critic of his age and country, admirable for his talents, and yet perhaps more admirable for his judgment in the proper application of them; I cannot help remarking the resemblance betwixt him and our author, in qualities, fame, and fortune; in the distinctions shown them by their superiors, in the general esteem of their equals, and in their extended reputation amongst foreigners; in the latter of which ours has met with the better fate, as he has had for his translators persons of the most eminent rank and abilities in their respective nations. But the resemblance holds in nothing more, than in their being equally abused by the ignorant pretenders to poetry of their times; of which not the least memory will remain but in their own writings, and in the notes made upon them. What BOILEAU has done in almost all his poems, our author has only in this: I dare answer for him he will do it in no more; and on this principle, of attacking few but who had slandered him, he could not have done it at all, had he been confined from censuring obscure and worthless persons, for scarce any other were his enemies. However, as the parity is so remarkable, I hope it will continue to the last; and if ever he shall give us an edition of this poem himself, I may see some of them treated as gently, on their repentance or better merit, as Perrault and Quinault were at last by BOILEAU.

In one point I must be allowed to think the character of our English poet the more amiable. He has not been a follower of fortune or success; he has lived with the great without flattery; been a friend to men in power, without pensions, from whom, as he asked, so he received no favour, but what was done him in his friends. As his satires were the more just for being delayed, so were his panegyrics; bestowed only on such persons as he had familiarly known, only for such virtues as he had long observed in them, and only at such times as others cease to praise, if not begin to calumniate them, I mean when out of power or out of fashion. A satire, therefore, on writers so notorious for the contrary practice, became no man so well as himself; as none, it is plain, was so little in their friendships, or so much in that of those whom they had most abused, namely, the greatest and best of all parties. Let me add a further reason, that, though engaged in their friendships, he never espoused their animosities; and can almost singly challenge this honour, not to have written a line of any man, which, through guilt, through shame, or through fear, through variety of fortune, or change of interests, he was ever unwilling to own.

I shall conclude with remarking what a pleasure it must be to every reader of humanity, to see all along, that our author in his very laughter is not indulging his own ill-nature, but only punishing that of others. As to his poem, those alone are capable of doing it justice, who, to use the words of a great writer, know how hard it is (with regard both to his subject and his manner) VETUSTIS DARE NOVITATEM, OBSOLETIS NITOREM, OBSCURIS LUCEM, FASTIDITIS GRATIAM. I am,

Your most humble servant,

St. James's, Dec. 22, 1728. WILLIAM CLELAND.

DENNIS, REMARKS ON PRINCE ARTHUR.

I cannot but think it the most *reasonable* thing in the world, to distinguish good writers by discouraging the bad. Nor is it an *ill-natured* thing, in relation even to the very *persons* upon whom the reflections are made. It is true, it may deprive them, a little the sooner, of a *short profit* and a *transitory reputation;* but then it may have a good effect, and oblige them (before it be too late) to decline that for which they are so very *unfit*, and to have recourse to *something* in which they may be more successful.

CHARACTER OF MR. P. 1716.

The *persons* whom Boileau has attacked in his writings, have been for the most part *authors*, and most of those authors, *poets:* and the censures he hath passed upon them have been confirmed by all Europe.

GILDON, PREFACE TO HIS NEW REHEARSAL.

It is the common cry of the *poetasters* of the town, and their fautors, that it is an *ill-natured thing* to expose the *pretenders* to wit and poetry. The judges and magistrates may with full as good reason be reproached with *ill-nature* for putting the laws in execution against a thief or impostor.—The same will hold in the republic of letters, if the critics and judges will let every *ignorant pretender* to scribbling pass on the world.

THEOBALD, LETTER TO MIST, JUNE 22, 1728.

Attacks may be levelled, either against *failures* in *genius*, or against the *pretensions* of *writing without one.*

CONCANEN, DEDICATION TO THE AUTHOR OF THE DUNCIAD.

A *satire* upon *dullness* is a thing that has been *used* and *allowed* in *all ages.*

Out of thine own mouth will I judge thee, wicked scribbler!

TESTIMONIES OF AUTHORS

CONCERNING OUR POET AND HIS WORKS.

M. SCRIBLERUS Lectori S.

BEFORE we present thee with our exercitations on this most delectable poem (drawn from the many volumes of our Adversaria on modern authors) we shall here, according to the laudable usage of editors, collect the various judgments of the learned concerning our poet: various indeed, not only of different authors, but of the same author at different seasons. Nor shall we gather only the testimonies of such eminent wits, as would of course descend to posterity, and consequently be read without our collection; but we shall likewise with incredible labour seek out for divers others, which, but for this our diligence, could never at the distance of a few months appear to the eye of the most curious. Hereby thou may'st not only receive the delectation of variety, but also arrive at a more certain judgment, by a grave and circumspect comparison of the witnesses with each other, or of each with himself. Hence also thou wilt be enabled to draw reflections, not only of a critical, but a moral nature, by being let into many particulars of the person as well as genius, and of the fortune as well as merit, of our author: In which if I relate some things of little concern peradventure to thee, and some of as little even to him: I entreat thee to consider how minutely all true critics and commentators are wont to insist upon such, and how material they seem to themselves, if to none other. Forgive me gentle reader, if (following learned example) I ever and anon become tedious: allow me to take the same pains to find whether my author were good or bad, well or ill-natured, modest or arrogant; as another, whether his author was fair or brown, short or tall, or whether he wore a coat or a cassock.

We purposed to begin with his life, parentage, and education: but as to these, even his contemporaries do exceedingly differ. One saith, he was educated at home; another, that he was bred at St. Omer's by Jesuits; a third, not at St. Omer's, but at Oxford; a fourth, that he had no university education at all. Those who allow him to be bred at home, differ as much concerning his tutor: one saith, he was kept by his father on purpose; a second, that he was an itinerant priest; a third, that he was a parson; one calleth him a secular clergyman of the church of Rome; another, a monk. As little do they agree about his father, whom one supposeth, like the father of Hesiod, a tradesman or merchant; another, a husbandman; another, a hatter, &c. Nor has an author been wanting to give our poet such a father as Apuleius hath to Plato, Jamblicus to Pythagoras, and divers to Homer, namely, a demon: for thus Mr. Gildon: "Certain it is, that his original is not from Adam, but the devil; and that he wanteth nothing but horns and tail to be the exact resemblance of his infernal father." Finding, therefore, such contrariety of opinions, and (whatever be ours of this sort of generation) not being fond to enter into controversy, we shall defer writing the life of our poet, until authors can determine among themselves what parents or education he had, or whether he had any education or parents at all.

Proceed we to what is more certain, his works, though not less uncertain the judgments concerning them; beginning with his ESSAY on CRITICISM, of which hear first the most ancient of critics.

MR. JOHN DENNIS.

"His precepts are false, or trivial, or both; his thoughts are crude and abortive, his expressions absurd, his numbers harsh and unmusical, his rhymes trivial and common;—instead of majesty, we have something that is very mean; instead of gravity, something that is very boyish; and instead of perspicuity and lucid order, we have but too often obscurity and confusion." And in another place: "What rare *numbers* are here! Would not one swear that this youngster had espoused some antiquated muse, who had sued out a divorce from some superannuated sinner, upon account of impotence, and who, being poxed by her former spouse, has got the gout in her decrepid age, which makes her *hobble so damnably*." No less peremptory is the censure of our hypercritical historian,

MR. OLDMIXON.

"I dare not say anything of the Essay on Criticism in verse; but if any more curious reader has discovered in it something *new* which is not in Dryden's prefaces, dedications, and his essay on dramatic poetry, not to mention the French critics, I should be very glad to have the benefit of the discovery."

He is followed (as in fame, so in judgment) by the modest and simple-minded

MR. LEONARD WELSTED;

who, out of great respect to our poet, not naming him, doth yet glance at his Essay, together with the Duke of Buckingham's, and the criticisms of Dryden, and of Horace, which he more openly taxeth: "As to the numerous treatises, essays, arts, &c. both in verse and prose, that have been written by the moderns on this ground-work, they do but *hackney the same thoughts over again*, making them still more *trite*. Most of their pieces are nothing but a pert, insipid heap of *commonplace*. Horace has even in his Art of Poetry thrown out several things which plainly show, he thought an art of poetry was of no use, even while he was writing one."

To all which great authorities, we can only oppose that of

MR. ADDISON.

"The Art of Criticism (saith he) which was published some months since, is a master-piece in its kind. The observations follow one another, like those in Horace's Art of Poetry, without that methodical regularity which would have been requisite in a prose writer. They are some of them *uncommon,* but such as the reader must assent to, when he sees them explained with that ease and perspicuity in which they are delivered. As for those which are the *most known* and the most *received,* they are placed in so beautiful a light, and illustrated with such apt allusions, that they have in them all the graces of novelty; and make the reader, who was before acquainted with them, still more convinced of their truth and solidity. And here give me leave to mention what Monsieur Boileau has so well enlarged upon in the preface to his works: That wit and fine writing doth not consist so much in advancing things that are new, as in giving things that are known an agreeable turn. It is impossible for us who live in the latter ages of the world, to make observations in criticism, morality, or any art or science, which have not been touched upon by others: we have little else left us, but to represent the common sense of mankind in more strong, more beautiful, or more uncommon lights. If a reader examines Horace's Art of Poetry, he will find but few precepts in it, which he may not meet with in Aristotle, and which were not commonly known by all the poets of the Augustan age. His way of expressing, and applying them, not his invention of them, is what we are chiefly to admire.

"Longinus, in his reflections, has given us the same kind of sublime, which he observes in the several passages that occasioned them: I cannot but take notice that our English author has after the same manner exemplified several of the precepts in the very precepts themselves." He then produces some instances of a particular beauty in the numbers, and concludes with saying, that "there are three poems in our tongue of the same nature, and each a master-piece in its kind; the Essay on Translated Verse; the Essay on the Art of Poetry; and the Essay on Criticism."

Of WINDSOR FOREST, positive is the judgment of the affirmative

MR. JOHN DENNIS

"That it is a wretched rhapsody, impudently written in emulation of the Cooper's Hill of Sir John Denham: the author of it is obscure, is ambiguous, is affected, is temerarious, is barbarous."

But the author of the Dispensary,

DR. GARTH,

in the preface to his poem of Claremont, differs from this opinion: "those who have seen these two excellent poems of Cooper's Hill, and Windsor Forest, the one written by Sir John Denham, the other by Mr. Pope, will show a great deal of candour if they approve of this."

Of the epistle of ELOISA, we are told by the obscure writer of a poem called Sawney, "that because Prior's Henry and Emma charmed the finest tastes, our author writ his Eloise, *in opposition to it*; but forgot innocence and virtue: if you take away her tender thoughts, and her fierce desires, all the rest is of no value." In which, methinks, his judgment resembleth that of a French tailor on a villa and gardens by the Thames: "All this is very fine, but take away the river, and it is good for nothing."

But very contrary hereunto was the opinion of

MR. PRIOR

himself, saying in his *Alma*,

O *Abelard!* ill fated youth,
Thy tale will justify this truth.
But well I weet thy cruel wrong
Adorns a nobler poet's song:
Dan *Pope*, for thy misfortune grieved,
With kind concern and skill has weaved
A silken web; and ne'er shall fade
Its colours: gently has he laid
The mantle o'er thy sad distress,
And Venus shall the texture bless, &c.

Come we now to his translation of the ILIAD, celebrated by numerous pens, yet shall it suffice to mention the indefatigable

SIR RICHARD BLACKMORE, KT.

who (though otherwise a severe censurer of our author) yet styleth this a "laudable translation." That ready writer,

MR. OLDMIXON,

in his forementioned Essay, frequently commends the same. And the painful

MR. LEWIS THEOBALD

thus extols it, "The spirit of Homer breathes all through this translation. I am in doubt, whether I should most admire the justness to the original, or the force and beauty of the language, or the sounding variety of the numbers: but when I find all these meet, it puts me in mind of what the poet says of one of his heroes, that he alone raised and flung with ease a weighty stone, that two common men could not lift from the ground; just so, one single person has performed in this translation, what I once despaired to have seen done by the force of several masterly hands." Indeed the same gentleman appears to have changed his sentiment in his Essay on the Art of Sinking in Reputation, (printed in Mist's Journal, March 30, 1728) where he says thus: "In order to sink in reputation, let him take it into his head to descend into Homer (let the world wonder, as it will, how the devil he got there,) and pretend to do him into English, so his version denote his neglect of the manner how." Strange variation! We are told in

MIST'S JOURNAL, June 8,

"That this translation of the Iliad was not in all respects conformable to the fine taste of his friend Mr. Addison; insomuch that he employed a *younger muse*, in an undertaking of this kind, which he supervised himself." Whether Mr. Addison did find it conformable to his taste, or not, best appears from his own testimony the year following its publication, in these words:

MR. ADDISON, FREEHOLDER, No. 40.

"When I consider myself as a British freeholder, I am in a particular manner pleased with the labours of those who have improved our language with the translations of old Greek and Latin authors.—We have already most of their historians in our own tongue, and what is more for the honour of our language, it has been taught to express with elegance the greatest of their poets in each nation. The illiterate among our own countrymen may learn to judge from Dryden's Virgil of the most perfect epic performance. And those parts of Homer which have been published already by Mr. Pope, give us reason to think that the Iliad will appear in English with as little disadvantage to that immortal poem."

As to the rest, there is a slight mistake, for this *younger muse* was an *elder:* nor was the gentleman (who is a friend of our author) employed by Mr. Addison to translate it *after him*, since he saith himself that he did it *before*. Contrariwise that Mr. Addison engaged our author in this work appeareth by declaration thereof in the preface to the Iliad, printed some time before his death, and by his own letters of October 26, and November 2, 1713, where he declares it as his opinion, that no other person was equal to it.

Next comes his Shakspeare on the stage: "Let him (quoth one, whom I take to be

MR. THEOBALD, MIST'S JOURNAL, June 8, 1728,)

publish such an author as he has least studied, and forget to discharge even the dull duty of an editor. In this project let him lend the bookseller his name (for a competent sum of money) to promote the credit of an exorbitant subscription." Gentle reader, be pleased to cast thine eye on the *proposal* below quoted, and on what follows (some months after the former assertion) in the same Journalist of June 8. "The bookseller proposed the book by subscription, and raised some thousands of pounds for the same: I believe the gentleman did *not* share in the profits of this extravagant subscription.

"After the Iliad, he undertook (saith

MIST'S JOURNAL, June 8, 1728,)

the sequel of that work, the Odyssey; and having secured the success by a numerous subscription, he employed some *underlings* to perform what, according to his proposals, should come from his own hands." To which heavy charge we can in truth oppose nothing but the words of

MR. POPE'S PROPOSAL FOR THE ODYSSEY.

(Printed by J. Watts, Jan. 10, 1724.)

"I take this occasion to declare that the subscription for Shakspeare belongs wholly to Mr. Tonson: And that the benefit of *this proposal* is not solely for my own use, but for that of *two of my friends*, who have *assisted me in this work*." But these very gentlemen are extolled above our poet himself in another of Mist's Journals, March 30, 1728, saying, "That he would not advise Mr. Pope to try the experiment again of getting a great part of a book done by assistants, lest those extraneous parts should unhappily ascend to the sublime, and retard the declension of the whole." Behold! these *underlings* are become good writers!

If any say, that before the said proposals were printed, the subscription was begun without declaration of such assistance; verily, those who set it on foot, or (as their term is) secured it, to wit, the right honourable the Lord Viscount HARCOURT, were he living, would testify, and the right honourable the Lord BATHURST, now living, doth testify, the same is a falsehood.

Sorry I am, that persons professing to be learned, or of whatever rank of authors, should either falsely tax, or be falsely taxed. Yet let us, who are only reporters, be impartial in our citations, and proceed.

MIST'S JOURNAL, June 8, 1728.

"Mr. Addison raised this author from obscurity, obtained him the acquaintance and friendship of the *whole body of our nobility*, and transferred his powerful interests with those great men to this rising bard, who frequently levied by that means unusual contributions on the public." Which surely cannot be, if, as the author of the Dunciad Dissected reporteth; "Mr. Wycherley had before introduced him into a familiar acquaintance with the *greatest peers* and *brightest wits* then living."

"No sooner (saith the same Journalist) was his body lifeless, but this author, reviving his resentment, libelled the memory of his departed friend; and, what was still more heinous, made the scandal public." Grievous the accusation! unknown the accuser! the person accused no witness in his own cause; the person, in whose regard accused, dead! But if there be living any one nobleman whose friendship, yea, any one gentleman whose subscription Mr. Addison procured to our author; let him stand forth, that truth may appear! *Amicus Plato, amicus Socrates, sed magis amica veritas.* In verity, the whole story of the libel is a lie; witness those persons of integrity who several years before Mr. Addison's decease, did see and approve of the said verses, in no wise a libel, but a friendly rebuke sent privately in our author's own hand to Mr. Addison himself, and never made public, until after their own journal and Curl had printed the same. One name alone, which I am here authorized to declare, will sufficiently evince this truth, that of the right honourable the Earl of BURLINGTON.

Next is he taxed with a crime (in the opinion of some authors, I doubt, more heinous than any morality), to wit, plagiarism, from the inventive and quaint-conceited

JAMES MOORE SMITH, GENT.

"Upon reading the third volume of Pope's Miscellanies, I found five lines which I thought excellent; and happening to praise them, a gentleman produced a modern comedy (the Rival Modes) published last year, where were the same verses to a tittle.

"These gentlemen are undoubtedly the first plagiaries, that pretend to make a reputation by stealing from a man's works in his own life-time, and out of a public print." Let us join to this what is written by the author of the Rival Modes, the said Mr. James Moore Smith, in a letter to our author himself, who had informed him, a month before that play was acted, Jan. 27, 1726-7, that "These verses, which he had before given him leave to insert in it, would be known for his, some copies being got abroad. He desires, nevertheless, that, since the lines had been read in his comedy to several, Mr. P. would not deprive it of them," &c. Surely if we add the testimonies of the Lord BOLINGBROKE, of the Lady to whom the said verses were originally addressed, of Hugh Bethel, Esq., and others, who knew them as our author's, long before the said gentleman composed his play; it is hoped, the ingenuous that affect not error, will rectify their opinion by the suffrage of so honourable personages.

And yet followeth another charge, insinuating no less than his enmity both to Church and State, which could come from no other informer than the said

MR. JAMES MOORE SMITH.

"The Memoirs of a Parish Clerk was a very dull and unjust abuse of a person who wrote in defence of our religion and constitution, and who has been dead many years." This seemeth also most untrue; it being known to divers that these memoirs were written at the seat of the Lord Harcourt in Oxfordshire, before that excellent person (bishop Burnet's) death, and many years before the appearance of that history, of which they are pretended to be an abuse. Most true it is, that Mr. Moore had such a design, and was himself the man who pressed Dr. Arbuthnot and Mr. Pope to assist him therein; and that he borrowed those Memoirs of our author, when that history came forth, with intent to turn them to such abuse. But being able to obtain from our author but one single hint, and either changing his mind, or having more mind than ability, he contented himself to keep the said Memoirs, and read them as his own to all his acquaintance. A noble person there is, into whose company Mr. Pope once chanced to introduce him, who well remembereth the conversation of Mr. Moore to have turned upon the "contempt he had for the work of that reverend prelate, and how full he was of a design he declared himself to have of exposing it." This noble person is the Earl of PETERBOROUGH.

Here in truth should we crave pardon of all the foresaid right honourable and worthy personages, for having mentioned them in the same page with such weekly riff-raff railers and rhymers; but that we had their ever-honoured commands for the same; and that they are introduced, not as witnesses in the controversy, but as witnesses that cannot be controverted; not to dispute, but to decide.

Certain it is, that dividing our writers into two classes, of such who were acquaintance, and of such who were strangers, to our author; the former are those who speak well, and the other those who speak evil of him. Of the first class, the most noble

JOHN, DUKE OF BUCKINGHAM,

sums up his character in these lines:

"And yet so wondrous, so sublime a thing,
As the great Iliad, scarce could make me sing,
Unless I justly could at once commend
A *good companion*, and as *firm a friend;*
One *moral*, or a mere *well-natured deed*,
Can all desert in sciences exceed."

So also is he deciphered by the honourable

SIMON HARCOURT.

"Say, wondrous youth, what column wilt thou chuse,
What laurel'd arch, for thy triumphant muse?
Though each great ancient court thee to his shrine,
Though every laurel through the dome be thine,
Go to the *good* and *just*, an awful train!
Thy soul's delight."——

Recorded in like manner for his virtuous disposition, and gentle bearing, by the ingenious

MR. WALTER HART,

in this apostrophe:

"O! ever worthy, ever crown'd with praise!
Blest in thy *life*, and blest in all thy *lays*.
Add, that the Sisters every thought refine,
And even thy *life*, be *faultless* as thy line.
Yet envy still, with fiercer rage pursues,
Obscures the *virtue*, and defames the muse.
A soul like thine, in pain, in grief, resign'd,
Views with just scorn the malice of mankind."

The witty and moral satirist,

DR. EDWARD YOUNG.

wishing some check to the corruption and evil manners of the times, calleth out upon our poet to undertake a task so worthy of his virtue:

"Why slumbers Pope, who leads the muses' train,
Nor hears that *Virtue*, which he *loves*, complain?"

MR. MALLET,

in his epistle on Verbal Criticism:

"Whose life, severely scann'd, transcends his lays;
For wit supreme is but his second praise."

MR. HAMMOND,

that delicate and correct imitator of Tibullus, in his Love Elegies, Elegy xiv.,

"Now, fired by Pope and *Virtue*, leave the age,
In low pursuit of self-undoing wrong,
And trace the author through his moral page,
Whose blameless life still answers to his song."

MR. THOMSON,

In his elegant and philosophical poem of The Seasons:

"Although not sweeter his own Homer sings,
Yet is his *life* the more endearing song."

To the same tune also singeth that learned clerk of Suffolk,

MR. WILLIAM BROOME:

"Thus, nobly rising in fair *Virtue's* cause,
From thy own *life* transcribe the *unerring laws*."

And, to close all, hear the reverend Dean of St. **Patrick's:**

"A soul with every virtue fraught,
By patriots, priests, and poets taught.
Whose filial piety excels
Whatever Grecian story tells.
A genius for each business fit,
Whose meanest talent is his wit," &c.

Let us now recreate thee by turning to the other side, and showing his character drawn by those with whom he never conversed, and whose countenances he could not know, though turned against him. First again commencing with the high-voiced and never enough quoted

MR. JOHN DENNIS,

who, in his Reflections on the Essay on Criticism, thus describeth him: "A little affected hypocrite, who has nothing in his mouth but candour, truth, friendship, good-nature, humanity, and magnanimity. He is so great a lover of falsehood, that, whenever he has a mind to calumniate his contemporaries, he brands them with some defect which is just *contrary to some good quality*, for which all their *friends and their acquaintance* commend them. He seems to have a particular pique to *people of quality*, and authors of that rank.—He must derive his religion from St. Omer's."—But in the Character of Mr. P. and his Writings (printed by S. Popping, 1716), he saith, "Though he is a professor of the worst religion, yet he *laughs at it;*" but that, "nevertheless, he is a *virulent papist;* and yet a *pillar* for the *church of England.*"

Of both which opinions

MR. LEWIS THEOBALD

seems also to be; declaring, in Mist's Journal of June 22, 1718, "That, if he is not shrewdly abused, he made it his practice to cackle to both *parties* in their own sentiments." But, as to his *pique* against *people of quality*, the same journalist doth not agree, but saith (May 8, 1728), "He had, by some means or other, the *acquaintance* and *friendship* of the *whole body of our nobility*."

However contradictory this may appear, Mr. Dennis and Gildon, in the character last cited, make it all plain, by assuring us, "That he is a creature that reconciles all contradictions; he is a beast, and a man; a whig, and a tory; a writer (at one and the same time) of Guardians and Examiners; an asserter of liberty, and of the dispensing power of kings; a jesuitical professor of truth; a base and a foul pretender to candour." So that, upon the whole account, we must conclude him either to have been a great hypocrite, or a very honest man; a terrible imposer upon both parties, or very moderate to either.

Be it as to the judicious reader shall seem good. Sure it is, he is little favoured of certain authors, whose wrath is perilous: for one declares he ought to have a *price set on his head*, and to be hunted down as a *wild beast*. Another protests that he does not know *what may happen;* advises him to *insure his person;* says he has *bitter enemies*, and expressly declares it will be well if he *escapes with his life.* One desires he would *cut his own throat, or hang himself.* But Pasquin seemed rather inclined it should be done by the government, representing him engaged in grievous designs with a lord of parliament, then under prosecution. Mr. Dennis himself hath written to a *minister*, that he is one of the most *dangerous persons in this kingdom;* and assureth the public, that he is an *open* and *mortal enemy* to his *country;* a monster, that *will*, one day, show as *daring a soul* as a *mad Indian*, who runs a *muck* to kill the first Christian he meets. Another gives information of *treason* discovered in his poem. Mr. Curl boldly supplies an imperfect verse with *kings* and *princesses.* And one Matthew Concanen, yet more impudent, publishes at length the two most SACRED NAMES in this nation, as members of the Dunciad!

This is prodigious! yet it is almost as strange, that in

the midst of these invectives his greatest enemies have (I know not how) borne testimony to some merit in him.

MR. THEOBALD,

in censuring his Shakspeare, declares, "He has so great an *esteem* for Mr. Pope, and so high an *opinion* of his *genius* and *excellencies*, that, notwithstanding he professes a *veneration almost rising to idolatry* for the writings of this inimitable poet, he would be very loth even to do *him* justice, at the expense of that *other gentleman's* character."

MR. CHARLES GILDON,

after having violently attacked him in many pieces, at last came to wish from his heart, "That Mr. Pope would be prevailed upon to give us Ovid's Epistles by his hand, for it is certain we see the original of Sappho to Phaon with much more life and likeness in his version, than in that of Sir Car. Scrope. And this," he adds, "is the more to be wished, because in the English tongue we have scarce anything truly and naturally written upon love." He also, in taxing Sir Richard Blackmore for his heterodox opinions of Homer, challengeth him to answer what Mr. Pope hath said in his preface to that poet.

MR. OLDMIXON

calls him a great master of our tongue; declares "the purity and perfection of the English language is to be found in his Homer; and saying there are more good verses in Dryden's Virgil than in any other work, excepts this of our author only."

THE AUTHOR OF A LETTER TO MR. CIBBER

says, "Pope *was* so good a versifier [*once*] that his predecessor, Mr. Dryden, and his contemporary, Mr. Prior, excepted, the harmony of his numbers *is* equal to anybody's. And that he *had* all the merit that a man can have that way." And

MR. THOMAS COOKE,

after much blemishing our author's Homer, crieth out,

"But in his other works what beauties shine!
While sweetest music dwells in every line,
These he admired, on these he stamp'd his praise,
And bade them live to brighten future days."

So also one who takes the name of

H. STANHOPE,

the maker of certain verses to Duncan Campbell, in that poem, which is wholly a satire on Mr. Pope, confesseth,

> "'Tis true, if finest notes alone could show
> (Tuned justly high, or regularly low)
> That we should fame to these mere vocals give;
> Pope more than we can offer should receive:
> For when some gliding river is his theme,
> His lines run smoother than the smoothest stream," &c.

MIST'S JOURNAL, June 8, 1728.

Although he says, "The smooth numbers of the Dunciad are all that recommend it, nor has it any other merit;" yet that same paper hath these words: "The author is allowed to be a perfect master of an easy and elegant versification. *In all his works* we find the most *happy turns*, and *natural similes*, wonderfully short and thick sown."

The Essay on the Dunciad, p. 25, also owns, "It is very full of *beautiful images*." But the panegyric, which crowns all that can be said on this poem, is bestowed by our Laureate

MR. COLLEY CIBBER,

who "grants it to be a better poem of its kind than ever was writ;" but adds, "it was a victory over a parcel of poor wretches, whom it was almost cowardice to conquer. A man might as well triumph for having killed so many silly flies that offended him. Could he have let them alone, by this time, poor souls! they had all been buried in oblivion." Here we see our excellent Laureate allows the justice of the satire on every man in it, but *himself;* as the great Mr. Dennis did before him.

The said

MR. DENNIS, AND MR. GILDON,

in the most furious of all their works (the forecited character, p. 5,) do in concert confess, "That some men of *good understanding* value him for his rhymes." And (p. 17,) "That he has got, like Mr. Bayes in the Rehearsal, (that is, like Mr. Dryden) a notable knack at rhyming, and writing smooth verse."

Of his Essay on Man, numerous were the praises bestowed by his avowed enemies, in the imagination that the same was not written by him, as it was printed anonymously.

Thus sung of it even

BEZALEEL MORRIS.

"Auspicious bard, while all admire thy strain,
All but the selfish, ignorant, and vain;
I, whom no bribe to servile flattery drew,
Must pay the tribute to thy merit due:
Thy muse, sublime, significant, and clear,
Alike informs the soul, and charms the ear," &c.

And

MR. LEONARD WELSTED

thus wrote to the unknown author, on the first publication of the said Essay: "I must own, after the reception which the vilest and most immoral ribaldry hath lately met with, I was surprised to see what I had long despaired, a performance deserving the name of a poet. Such, sir, is your work. It is, indeed, above all commendation, and ought to have been published in an age and country more worthy of it. If my testimony be of weight anywhere, you are sure to have it in the amplest manner," &c. &c. &c.

Thus we see every one of his works hath been extolled by one or other of his most inveterate enemies; and to the success of them all they do unanimously give testimony. But it is sufficient, *instar omnium*, to behold the great critic, Mr. Dennis, sorely lamenting it, even from the Essay on Criticism to this day of the Dunciad! "A most notorious instance," quoth he, "of the depravity of genius and taste, the *approbation* this essay meets with.—I can safely affirm, that I never attacked any of these writings, unless they had *success* infinitely beyond their merit.—This, though an empty, has been a *popular* scribbler. The epidemic madness of the times has given him *reputation*. If, after the cruel treatment so many extraordinary men (Spenser, Lord Bacon, Ben Jonson, Milton, Butler, Otway, and others) have received from this country for these last hundred years, I should shift the scene, and show all that penury changed at once to riot and profuseness; and more squandered away upon *one object*, than would have satisfied the greater part of those extraordinary men; the reader, to whom this one creature should be unknown, would fancy him a prodigy of art and nature, would believe that all the great qualities of these persons were centred in him alone.—But if I should venture to assure him, that the PEOPLE of ENGLAND had made such a choice—the reader would either believe me a *malicious enemy*, and *slanderer;* or that the reign of the last (queen Anne's) *ministry* was designed by fate to encourage *fools*."

But it happens, that this our poet never had any place, pension, or gratuity, in any shape, from the said glorious queen, or any of her ministers. All he owed, in the whole course of his life, to any court, was a subscription for his Homer of 200*l*. from king George I., and 100*l*. from the prince and princess.

However, lest we imagine our author's success was constant and universal, they acquaint us of certain works in a less degree of repute, whereof, although owned by others, yet do they assure us he is the writer. Of this sort Mr. DENNIS ascribes to him *two farces*, whose names he does not tell, but assures us that *there is not one jest in them;* and an imitation of Horace, whose title he does not mention, but assures us *it is much more execrable than all his works*. The DAILY JOURNAL, May 11, 1728, assures us, "He is below Tom Durfey in the drama, because (as that writer thinks) the Marriage Hater Matched, and the Boarding School are better than the What-d'ye-call-it;" which is not Mr. P.'s, but Mr. Gay's. Mr. GILDON assures us, in his new Rehearsal, p. 48, "That he was writing a *play* of the Lady Jane Grey;" but it afterwards proved to be Mr. Rowe's. We are assured by another, "He wrote a pamphlet, called Dr. Andrew Tripe;" which proved to be one Dr. Wagstaff's. Mr. THEOBALD assures us, in the Mist of the 27th of April, "That the treatise of the *Profound* is very dull, and that Mr. Pope is the author of it." The writer of Gulliveriana is of another opinion; and says, "the whole, or greatest part, of the merit of this treatise must and can only be ascribed to Gulliver." [Here, gentle reader, cannot I but smile at the strange blindness and positiveness of men knowing the said treatise to appertain to none other but to me, Martinus Scriblerus.]

We are assured, in Mist's Journal of June 8th, "that his own *plays* and *farces* would better have adorned the Dunciad than those of Mr. Theobald; for he had neither genius for tragedy nor comedy." Which whether true or not, is not easy to judge, inasmuch as he hath attempted neither; unless we will take it for granted, with Mr. Cibber, that his being once very angry at hearing a friend's play abused, was an infallible proof the play was his own; the said Mr. Cibber thinking it impossible for a man to be much concerned for any but himself: "Now let any man judge," saith he, "by this concern, who was the true mother of the child."

But from all that hath been said, the discerning reader will collect, that it little availed our author to have any candour, since, when he declared he did not write for others, it was not credited; as little to have any modesty, since, when he declined writing in any way himself, the presumption of others was imputed to him. If he singly enterprised one great work, he was taxed of boldness and madness to a prodigy: if he took assistants in another, it was complained of, and represented as a great injury to the public. The loftiest heroics, the lowest ballads, treatises against the state or church, satires on lords and ladies, raillery on wits and authors, squabbles with booksellers, or even full and true accounts of monsters, poisons, and murders; of any hereof was there nothing so good, nothing so bad, which hath not at one or other season been to him ascribed. If it bore no author's name, then lay he concealed; if it did, he fathered it upon that author to be yet better concealed: if it resembled any of his styles, then was it evident; if it did not, then disguised he it on set purpose. Yea, even direct oppositions in religion, principles, and politics, have equally been supposed in him inherent. Surely a most rare and singular character! of which let the reader make what he can.

Doubtless most commentators would hence take occasion to turn all to their author's advantage, and from the testimony of his very enemies would affirm, that his capacity was boundless, as well as his imagination; that he was a perfect master of all styles, and all arguments; and that there was in those times no other writer, in any kind, of any degree of excellence, save himself. But as this is not our own sentiment, we shall determine on nothing; but leave thee, gentle reader, to steer thy judgment equally between various opinions, and to choose whether thou wilt incline to the testimonies of authors avowed, or of authors concealed; of those who knew him, or of those who knew him not.

MARTINUS SCRIBLERUS,

OF THE POEM

THIS poem, as it celebrateth the most grave and ancient of things, Chaos, Night, and Dulness, so is it of the most grave and ancient kind. Homer, saith Aristotle, was the first who gave the *form*, and, saith Horace, who adapted the *measure*, to heroic poesy. But even before this, may be rationally presumed from what the ancients have left written, was a piece by Homer composed, of like nature and matter with this of our poet; for of epic sort it appeareth to have been, yet of matter surely not unpleasant, witness what is reported of it by the learned Archbishop Eustathius, in Odyss. x. And accordingly Aristotle, in his Poetic, chap. iv., doth further set forth, that as the Iliad and Odyssey gave examples to tragedy, so did this poem to comedy its first idea.

From these authors also it should seem that the hero, or chief personage of it, was no less *obscure*, and his understanding and sentiments no less quaint and strange (if indeed not more so) than any of the actors of our poem. MARGITES was the name of this personage, whom Antiquity recordeth to have been *Dunce the first;* and surely from what we hear of him, not unworthy to be the root of so spreading a tree, and so numerous a posterity. The poem therefore celebrating him, was properly and absolutely a *Dunciad;* which, though now unhappily lost, yet is its nature sufficiently known by the infallible tokens aforesaid. And thus it doth appear that the first Dunciad was the first epic poem, written by Homer himself, and anterior even to the Iliad or Odyssey.

Now, forasmuch as our poet had translated those two famous works of Homer which are yet left, he did conceive it in some sort his duty to imitate that also which was lost; and was therefore induced to bestow on it the same form which Homer's is reported to have had, namely, that of epic poem, with a title also framed after the ancient Greek manner, to wit, that of *Dunciad.*

Wonderful it is that so few of the moderns have been stimulated to attempt some Dunciad! since, in the opinion of the multitude, it might cost less pain and oil than imitation of the greater epic. But possible it is also, that, on due reflection, the maker might find it easier to paint a Charlemagne, a Brute, or a Godfrey, with just pomp and dignity heroic, than a Margites, a Codrus, or a Fleckno.

We shall next declare the occasion and the cause which moved our poet to this particular work. He lived in those days when (after Providence had permitted the invention of printing as a scourge for the sins of the learned) paper also became so cheap, and printers so numerous, that a deluge of authors covered the land; whereby not only the peace of the honest unwriting subject was daily molested, but unmerciful demands were made of his applause, yea of his money, by such as would neither earn the one, nor deserve the other. At the same time the licence of the press was such, that it grew dangerous to refuse them either; for they would forthwith publish slanders unpunished, the authors being anonymous, and skulking under the wings of publishers—a set of men who never scrupled to vend either calumny or blasphemy, as long as the town would call for it.

Now our author, living in those times, did conceive it an endeavour well worthy an honest satirist to dissuade the dull, and punish the wicked, *the only way that was left.* In that public-spirited view he laid the plan of this poem, as the greatest service he was capable (without much hurt, or being slain) to render his dear country. First, taking things from their original, he considereth the causes creative of such authors, namely, *dulness* and *poverty;* the one born with them, the other contracted by neglect of their proper talents, through self-conceit of greater abilities. This truth he wrappeth in an *allegory,* (as the construction of epic poesy requireth) and feigns that one of these goddesses had taken up her abode with the other, and that they jointly inspired all such writers and such works. He proceedeth to show the *qualities* they bestow on these authors, and the *effects* they produce; then the *materials,* or *stock,* with which they furnish them; and, above all, that *self-opinion* which causeth it to seem to themselves vastly greater than it is, and is the prime motive of their setting up in this sad and sorry merchandise. The great power of these goddesses acting in alliance (whereof as the one is the mother of industry, so is the other of plodding) was to be exemplified in some *one great* and *remarkable action:* and none could be more so than that which our poet hath chosen, viz. the restoration of the reign of Chaos and Night, by the ministry of Dulness, their daughter, in the removal of her imperial seat from the city to the polite world; as the action of the Æneid is the restoration of the empire of Troy, by the removal of the race from thence to Latium. But as Homer singing only the *wrath* of Achilles, yet includes in his poem the whole history of the Trojan war, in like manner our author hath drawn into this *single action* the whole history of Dulness and her children.

A *person* must next be fixed upon to support this action. This *phantom* in the poet's mind must have a *name:* he finds it to be ——, and he becomes of course the hero of the poem.

The *fable* being thus, according to the best example, one and entire, as contained in the proposition; the *machinery* is a continued chain of allegories, setting forth the whole power, ministry, and empire of Dulness, extended through her subordinate instruments, in all her various operations.

This is branched into *episodes*, each of which hath its moral apart, though all conducive to the main end. The crowd assembled in the second book demonstrates the design to be more extensive than to bad poets only, and that we may expect other episodes of the patrons, encouragers, or paymasters of such authors, as occasion shall bring them forth. And the third book, if well considered, seemeth to embrace the whole world. Each of the games relateth to some or other of the vile class of writers. The first concerneth the Plagiary, to whom he giveth the name of Moore; the second, the libellous Novelist, whom he styleth Eliza; the third, the flattering Dedicator; the fourth, the bawling Critic, or noisy Poet; the fifth, the dark and dirty Party-writer; and so of the rest: assigning to each some *proper name* or other, such as he could find.

As for the *characters*, the public hath already acknowledged how justly they are drawn: the manners are so depicted, and the sentiments so peculiar to those to whom applied, that surely to transfer them to any other or wiser personages, would be exceeding difficult: and certain it is, that every person concerned, being consulted apart, hath readily owned the resemblance of every portrait, his own excepted. So Mr. Cibber calls them, "a parcel of *poor wretches, silly flies:*" but adds, "our author's wit is remarkably more bare and barren, whenever it would fall foul on *Cibber*, than upon any other person whatever."

The *descriptions* are singular, the *comparisons* very quaint, the *narration* various, yet of one colour: the purity and chastity of *diction* is so preserved, that in the places most suspicious, not the *words* but only the *images* have been censured, and yet are those images no other than have been sanctified by ancient and classical authority, (though, as was the manner of those good timés, not so curiously wrapped up) yea, and commented upon by most grave doctors, and approved critics.

As it beareth the name of *epic*, it is thereby subjected to such severe indispensable rules as are laid on all neoterics, a strict imitation of the ancients; insomuch, that any deviation, accompanied with whatever poetic beauties, hath always been censured by the sound critic. How exact that imitation hath been in this piece, appeareth not only by its general structure, but by particular allusions infinite, many whereof have escaped both the commentator and poet himself; yea, divers by his exceeding diligence are so altered and interwoven with the rest, that several have already been, and more will be, by the ignorant abused, as altogether and originally his own.

In a word, the whole poem proveth itself to be the work of our Author, when his faculties were in full vigour and perfection; at that exact time when years have ripened the judgment, without diminishing the imagination: which, by good critics, is held to be punctually at *forty*. For at that season it was that Virgil finished his Georgics; and Sir Richard Blackmore at the like age composing his Arthurs, declared the same to be the very *acme* and pitch of life for epic poesy: though since he hath altered it to *sixty*, the year in which he published his Alfred. True it is, that the talents for *criticism*, namely, smartness, quick censure, vivacity of remark, certainty of asseveration; indeed, all but acerbity, seem rather the gifts of youth than of riper age. But it is far otherwise in *poetry;* witness the works of Mr. Rymer and Mr. Dennis, who, beginning with criticism, became afterwards such poets as no age hath paralleled. With good reason, therefore, did our author choose to write his Essay on that subject at twenty, and reserve for his maturer years this great and wonderful work of the Dunciad.

RICARDUS ARISTARCHUS

OF

THE HERO OF THE POEM.

Of the nature of *Dunciad* in general, whence derived, and on what authority founded, as well as of the art and conduct of this our poem in particular, the learned and laborious Scriblerus hath, according to his manner, and with tolerable share of judgment, dissertated. But when he cometh to speak of the *person* of the *hero* fitted for such poem, in truth he miserably halts and hallucinates. For misled by one Monsieur Bossu, a Gallic critic, he prateth of I cannot tell what *phantom of a hero*, only raised up to support the fable. A putrid conceit! as if Homer and Virgil, like modern undertakers, who first build their house and then seek out for a tenant, had contrived the story of a war and a wandering, before they once thought either of Achilles or Æneas. We shall therefore set our good brother and the world also right in this particular, by giving our word, that in the *greater epic*, the prime invention of the muse is to exalt heroic virtue, in order to propagate the love of it among the children of men; and consequently that the poet's first thought must needs be turned upon a real subject meet for laud and celebration; not one whom he is to make, but one whom he may find, truly illustrious. This is the *primum mobile* of his poetic world, whence everything is to receive life and motion. For this subject being found, he is immediately ordained, or rather acknowledged, a *hero*, and put upon such action as befitteth the dignity of his character.

But the muse ceases not here her eagle-flight. Sometimes, satiated with the contemplation of these *suns* of glory, she turneth downward on her wing, and darts like lightning on the *goose* and *serpent* kind. For we may apply to the muse in her various moods, what an ancient master of wisdom affirmeth of the gods in general: *Si dii non irascuntur impiis et injustis, nec pios utique justosque diligunt. In rebus enim diversis, aut in utramque partem moveri necesse est, aut in neutram. Itaque qui bonos diligit, et malos odit; et qui malos non odit, nec bonos diligit. Quia et diligere bonos ex odio malorum venit; et malos odisse ex bonorum caritate descendit.* Which in the vernacular idiom may be thus interpreted: "If the gods be not provoked at evil men, neither are they delighted with the good and just. For contrary objects must either excite contrary affections, or no affections at all. So that he who loveth good men, must at the same time hate the bad; and he who hateth not bad men, cannot love the good; because to love good men proceedeth from an aversion to evil, and to hate evil men from a tenderness to the good." From this delicacy of the muse arose the *little epic,* (more lively and choleric than her elder sister, whose bulk and complexion incline her to the flegmatic,) and for this some notorious vehicle of vice and folly was sought out, to make thereof an example. An early instance of which, (nor could it escape the accurate Scriblerus) the father of epic poem himself affordeth us. From him the practice descended to the Greek dramatic poets, his offspring; who, in the composition of their *tetralogy,* or set of four pieces, were wont to make the last a *satiric tragedy.* Happily one of these ancient *Dunciads* (as we may well term it) is come down to us amongst the tragedies of Euripides. And what doth the reader think may be the subject? Why truly, and it is worth his observation, the unequal contention of an *old, dull, debauched, buffoon Cyclops,* with the heaven-directed *favourite* of Minerva; who, after having quietly borne all the monster's obscene and impious ribaldry, endeth the farce in punishing him with the mark of an indelible brand in his *forehead.* May we not then be excused, if for the future we consider the epics of Homer, Virgil, and Milton, together with this our poem, as a complete *tetralogy,* in which the last worthily holdeth the place or station of the *satiric* piece?

Proceed we therefore in our subject. It hath been long, and, alas for pity! still remaineth a question, whether the hero of the *greater epic* should be an *honest man?* or, as the French critics express it, *un honnête homme;* but it never admitted of any doubt but that the hero of the *little epic* should *not* be so. Hence, to the advantage of our Dunciad, we may observe how much juster the *moral* of that poem must needs be, where so important a question is previously decided.

But then it is not every knave, nor (let me add) fool, that is a fit subject for a Dunciad. There must still exist some analogy, if not resemblance of qualities, between the heroes of the two poems: and this in order to admit what neoteric critics call the *parody*, one of the liveliest graces of the little epic. Thus, it being agreed that the constituent qualities of the greater epic hero are *wisdom*, *bravery*, and *love*, from whence springeth *heroic virtue*, it followeth that those of the lesser epic hero should be *vanity*, *impudence*, and *debauchery*, from which happy assemblage resulteth *heroic dulness*, the never-dying subject of this our Poem.

This being confessed, come we now to particulars. It is the character of true *wisdom*, to seek its chief support and confidence within itself; and to place that support in the resources which proceed from a conscious rectitude of will. —And are the advantages of *vanity*, when arising to the heroic standard, at all short of this self-complacence? Nay, are they not, in the opinion of the enamoured owner, far beyond it? "Let the world (will such a one say) impute to me what folly or weakness they please; but till *wisdom* can give me something that will make me more heartily happy, I am content to be GAZED at." This we see is *vanity* according to the *heroic* gage or measure; not that low and ignoble species which pretendeth to *virtues we have not*, but the laudable ambition of being *gazed at* for glorying in those *vices* which all the world know *we have*. "The world may ask," says he, "why I make my follies public? Why not? I have passed my time very pleasantly with them." In short, there is no sort of vanity such a hero would scruple, but that which might go near to degrade him from his high station in this our Dunciad, namely, "whether it would not be *vanity* in him, to take shame to himself for *not being a wise man?*"

Bravery, the second attribute of the true hero, is courage, manifesting itself in every limb; while, in its correspondent virtue in the mock hero, that courage is all collected into the *face*. And as power when drawn together, must needs be more strong than when dispersed, we generally find this kind of courage in so high and heroic a degree, that it insults not only men, but gods. Mezentius is without doubt the bravest character in all the Æneis; but how? His bravery, we know, was a high courage of blasphemy. And can we say less of this brave man's, who, having told us that he placed "his *summum bonum* in those follies, which he was not content barely to possess but would likewise glory in," adds, "*If I am misguided*, 'TIS NATURE'S FAULT, *and I follow* HER." Nor can we be mistaken in making this happy quality a species of *courage*, when we consider those illustrious marks of it, which made his *face* "more known (as he justly boasteth) than most in the kingdom," and his *language* to consist of what we must allow to be the most *daring* figure of speech, that which is taken from the *name of God.*

Gentle love, the next ingredient in the true hero's composition, is a mere bird of passage, or (as Shakspeare calls it) *summer-teeming lust*, and evaporates in the heat of *youth;* doubtless by that refinement it suffers in passing through those *certain strainers* which our poet somewhere speaketh of. But when it is let alone to work upon the *lees*, it acquireth strength by *old age:* and becometh a standing ornament to the little epic. It is true, indeed, there is one objection to its fitness for such a use: for not only the ignorant may think it *common*, but it is admitted to be so, even by him who best knoweth its nature. "Don't you think," saith he, "to say only *a man has his whore*, ought to go for little or nothing? Because *defendit numerus*, take the first ten thousand men you meet, and I believe you would be no loser if you betted ten to one, that every single sinner of them, one with another, had been guilty of the same frailty." But here he seemeth not to have done himself justice: the man is sure enough a hero who hath his lady at fourscore. How doth his modesty herein lessen the merit of a *whole well-spent* life: not taking to himself the commendation (which *Horace* accounted the greatest in a theatrical character) of continuing to the very *dregs* the same he was from the beginning—

Servetur ad IMUM
Qualis ab incepto processerat——

But let us farther remark, that the calling her *his* whore, implieth she was *his own*, and not his *neighbour's*. Truly a commendable continence! and such as Scipio himself must have applauded. For how much self-denial was necessary not to covet his neighbour's whore? and what disorders must the coveting her have occasioned, in that society, where (according to this political calculator) *nine* in *ten* of all ages have their *concubines?*

We have now, as briefly as we could devise, gone through the three constituent qualities of either hero. But it is not in any, or all of these, that heroism properly or essentially resideth. It is a lucky result rather from the collision of these lively qualities against one another. Thus, as from wisdom, bravery, and love, ariseth *magnanimity*, the object of *admiration*, which is the aim of the greater epic; so from vanity, impudence, and debauchery, springeth *buffoonery*, the source of *ridicule*, that "laughing ornament," as he well termeth it, of the little epic.

He is not ashamed (God forbid he ever should be ashamed!) of this character, who deemeth, that not *reason* but *risibility* distinguisheth the human species from the brutal. "As nature (saith this profound philosopher) distinguished our species from the mute creation by our risibility, her design MUST have been by *that faculty* as evidently to raise our HAPPINESS, as by OUR *os sublime* (OUR ERECTED FACES) to lift the dignity of our FORM above them." All this considered, how complete a hero must he be, as well as how *happy* a man, whose risibility lieth not barely in his *muscles* as in the common sort, but (as himself informeth us) in his very *spirits?* And whose *os sublime* is not simply an *erect face*, but a brazen head, as should seem by his comparing it with one of iron, said to belong to the late king of Sweden!

But whatever personal qualities a hero may have, the examples of Achilles and Æneas show us, that all those are of small avail, without the constant *assistance of the* GODS: for the subversion and erection of empires have never been judged the work of man. How greatly soever then we may esteem of his high talents, we can hardly conceive his personal prowess alone sufficient to restore the decayed empire of Dulness. So weighty an achievement must require the particular favour and protection of the GREAT; who being the natural patrons and supporters of *letters*, as the ancient gods were of *Troy*, must first be drawn off and engaged in another interest, before the total subversion of them can be accomplished. To surmount, therefore, this last and greatest difficulty, we have in this excellent man a professed favourite and intimado of the great. And look of what force ancient piety was to draw the gods into the party of Æneas, that, and much stronger is modern incense, to engage the great in the party of Dulness.

Thus have we essayed to portray or shadow out this noble imp of fame. But now the impatient reader will be apt to say, if so many and various graces go to the making up a hero, what mortal shall suffice to bear this character?

Ill hath he read, who sees not in every trace of this picture, that *individual*, ALL-ACCOMPLISHED PERSON, in whom these rare virtues and lucky circumstances have agreed to meet and concentre with the strongest lustre and fullest harmony.

The good Scriblerus indeed, nay, the world itself, might be imposed on in the late spurious editions, by I can't tell what *sham-hero*, or *phantom:* But it was not so easy to impose on HIM whom this egregious error most of all concerned. For no sooner had the fourth book laid open the high and swelling scene, but he recognised his own heroic acts: And when he came to the words,

Soft on her lap her Laureat son reclines,

(though *laureat* imply no more than *one crowned with laurel*, as befitteth any associate or consort in empire) he ROARED (like a lion) and VINDICATED HIS RIGHT OF FAME. Indeed not without cause, he being there represented as *fast asleep;* so unbeseeming the eye of empire, which, like that of Providence, should never slumber. "Hah!" said he, "fast asleep it seems! that's a little too strong. Pert and dull at least you might have allowed me, but as seldom asleep as any fool." However, the injured hero may comfort himself with this reflection, that though it be *sleep*, yet it is not the *sleep of death*, but of *immortality*. Here he will *live* at least, though not *awake;* and in no worse condition than many an enchanted warrior before him. The famous Durandarte, for instance, was, like him, cast into a long slumber by Merlin, the *British bard* and necromancer; and his example for submitting to it with so good a grace might be of use to our hero. For this disastrous knight being sorely pressed or driven to make his answer by several *persons of quality*, only replied with a sigh, *Patience, and shuffle the cards.*

But now, as nothing in this world, no, not the most sacred or perfect things either of religion or government, can escape the teeth or tongue of envy, methinks I already hear these carpers objecting to the clear title of our hero.

"It would never," say they, "have been esteemed sufficient to make a hero for the Iliad or Æneis, that Achilles was brave enough to overturn one empire, or Æneas pious enough to raise another, had they not been goddess-born and princes bred. What then did this author mean by erecting a player instead of one of his patrons, (a person 'never a hero even on the stage') to this dignity of colleague in the empire of Dulness, and achiever of a work that neither old Omar, Attila, nor John of Leyden could entirely compass."

To all this we have, as we conceive, a sufficient answer from the Roman historian, *Fabrum esse suæ quemque fortunæ: Every man is the* Smith *of his own fortune.* The politic Florentine Nicholas Machiavel goeth still farther, and affirms that a man needs but to *believe himself a hero* to be one of the best. "Let him," saith he, "but fancy himself capable of the highest things, and he will of course be able to achieve them." Laying this down as a principle, it will certainly and incontestably follow, that, if ever hero *was* such a character, OURS *is:* for if ever man *thought* himself such, OURS *doth.* Hear how he constantly paragons himself, at one time to ALEXANDER THE GREAT and CHARLES XII. of Sweden, for the excess and delicacy of his ambition; to HENRY IV. of France, for honest policy; to the first BRUTUS for love of liberty; and to SIR ROBERT WALPOLE, for good government while in power. At another time, to the godlike SOCRATES, for his diversions and amusements; to HORACE, MONTAIGNE, and SIR WILLIAM TEMPLE, for an elegant vanity that makes them for ever read and admired; to TWO LORD CHANCELLORS, for law, from whom, when confederate against him at the bar, he carried away the prize of eloquence; and, to say all in a word, to the right reverend the LORD BISHOP OF LONDON himself, in the art of writing *pastoral letters.*

Nor did his *actions* fall short of the sublimity of his conceptions. In his early youth he *met the revolution* at Nottingham face to face, at a time when his betters contented themselves with *following* her. But he shone in courts as well as camps. He was *called up* when *the nation fell in labour* of this *revolution,* and was a gossip at her christening with the bishop and the ladies.

As to his *birth,* it is true he pretendeth no relation either to heathen god or goddess; but, what is as good, he was descended from a *maker* of both. And that he did not pass himself on the world for a hero, as well by birth as education, was his own fault; for his lineage he bringeth into his life as an anecdote, and is sensible he had it in his power *to be thought nobody's son at all:* and what is that but coming into the world a hero?

There is in truth another objection of greater weight, namely, "That this hero still existeth, and hath not yet finished his earthly course. For if Solon said well, that 'no man could be called happy till his death,' surely much less can any one, till then, be pronounced a hero; this species of men being far more subject than others to the caprices of fortune and humour." But to this also we have an answer, that will be deemed (we hope) decisive. It cometh from *himself*, who, to cut this dispute short, hath solemnly protested that *he will never change or amend.*

With regard to his *vanity*, he declareth that nothing shall ever part them. "Nature," saith he, "hath amply supplied me in vanity; a pleasure which neither the pertness of wit nor the gravity of wisdom will ever persuade me to part with." Our poet had charitably endeavoured to administer a cure to it, but he telleth us plainly, "My superiors perhaps may be mended by him, but for my part I own myself incorrigible. I look upon my follies as the best part of my fortune." And with good reason.—We see to what they have brought him!

Secondly, as to *buffoonery*. "Is it," saith he, "a time of day for me to leave off these fooleries, and set up a new character? I can no more put off my follies than my skin; I have often tried, but they stick too close to me; nor am I sure my friends are displeased with them, for in this light I afford them frequent matter of mirth," &c. &c. Having then so publicly declared himself *incorrigible*, he is become *dead in law*, (I mean the *law Epopœian*) and descendeth to the poet as his property, who may take him, and deal with him, as if he had been dead as long as an old Egyptian hero; that is to say, *embowel* and *embalm him for posterity.*

Nothing therefore, we conceive, remains to hinder his own prophecy of himself from taking immediate effect. A rare felicity! and what few prophets have had the satisfaction to see alive! Nor can we conclude better than with that extraordinary one of his, which is conceived in these oraculous words, MY DULNESS WILL FIND SOMEBODY TO DO IT RIGHT.

THE DUNCIAD.

TO DR. JONATHAN SWIFT.

BOOK THE FIRST

ARGUMENT.

The Proposition, the Invocation, and the Inscription. Then the original of the great empire of *Dulness*, and cause of the continuance thereof. The College of the *Goddess* in the City, with her private Academy for poets in particular; the governors of it, and the four Cardinal Virtues. Then the Poem *hastes into the midst of things*, presenting her, on the evening of a Lord Mayor's day, revolving the long succession of her sons, and the glories past and to come. She fixes her eye on *Bays* to be the instrument of that great event which is the subject of the poem. He is described pensive among his books, giving up the cause, and apprehending the period of her empire: after debating whether to betake himself to the Church, or to Gaming, or to Party-writing, he raises an altar of proper books, and (making first his solemn prayer and declaration) purposes thereon to sacrifice all his unsuccessful writings. As the pile is kindled, the Goddess, beholding the flame from her seat, flies and puts it out by casting upon it the poem of *Thulé*. She forthwith reveals herself to him, transports him to her temple, unfolds her arts, and initiates him into her mysteries; then announcing the death of *Eusden*, the Poet Laureate, anoints him, carries him to court, and proclaims him successor.

The mighty mother, and her son who brings
The Smithfield muses[1] to the ear of kings,
I sing. Say you, her instruments the great!
Call'd to this work by Dulness, Jove, and Fate;
You by whose care, in vain decried and curs'd,
Still Dunce the second reigns like Dunce the first;
Say how the goddess bade Britannia sleep,
And pour'd her spirit o'er the land and deep.

[1] *Smithfield* is the place where Bartholomew Fair was kept, whose shows, machines, and dramatical entertainments, formerly agreeable only to the taste of the rabble, were, by the hero of this poem and others of equal genius, brought to the theatres of Covent-Garden, Lincoln's-Inn-fields, and the Haymarket, to be the reigning pleasures of the court and town. This happened in the reigns of King George I. and II.

In eldest time, ere mortals writ or read,
Ere Pallas issued from the Thunderer's head,
Dulness o'er all possess'd her ancient right,
Daughter of Chaos and eternal Night:
Fate in their dotage this fair idiot gave,
Gross as her sire, and as her mother grave,
Laborious, heavy, busy, bold, and blind,
She ruled, in native anarchy, the mind.
Still her old empire to restore she tries,
For, born a goddess, Dulness never dies.
O thou! whatever title please thine ear,
Dean, Drapier, Bickerstaff, or Gulliver!
Whether thou choose Cervantes' serious air,
Or laugh and shake in Rabelais' easy chair,
Or praise the court, or magnify mankind,
Or thy grieved country's copper chains unbind;
From thy Bœotia though her power retires,
Mourn not, my Swift, at aught our realm acquires,
Here pleased behold her mighty wings outspread
To hatch a new Saturnian age of lead.
Close to those walls where Folly holds her throne,
And laughs to think Monro would take her down,
Where o'er the gates, by his famed father's hand[1]
Great Cibber's brazen brainless brothers stand;
One cell there is, conceal'd from vulgar eye,
The cave of Poverty and Poetry.
Keen hollow winds howl thro' the bleak recess,
Emblem of music caus'd by emptiness.
Hence bards, like Proteus long in vain tied down,
Escape in monsters, and amaze the town.
Hence Miscellanies spring, the weekly boast
Of Curl's chaste press, and Lintot's rubric post:[2]
Hence hymning Tyburn's elegiac lines,[3]
Hence Journals, Medleys, Merc'ries, Magazines,

[1] Mr. Caius Gabriel Cibber, father of the poet laureate. The two statues of the lunatics formerly placed over the gates of Bedlam Hospital were done by him, and (as the son justly says of him) are no ill monuments of his fame as an artist.

[2] Two booksellers. The former was fined by the Court of King's Bench for publishing obscene books; the latter usually adorned his shop with titles in red letters.

[3] It was an ancient English custom for the malefactors to sing a psalm at their execution at Tyburn, and no less customary to print elegies on their deaths, at the same time, or before.

Sepulchral lies, our holy walls to grace,
And new-year odes, and all the Grub-street race.
In clouded majesty here Dulness shone;
Four guardian Virtues, round, support her throne:
Fierce champion Fortitude, that knows no fears
Of hisses, blows, or want, or loss of ears:
Calm Temperance, whose blessings those partake
Who hunger and who thirst for scribbling sake:
Prudence, whose glass presents the approaching gaol;
Poetic Justice, with her lifted scale,
Where, in nice balance, truth with gold she weighs,
And solid pudding against empty praise.
Here she beholds the chaos dark and deep,
Where nameless somethings in their causes sleep,
'Til genial Jacob,[1] or a warm third day,
Call forth each mass, a poem, or a play:
How hints, like spawn, scarce quick in embryo lie,
How new-born nonsense first is taught to cry;
Maggots half-form'd in rhyme exactly meet,
And learn to crawl upon poetic feet.
Here one poor word an hundred clenches makes,
And ductile Dulness new meanders takes;
There motley images her fancy strike,
Figures ill pair'd, and similes unlike.
She sees a mob of metaphors advance,
Pleased with the madness of the mazy dance:
How Tragedy and Comedy embrace;
How Farce and Epic get a jumbled race;
How Time himself stands still at her command,
Realms shift their place, and ocean turns to land.
Here gay description Ægypt glads with showers,[2]
Or gives to Zembla fruits, to Barca flowers;
Glittering with ice here hoary hills are seen,
There painted valleys of eternal green,
In cold December fragrant chaplets blow,
And heavy harvests nod beneath the snow.
All these, and more, the cloud-compelling queen
Beholds through fogs, that magnify the scene:

[1] Jacob Tonson, the publisher.

[2] In the Lower Ægypt rain is of no use, the overflowing of the Nile being sufficient to impregnate the soil.—These six verses represent the inconsistencies in the descriptions of poets, who heap together al glittering and gaudy images, though incompatible in one season, or in one scene.

She, tinsel'd o'er in robes of varying hues,
With self-applause her wild creation views;
Sees momentary monsters rise and fall,
And with her own fools-colours gilds them all.
'Twas on the day, when * * rich and grave,[1]
Like Cimon, triumph'd both on land and wave:
(Pomps without guilt, of bloodless swords and maces.
Glad chains, warm furs, broad banners, and broad faces:)
Now night descending, the proud scene was o'er,
But lived, in Settle's numbers, one day more:[2]
Now mayors and shrieves all hush'd and satiate lay,
Yet eat, in dreams, the custard of the day;
While pensive poets painful vigils keep,
Sleepless themselves, to give their readers sleep.
Much to the mindful queen the feast recals
What city swans once sung within the walls;
Much she revolves their arts, their ancient praise,
And sure succession down from Heywood's days,[3]
She saw, with joy, the line immortal run,
Each sire impress'd and glaring in his son:
So watchful Bruin forms, with plastic care,
Each growing lump, and brings it to a bear,
She saw old Prynne in restless Daniel shine,[4]
And Eusden[5] eke out Blackmore's endless line;

1 Viz., a Lord Mayor's day; his name the author had left in blanks, but most certainly could never be that which the editor foisted in formerly, and which no ways agrees with the chronology of the poem.

The procession of a Lord Mayor is made partly by land, and partly by water.—Cimon, the famous Athenian general, obtained a victory by sea, and another by land, on the same day, over the Persians and barbarians.

2 Settle was poet to the city of London. His office was to compose yearly panegyrics upon the Lord Mayors, and verses to be spoken in the pageants; but that part of the show being at length frugally abolished, the employment of city poet ceased, so that upon Settle's demise there was no successor to that place. His productions are carefully preserved in the City library.

3 John Heywood, whose interludes were printed in the time of Henry VIII.

4 The first edition had it,

She saw in Norton all his father shine.

A great mistake; for Daniel De Foe had parts, but Norton de Foe was a wretched writer, and never attempted poetry. Much more justly is Daniel himself made successor to W. Prynne, both of whom wrote verses as well as politics.

5 Laurence Eusden, poet laureate. Mr. Jacob gives a catalogue of some few only of his works, which were very numerous.

She saw slow Phillips creep like Tate's poor page;
And all the mighty mad in Dennis[2] rage.
  In each she marks her image full express'd,
But chief in Bays's monster-breeding breast;
Bays, form'd by nature stage and town to bless,
And act, and be, a coxcomb, with success.
Dulness with transport eyes the lively dunce,
Remembering she herself was Pertness once.
Now (shame to Fortune!) an ill run at play
Blank'd his bold visage, and a thin third day:
Swearing and supperless the hero sate,
Blasphemed his gods, the dice, and damn'd his fate.
Then gnaw'd his pen, then dash'd it on the ground,
Sinking from thought to thought, a vast profound!
Plunged for his sense, but found no bottom there,
Yet wrote and flounder'd on, in mere despair.
Round him much embryo, much abortion lay,
Much future ode, and abdicated play;
Nonsense precipitate, like running lead,
That slipp'd through cracks and zig-zags at the head;
All that on Folly Frenzy could beget,
Fruits of dull heat, and sooterkins of wit.
Next, o'er his books his eyes began to roll,
In pleasing memory of all he stole,
How here he sipp'd, how there he plunder'd snug,
And suck'd all o'er, like an industrious bug.
Here lay poor Fletcher's half-eat scenes, and here
The frippery of crucified Moliere;
There hapless Shakspeare, yet of Tibbald sore,
Wish'd he had blotted for himself before.
The rest on outside merit but presume,
Or serve (like other fools) to fill a room;
Such with their shelves as due proportion hold,
Or their fond parents dress'd in red and gold;
Or where the pictures for the page atone,
And Quarles is saved by beauties not his own.

1 Nahum Tate was poet laureate, a cold writer, of no invention; but sometimes translated tolerably when befriended by Mr. Dryden.

2 Mr. John Dennis was the son of a saddler in London, born in 1657. He paid court to Mr. Dryden; and having obtained some correspondence with Mr. Wycherley and Mr. Congreve, he immediately obliged the public with their letters. He made himself known to the government by many admirable schemes and projects, which the ministry, for reasons best known to themselves, constantly kept private.

Here swells the shelf with Ogilby the great;[1]
There, stamp'd with arms, Newcastle[2] shines complete:
Here all his suffering brotherhood retire,
And 'scape the martyrdom of jakes and fire:
A Gothic library! of Greece and Rome
Well purged, and worthy Settle,[3] Banks and Broome.
But, high above, more solid learning shone,
The classics of an age that heard of none;
There Caxton[4] slept, with Wynkyn at his side,
One clasp'd in wood, and one in strong cow-hide;
There, saved by spice, like mummies, many a year,
Dry bodies of divinity appear:
De Lyra[5] there a dreadful front extends,
And here the groaning shelves Philemon[6] bends.
Of these twelve volumes, twelve of amplest size,
Redeem'd from tapers and defrauded pies,
Inspired he seizes: these an altar raise:
An hecatomb of pure unsullied lays
That altar crowns: a folio common-place
Founds the whole pile, of all his works the base:

1 "John Ogilby was one, who, from a late initiation into literature, made such a progress as might well style him the prodigy of his time in sending into the world so many *large volumes!*"

2 "The *Duchess of Newcastle* was one who busied herself in the ravishing delights of poetry; leaving to posterity in print three *ample volumes* of her studious endeavours." Langbaine reckons up *eight* folios of her Grace's; which were usually adorned with gilded covers, and had her coat of arms upon them.

3 The poet has mentioned these three authors in particular, as they are parallel to our hero in his three capacities: 1. Settle was his brother laureate; only indeed upon half-pay, for the city instead of the court; but equally famous for unintelligible flights in his poems on public occasions, such as shows, birth-days, &c. 2. Banks was his rival in *tragedy*, though more successful in one of his tragedies, the *Earl of Essex*, which is yet alive: *Anna Boleyn*, the *Queen of Scots*, and *Cyrus the Great*, are dead and gone. Those he dressed in a sort of *beggar's velvet*, or a happy mixture of the *thick fustian* and *thin prosaic;* exactly imitated in *Perolla and Isidora*, *Cæsar in Egypt*, and the *Heroic Daughter*. 3. Broome was a serving-man of Ben Jonson, who once picked up a *comedy* from his betters, or from some cast scenes of his master, not entirely contemptible.

4 A printer in the time of Ed. IV., Rich. III., and Hen. VII.; Wynkyn de Worde, his successor, in that of Hen. VII and VIII.

5 *Nich. de Lyra*, or Harpsfield, a very voluminous commentator, whose works, in five vast folios, were printed in 1472.

6 *Philemon Holland*, doctor in physic. He translated *so many books*, that a man would think he had done *nothing else*, insomuch that he might be called *translator general of his age.*

Quartos, octavos, shape the lessening pyre;
A twisted birth-day ode completes the spire.
Then he: Great tamer of all human art!
First in my care, and ever at my heart;
Dulness! whose good old cause I yet defend,
With whom my muse began, with whom shall end;
E'er since Sir Fopling's periwig was praise,
To the last honours of the Butt and Bays:
O thou! of business the directing soul!
To this our head like bias to the bowl,
Which, as more ponderous, made its aim more true,
Obliquely waddling to the mark in view:
O! ever gracious to perplex'd mankind,
Still spread a healing mist before the mind;
And lest we err by wit's wild dancing light,
Secure us kindly in our native night.
Or, if to wit a coxcomb make pretence,
Guard the sure barrier between that and sense;
Or quite unravel all the reasoning thread,
And hang some curious cobweb in its stead!
As, forced from wind-guns, lead itself can fly,
And ponderous slugs cut swiftly through the sky;
As clocks to weight their nimble motion owe,
The wheels above urged by the load below:
Me emptiness, and dulness could inspire,
And were my elasticity, and fire.
Some demon stole my pen (forgive the offence)
And once betray'd me into common sense:
Else all my prose and verse were much the same;
This, prose on stilts; that, poetry fallen lame.
Did on the stage my fops appear confined?
My life gave ampler lessons to mankind.
Did the dead letter unsuccessful prove?
The brisk example never fail'd to move.
Yet sure had heaven decreed to save the state,
Heaven had decreed these works a longer date.
Could Troy be saved by any single hand,
This grey-goose weapon must have made her stand.
What can I now? my Fletcher cast aside,
Take up the Bible, once my better guide?
Or tread the path by venturous heroes trod,
This box my thunder, this right hand my god?
Or chair'd at White's amidst the doctors sit,
Teach oaths to gamesters, and to nobles wit?

Or bidst thou rather party to embrace?
(A friend to party thou, and all her race;
'Tis the same rope at different ends they twist;
To Dulness Ridpath is as dear as Mist.[1])
Shall I, like Curtius, desperate in my zeal,
O'er head and ears plunge for the commonweal?
Or rob Rome's ancient geese of all their glories,
And cackling save the monarchy of tories?
Hold—to the minister I more incline;
To serve his cause, O queen! is serving thine.
And see! thy very gazetteers[2] give o'er,
Even Ralph repents, and Henly writes no more.
What then remains? Ourself. Still, still remain
Cibberian forehead, and Cibberian brain.
This brazen brightness, to the squire so dear;
This polish'd hardness, that reflects the peer;
This arch absurd, that wit and fool delights;
This mess, toss'd up of Hockley-hole and White's;
Where dukes and butchers join to wreathe my crown,
At once the bear and fiddle of the town.
O born in sin, and forth in folly brought!
Works damn'd, or to be damn'd! (your father's fault)
Go, purified by flames, ascend the sky,
My better and more christian progeny!
Unstain'd, untouch'd, and yet in maiden sheets;
While all your smutty sisters walk the streets.
Ye shall not beg, like gratis-given Bland,
Sent with a pass, and vagrant through the land;
Not sail, with Ward,[3] to ape-and-monkey climes,
Where vile Mundungus trucks for viler rhymes;

1 George Ridpath, author of a Whig paper, called the Flying Post; Nathaniel Mist, of a famous Tory journal.

2 A band of ministerial writers, who, on the very day their patron quitted his post, laid down their paper, and declared they would never more meddle in politics.

3 "Edward Ward, a very voluminous poet in Hudibrastic verse, but best known by the London Spy, in prose. He has of late years kept a public-house in the City, (but in a genteel way,) and with his wit, humour, and good liquor (ale) afforded his guests a pleasurable entertainment, especially those of the high-church party."—JACOB, Lives of Poets, vol. ii. p 225. Great numbers of his works were yearly sold into the Plantations. Ward, in a book called Apollo's Maggot, declared this account to be a great falsity, protesting that his public-house was not in the *City*, but in *Moorfields*.

Not sulphur-tipp'd, emblaze an ale-house fire!
Not wrap up oranges, to pelt your sire!
O! pass more innocent, in infant state,
To the mild limbo of our father Tate:[1]
Or peaceably forgot, at once be blest
In Shadwell's bosom with eternal rest!
Soon to that mass of nonsense to return,
Where things destroy'd are swept to things unborn.
With that, a tear (portentous sign of grace!)
Stole from the master of the sevenfold face:
And thrice he lifted high the birth-day brand,
And thrice he dropp'd it from his quivering hand;
Then lights the structure, with averted eyes:
The rolling smokes involve the sacrifice,
The opening clouds disclose each work by turns,
Now flames the Cid, and now Perolla burns;
Great Cæsar roars, and hisses in the fires;
King John in silence modestly expires:
No merit now the dear Nonjuror claims,
Moliere's old stubble in a moment flames.
Tears gush'd again, as from pale Priam's eyes
When the last blaze sent Ilion to the skies.
Roused by the light, old Dulness heaved the head;
Then snatch'd a sheet of Thulè[2] from her bed,
Sudden she flies, and whelms it o'er the pyre,
Down sink the flames, and with a hiss expire.
Her ample presence fills up all the place:
A veil of fogs dilates her awful face:
Great in her charms! as when on shrieves and mayors
She looks, and breathes herself into their airs.
She bids him wait her to her sacred dome:
Well pleased he entered, and confess'd his home.
So spirits, ending their terrestial race,
Ascend, and recognise their native place.
This the great mother dearer held than all
The clubs of quidnuncs, or her own Guild-hall:
Here stood her opium, here she nursed her owls,
And here she plann'd the imperial seat of fools.
Here to her chosen all her works she shows;
Prose swell'd to verse, verse loitering into prose:

[1] Tate and Shadwell, two of his predecessors in the Laurel.

[2] An unfinished poem of that name, of which one sheet was printed many years ago, by Amb. Phillips.

How random thoughts now meaning chance to find,
Now leave all memory of sense behind:
How prologues into prefaces decay,
And these to notes are fritter'd quite away:
How index-learning turns no student pale,
Yet holds the eel of science by the tail;
How, with less reading than makes felons 'scape,
Less human genius than God gives an ape,
Small thanks to France, and none to Rome or Greece,
A past, vamp'd future, old, revived, new piece,
'Twixt Plautus, Fletcher, Shakspere, and Corneille,
Can make a Cibber, Tibbald, or Ozell.[1]
  The goddess then, o'er his anointed head,
With mystic words, the sacred opium shed.
And lo! her bird, (a monster of a fowl,
Something betwixt a Heideggre[2] and owl)
Perch'd on his crown. "All hail! and hail again,
My son! the promised land expects thy reign.
Know, Eusden thirsts no more for sack or praise;
He sleeps among the dull of ancient days;
Safe, where no critics damn, no duns molest,
Where wretched Withers, Ward, and Gildon rest,[3]
And high-born Howard,[4] more majestic sire,
With fool of quality completes the choir.

[1] Lewis Tibbald (as pronounced) or Theobald (as written) was bred an attorney, and son to an attorney (says Mr. Jacob) of Sittingbourn, in Kent. He was author of some forgotten plays, translations, and other pieces. He was concerned in a paper called the Censor, and a translation of Ovid.

"Mr. John Ozell (if we may credit Mr. Jacob) did go to school in Leicestershire, where *somebody* left him *something* to live on, when he shall retire from business. He was designed to be sent to Cambridge, in order for priesthood; but he chose rather to be placed in an *office* of *accounts*, in the City, being qualified for the same by his skill in *arithmetic*, and writing the necessary *hands*. He has obliged the world with many translations of French plays."

[2] A strange bird from Switzerland, and not (as some have supposed) the name of an eminent person who was a man of parts, and, as was said of Petronius, *Arbiter Elegantiarum*.

[3] "George Withers was a great pretender to poetical zeal, and abused the greatest personages in power, which brought upon him frequent correction."

Charles Gildon, a writer of criticisms and libels of the last age, bred at St. Omer's with the Jesuits; but renouncing popery, he published Blount's books against the divinity of Christ, the Oracles of Reason, &c.

[4] Hon. Edward Howard, author of the British Princes, and a great number of wonderful pieces, celebrated by the late Earls of Dorset and Rochester, Duke of Buckingham, Mr. Waller, &c.

Thou Cibber! thou, his laurel shalt support,
Folly, my son, has still a friend at court.
Lift up your gates, ye princes, see him come!
Sound, sound ye viols, be the cat-call dumb!
Bring, bring the madding bay, the drunken vine;
The creeping, dirty, courtly ivy join.
And thou! his aide-de-camp, lead on my sons,
Light-arm'd with points, antitheses, and puns.
Let Bawdry, Billingsgate, my daughters dear,
Support his front, and oaths bring up the rear:
And under his, and under Archer's wing,
Gaming and Grub-street skulk behind the king.
  Oh! when shall rise a monarch all our own,
And I, a nursing-mother, rock the throne,
'Twixt prince and people close the curtain draw,
Shade him from light, and cover him from law:
Fatten the courtier, starve the learned band,
And suckle armies, and dry-nurse the land:
'Till senates nod to lullabies divine,
And all be sleep, as at an ode of thine."

  She ceased. Then swells the chapel-royal throat:
"God save king Cibber!" mounts in every note.
Familiar White's, "God save king Colley!" cries;
"God save king Colley!" Drury-lane replies:
To Needham's quick the voice triumphal rode,
But pious Needham[1] dropt the name of God;
Back to the Devil[2] the last echoes roll,
And Coll! each butcher roars at Hockley-hole.
  So when Jove's block descended from on high
(As sings thy great forefather Ogilby)[3]
Loud thunder to its bottom, shook the bog,
And the hoarse nation croak'd, God save king Log!

[1] A matron of great fame, and very religious in her way; whose constant prayer it was, that she might "get enough by her profession to leave it off in time, and make her peace with God." But her fate was not so happy; for being convicted, and set in the pillory, she was (to the lasting shame of all her great friends and votaries) so ill-used by the populace, that it put an end to her days.

[2] The Devil Tavern in Fleet-street, where these odes are usually rehearsed before they are performed at Court.

[3] See Ogilby's Æsop's Fables, where, in the story of the Frogs and their King, this excellent hemistitch is to be found.

BOOK THE SECOND.

ARGUMENT.

The king being proclaimed, the solemnity is graced with public games and sports of various kinds; not instituted by the hero, as by Æneas in Virgil, but for greater honour by the Goddess in person (in like manner as the games Pythia, Isthmia, &c., were anciently said to be ordained by the gods, and as Thetis herself appearing, according to Homer, Odyss. 24, proposed the prizes in honour of her son Achilles.) Hither flock the poets and critics, attended, as is but just, with their patrons and booksellers. The Goddess is first pleased, for her disport, to propose games to the *booksellers*, and setteth up the phantom of a poet, which they contend to overtake. The race is described with their divers accidents. Next, the game for a *poetess*. Then follow the exercises for the *poets*, of *tickling*, *vociferating*, *diving:* the first holds forth the arts and practices of *dedicators;* the second of *disputants* and *fustian poets;* the third of *profound, dark*, and *dirty party-writers*. Lastly, for the *critics*, the Goddess proposes (with great propriety) an exercise, not of their parts, but their patience, in hearing the works of two voluminous authors, one in *verse* and the other in *prose*, deliberately read, without sleeping; the various effects of which with the several degrees and manners of their operation, are here set forth, till the whole number, not of critics only, but of spectators, actors, and all present, fall fast asleep, which naturally and necessarily ends the games.

High on a gorgeous seat, that far out-shone
Henley's gilt tub,[1] or Fleckno's Irish throne,
Or that where on her Curls[2] the public pours,
All-bounteous, fragrant grains and golden showers,
Great Cibber sate; the proud Parnassian sneer,
The conscious simper and the jealous leer
Mix on his look: all eyes direct their rays
On him, and crowds turn coxcombs as they gaze.

[1] The pulpit of a dissenter is usually called a tub; but that of Mr. Orator Henley was covered with velvet, and adorned with gold. He had also a fair altar, and over it this extraordinary inscription, "*The Primitive Eucharist.*"

Richard Fleckno was an Irish priest, but had laid aside (as himself expressed it) the mechanic part of priesthood. He printed some plays, poems, letters, and travels.

[2] Edmund Curl stood in the pillory at Charing-cross, in March 1727-8.

His peers shine round him with reflected grace,
New edge their dulness, and new bronze their face.
So from the sun's broad beam, in shallow urns
Heaven's twinkling sparks draw light and point their horns.
Not with more glee, by hands pontific crown'd,
With scarlet hats wide-waving circled round,
Rome in her capitol saw Querno sit,[1]
Throned on seven hills, the antichrist of wit.
And now the Queen, to glad her sons, proclaims
By herald hawkers, high heroic games,
They summon all her race: an endless band
Pours forth, and leaves unpeopled half the land.
A motley mixture! in long wigs, in bags,
In silks, in crapes, in garters, and in rags;
From drawing-rooms, from colleges, from garrets,
On horse, on foot, in hacks, and gilded chariots:
All who true Dunces in her cause appear'd,
And all who knew those Dunces to reward.
Amid that area wide they took their stand,
Where the tall May-pole once o'er-looked the Strand;
But now (so Anne and Piety ordain)
A church collects the saints of Drury-lane.
With authors, stationers obeyed the call,
(The field of glory is a field for all).
Glory and gain, the industrious tribe provoke;
And gentle Dulness ever loves a joke.
A poet's form she placed before their eyes,
And bade the nimblest racer seize the prize;
No meagre, muse-rid mope, adust and thin,
In a dun night-gown of his own loose skin;
But such a bulk as no twelve bards could raise,
Twelve starveling bards of these degenérate days,
All as a partridge plump, full-fed, and fair,
She form'd this image of well-bodied air;
With pert flat eyes she window'd well its head;
A brain of feathers, and a heart of lead;
And empty words she gave, and sounding strain,
But senseless, lifeless! idol void and vain!
Never was dash'd out, at one lucky hit,
A fool, so just a copy of a wit:

[1] Camillo Querno was of Apulia, who hearing the great encouragement which Leo X. gave to poets, travelled to Rome with a harp in his hand, and sung to it twenty thousand verses of a poem called Alexias.

So like, that critics said, and courtiers swore,
A wit it was, and call'd the phantom Moore.[1]
All gaze with ardour: some a poet's name,
Others a sword-knot and laced suit inflame.
But lofty Lintot[2] in the circle rose:
"This prize is mine, who tempt it are my foes;
With me began this genius, and shall end."
He spoke: and who with Lintot shall contend?
Fear held them mute. Alone, untaught to fear,
Stood dauntless Curl;[3] "Behold that rival here!
The race by vigour, not by vaunts, is won;
So take the hindmost, Hell,"—he said and run.
Swift as a bard the bailiff leaves behind,
He left huge Lintot, and outstripp'd the wind.
As when a dab-chick waddles through the copse
On feet and wings, and flies, and wades, and hops;
So labouring on, with shoulders, hands, and head,
Wide as a windmill all his figure spread,
With arms expanded Bernard rows his state,
And left-legg'd Jacob seems to emulate.
Full in the middle way there stood a lake,
Which Curl's Corinna[4] chanced that morn to make;

[1] Curl, in his Key to the Dunciad, affirmed this to be James Moore Smith, Esq. His only work was a comedy called the Rival Modes; the town condemned it in the action.

[2] We enter here upon the episode of the booksellers; persons whose names being more known and famous in the learned world than those of the authors in this poem, do therefore need less explanation. The action of Mr. Lintot here imitates that of Dares in Virgil, rising just in this manner to lay hold on a *bull*. This eminent bookseller printed the *Rival Modes* before-mentioned.

[3] We come now to a character of much respect, that of Mr. Edmund Curl. As a plain repetition of great actions is the best praise of them, we shall only say of this eminent man, that he carried the trade many lengths beyond what it ever before had arrived at, and that he was the envy and admiration of all his profession. He possessed himself of a command over all authors whatever; he caused them to write what he pleased; they could not call their very *names* their own. He was not only famous among these; he was taken notice of by the *state*, the *church*, and the *law*, and received particular marks of distinction from each.

[4] This name, it seems, was taken by one Mrs. T——, who procured some private letters of Mr. Pope's, while almost a boy, to Mr. Cromwell, and sold them without the consent of either of those gentlemen to Curl, who printed them in 12mo, 1727. He discovered her to be the publisher, in his Key.

(Such was her wont, at early dawn to drop
Her evening cates before his neighbour's shop)
Here fortuned Curl to slide: loud shout the band,
And Bernard! Bernard! rings thro' all the Strand.
Obscene with filth the miscreant lies bewray'd,
Fallen in the plash his wickedness had laid:
Then first (if poets aught of truth declare)
The caitiff vaticide conceived a prayer.
  Hear Jove! whose name my bards and I adore,
As much at least as any god's, or more:
And him and his, if more devotion warms,
Down with the Bible, up with the pope's arms.[1]
  A place there is, betwixt earth, air, and seas,
Where, from ambrosia, Jove retires for ease.
There in his seat two spacious vents appear,
On this he sits, to that he leans his ear,
And hears the various vows of fond mankind;
Some beg an eastern, some a western wind:
All vain petitions, mounting to the sky,
With reams abundant this abode supply;
Amused he reads, and then returns the bills
Sign'd with that ichor which from gods distils.
  In office here fair Cloacina[2] stands,
And ministers to Jove with purest hands.
Forth from the heap she pick'd her votary's prayer
And placed it next him, a distinction rare!
Oft had the goddess heard her servant's call,
From her black grottos near the Temple-wall,
Listening delighted to the jest unclean
Of link-boys vile, and watermen obscene;
Where as he fished her nether realms for wit,
She oft had favour'd him, and favours yet.
Renew'd by ordure's sympathetic force,
As oil'd with magic juices for the course,
Vigorous he rises: from the effluvia strong,
Imbibes new life, and scours and stinks along:
Re-passes Lintot, vindicates the race,
Nor heeds the brown dishonours of his face.
  And now the victor stretch'd his eager hand,
Where the tall nothing stood, or seem'd to stand;
A shapeless shade, it melted from his sight,
Like forms in clouds, or visions of the night.

1 The Bible was Curl's sign; the Cross Keys, Lintot's.

2 The Roman goddess of the common sewers. Her black grottos near the Temple still pour forth their odoriferous streams.

To seize his papers, Curl, was next thy care;
His papers light, fly diverse, tost in air;
Songs, sonnets, epigrams the winds uplift,
And whisk 'em back to Evans, Young, and Swift.
The embroider'd suit at least he deem'd his prey;
That suit an unpaid tailor snatch'd away.
No rag, no scrap, of all the beau, or wit,
That once so flutter'd, and that once so writ.
Heaven rings with laughter: of the laughter vain,
Dulness, good queen, repeats the jest again.
Three wicked imps, of her own Grub-street choir,
She deck'd like Congreve, Addison, and Prior;[1]
Mears, Warner, Wilkins,[2] run: delusive thought!
Breval, Bond, Bezaleel, the varlets caught.
Curl stretches after Gay, but Gay is gone,
He grasps an empty Joseph[3] for a John:
So Proteus, hunted in a nobler shape,
Became, when seized, a puppy, or an ape.
To him the goddess: Son! thy grief lay down,
And turn this whole illusion on the town:[4]
As the sage dame, experienced in her trade,
By names of toasts retails each batter'd jade;
(Whence hapless Monsieur much complains at Paris
Of wrongs from duchesses and lady Marys;)
Be thine, my stationer! this magic gift;
Cook shall be Prior,[5] and Concanen, Swift:
So shall each hostile name become our own,
And we too boast our Garth and Addison.

[1] These authors being such whose names will reach posterity, we shall not give any account of them, but proceed to those of whom it is necessary. Bezaleel Morris was author of some satires on the translators of Homer, with many other things printed in newspapers.—"Bond wrote a satire against Pope. Captain Breval was author of The Confederates, an ingenious dramatic performance to expose Mr. P., Mr. Gay, Dr. Arbuthnot and some ladies of quality," says Curl.

[2] Booksellers, and printers of much anonymous stuff.

[3] *Joseph Gay*, a fictitious name put by Curl before several pamphlets, which made them pass with many for Mr. Gay's.

[4] It was a common practice of this bookseller to publish vile pieces of obscure hands under the names of eminent authors.

[5] The man here specified wrote a thing called The Battle of Poets, in which Phillips and Welsted were the heroes, and Swift and Pope utterly routed. He also published some malevolent things in the British, London, and Daily Journals; and at the same time wrote letters to Mr. Pope, protesting his innocence. His chief work was a translation of Hesiod, to which Theobald put notes and half-notes, which he carefully owned.

With that she gave him (piteous of his case,
Yet smiling at his rueful length of face)
A shaggy tapestry, worthy to be spread
On Codrus' old, or Dunton's[1] modern bed;
Instructive work! whose wry-mouth'd portraiture
Display'd the fates her confessors endure.
Earless on high, stood unabash'd De Foe,
And Tutchin flagrant from the scourge below.[2]
There Ridpath, Roper,[3] cudgell'd might ye view,
The very worsted still look'd black and blue.
Himself among the storied chiefs he spies,
As from the blanket high in air he flies,
And oh! (he cried) what street, what lane but knows,
Our purgings, pumpings, blanketings, and blows?[4]
In every loom our labours shall be seen,
And the fresh vomit run for ever green!
See in the circle next, Eliza placed,[5]
Two babes of love close clinging to her waist;
Fair as before her works she stands confess'd,
In flowers and pearls by bounteous Kirkall dress'd.
The Goddess then: "Who best can send on high
The salient spout, far streaming to the sky;
His be yon Juno of majestic size,
With cow-like udders, and with ox-like eyes.
This china jordan let the chief o'ercome
Replenish, not ingloriously, at home."

[1] John Dunton was a broken bookseller and abusive scribbler; he wrote Neck or Nothing, a violent satire on some ministers of state; a libel on the Duke of Devonshire and the Bishop of Peterborough. He also left his autobiography entitled The Life and Errors of John Dunton.

[2] John Tutchin, author of some vile verses, and of a weekly paper called the Observator. He was sentenced to be whipped through several towns in the west of England, upon which he petitioned king James II. to be hanged. When that prince died in exile, he wrote an invective against his memory, occasioned by some humane elegies on his death. He lived to the time of Queen Anne.

[3] Authors of the Flying-post and Post-boy, two scandalous papers on different sides, for which they equally and alternately deserved to be cudgeled, and were so.

[4] The history of Curl's being tossed in a blanket, and whipped by the scholars of Westminster, is well known.

[5] *Eliza Haywood;* this woman was authoress of two scandalous books called the Court of Carimania, and the New Utopia. Some of this lady's works were printed in four volumes in 12mo.; her picture, engraved by Kirkall, was thus dressed up before them.

Osborne[1] and Curl accept the glorious strife,
(Though this his son dissuades, and that his wife.)
One on his manly confidence relies,
One on his vigour and superior size.
First Osborne lean'd against his letter'd post;
It rose, and labour'd to a curve at most.
So Jove's bright bow displays its watery round,
(Sure sign, that no spectator shall be drown'd)
A second effort brought but new disgrace,
The wild meander wash'd the artist's face:
Thus the small jet, which hasty hands unlock,
Spirts in the gardener's eyes who turns the cock.
Not so from shameless Curl; impetuous spread
The stream, and smoking flourish'd o'er his head.
So (famed like thee for turbulence and horns)
Eridanus his humble fountain scorns:
Through half the heavens he pours the exalted urn;
His rapid waters in their passage burn.
Swift as it mounts, all follow with their eyes:
Still happy Impudence obtains the prize.
Thou triumph'st, victor of the high-wrought day,
And the pleased dame, soft smiling, lead'st away.
Osborne, through perfect modesty o'ercome,
Crown'd with the jordan, walks contented home.
But now for authors nobler palms remain;
Room for my Lord! three jockeys in his train;
Six huntsmen with a shout precede his chair:
He grins, and looks broad nonsense with a stare.
His Honour's meaning Dulness thus express'd—
"He wins this patron, who can tickle best."
He chinks his purse, and takes his seat of state:
With ready quills the dedicators wait;
Now at his head the dexterous task commence,
And, instant, fancy feels the imputed sense:
Now gentle touches wanton o'er his face,
He struts Adonis, and affects grimace:
Rolli[2] the feather to his ear conveys,
Then his nice taste directs our Operas:

[1] A bookseller in Gray's Inn, very well qualified by his impudence to act this part; and therefore placed here instead of a less deserving predecessor.

[2] Paolo Antonio Rolli, an Italian poet, and writer of many operas in that language, which, partly by the help of his genius, prevailed in England near twenty years.

Bentley[1] his mouth with classic flattery opes,
And the puff'd orator bursts out in tropes.
But Welsted[2] most the poet's healing balm
Strives to extract from his soft, giving palm;
Unlucky Welsted! thy unfeeling master,
The more thou ticklest, gripes his fist the faster.
While thus each hand promotes the pleasing pain,
And quick sensations skip from vein to vein;
A youth unknown to Phœbus, in despair,
Puts his last refuge all in heaven and prayer.
What force have pious vows! The Queen of Love
His sister sends, her votaress, from above.
As taught by Venus, Paris learnt the art
To touch Achilles' only tender part;
Secure, through her, the noble prize to carry,
He marches off, his grace's secretary.
Now turn to different sports (the goddess cries)
And learn, my sons, the wondrous power of noise.
To move, to raise, to ravish every heart,
With Shakspere's nature, or with Jonson's art,
Let others aim: 'Tis yours to shake the soul
With thunder rumbling from the mustard bowl;
With horns and trumpets now to madness swell,
Now sink in sorrows with a tolling bell!
Such happy arts attention can command,
When fancy flags, and sense is at a stand.
Improve we these. Three cat-calls be the bribe
Of him, whose chattering shames the monkey tribe;
And his this drum, whose hoarse heroic base
Drowns the loud clarion of the braying ass.
Now thousand tongues are heard in one loud din;
The monkey-mimics rush discordant in;
'Twas chattering, grinning, mouthing, jabbering all,
And noise and Norton,[3] brangling and Breval,
Dennis and dissonance, and captious art,
And snip-snap short, and interruption smart,

[1] Not spoken of the famous Dr. Richard Bentley, but of one Thomas Bentley, a small critic, who aped his uncle in a *little Horace*.

[2] Leonard Welsted, author of The Triumvirate, or a letter in verse from Palæmon to Celia at Bath, which was meant for a satire on Mr. Pope and some of his friends, about the year 1718.

[3] See ver. 417—J. Durant Breval, author of a very extraordinary book of travels, and some poems.

And demonstration thin, and theses thick,
And major, minor, and conclusion quick.
Hold (cried the queen) a cat-call each shall win;
Equal your merits! equal is your din!
But that this well-disputed game may end,
Sound forth my brayers, and the welkin rend.
As when the long-ear'd milky mothers wait
At some sick miser's triple-bolted gate,
For their defrauded absent foals they make
A moan so loud, that all the guild awake;
Sore sighs sir Gilbert, starting at the bray,
From dreams of millions, and three groats to pay.
So swells each windpipe; ass intones to ass,
Harmonic twang! of leather, horn, and brass;
Such as from labouring lungs the enthusiast blows,
High sound, attemper'd to the vocal nose;
Or such as bellow from the deep divine;
There Webster! peal'd thy voice, and Whitfield![1] thine.
But far o'er all, sonorous Blackmore's strain;
Walls, steeples, skies, bray back to him again.
In Tottenham fields, the brethren, with amaze,
Prick all their ears up, and forget to graze;[2]
Long Chancery-lane retentive rolls the sound,[3]
And courts to courts return it round and round;
Thames wafts it thence to Rufus' roaring hall,
And Hungerford re-echoes bawl for bawl.
All hail him victor in both gifts of song,
Who sings so loudly, and who sings so long.[4]
This labour past, by Bridewell all descend,
(As morning prayer, and flagellation end)
To where Fleet-ditch with disemboguing streams
Rolls the large tribute of dead dogs to Thames,
The king of dykes! than whom no sluice of mud
With deeper sable blots the silver flood.

[1] Webster was the writer of a newspaper called the Weekly Miscellany; Whitfield, the celebrated Rev. George.

[2] The progress of the sound from place to place, and the scenery here of the bordering regions, Tottenham-fields, Chancery-lane, the Thames, Westminster-hall, and Hungerford-stairs, are imitated from Virgil.

[3] The place where the offices of Chancery are kept. The long detention of clients in that court, and the difficulty of getting out, is humorously allegorised in these lines.

[4] A just character of Sir Richard Blackmore, knight.

"Here strip, my children! here at once leap in,
Here prove who best can dash through thick and thin,
And who the most in love of dirt excel,
Or dark dexterity of groping well.[1]
Who flings most filth, and wide pollutes around
The stream, be his the Weekly Journals bound,[2]
A pig of lead to him who dives the best;
A peck of coals a-piece shall glad the rest."
In naked majesty Oldmixon stands,[3]
And, Milo-like, surveys his arms and hands;
Then sighing thus, "and am I now three-score?
Ah why, ye gods! should two and two make four?"
He said, and climb'd a stranded lighter's height,
Shot to the black abyss, and plunged down-right.
The senior's judgment all the crowd admire,
Who but to sink the deeper, rose the higher.
  Next Smedley dived; slow circles dimpled o'er[4]
The quaking mud, that closed, and oped no more.
All look, all sigh, and call on Smedley lost;
Smedley! in vain resounds through all the coast.
  Then * essay'd;[5] scarce vanish'd out of sight,
He buoys up instant, and returns to light:
He bears no token of the sabler streams,
And mounts far off among the swans of Thames.
  True to the bottom, see Concanen creep,[6]
A cold, long-winded, native of the deep:

1 The three chief qualifications of party writers; to stick at nothing, to delight in flinging dirt, and to slander in the dark by guess.

2 Papers of news and scandal intermixed, on different sides and parties, and frequently shifting from one side to the other, called the London Journal, British Journal, Daily Journal, &c., the concealed writers of which for some time were Oldmixon, Roome, Arnall, Concanen, and others; persons never seen by our author.

3 Mr. John Oldmixon, next to Mr. Dennis, the most ancient critic of our nation; an unjust censurer of Mr. Addison in his prose Essay on Criticism, whom also in his imitation of Bouhours, he misrepresents in plain matter of fact.

4 The person here mentioned, an Irishman, was author and publisher of many scurrilous pieces, a weekly Whitehall Journal, in the year 1722, in the name of Sir James Baker.

5 A gentleman of genius and spirit, who was secretly dipped in some papers of this kind, on whom our poet bestows a panegyric instead of a satire, as deserving to be better employed than in party-quarrels and personal invectives; by some supposed to be Aaron Hill.

6 Matthew Concanen, an Irishman, bred to the law. He was author of several dull and dead scurrilities in the British and London Journals, and in a paper called the Speculatist

If perseverance gain the diver's prize,
Not everlasting Blackmore this denies:
No noise, no stir, no motion canst thou make;
The unconscious stream sleeps o'er thee like a lake.
Next plunged a feeble, but a desperate pack,
With each a sickly brother at his back:
Sons of a day! just buoyant on the flood,[1]
Then number'd with the puppies in the mud.
Ask ye their names? I could as soon disclose
The names of these blind puppies as of those.
Fast by, like Niobe (her children gone)
Sits Mother Osborne, stupified to stone![2]
And monumental brass this record bears,
"These are,—ah no! these were, the Gazetteers!"
Not so bold Arnall; with a weight of skull,
Furious he dives, precipitately dull.
Whirlpools and storms his circling arm invest,[3]
With all the might of gravitation blest.
No crab more active in the dirty dance,
Downward to climb, and backward to advance.
He brings up half the bottom on his head,
And loudly claims the journals and the lead.
The plunging prelate, and his ponderous grace,
With holy envy gave one layman place.
When lo! a burst of thunder shook the flood,
Slow rose a form, in majesty of mud;
Shaking the horrors of his sable brows,
And each ferocious feature grim with ooze.
Greater he looks, and more than mortal stares:
Then thus the wonders of the deep declares.
First he relates, how sinking to the chin,
Smit with his mien, the mud-nymphs suck'd him in:
How young Lutetia, softer than the down,
Nigrina black, and Merdamante brown,
Vied for his love in jetty bowers below,
As Hylas fair[4] was ravish'd long ago.

[1] These were daily papers, a number of which, to lessen the expense, were printed one on the back of another.

[2] A name assumed by the eldest and gravest of these writers, who at last being ashamed of his pupils, gave his paper over, and in his age remained silent.

[3] William Arnall, bred an attorney, was a perfect genius in this sort of work. He began under twenty, with furious party-papers; then succeeded Concanen in the British Journal.

[4] Who was ravished by the water-nymphs and drawn into the river. The story is told at large by Valerius Flaccus.

Then sung, how shown him by the nut-brown maids
A branch of Styx here rises from the shades,
That tinctured as it runs with Lethe's streams,
And wafting vapours from the land of dreams,
(As under seas Alphæus' secret sluice
Bears Pisa's offerings to his Arethuse)
Pours into Thames: and hence the mingled wave
Intoxicates the pert, and lulls the grave:
Here brisker vapours o'er the Temple creep,
There, all from Paul's to Aldgate drink and sleep.
Thence to the banks where reverend bards repose,
They led him soft; each reverend bard arose;
And Milbourn[1] chief, deputed by the rest,
Gave him the cassock, surcingle, and vest.
"Receive (he said) these robes which once were mine,
Dulness is sacred in a sound divine."
He ceased, and spread the robe; the crowd confess
The reverend flamen in his lengthen'd dress.
Around him wide a sable army stand,
A low-born, cell-bred, selfish, servile band,
Prompt or to guard or stab, to saint or damn,
Heaven's Swiss, who fight for any god, or man.
Through Lud's famed gates,[2] along the well-known Fleet
Rolls the black troop, and overshades the street,
'Till showers of sermons, characters, essays,
In circling fleeces whiten all the ways:
So clouds, replenish'd from some bog below,
Mount in dark volumes, and descend in snow.
Here stopp'd the goddess; and in pomp proclaims
A gentle exercise to close the games.
"Ye critics! in whose heads, as equal scales,
I weigh what author's heaviness prevails;
Which most conduce to soothe the soul in slumbers,
My Henley's periods, or my Blackmore's numbers;
Attend the trial we propose to make:
If there be man, who o'er such works can wake,

1 Luke Milbourn, a clergyman, the fairest of critics; who, when he wrote against Mr. Dryden's Virgil, did him justice in printing at the same time his own intolerable translations.

2 "King Lud repairing the City, called it after his own name, Lud's Town; the strong gate which he built in the west part he likewise, for his own honour, named Ludgate. In the year 1260, this gate was beautified with images of Lud and other kings. Those images, in the reign of Edward VI., had their heads smitten off, and were otherwise defaced by unadvised folks."—*Stow's Survey of London.*

Sleep's all-subduing charms who dares defy,
And boasts Ulysses' ear with Argus' eye;
To him we grant our amplest powers to sit
Judge of all present, past, and future wit;
To cavil, censure, dictate, right or wrong,
Full and eternal privilege of tongue."
  Three college sophs, and three pert templars came,
The same their talents, and their tastes the same;
Each prompt to query, answer, and debate,
And smit with love of poesy and prate.
The ponderous books two gentle readers bring;
The heroes sit, the vulgar form a ring.
The clamorous crowd is hush'd with mugs of mum,
'Till all tuned equal, send a general hum.
Then mount the clerks, and in one lazy tone
Through the long, heavy, painful page drawl on;
Soft creeping, words on words, the sense compose,
At every line they stretch, they yawn, they doze.
As to soft gales top-heavy pines bow low:
Their heads, and lift them as they cease to blow:
Thus oft they rear, and oft the head decline,
As breath, or pause, by fits, the airs divine.
And now to this side, now to that they nod,
As verse, or prose, infuse the drowsy god.
Thrice Budgel aim'd to speak, but thrice suppress'd[1]
By potent Arthur, knock'd his chin and breast
Toland and Tindal, prompt at priests to jeer,[2]
Yet silent bow'd to "Christ's no kingdom here."[3]
Who sate the nearest, by the words o'ercome,
Slept first; the distant nodded to the hum.
Then down are roll'd the books; stretch'd o'er 'em lies
Each gentle clerk, and muttering seals his eyes.
As what a Dutchman plumps into the lakes,
One circle first, and then a second makes;
What Dulness dropp'd among her sons impress'd
Like motion from one circle to the rest;
So from the midmost the nutation spreads
Round and more round, o'er all the "sea of heads."

[1] Famous for his speeches on many occasions about the South Sea scheme.

[2] Two persons, not so happy as to be obscure, who wrote against the religion of their country.

[3] This is said by Curl, Key to Dunc., to allude to a sermon of a reverend bishop.

At last Centlivre[1] felt her voice to fail,
Motteux himself unfinish'd left his tale,
Boyer the state, and Law the stage gave o'er,[2]
Morgan[3] and Mandeville[4] could prate no more;
Norton,[5] from Daniel and Ostrœa sprung,
Bless'd with his father's front, and mother's tongue,
Hung silent down his never-blushing head;
And all was hush'd, as Folly's self lay dead.
  Thus the soft gifts of Sleep conclude the day,
And stretch'd on bulks, as usual, poets lay.
Why should I sing what bards the nightly muse
Did slumbering visit, and convey to stews;
Who prouder march'd, with magistrates in state,
To some famed round-house' ever-open gate!
How Henley lay inspired beside a sink,
And to mere mortals seem'd a priest in drink:
While others, timely, to the neighbouring Fleet[6]
(Haunt of the muses) made their safe retreat.

1 Mrs. Susanna Centlivre, authoress of many plays.

2 A. Boyer, a voluminous compiler of annals, political collections, &c.—William Law, A.M., wrote with great zeal against the stage. Mr. Law was the author of several works, in which he recommends the exercise of a piety almost approaching to the character of an ascetic. The best known is "A Serious Call to a Devout and Holy Life," which has had great influence on many minds. Dr. Johnson said it was this work that first led to his thinking of religion in earnest.

3 A writer against religion, distinguished no otherwise from the rabble of his tribe than by the pompousness of his title; for having stolen his morality from Tindal, and his philosophy from Spinoza, he calls himself, by the courtesy of England, a *moral philosopher.*

4 This writer, who prided himself as much in the reputation of an *immoral philosopher*, was author of a famous book called the Fable of the Bees, which may seem written to prove, that moral virtue is the invention of knaves, and christian virtue the imposition of fools; and that vice is necessary, and alone sufficient to render society flourishing and happy.

5 Norton de Foe, son of the famous Daniel; he was one of the authors of the Flying Post, in which well-bred work Mr. P. had sometime the honour to be abused with his betters; and of many hired scurrilities and daily papers, to which he never set his name.

6 A prison for insolvent debtors on the bank of the ditch. The ditch has been filled up and the prison pulled down.

BOOK THE THIRD.

ARGUMENT.

After the other persons are disposed in their proper places of rest, the goddess transports the king to her temple, and there lays him to slumber with his head on her lap; a position of marvellous virtue, which causes all the visions of wild enthusiasts, projectors, politicians, inamoratos, castle-builders, chemists, and poets. He is immediately carried on the wings of fancy, and led by a mad poetical sibyl to the *Elysian shade;* where, on the banks of *Lethe,* the souls of the dull are dipped by *Bævius,* before their entrance into this world. There he is met by the ghost of *Settle,* and by him made acquainted with the wonders of the place, and with those which he himself is destined to perform. He takes him to a *Mount of Vision,* from whence he shows him the past triumphs of the Empire of Dulness, then the present, and lastly the future: how small a part of the world was ever conquered by science, how soon those conquests were stopped, and these very nations again reduced to her dominion. Then distinguishing the island of *Great Britain,* shows by what aids, by what persons, and by what degrees it shall be brought to her empire. Some of the persons he causes to pass in review before his eyes, describing each by his proper figure, character, and qualifications. On a sudden the scene shifts, and a vast number of miracles and prodigies appear, utterly surprising and unknown to the king himself, till they are explained to be the wonders of his own reign now commencing. On this subject *Settle* breaks into a congratulation, yet not unmixed with concern, that his own times were but the types of these. He prophesies how first the nation shall be over-run with *farces, operas,* and *shows;* how the throne of Dulness shall be advanced over the *theatres,* and set up even at *court:* then how her sons shall preside in the seats of *arts* and *sciences:* giving a glimpse, or Pisgah-sight, of the future fulness of her glory, the accomplishment whereof is the subject of the fourth and last book.

But in her temple's last recess inclosed,
On Dulness' lap the anointed head reposed.
Him close she curtains round with vapours blue,
And soft besprinkles with Cimmerian dew.
Then raptures high the seat of sense o'erflow,
Which only heads refined from reason know.
Hence, from the straw where Bedlam's prophet nods,
He hears loud oracles, and talks with gods:
Hence the fool's paradise, the statesman's scheme,
The air-built castle, and the golden dream,
The maid's romantic wish, the chemist's flame,
And poet's vision of eternal fame.

And now, on fancy's easy wing convey'd,
The king descending, views the Elysian shade.
A slip-shod sibyl led his steps along,
In lofty madness meditating song;
Her tresses staring from poetic dreams,
And never wash'd, but in Castalia's streams.
Taylor,[1] their better Charon, lends an oar,
(Once swan of Thames, though now he sings no more)
Benlowes,[2] propitious still to blockheads bows;
And Shadwell nods the poppy on his brows.[3]
Here, in a dusky vale where Lethe rolls,
Old Bævius sits to dip poetic souls,[4]
And blunt the sense, and fit it for a skull
Of solid proof, impenetrably dull:
Instant, when dipp'd, away they wing their flight,
Where Brown and Mears[5] unbar the gates of light,
Demand new bodies, and in calf's array,
Rush to the world impatient for the day.
Millions and millions on these banks he views,
Thick as the stars of night, or morning dews,
As thick as bees o'er vernal blossoms fly,
As thick as eggs at Ward in pillory.[6]

1 John Taylor, the water-poet, an honest man who owns he learned not so much as the accidence: a rare example of modesty in a poet! He wrote fourscore books in the reign of James I. and Charles I. and afterwards (like Edward Ward) kept an alehouse in Long Acre. He died in 1654.

2 A country gentleman, famous for his own bad poetry, and for patronising bad poets, as may be seen from many dedications of Quarles and others to him. Some of these anagramed his name, *Benlowes*, into *Benevolus*: to verify which, he spent his whole estate upon them.

3 Shadwell took opium for many years, and died of too large a dose, in the year 1692.

4 Bævius was an ancient poet, celebrated by Virgil for the like cause as Bays by our author, though not in so christian-like a manner.

Ver. 24 alludes to the story of Thetis dipping Achilles to render him impenetrable.

5 Booksellers, printers for anybody.—The allegory of the souls of the dull coming forth in the form of books, dressed in calf's skin, and being let abroad in vast numbers by booksellers, is sufficiently intelligible.

6 John Ward, of Hackney, Esq., Member of Parliament, being convicted of forgery, was first expelled the House, and then sentenced to the pillory, on the 17th of February, 1727. Mr. Curl (having likewise stood there) looks upon the mention of such a gentleman in a satire as a *great act of barbarity*. But it is evident this verse could not be meant of him; it being notorious, that no *eggs* were thrown at that gentleman. Perhaps, therefore, it might be intended of Mr. Edward Ward the poet, when he stood there.

Wondering he gazed: when lo! a sage appears,
By his broad shoulders known, and length of ears,
Known by the band and suit which Settle[1] wore
(His only suit) for twice three years before:
All as the vest, appear'd the wearer's frame,
Old in new state, another, yet the same.
Bland and familiar as in life, begun
Thus the great father to the greater son.
O born to see what none can see awake!
Behold the wonders of the oblivious lake.
Thou, yet unborn, hast touch'd this sacred shore;
The hand of Bævius drench'd thee o'er and o'er.
But blind to former as to future fate,
What mortal knows his pre-existent state?
Who knows how long thy transmigrating soul
Might from Bœotian to Bœotian roll?[2]
How many Dutchmen she vouchsafed to thrid?
How many stages through old monks she rid?
And all who since, in mild benighted days,
Mix'd the owl's ivy with the poet's bays.
As man's mæanders to the vital spring
Roll all their tides, then back their circles bring;
Or whirligigs twirl'd round by skilful swain,
Suck the thread in, then yield it out again:
All nonsense thus, of old or modern date,
Shall in thee centre, from thee circulate.
For this our queen unfolds to vision true
Thy mental eye, for thou hast much to view:
Old scenes of glory, times long cast behind,
Shall first recall'd, rush forward to thy mind:
Then stretch thy sight o'er all her rising reign,
And let the past and future fire thy brain.
Ascend this hill, whose cloudy point commands
Her boundless empire over seas and lands.
See, round the Poles where keener spangles shine,
Where spices smoke beneath the burning line,

[1] Elkanah Settle was once a writer in vogue, as well as Cibber, both for dramatic poetry and politics. Mr. Dennis tells us that "he was a formidable rival to Mr. Dryden, and that in the University of Cambridge there were those who gave him the *preference*." He was author or publisher of many noted pamphlets in the time of king Charles II.: for which see the library at the Guildhall of the City of London.

[2] Bœotia lay under the ridicule of the Wits formerly, as Ireland does now: though it produced one of the greatest poets and one of the greatest generals of Greece.

(Earth's wide extremes) her sable flag display'd,
And all the nations cover'd in her shade!
  Far eastward cast thine eye, from whence the sun
And orient science their bright course begun:
One god-like monarch all that pride confounds,[1]
He, whose long wall the wandering Tartar bounds;
Heavens! what a pile! whole ages perish there,
And one bright blaze turns learning into air.
  Thence to the south extend thy gladden'd eyes;
There rival flames with equal glory rise,
From shelves to shelves see greedy Vulcan roll,
And lick up all their physic of the soul.[2]
  How little, mark! that portion of the ball,
Where, faint at best, the beams of science fall:
Soon as they dawn, from hyperborean skies
Embodied dark, what clouds of Vandals rise!
Lo! where Mæotis sleeps, and hardly flows
The freezing Tanais through a waste of snows,
The North by myriads pours her mighty sons,
Great nurse of Goths, of Alans, and of Huns!
See Alaric's stern port! the martial frame
Of Genseric! and Attila's dread name!
See the bold Ostrogoths on Latium fall;
See the fierce Visigoths on Spain and Gaul!
See where the morning gilds the palmy shore,
(The soil that arts and infant letters bore)[3]
His conquering tribes the Arabian prophet draws,
And saving ignorance enthrones by laws.
See Christians, Jews, one heavy sabbath keep,
And all the western world believe and sleep.
  Lo! Rome herself, proud mistress now no more
Of arts, but thundering against heathen lore;[4]

1 Chi Ho-am-ti, emperor of China, the same who built the great wall between China and Tartary, destroyed all the books and learned men of that empire.

2 The caliph, Omar I., having conquered Egypt, caused his general to burn the Ptolemæan library, on the gates of which was this inscription: ΨΥΧΗΣ ΙΑΤΡΕΙΟΝ, the physic of the soul.

3 Phœnicia, Syria, &c., where letters are said to have been invented. In these countries Mahomet began his conquests.

4 A strong instance of this pious rage is placed to Pope Gregory's account. The same Pope is accused by Vossius, and others, of having caused the noble monuments of the old Roman magnificence to be destroyed, lest those who came to Rome should give more attention to triumphal arches, &c., than to holy things.

Her grey-hair'd synods damning books unread,
And Bacon trembling for his brazen head.
Padua, with sighs, beholds her Livy burn,
And even the Antipodes Virgilius mourn.
See, the cirque falls, the unpillar'd temple nods,
Streets paved with heroes, Tiber chok'd with gods:
Till Peter's keys some christen'd Jove adorn,[1]
And Pan to Moses lends his pagan horn;
See graceless Venus to a virgin turn'd,
Or Phidias broken, and Apelles burn'd.
  Behold yon isle, by palmers, pilgrims trod,
Men bearded, bald, cowl'd, uncowl'd, shod, unshod,
Peel'd, patch'd, and piebald, linsey-woolsey brothers,
Grave mummers! sleeveless some, and shirtless others.
That once was Britain—happy, had she seen[2]
No fiercer sons, had Easter never been!
In peace, great goddess, ever be adored;
How keen the war, if Dulness draw the sword!
Thus visit not thy own! on this blest age
O spread thy influence, but restrain thy rage.
  And see, my son! the hour is on its way,
That lifts our goddess to imperial sway;
This favourite isle, long sever'd from her reign,
Dove-like, she gathers to her wings again.[3]
Now look through fate! behold the scene she draws![4]
What aids, what armies, to assert her cause!
See all her progeny, illustrious sight!
Behold, and count them, as they rise to light.
As Berecynthia, while her offspring vie
In homage to the mother of the sky,

[1] After the government of Rome devolved to the Popes, their zeal was for some time exerted in demolishing the heathen temples and statues, so that the Goths scarce destroyed more monuments of antiquity out of rage, than these out of devotion. At length they spared some of the temples, by converting them to churches; and some of the statues, by modifying them into images of saints. In much later times, it was thought necessary to change the statues of Apollo and Pallas, on the tomb of Sannazarius, into David and Judith; the lyre easily became a harp, and the Gorgon's head turned to that of Holofernes.

[2] Wars in England anciently, about the right time of celebrating Easter.

[3] This is fulfilled in the fourth book.

[4] Of poets, antiquaries, critics, divines, free-thinkers. But as this revolution is only here set on foot by the first of these classes, the poets, they only are here particularly celebrated, and they only properly fall under the care and review of this colleague of Dulness, the Laureate.

Surveys around her, in the blest abode,
An hundred sons, and every son a god:
Not with less glory mighty Dulness crown'd,
Shall take through Grub-street her triumphant round;
And her Parnassus glancing o'er at once,
Behold an hundred sons, and each a dunce.
  Mark first that youth who takes the foremost place,
And thrusts his person full into your face.
With all thy father's virtues blest, be born!
And a new Cibber shall the stage adorn.
  A second see, by meeker manners known,
And modest as the maid that sips alone;
From the strong fate of drams if thou get free,
Another Durfey, Ward! shall sing in thee.
Thee shall each ale-house, thee each gill-house mourn,
And answering gin-shops sourer sighs return.
  Jacob, the scourge of grammar, mark with awe,[1]
Nor less revere him, blunderbuss of law.
Lo! P—p—le's brow, tremendous to the town,
Horneck's fierce eye, and Roome's funereal frown,[2]
Lo! sneering Goode,[3] half malice and half whim,
A fiend in glee, ridiculously grim.
Each cygnet sweet of Bath and Tunbridge race,
Whose tuneful whistling makes the waters pass:[4]

1 "This *gentleman* is son of a *considerable maltster* of Romsey, in Southamptonshire, and bred to the law under a *very eminent attorney:* who, between his *more laborious* studies, has *diverted* himself with poetry. He is a great admirer of poets and their works, which has occasioned him to try his genius that way.—He has writ in prose the *Lives* of the *Poets*, *Essays*, and a great many law-books, *The Accomplished Conveyancer*, *Modern Justice*, *&c.*" GILES JACOB of himself, *Lives of Poets*.

2 These two were virulent party-writers, worthily coupled together, and one would think prophetically, since, after the publishing of this piece, the former dying, the latter succeeded him in *honour* and *employment*. The first was Philip Horneck, author of a Billingsgate paper, called The High German Doctor. Edward Roome was son of an undertaker for funerals in Fleet Street, and writ some of the papers called Pasquin, where by malicious innuendos he endeavoured to represent our author guilty of malevolent practices with a great man then under prosecution of Parliament. P—le was the author of some vile plays and pamphlets. He published abuses on our author in a paper called The Prompter.

3 ill-natured critic, who wrote a satire on our author, called *The mock Æsop*, and many anonymous libels in newspapers for hire.

4 There were several successions of these sort of minor poets, at Tunbridge, Bath, &c., singing the praise of the annuals flourishing for that season; whose names indeed would be nameless, and therefore the poet slurs them over with others in general.

Each songster, riddler, every nameless name,
All crowd, who foremost shall be damned to fame.
Some strain in rhyme; the Muses on their racks,
Scream like the winding of ten thousand jacks:
Some free from rhyme or reason, rule or check,
Break Priscian's head, and Pegasus's neck;
Down, down they larum, with impetuous whirl,
The Pindars, and the Miltons of a Curl.
Silence, ye wolves! while Ralph[1] to Cynthia howls,
And makes night hideous—Answer him, ye owls!
Sense, speech, and measure, living tongues and dead,
Let all give way—and Morris may be read.
Flow, Welsted,[2] flow! like thine inspirer, beer,
Though stale, not ripe; though thin, yet never clear;
So sweetly mawkish, and so smoothly dull;
Heady, not strong; o'erflowing, though not full.
Ah, Dennis! Gildon, ah! what ill-starr'd rage
Divides a friendship long confirm'd by age?
Blockheads with reason wicked wits abhor,
But fool with fool is barbarous civil war.
Embrace, embrace, my sons! be foes no more!
Nor glad vile poets with true critics' gore.
Behold yon pair,[3] in strict embraces join'd:
How like in manners, and how like in mind!
Equal in wit, and equally polite,
Shall this a Pasquin, that a Grumbler write;
Like are their merits, like rewards they share,
That shines a consul, this commissioner.

1 James Ralph, a name inserted after the first editions, not known to our author till he wrote a swearing piece, called *Sawney*, very abusive of Dr. Swift, Mr. Gay, and himself. This low writer attended his own works with panegyrics in the journals, and once in particular praised himself highly above Mr. Addison, in wretched remarks upon that author's account of English poets, printed in a London journal, Sept. 1728. He ended at last in the common sink of all such writers, a political newspaper, to which he was recommended by his friend Arnall, and received a small pittance for pay.

2 "Mr. *Welsted* had, in his youth, raised so great expectations of his future genius, that there was a *kind of struggle* between the most eminent in the two universities, which should have the *honour* of his education. To *compound* this, he (*civilly*) became a member of both, and after having passed some time at the one, he removed to the other.

3 One of these was author of a weekly paper called *The Grumbler*, as the other was concerned in another called *Pasquin*, in which Mr. Pope was abused with the Duke of Buckingham and Bishop of Rochester. They also joined in a piece against his first undertaking to translate the Iliad, entitled *Homerides, by Sir Iliad Doggrel*, printed 1715.

"But who is he, in closet close y-pent,
Of sober face, with learned dust besprent?
Right well mine eyes arede[1] the myster wight,
On parchment scraps y-fed, and Wormius hight.[2]
To future ages may thy dulness last,
As thou preserv'st the dulness of the past!
There, dim in clouds, the poring scholiasts mark,
Wits, who like owls, see only in the dark,[3]
A lumberhouse of books in every head,
For ever reading, never to be read!
But, where each silence lifts its modern type,
History her pot, Divinity her pipe,
While proud Philosophy repines to show,
Dishonest sight! his breeches rent below;
Imbrown'd with native bronze, lo! Henley stands,[4]
Tuning his voice, and balancing his hands.

[1] *Read*, or *peruse;* though sometimes used for *counsel*. "READE THY READ, *take thy consaile*." Thomas Sternhold, in his translation of the first Psalm into English metre, hath *wisely* made use of this word,

The man is blest that hath not bent
To wicked READ *his ear*.

But in the last spurious editions of the singing Psalms the word READ is changed into *men*. I say *spurious* editions, because not only here, but quite throughout the whole book of Psalms, are *strange alterations*, all for the worse; and yet the title-page stands as it used to do! and all (which is *abominable* in any book, much more in a sacred work) is ascribed to Thomas Sternhold, John Hopkins, and others; I am confident, were Sternhold and Hopkins now living, they would proceed against the innovators as cheats.

[2] Let not this name, purely fictitious, be conceited to mean the learned Olaus Wormius; much less (as it was unwarrantably foisted into the surreptitious editions) our own antiquary, Mr. Thomas Hearne, who had no way aggrieved our Poet, but on the contrary published many curious tracts which he hath to his great contentment perused.

[3] These few lines exactly describe the right verbal critic: The darker his author is, the better he is pleased; like the famous quack doctor, who put up in his bills, *he delighted in matters of difficulty*. Somebody said well of these men, that their heads were *libraries out of order*.

[4] J. Henley the orator, who was a member of St. John's College, Cambridge, and had been admitted to priest's orders, commenced preaching at what he styled his "*Oratory*," in Newport Market, on the Sundays upon theological matters, and on the Wednesdays lectured upon all other sciences. Each auditor paid one shilling. He declaimed some years against the greatest persons, and occasionally did our author that honour. After having stood some prosecutions, he turned his rhetoric to buffoonery upon all public and private occurrences. All this passed in the same room; where sometimes he broke jests, and sometimes that bread which he called the *primitive eucharist*.

How fluent nonsense trickles from his tongue!
How sweet the periods, neither said nor sung!
Still break the benches, Henley, with thy strain,
While Sherlock, Hare, and Gibson[1] preach in vain.
O great restorer of the good old stage,
Preacher at once, and zany of thy age!
O worthy thou of Egypt's wise abodes,
A decent priest, where monkeys were the gods!
But fate with butchers placed thy priestly stall,
Meek modern faith to murder, hack, and maul;
And bade thee live, to crown Britannia's praise,
In Toland's, Tindal's, and in Woolston's days.[2]
Yet oh, my sons! a father's words attend:
(So may the fates preserve the ears you lend)
'Tis yours, a Bacon or a Locke to blame,
A Newton's genius, or a Milton's flame:
But oh! with One, immortal One, dispense,
The source of Newton's light, of Bacon's sense!
Content, each emanation of his fires
That beams on earth, each virtue he inspires,
Each art he prompts, each charm he can create,
Whate'er he gives, are given for you to hate.
Persist by all divine in man unawed,
But "Learn, ye DUNCES! not to scorn your GOD."
Thus he, for then a ray of reason stole
Half through the solid darkness of his soul;
But soon the cloud return'd—and thus the sire:
See now, what Dulness and her sons admire!
See what the charms, that smite the simple heart
Not touch'd by nature, and not reach'd by art.
His never-blushing head he turn'd aside,
(Not half so pleased when Goodman prophesied)
And look'd, and saw a sable Sorcerer[3] rise,
Swift to whose hand a winged volume flies:
All sudden, gorgons hiss, and dragons glare,
And ten-horn'd fiends and giants rush to war.

[1] Bishops of Salisbury, Chichester, and London.

[2] Of Toland and Tindal, see Book II. Tho. Woolston was an impious madman, who wrote in a most insolent style against the Miracles of the Gospel, in the year 1726.

[3] Dr. Faustus, the subject of a set of farces, which lasted in vogue two or three seasons, in which both playhouses strove to outdo each other for some years. All the extravagancies in the sixteen lines following were introduced on the stage, and frequented by persons of the first quality in England, to the twentieth and thirtieth time.

Hell rises, Heaven descends, and dance on earth :[1]
Gods, imps, and monsters, music, rage, and mirth,
A fire, a jig, a battle, and a ball,
Till one wide conflagration swallows all.
  Thence a new world, to nature's laws unknown,
Breaks out refulgent, with a heaven its own:
Another Cynthia her new journey runs,
And other planets circle other suns.
The forests dance, the rivers upward rise,
Whales sport in woods, and dolphins in the skies;
And last, to give the whole creation grace,
Lo! one vast egg produces human race.
  Joy fills his soul, joy innocent of thought;
What power, he cries, what power these wonders wrought?
Son, what thou seek'st is in thee! Look, and find
Each monster meets his likeness in thy mind.
Yet wouldst thou more? In yonder cloud behold,
Whose sarsnet skirts are edged with flamy gold.
A matchless youth! his nod these worlds controls,
Wings the red lightning, and the thunder rolls.
Angel of Dulness, sent to scatter round
Her magic charms o'er all unclassic ground:
Yon stars, yon suns, he rears at pleasure higher,
Illumes their light, and sets their flames on fire.
Immortal Rich![2] how calm he sits at ease,
'Mid snows of paper, and fierce hail of pease;
And, proud his mistress' orders to perform,
Rides in the whirlwind, and directs the storm.
  But lo! to dark encounter in mid air
New wizards rise; I see my Cibber there!
Booth[3] in his cloudy tabernacle shrined,
On grinning dragons thou shalt mount the wind.
Dire is the conflict, dismal is the din,
Here shouts all Drury, there all Lincoln's-inn;
Contending theatres our empire raise,
Alike their labours, and alike their praise.
  And are these wonders, son, to thee unknown?
Unknown to thee? These wonders are thy own.

1 This monstrous absurdity was actually represented in Theobald's Rape of Proserpine.

2 Mr. John Rich, Manager of the Theatre Royal, Covent-garden, was the first that excelled this way.

3 Booth and Cibber were joint managers of the Theatre in Drury-lane.

These Fate reserved to grace thy reign divine,
Foreseen by me, but ah! withheld from mine.
In Lud's old walls, though long I ruled, renown'd
Far as loud Bow's stupendous bells resound;
Though my own Aldermen conferr'd the bays,
To me committing their eternal praise,
Their full-fed heroes, their pacific mayors,
Their annual trophies,[1] and their monthly wars:
Though long my party[2] built on me their hopes,
For writing pamphlets, and for roasting popes;
Yet lo! in me what authors have to brag on!
Reduced at last to hiss in my own dragon.
Avert it, Heaven! that thou, my Cibber, e'er
Shouldst wag a serpent-tail in Smithfield fair!
Like the vile straw that's blown about the streets,
The needy poet sticks to all he meets,
Coach'd, carted, trod upon; now loose, now fast,
And carried off in some dog's tail at last.
Happier thy fortunes! like a rolling stone,
Thy giddy dulness still shall lumber on,
Safe in its heaviness, shall never stray,
But lick up every blockhead in the way.
Thee shall the patriot, thee the courtier taste,
And every year be duller than the last.
Till raised from booths, to theatre, to court,
Her seat imperial Dulness shall transport.
Already opera prepares the way,
The sure fore-runner of her gentle sway:
Let her thy heart; next drabs and dice, engage,
The third made passion of thy doting age.
Teach thou the warbling Polypheme[3] to roar,
And scream thyself as none e'er scream'd before!

1 *Annual trophies*, on the Lord-mayor's day; and *monthly wars* in the Artillery-ground.

2 Settle, like most party-writers, was very uncertain in his political principles. He was employed to hold the pen in the *character* of a *popish successor*, but afterwards printed his *Narrative* on the other side. He had managed the ceremony of a famous Pope-burning on Nov. 17, 1680, then became a trooper in King James's army, at Hounslow-heath. After the Revolution he kept a booth at Bartholomew-fair, where in the droll called *St. George for England*, he acted in his old age in a dragon of green leather of his own invention; he was at last taken into the Charter-house, and there died, aged sixty years.

3 He translated the Italian opera of Polifemo; but unfortunately lost the whole jest of the story. The Cyclops asks Ulysses his *name*, who

To aid our cause, if Heaven thou canst not bend,
Hell thou shalt move; for Faustus is our friend:
Pluto with Cato[1] thou for this shalt join,
And link the Mourning Bride to Proserpine.
Grub-street! thy fall should men and gods conspire,
Thy stage shall stand, ensure it but from fire.[2]
Another Æschylus appears![3] prepare
For new abortions, all ye pregnant fair!
In flames, like Semele's, be brought to bed,
While opening Hell spouts wild-fire at your head.
  Now, Bavius, take the poppy from thy brow,
And place it here! here all ye heroes bow!
This, this is he, foretold by ancient rhymes:
The Augustus born to bring Saturnian times.
Signs following signs lead on the mighty year!
See! the dull stars roll round and re-appear.
See, see, our own true Phœbus wears the bays!
Our Midas sits lord chancellor of plays!
On poets' tombs see Benson's titles writ![4]
Lo! Ambrose Philips is preferr'd for wit!

tells him his name is *Noman*. After his eye is put out, he roars and calls the brother Cyclops to his aid: They inquire *who has hurt him?* he answers *Noman;* whereupon they all go away again. Our ingenious translator made Ulysses answer, *I take no name*, whereby all that followed became unintelligible.

1 Names of miserable farces which it was the custom to act at the end of the best tragedies, to spoil the digestion of the audience.

2 In the farce of Proserpine a corn-field was set on fire: whereupon the other play-house had a barn burnt down for the recreation of the spectators. They also rivalled each other in showing the burnings of hell-fire, in Dr. Faustus.

3 It is reported of Æschylus, that when his tragedy of the Furies was acted, the audience were so terrified that the children fell into fits, and the women miscarried.

4 Benson (Surveyor of the buildings to his Majesty King George I.) gave in a report to the Lords, that their house and the Painted Chamber adjoining were in immediate danger of falling. Whereupon the lords met in committee to appoint some other place to sit in, while the house should be taken down. But it being proposed to cause some other builders first to inspect it, they found it in very good condition. The lords, upon this, were going upon an address to the king against Benson, for such a misrepresentation; but the Earl of Sunderland, then secretary, gave them an assurance that his Majesty would remove him, which was done accordingly. In favour of this man, the famous Sir Christopher Wren, who had been architect to the crown for above fifty years, who built most of the churches in London, laid the first stone of St. Paul's, and lived to finish it, had been displaced from his employment at the age of near ninety years.

See under Ripley rise a new Whitehall,
While Jones' and Boyle's united labours fall;[1]
While Wren with sorrow to the grave descends,
Gay dies unpension'd[2] with a hundred friends,
Hibernian politics, O Swift! thy fate;
And Pope's ten years to comment and translate.
Proceed, great days! till learning fly the shore,
Till birch shall blush with noble blood no more,
Till Thames see Eton's sons for ever play,
Till Westminster's whole year be holiday,
Till Isis' elders reel, their pupils sport,
And Alma mater lie dissolved in port!
Enough! enough! the raptured monarch cries,
And through the ivory gate the vision flies.

BOOK THE FOURTH.

ARGUMENT.

THE Poet being, in this book, to declare the *completion* of the *prophecies* mentioned at the end of the former, makes a new *invocation;* as the greater poets are wont, when some high and worthy matter is to be sung. He shows the goddess coming in her majesty, to destroy *order* and *science*, and to substitute the *kingdom* of the *dull* upon earth. How she leads captive the *sciences*, and silenceth the *muses;* and *what* they be who succeed in their stead. All her children, by a wonderful attraction, are drawn about her; and bear along with them divers others, who promote her empire by connivance, weak resistance, or discouragement of arts; such as half-wits, tasteless admirers, vain pretenders, the flatterers of dunces, or the patrons of them. All these crowd round her; one of them, offering to approach her, is driven back by a rival, but she commends and encourages both. The first who speak in form

---

[1] At the time when this poem was written, the Banqueting-house of Whitehall, the church and piazza of Covent-garden, and the palace and chapel of Somerset-house, the works of the famous Inigo Jones, had been for many years so neglected, as to be in danger of ruin. The portico of Covent-garden church had been just then restored and beautified at the expense of the Earl of Burlington, who, at the same time, by his publication of the designs of that great master and Palladio, as well as by many noble buildings of his own, revived the true taste of architecture in this kingdom.

[2] See Mr. Gay's fable of the *Hare and many Friends.* This gentleman was early in the friendship of our Author, which continued to his death. He wrote several works of humour with great success, the Shepherd's Week, Trivia, the What-d'ye-call it, Fables, and lastly, the celebrated Beggar's Opera, a piece of satire, which hit all tastes and degrees of men, from those of the highest quality to the very rabble.

are the *Geniuses* of the *schools*, who assure her of their care to advance her cause, by confining youth to *words*, and keeping them out of the way of real knowledge. Their address, and her gracious answer; with her charge to them and the Universities. The *Universities* appear by their proper deputies, and assure her that the same method is observed in the progress of *education*, the speech of *Aristarchus* on this subject. They are driven off by a band of young gentlemen returned from *travel* with their *tutors*, one of whom delivers to the goddess, in a polite oration, an account of the whole conduct and fruits of their *travels*, presenting to her at the same time a young nobleman perfectly accomplished. She receives him graciously, and indues him with the happy quality of *want of shame*. She sees loitering about her a number of *indolent persons* abandoning all business and duty, and dying with laziness: to these approaches the antiquary *Annius*, intreating her to make them *virtuosos*, and assign them over to him: but *Mummius*, another antiquary, complaining of his fraudulent proceeding, she finds a method to reconcile their difference. Then enter a troop of people fantastically adorned, offering her strange and exotic presents: amongst them one stands forth and demands justice on another, who had deprived him of one of the greatest curiosities in nature: but he justifies himself so well, that the goddess gives them both her approbation. She recommends to them to find proper employment for the *indolents* before mentioned in the study of *butterflies, shells, birds'-nests, moss, &c.*, but with particular caution, not to proceed beyond *trifles*, to any useful or extensive views of nature, or of the Author of nature. Against the last of these apprehensions, she is secured by a hearty address from the *minute philosophers* and *freethinkers*, one of whom speaks in the name of the rest. The youth thus instructed and principled, are delivered to her in a body, by the hands of *Silenus;* and then admitted to taste the cup of the *Magus* her high priest, which causes a total oblivion of all obligations, divine, civil, moral, or rational. To these her adepts she sends *priests, attendants*, and *comforters*, of various kinds; confers on them *orders* and *degrees;* and then, dismissing them with a speech, confirming to each his *privileges*, and telling what she expects from each, concludes with a *yawn* of extraordinary virtue; the progress and effects whereof on all orders of men, and the consummation of all, in the restoration of *night* and *chaos*, conclude the poem.

Yet, yet a moment, one dim ray of light
Indulge, dread Chaos, and eternal Night!
Of darkness visible so much be lent,
As half to show, half veil the deep intent.
Ye powers! whose mysteries restored I sing,
To whom Time bears me on his rapid wing,
Suspend awhile your force, inertly strong,
Then take at once the poet and the song.
  Now flamed the dog-star's unpropitious ray,
Smote every brain, and wither'd every bay;
Sick was the sun, the owl forsook his bower,
The moon-struck prophet felt the madding hour:

Then rose the seed of Chaos, and of Night,
To blot out order, and extinguish light.
Of dull and venal a new world to mould,
And bring Saturnian days of lead and gold.
 She mounts the throne: her head a cloud conceal'd,
In broad effulgence all below reveal'd,
('Tis thus aspiring Dulness ever shines)
Soft on her lap her laureate son reclines.
 Beneath her foot-stool, *Science* groans in chains,
And *Wit* dreads exile, penalties, and pains.
There foam'd rebellious *Logic*, gagg'd and bound,
There, stript, fair *Rhetoric* languish'd on the ground;
His blunted arms by *Sophistry* are borne,
And shameless *Billingsgate* her robes adorn
Morality, by her false guardians drawn,[1]
Chicane in furs, and *Casuistry* in lawn,
Gasps, as they straiten at each end the cord,
And dies, when Dulness gives her Page the word.
Mad *Mathesis* alone was unconfined,
Too mad for mere material chains to bind,
Now to pure space lifts her ecstatic stare,
Now running round the circle, finds it square.
But held in ten-fold bonds the *Muses* lie,
Watch'd both by Envy's and by Flattery's eye:
There to her heart sad Tragedy addrest
The dagger wont to pierce the tyrant's breast;
But sober History restrain'd her rage,
And promised vengeance on a barbarous age.
There sunk Thalia, nerveless, cold, and dead,
Had not her sister Satire held her head:
Nor could'st thou,[3] Chesterfield! a tear refuse;
Thou wept'st, and with thee wept each gentle Muse.

[1] *Morality* is the daughter of *Astræa*. This alludes to the mythology of the ancient poets; who tell us that in the *gold* and *silver* ages, or in the *state of nature*, the gods cohabited with men here on earth; but when, by reason of human degeneracy, men were forced to have recourse to a *magistrate*, and that the ages of *brass* and *iron* came on, (that is, when laws were wrote on brazen tablets and inforced by the sword of justice,) the celestials soon retired from earth, and Astræa last of all; and then it was she left this her orphan daughter in the hands of the *guardians* aforesaid.

[2] There was a judge of this name, always ready to hang any man, of which he was suffered to give a hundred miserable examples during a long life, even to his dotage.

[3] This noble person, in the year 1737, when the act aforesaid was brought into the House of Lords, opposed it in an excellent speech (says Mr. Cibber) "with a lively spirit and uncommon eloquence."

When lo! a harlot form soft sliding by,
With mincing step, small voice, and languid eye;
Foreign her air, her robe's discordant pride
In patchwork fluttering, and her head aside:
By singing peers upheld on either hand,
She tripp'd and laugh'd, too pretty much to stand;
Cast on the prostrate Nine a scornful look,
Then thus in quaint recitativo spoke.
O cara! cara! silence all that train:
Joy to great Chaos! let division reign:
Chromatic tortures soon shall drive them hence,
Break all their nerves, and fritter all their sense:
One trill shall harmonize joy, grief, and rage,
Wake the dull church, and lull the ranting stage;
To the same notes thy sons shall hum, or snore,
And all thy yawning daughters cry *encore.*
Another Phœbus, thy own Phœbus, reigns,
Joys in my jigs, and dances in my chains.
But soon, ah soon, rebellion will commence,
If music meanly borrows aid from sense:
Strong in new arms, lo! giant Handel stands,
Like bold Briareus, with a hundred hands;
To stir, to rouse, to shake the soul he comes,
And Jove's own thunders follow Mars's drums.
Arrest him, empress; or you sleep no more—
She heard, and drove him to the Hibernian shore.
And now had Fame's posterior trumpet blown,
And all the nations summon'd to the throne.
The young, the old, who feel her inward sway,
One instinct seizes, and transports away.
None need a guide, by sure attraction led,
And strong impulsive gravity of head:
None want a place, for all their centre found,
Hung to the goddess, and cohered around.
Not closer, orb in orb, conglobed are seen
The buzzing bees about their dusky queen.
The gathering number, as it moves along,
Involves a vast involuntary throng,
Who gently drawn, and struggling less and less,
Roll in her vortex, and her power confess.
Not those alone who passive own her laws,
But who, weak rebels, more advance her cause.
Whate'er of dunce in college or in town
Sneers at another, in toupee or gown;

Whate'er of mongrel no one class admits,
A wit with dunces, and a dunce with wits,
Nor absent they, no members of her state,
Who pay her homage in her sons, the great;
Who, false to Phœbus, bow the knee to Baal;
Or, impious, preach his word without a call.
Patrons, who sneak from living worth to dead,
Withhold the pension, and set up the head;
Or vest dull Flattery in the sacred gown;
Or give from fool to fool the laurel crown.
And (last and worst) with all the cant of wit,
Without the soul, the Muse's hypocrite.
There march'd the bard and blockhead, side by side,
Who rhymed for hire, and patronised for pride.
Narcissus, praised with all a parson's power,
Look'd a white lily sunk beneath a shower.
There moved Montalto with superior air;
His stretch'd-out arm display'd a volume fair;
Courtiers and patriots in two ranks divide,
Through both he pass'd, and bow'd from side to side:
But as in graceful act, with awful eye
Composed he stood, bold Benson[1] thrust him by:
On two unequal crutches propp'd he came,
Milton's on this, on that one Johnston's name.
The decent knight[2] retired with sober rage,
Withdrew his hand, and closed the pompous page.
But—happy for him as the times went then—
Appear'd Appollo's mayor and aldermen,
On whom three hundred gold-capp'd youth await,
To lug the ponderous volume off in state.
When Dulness, smiling—"Thus revive the wits!
But murder first, and mince them all to bits;
As erst Medea (cruel, so to save!)
A new edition of old Æson gave;
Let standard authors, thus like trophies borne,
Appear more glorious as more hack'd and torn,
And you, my critics! in the chequer'd shade,
Admire new light through holes yourselves have made.

1 This man endeavoured to raise himself to fame by erecting monuments, striking coins, setting up heads, and procuring translations, of *Milton*; and afterwards by a great passion for *Arthur Johnston's* version of the Psalms, of which he printed many fine editions. He was also the means of raising the monument to Milton in Westminster Abbey.

2 Sir Thomas Hanmer, who was about to publish a very pompous edition of Shakspere.

Leave not a foot of verse, a foot of stone,
A page, a grave, that they can call their own;
But spread, my sons, your glory thin or thick,
On passive paper, or on solid brick.
So by each bard an alderman shall sit,
A heavy lord shall hang at every wit,
And while on Fame's triumphal car they ride,
Some slave of mine be pinion'd to their side.
Now crowds on crowds around the goddess press,
Each eager to present the first address.
Dunce scorning dunce beholds the next advance,
But fop shows fop superior complaisance.
When lo! a spectre rose, whose index-hand
Held forth the virtue of the dreadful wand;
His beaver'd brow a birchen garland wears,
Dropping with infants' blood, and mothers' tears.
O'er every vein a shuddering horror runs;
Eton and Winton shake through all their sons.
All flesh is humbled, Westminster's bold race
Shrink, and confess the genius of the place:
The pale boy-senator yet tingling stands,
And holds his breeches close with both his hands.
Then thus. Since man from beast by words is known,
Words are man's province, words we teach alone.
When reason, doubtful, like the Samian letter,[1]
Points him two ways, the narrower is the better.
Placed at the door of learning, youth to guide,
We never suffer it to stand too wide.
To ask, to guess, to know as they commence,
As fancy opens the quick springs of sense,
We ply the memory, we load the brain,
Bind rebel wit, and double chain on chain,
Confine the thought, to exercise the breath;
And keep them in the pale of words till death.
Whate'er the talents, or howe'er design'd,
We hang one jingling padlock on the mind:
A poet the first day he dips his quill;
And what the last? a very poet still.
Pity! the charm works only in our wall,
Lost, lost too soon in yonder house or hall.[2]

1 The letter Y, used by Pythagoras as an emblem of the different roads to Virtue and Vice.
2 Westminster-Hall and the House of Commons.

There truant WYNDHAM every muse gave o'er,
There TALBOT sunk, and was a wit no more!
How sweet an Ovid, MURRAY was our boast!
How many Martials were in PULTENEY lost!
Else sure some bard, to our eternal praise,
In twice ten thousand rhyming nights and days,
Had reach'd the work, the all that mortal can;
And South beheld that master-piece of man.[1]
O (cried the goddess) for some pedant reign!
Some gentle JAMES, to bless the land again;[2]
To stick the doctor's chair into the throne,
Give law to words, or war with words alone,
Senates and courts with Greek and Latin rule,
And turn the council to a grammar school!
For sure, if Dulness sees a grateful day,
'Tis in the shade of arbitrary sway
O! if my sons may learn one earthly thing,
Teach but that one, sufficient for a king;
That which my priests, and mine alone, maintain,
Which, as it dies or lives, we fall or reign:
May you, may Cam, and Isis preach it long!
"The RIGHT DIVINE of Kings to govern wrong."
Prompt at the call, around the goddess roll
Broad hats, and hoods, and caps, a sable shoal:
Thick and more thick the black blockade extends,
A hundred head of Aristotle's friends.
Nor wert thou, Isis! wanting to the day,—
Tho' Christchurch long kept prudishly away.—
Each staunch polemic, stubborn as a rock,
Each fierce logician, still expelling Locke,[3]
Came whip and spur, and dash'd through thin and thick,
On German Crouzaz and Dutch Burgersdyck.
As many quit the streams[4] that murmuring fall
To lull the sons of Margaret and Clare-hall,

[1] Viz., an *epigram.* The famous Dr. South declared a perfect epigram to be as difficult a performance as an epic poem. And the critics say, "an epic poem is the greatest work human nature is capable of."

[2] Wilson tells us that this king, James the First, took upon himself to teach the Latin tongue to Car Earl of Somerset; and that Gondomar, the Spanish ambassador, would speak false Latin to him, on purpose to give him the pleasure of correcting it, whereby he wrought himself into his good graces.

[3] In the year 170- there was a meeting of the heads of the University of Oxford to censure Mr. Locke's Essay on Human Understanding, and to forbid the reading it.

[4] The river Cam, running by the walls of these colleges, which are particularly famous for their skill in disputation.

Where Bentley late tempestuous wont to sport
In troubled waters, but now sleeps in port.
Before them march'd that awful Aristarch;
Plough'd was his front with many a deep remark:
His hat, which never vail'd to human pride,
Walker with reverence took, and laid aside.
Low bow'd the rest: he, kingly, did but nod;
So upright Quakers please both man and God.
Mistress! dismiss that rabble from your throne:
Avaunt —— is Aristarchus[1] yet unknown?
Thy mighty scholiast, whose unwearied pains
Made Horace dull, and humbled Milton's strains.
Turn what they will to verse, their toil is vain,
Critics like me shall make it prose again.
Roman and Greek grammarians! know your better;
Author of something yet more great than letter;
While towering o'er your alphabet, like Saul,
Stands our Digamma, and o'ertops them all.
'Tis true, on words is still our whole debate,
Disputes of *me* or *te*, of *aut* or *at*,
To sound or sink in *cano*, O or A,
Or give up Cicero to C or K.
Let Freind[2] affect to speak as Terence spoke,
And Alsop[3] never but like Horace joke:
For me, what Virgil, Pliny may deny,
Manilius or Solinus shall supply:
For Attic phrase in Plato let them seek,
I poach in Suidas for unlicensed Greek.
In ancient sense if any needs will deal,
Be sure I give them fragments, not a meal;
What Gellius or Stobæus[4] hash'd before,
Or chew'd by blind old scholiasts o'er and o'er.
The critic eye, that microscope of wit,
Sees hairs and pores, examines bit by bit:
How parts relate to parts, or they to whole,
The body's harmony, the beaming soul,

[1] A famous commentator, and corrector of Homer, whose name has been frequently used to signify a complete critic.

[2] Dr. Robert Freind, master of Westminster-school, and canon of Christ-church.

[3] Dr. Anthony Alsop, a happy imitator of the Horatian style.

[4] *Suidas, Gellius, Stobæus.* The first a dictionary-writer, a collector of impertinent facts and barbarous words; the second a minute critic; the third an author, who gave his common-place book to the public, where we happen to find much mince-meat of old books.

Are things which Kuster, Burman, Wasse shall see,
When man's whole frame is obvious to a *flea*.
Ah, think not, mistress! more true dulness lies
In Folly's cap, than Wisdom's grave disguise.
Like buoys, that never sink into the flood,
On learning's surface we but lie and nod.
Thine is the genuine head of many a house,
And much divinity without a Νοῦς.
Nor could a BARROW work on every block,
Nor has one ATTERBURY[1] spoil'd the flock.
See! still thy own, the heavy canon roll,
And metaphysic smokes involve the pole.
For thee we dim the eyes, and stuff the head
With all such reading as was never read:
For thee explain a thing till all men doubt it,
And write about it, goddess, and about it:
So spins the silk-worm small its slender store,
And labours till it clouds itself all o'er.
What though we let some better sort of fool
Thrid every science, run through every school?
Never by tumbler through the hoops was shown
Such skill in passing all, and touching none.
He may, indeed (if sober all this time),
Plague with dispute, or persecute with rhyme.
We only furnish what he cannot use,
Or wed to what he must divorce, a Muse:
Full in the midst of Euclid dip at once,
And petrify a genius to a dunce:
Or set on metaphysic ground to prance,
Show all his paces, not a step advance.
With the same cement, ever sure to bind,
We bring to one dead level every mind.
Then take him to develope, if you can,
And hew the block off,[2] and get out the man.
But wherefore waste I words? I see advance
Whore, pupil, and laced governor from France.

[1] Isaac Barrow, Master of Trinity, Francis Atterbury, Dean of Christchurch, both great geniuses and eloquent preachers; one more conversant in the sublime geometry, the other in classical learning; but who equally made it their care to advance the polite arts in their several Societies.

[2] A notion of Aristotle, that there was originally in every block of marble, a statue, which would appear on the removal of the superfluous parts.

Walker! our hat—nor more he deign'd to say,
But, stern as Ajax' spectre, strode away.
In flow'd at once a gay embroider'd race,
And tittering push'd the pedants off the place:
Some would have spoken, but the voice was drown'd
By the French horn, or by the opening hound.
The first came forwards, with as easy mien
As if he saw St. James's and the queen.
When thus the attendant orator begun:
Receive, great empress! thy accomplish'd son:
Thine from the birth, and sacred from the rod,
A dauntless infant! never scared with God.
The sire saw, one by one, his virtues wake:
The mother begg'd the blessing of a rake.
Thou gavest that ripeness, which so soon began,
And ceased so soon, he ne'er was boy nor man.
Through school and college, thy kind cloud o'ercast,
Safe and unseen the young Æneas pass'd:
Thence bursting glorious, all at once let down,
Stunn'd with his giddy 'larum half the town.
Intrepid then, o'er seas and lands he flew:
Europe he saw, and Europe saw him too.
There all thy gifts and graces we display,
Thou, only thou, directing all our way!
To where the Seine, obsequious as she runs,
Pours at great Bourbon's feet her silken sons;
Or Tyber, now no longer Roman, rolls,
Vain of Italian arts, Italian souls:
To happy convents, bosom'd deep in vines,
Where slumber abbots, purple as their wines:
To isles of fragrance, lily-silver'd vales,
Diffusing languor in the panting gales:
To lands of singing, or of dancing slaves,
Love-whispering woods, and lute-resounding waves.
But chief her shrine where naked Venus keeps,
And Cupids ride the lion of the deeps;
Where, eased of fleets, the Adriatic main
Wafts the smooth eunuch and enamour'd swain.
Led by my hand, he saunter'd Europe round,
And gather'd every vice on Christian ground;
Saw every court, heard every king declare
His royal sense of operas or the fair;
The stews and palace equally explored,
Intrigued with glory, and with spirit whored;

Tried all *hors-d'œuvres*, all *liqueurs* defined,
Judicious drank, and greatly-daring dined;
Dropp'd the dull lumber of the Latin store,
Spoil'd his own language, and acquired no more;
All classic learning lost on classic ground;
And last turn'd *air*, the echo of a sound!
See now, half-cured, and perfectly well-bred,
With nothing but a solo in his head;
As much estate, and principle, and wit,
As Jansen, Fleetwood, Cibber[1] shall think fit;
Stolen from a duel, follow'd by a nun,
And, if a borough choose him, not undone;
See, to my country happy I restore
This glorious youth, and add one Venus more.
Her too receive (for her my soul adores),
So may the sons of sons of sons of whores,
Prop thine, O empress! like each neighbour throne,
And make a long posterity thy own.
Pleased she accepts the hero, and the dame
Wraps in her veil, and frees from sense of shame.
Then look'd, and saw a lazy, lolling sort,
Unseen at church, at senate, or at court,
Of ever-listless loiterers, that attend
No cause, no trust, no duty, and no friend.
Thee, too, my Paridel! she mark'd thee there,
Stretch'd on the rack of a too easy chair,
And heard thy everlasting yawn confess
The pains and penalties of idleness.
She pitied! but her pity only shed
Benigner influence on thy nodding head.
But Annius,[2] crafty seer, with ebon wand,
And well-dissembled emerald on his hand,
False as his gems, and canker'd as his coins,
Came, cramm'd with capon, from where Pollio dines.
Soft, as the wily fox is seen to creep,
Where bask on sunny banks the simple sheep,

[1] Three very eminent persons, all managers of *plays*: who, though not governors by profession, had, each in his way, concerned themselves in the education of youth; and regulated their wits, their morals, or their finances, at that period of their age which is the most important, their entrance into the polite world.

[2] The name taken from Annius, the monk of Viterbo, famous for many impositions and forgeries of ancient manuscripts and inscriptions, which he was prompted to by mere vanity, but our Annius had a more substantial motive.

Walk round and round, now prying here, now there;
So he; but pious whisper'd first his prayer:
Grant, gracious goddess! grant me still to cheat,
O may thy cloud still cover the deceit!
Thy choicer mists on this assembly shed,
But pour them thickest on the noble head.
So shall each youth, assisted by our eyes,
See other Cæsars, other Homers rise;
Through twilight ages hunt the Athenian fowl,[1]
Which Chalcis gods, and mortals call an owl,
Now see an Attys, now a Cecrops[2] clear,
Nay, Mahomet! the pigeon at thine ear;
Be rich in ancient brass, though not in gold,
And keep his Lares, though his house be sold;
To headless Phœbe his fair bride postpone,
Honour a Syrian prince above his own;
Lord of an Otho, if I vouch it true;
Bless'd in one Niger, till he knows of two.
Mummius o'erheard him; Mummius,[3] fool-renown'd,
Who, like his Cheops,[4] stinks above the ground,
Fierce as a startled adder, swell'd, and said.
Rattling an ancient sistrum at his head:
Speak'st thou of Syrian princes?[5] Traitor base!
Mine, goddess, mine is all the horned race.

[1] The owl stamped on the reverse of the ancient money of Athens.

[2] The first kings of Athens, of whom it is hard to suppose any coins are extant; but not so improbable as what follows, that there should be any of Mahomet, who forbade all images. Nevertheless, one of these Anniuses made a counterfeit one, now in the collection of a learned nobleman.

[3] This name is not merely an allusion to the mummies he was so fond of, but probably referred to the Roman general of that name, who burned Corinth, and committed the curious statues to the captain of a ship, assuring him, "that if any were lost or broken, he should procure others to be made in their stead:" by which it should seem (whatever may be pretended) that Mummius was no virtuoso.

[4] A king of Egypt, whose body was certainly to be known, as being buried alone in his pyramid, and is therefore more genuine than any of the Cleopatras. This royal mummy, being stolen by a wild Arab, was purchased by the consul of Alexandria, and transmitted to the museum of Mummius.

[5] The strange story following, which may be taken for a fiction of the Poet, is justified by a true relation in Spon's Voyages. Vaillant (who wrote the history of the Syrian kings as it is to be found on medals), coming from the Levant, where he had been collecting various coins, and being pursued by a corsair of Sallee, swallowed down twenty gold medals. A sudden bourasque freed him from the rover, and he got to

True he had wit, to make their value rise;
From foolish Greeks to steal them was as wise;
More glorious yet, from barbarous hands to keep,
When Sallee rovers chased him on the deep.
Then taught by Hermes, and divinely bold,
Down his own throat he risk'd the Grecian gold;
Receivèd each demi-god, with pious care,
Deep in his entrails—I revered them there,
I bought them, shrouded in that living shrine,
And, at their second birth, they issue mine.
Witness, great Ammon![1] by whose horns I swore,
(Replied soft Annius) this our paunch before
Still bears them, faithful; and that thus I eat,
Is to refund the medals with the meat.
To prove me, goddess! clear of all design,
Bid me with Pollio sup, as well as dine:
There all the learn'd shall at the labour stand,
And Douglas[2] lend his soft, obstetric hand.
The goddess, smiling, seem'd to give consent;
So back to Pollio, hand in hand, they went.
Then, thick as locusts blackening all the ground,
A tribe, with weeds and shells fantastic crown'd,
Each with some wondrous gift approach'd the power,
A nest, a toad, a fungus, or a flower.
But far the foremost, two, with earnest zeal,
And aspect ardent, to the throne appeal.
The first thus open'd: Hear thy suppliant's call,
Great queen, and common mother of us all!
Fair from its humble bed I rear'd this flower,
Suckled, and cheer'd, with air, and sun, and shower,

land with them in his belly. On his road to Avignon he met two physicians, of whom he demanded assistance. One advised purgations, the other vomits. In this uncertainty he took neither, but pursued his way to Lyons, where he found his ancient friend, the famous physician and antiquary, Dufour, to whom he related his adventure. Dufour first asked him *whether the medals were of the higher empire?* He assured him they were. Dufour was ravished with the hope of possessing such a treasure; he bargained with him on the spot for the most curious of them, and was to recover them at his own expense.

[1] Jupiter Ammon is called to witness, as the father of Alexander, to whom those kings succeeded in the division of the Macedonian empire, and whose *horns* they wore on their medals.

[2] A physician of great learning and no less taste; above all, curious in what related to *Horace*, of whom he collected every edition, translation, and comment, to the number of several hundred volumes.

Soft on the paper ruff its leaves I spread,
Bright with the gilded button tipp'd its head,
Then throned in glass, and named it CAROLINE:
Each maid cried, charming! and each youth, divine!
Did Nature's pencil ever blend such rays,
Such varied light in one promiscuous blaze?
Now prostrate! dead! behold that Caroline:
No maid cries, charming! and no youth, divine!
And lo the wretch! whose vile, whose insect lust
Laid this gay daughter of the spring in dust;
O punish him! or to the Elysian shades
Dismiss my soul, where no carnation fades.
He ceased, and wept. With innocence of mien,
The accused stood forth, and thus address'd the queen:
Of all the enamell'd race, whose silvery wing
Waves to the tepid zephyrs of the spring,
Or swims along the fluid atmosphere,
Once brightest shined this child of heat and air.
I saw, and started from its vernal bower
The rising game, and chased from flower to flower.
It fled, I follow'd; now in hope, now pain;
It stopp'd, I stopp'd; it moved, I moved again;
At last it fix'd, 'twas on what plant it pleased,
And where it fix'd, the beauteous bird I seized:
Rose or carnation was below my care;
I meddle, goddess! only in my sphere.
I tell the naked fact without disguise,
And, to excuse it, need but show the prize;
Whose spoils this paper offers to your eye,
Fair even in death! this peerless *butterfly*.
My sons! (she answer'd) both have done your parts:
Live happy both, and long promote our arts.
But hear a mother, when she recommends
To your fraternal care our sleeping friends.
The common soul, of Heaven's more frugal make,
Serves but to keep fools pert, and knaves awake:
A drowsy watchman, that just gives a knock,
And breaks our rest, to tell us what's o'clock.
Yet by some object every brain is stirr'd;
The dull may waken to a humming-bird;
The most recluse, discreetly open'd, find
Congenial matter in the cockle-kind;
The mind, in metaphysics at a loss,
May wander in a wilderness of moss

The head, that turns at super-lunar things,
Poised with a tail, may steer on Wilkins' wings.[1]
O! would the sons of men once think their eyes
And reason given them but to study *flies!*
See Nature in some partial narrow shape,
And let the Author of the whole escape:
Learn but to trifle; or, who most observe,
To wonder at their Maker, not to serve.
Be that my task (replies a gloomy clerk,
Sworn foe to mystery, yet divinely dark;
Whose pious hope aspires to see the day
When moral evidence shall quite decay,
And damns implicit faith, and holy lies,
Prompt to impose, and fond to dogmatize:)
Let others creep by timid steps, and slow,
On plain experience lay foundations low,
By common sense to common knowledge bred,
And last, to Nature's cause through Nature led.
All-seeing in thy mists, we want no guide,
Mother of arrogance, and source of pride!
We nobly take the high priori road,
And reason downward, till we doubt of God:
Make Nature still encroach upon his plan;
And shove him off as far as e'er we can:
Thrust some mechanic cause into his place;
Or bind in matter, or diffuse in space.
Or, at one bound o'erleaping all his laws,
Make God man's image, man the final cause,
Find virtue local, all relation scorn,
See all in *self*, and but for self be born:
Of nought so certain as our *reason* still,
Of nought so doubtful as of *soul* and *will*.
O hide the god still more! and make us see
Such as Lucretius drew, a god like thee:
Wrapp'd up in self, a god without a thought,
Regardless of our merit or default.
Or that bright image to our fancy draw,
Which Theocles in raptured vision saw,
While through poetic scenes the Genius roves,
Or wanders wild in academic groves;

[1] John Wilkins, bishop of Chester, a man of very superior talents. He was one of the first projectors of the Royal Society, who, among many enlarged and useful notions, entertained the extravagant hope of a possibility to fly to the moon; which has put some volatile geniuses upon making wings for that purpose.

That NATURE our society adores,
Where Tindal dictates, and Silenus snores.
Roused at his name, up rose the bouzy sire,
And shook from out his pipe the seeds of fire;
Then snapp'd his box, and stroked his belly down:
Rosy and reverend, though without a gown.
Bland and familiar to the throne he came,
Led up the youth, and call'd the goddess *dame*.
Then thus. From priestcraft happily set free,
Lo! every finish'd son returns to thee:
First slave to words, then vassal to a name,
Then dupe to party; child and man the same;
Bounded by nature, narrow'd still by art,
A trifling head, and a contracted heart.
Thus bred, thus taught, how many have I seen,
Smiling on all, and smiled on by a queen.
Mark'd out for honours, honour'd for their birth,
To thee the most rebellious things on earth:
Now to thy gentle shadow all are shrunk,
All melted down, in pension, or in punk!
So K*, so B** sneak'd into the grave,
A monarch's half, and half a harlot's slave.
Poor W**, nipp'd in folly's broadest bloom,
Who praises now? his chaplain on his tomb.
Then take them all, oh, take them to thy breast!
Thy *Magus*, Goddess! shall perform the rest.
With that, a WIZARD OLD his *cup* extends;
Which whoso tastes forgets his former friends,
Sire, ancestors, himself. One casts his eyes
Up to a *star*, and like Endymion dies:
A *feather* shooting from another's head,
Extracts his brain, and principle is fled,
Lost is his God, his country, everything;
And nothing left but homage to a king!
The vulgar herd turn off to roll with hogs,
To run with horses, or to hunt with dogs;
But, sad example! never to escape
Their infamy, still keep the human shape.[1]
But she, good goddess, sent to every child
Firm Impudence, or Stupefaction mild;

[1] The effects of the Magus's cup are just contrary to that of Circe. Hers took away the shape, and left the human mind: this takes away the mind, and leaves the human shape.

And straight succeeded, leaving shame no room,
Cibberian forehead, or Cimmerian gloom.
Kind Self-conceit to some her glass applies,
Which no one looks in with another's eyes:
But as the flatterer or dependant paint,
Beholds himself a patriot, chief, or saint.
On others Interest her gay livery flings,
Interest, that waves on party-colour'd wings:
Turn'd to the sun, she casts a thousand dyes,
And, as she turns, the colours fall or rise.
Others the Syren Sisters warble round,
And empty heads console with empty sound.
No more, alas! the voice of Fame they hear,
The balm of dulness trickling in their ear.
Great C**, H**, P**, R**, K*,
Why all your toils? your sons have learn'd to sing.
How quick ambition hastes to ridicule!
The sire is made a peer, the son a fool.
On some, a priest succinct in amice white
Attends; all flesh is nothing in his sight!
Beeves, at his touch, at once to jelly turn,
And the huge boar is shrunk into an urn:
The board with specious miracles he loads,
Turns hares to larks, and pigeons into toads.
Another (for in all what one can shine)
Explains the *sève* and *verdeur*[1] of the vine.
What cannot copious sacrifice atone?
Thy truffles, Perigord! thy hams, Bayonne!
With French libation, and Italian strain,
Wash Bladen white, and expiate Hays's[2] stain.
Knight lifts the head, for what are crowds undone
To three essential partridges in one?
Gone every blush, and silent all reproach,
Contending princes mount them in their coach.
Next bidding all draw near on bended knees,
The queen confers her *titles* and *degrees*.

[1] French terms relating to wines. St. Evremont has a very pathetic letter to a *nobleman in disgrace*, advising him to seek comfort in a *good table*, and particularly to be attentive to *these qualities* in his champagne.

[2] *Bladen—Hays*—Names of gamesters. Bladen was a black man. Robert Knight, cashier of the South Sea Company, who fled from England in 1720, (afterwards pardoned in 1742.)—These lived with the utmost magnificence at Paris, and kept open tables frequented by persons of the first quality of England, and even by princes of the blood of France.

Her children first, of more distinguish'd sort,
Who study Shakspere at the inns of court,
Impale a glow-worm, or vertù profess,
Shine in the dignity of F.R.S.
Some, deep Freemasons, join the silent race,
Worthy to fill Pythagoras's place:
Some botanists, or florists at the least,
Or issue members of an annual feast.
Nor pass'd the meanest unregarded, one
Rose a Gregorian, one a Gormogon.[1]
The last, not least in honour or applause,
Isis and Cam made doctors of her laws.
Then blessing all, Go, children of my care!
To practice now from theory repair.
All my commands are easy, short, and full:
My sons! be proud, be selfish, and be dull.
Guard my prerogative, assert my throne:
This nod confirms each privilege your own.
The cap and switch be sacred to his Grace;
With staff and pumps the marquis leads the race;
From stage to stage the licensed earl may run,
Pair'd with his fellow-charioteer, the sun;
The learned baron butterflies design,
Or draw to silk Arachne's subtile line;
The judge to dance his brother sergeant call;
The senator at cricket urge the ball;
The bishop stow (pontific luxury!)
An hundred souls of turkeys in a pie;
The sturdy 'squire to Gallic masters stoop,
And drown his lands and manors in a soup.
Others import yet nobler arts from France,
Teach kings to fiddle, and make senates dance.
Perhaps more high some daring son may soar,
Proud to my list to add one monarch more;
And, nobly conscious princes are but things
Born for first ministers, as slaves for kings,
Tyrant supreme! shall three estates command,
And MAKE ONE MIGHTY DUNCIAD OF THE LAND!
More she had spoke, but yawn'd—all nature nods:
What mortal can resist the yawn of gods?
Churches and chapels instantly it reach'd;
(St. James's first, for leaden Gilbert[2] preach'd)

[1] Societies then in existence said to have been *slips* from the root of the freemasonry.

[2] Gilbert Burnet, bishop of Salisbury.

Then catch'd the schools; the hall scarce kept awake;
The convocation gaped, but could not speak:
Lost was the nation's sense, nor could be found,
While the long solemn unison went round:
Wide, and more wide, it spread o'er all the realm
Even Palinurus nodded at the helm:
The vapour mild o'er each committee crept;
Unfinish'd treaties in each office slept;
And chiefless armies dozed out the campaign;
And navies yawn'd for orders on the main.
  O Muse! relate (for you can tell alone,
Wits have short memories, and dunces none)
Relate who first, who last resign'd to rest;
Whose heads she partly, whose completely blest;
What charms could faction, what ambition lull,
The venal quiet, and entrance the dull;
'Till drown'd was sense, and shame, and right, and wrong,—
O sing, and hush the nations with thy song!

* * * * * *

  In vain, in vain—the all-composing hour
Resistless falls: the Muse obeys the power.
She comes! she comes! the sable throne behold
Of *Night* primeval, and of *Chaos* old!
Before her, *Fancy's* gilded clouds decay,
And all its varying rainbows die away.
Wit shoots in vain its momentary fires,
The meteor drops, and in a flash expires.
As one by one, at dread Medea's strain,
The sickening stars fade off the ethereal plain;
As Argus' eyes by Hermes' wand oppress'd,
Closed one by one to everlasting rest;
Thus at her felt approach, and secret might,
Art after *art* goes out, and all is night.
See skulking *Truth* to her old cavern fled,
Mountains of casuistry heap'd o'er her head!
Philosophy, that lean'd on Heaven before,
Shrinks to her second cause, and is no more.
Physic of *Metaphysic* begs defence,
And *Metaphysic* calls for aid on *Sense!*
See *Mystery* to *Mathematics* fly!
In vain! they gaze, turn giddy, rave, and die.
Religion, blushing, veils her sacred fires,
And unawares *Morality* expires.

Nor *public* flame, nor *private*, dares to shine;
Nor *human* spark is left, nor glimpse *divine!*
Lo! thy dread empire, CHAOS! is restored;
Light dies before thy uncreating word:
Thy hand, great anarch! lets the curtain fall;
And universal darkness buries all.

APPENDIX.

I.

PREFACE.

PREFIXED TO THE FIVE FIRST IMPERFECT EDITIONS OF THE DUNCIAD, IN THREE BOOKS, PRINTED AT DUBLIN AND LONDON, IN OCTAVO AND DUODECIMO, 1727.

THE PUBLISHER[1] TO THE READER.

It will be found a true observation, though somewhat surprising, that when any scandal is vented against a man of the highest distinction and character, either in the state or in literature, the public in general afford it a most quiet reception; and the larger part accept it as favourably as if it were some kindness done to themselves:—whereas if a known scoundrel or blockhead but chance to be touched upon, a whole legion is up in arms, and it becomes the common cause of all scribblers, booksellers, and printers whatsoever.

Not to search too deeply into the reason hereof, I will only observe as a fact, that every week for these two months past, the town has been persecuted with pamphlets,

[1] Who he was is uncertain; but Edward Ward tells us, in his preface to Durgen, "that most judges are of opinion this preface is not of English extraction, but Hibernian," &c. He means it was written by Dr. Swift, who, whether publisher or not, may be said in a sort to be author of the poem: for when he, together with Mr. Pope, (for reasons specified in the preface to their Miscellanies), determined to own the most trifling pieces in which they had any hand, and to destroy all that remained in their power, the first sketch of this poem was snatched from the fire by Dr. Swift, who persuaded his friend to proceed in it,

advertisements, letters, and weekly essays, not only against the wit and writings, but against the character and person, of Mr. Pope. And that of all those men who have received pleasure from his works, which by modest computation may be about a hundred thousand in these kingdoms of England and Ireland (not to mention Jersey, Guernsey, the Orcades, those in the new world, and foreigners who have translated him into their languages); of all this number not a man hath stood up to say one word in his defence.

The only exception is the author of the following poem, who doubtless had either a better insight into the grounds of this clamour, or a better opinion of Mr. Pope's integrity, joined with a greater personal love for him, than any other of his numerous friends and admirers.

Farther, that he was in his peculiar intimacy, appears from the knowledge he manifests of the most private authors of all the anonymous pieces against him, and from his having in this poem attacked no man living, who had not before printed, or published, some scandal against this gentleman.

---

and to him it was therefore inscribed. But the occasion of printing it was as follows.

There was published in those miscellanies, a Treatise of the Bathos, or Art of Sinking in Poetry, in which was a chapter, where the species of bad writers were ranged in classes, and initial letters of names prefixed, for the most part at random. But such was the number of poets eminent in that art, that some one or other took every letter to himself. All fell into so violent a fury, that for half a year, or more, the common newspapers (in most of which they had some property, as being hired writers) were filled with the most abusive falsehoods and scurrilities they could possibly devise: a liberty noways to be wondered at in those people, and in those papers, that for many years, during the uncontrolled licence of the press, had aspersed almost all the great characters of the age; and this with impunity, their own persons and names being utterly secret and obscure. This gave Mr. Pope the thought, that he had now some opportunity of doing good, by detecting and dragging into light these common enemies of mankind; since to invalidate this universal slander, it sufficed to show what contemptible men were the authors of it. He was not without hopes, that by manifesting the dulness of those who had only malice to recommend them, either the booksellers would not find their account in employing them, or the men themselves, when discovered, want courage to proceed in so unlawful an occupation. This it was that gave birth to the Dunciad: and he thought it a happiness, that by the late flood of slander on himself, he had acquired such a peculiar right over their names as was necessary to his design.

How I came possessed of it, is no concern to the reader; but it would have been a wrong to him had I detained the publication; since those names which are its chief ornaments die off daily so fast, as must render it too soon unintelligible. If it provoke the author to give us a more perfect edition, I have my end.

Who he is I cannot say, and (which is great pity) there is certainly nothing in his style and manner of writing which can distinguish or discover him: for if it bears any resemblance to that of Mr. Pope, 'tis not improbable but it might be done on purpose, with a view to have it pass for his. But by the frequency of his allusions to Virgil, and a laboured (not to say affected) *shortness* in imitation of him, I should think him more an admirer of the Roman poet than of the Grecian, and in that not of the same taste with his friend.

I have been well informed, that this work was the labour of full six years of his life, and that he wholly retired himself from all the avocations and pleasures of the world, to attend diligently to its correction and perfection; and six years more he intended to bestow upon it, as it should seem by this verse of Statius which was cited at the head of his manuscript,

> *Oh mihi bissenos multum vigilata per annos,*
> *Duncia!*

Hence also we learn the true title of the poem; which, with the same certainty as we call that of Homer the Iliad, of Virgil the Æneid, of Camoens the Lusiad, we may pronounce could have been, and can be, no other than the DUNCIAD.

It is styled *heroic*, as being *doubly* so; not only with respect to its nature, which, according to the best rules of the ancients, and strictest ideas of the moderns, is critically such; but also with regard to the heroical disposition and high courage of the writer, who dared to stir up such a formidable, irritable, and implacable race of mortals.

There may arise some obscurity in chronology from the *names* in the poem, by the inevitable removal of some authors, and insertion of others, in their niches. For whoever will consider the unity of the whole design, will be sensible, that the *poem was not made for these authors, but these authors for the poem.* I should judge that they were clapped in as they rose, fresh and fresh, and changed from day to day; in like manner as when the old boughs wither, we thrust new ones into a chimney.

I would not have the reader too much troubled or anxious, if he cannot decipher them; since, when he shall have found them out, he will probably know no more of the persons than before.

Yet we judged it better to preserve them as they are, than to change them for fictitious names; by which the satire would only be multiplied, and applied to many instead of one. Had the hero, for instance, been called Codrus, how many would have affirmed him to have been Mr. T., Mr. E., Sir R. B., &c., but now all that unjust scandal is saved by calling him by a name, which by good luck happens to be that of a real person.

II.

A LIST OF BOOKS, PAPERS, AND VERSES,

IN WHICH OUR AUTHOR WAS ABUSED, BEFORE THE PUBLICATION OF THE DUNCIAD; WITH THE TRUE NAMES OF THE AUTHORS.

REFLECTIONS critical and satirical on a late Rhapsody, called An Essay on Criticism. By Mr. Dennis, printed by B. Lintot, price 6*d.*

A New Rehearsal, or Bays the younger; containing an Examen of Mr. Row's plays, and a word or two on Mr. Pope's Rape of the Lock. Anon. [by Charles Gildon] printed for J. Roberts, 1714, price 1*s.*

Homerides, or a Letter to Mr. Pope, occasioned by his intended translation of Homer. By Sir Iliad Dogrel. [Tho. Burnet and G. Ducket esquires] printed for W. Wilkins, 1715, price 9*d.*

Æsop at the Bear Garden; a vision, in imitation of the Temple of Fame. By Mr. Preston. Sold by John Morphew, 1715, price 6*d.*

The Catholic Poet, or Protestant Barnaby's Sorrowful Lamentation; a Ballad about Homer's Iliad. By Mrs. Centlivre, and others, 1715, price 1*d.*

An Epilogue to a Puppet-show at Bath, concerning the said Iliad. By George Ducket, Esq., printed by E. Curl.

A complete Key to the What d'ye call it. Anon. [by Griffin, a player, supervised by Mr. Th——] printed by J. Roberts, 1715.

A true character of Mr. P. and his writings, in a letter to a friend. Anon. [Dennis] printed for S. Popping, 1716, price 3*d.*

The Confederates, a Farce. By Joseph Gay [J. D. Breval] printed for R. Burleigh, 1717, price 1*s.*

Remarks upon Mr. Pope's translation of Homer; with two letters concerning the Windsor Forest, and the Temple of Fame. By Mr. Dennis, printed for E. Curl, 1717, price 1*s.* 6*d.*

Satyrs on the translators of Homer, Mr. P. and Mr. T. Anon. [Bez. Morris] 1717, price 6*d.*

The Triumvirate; or, a Letter from Palæmon to Celia at Bath. Anon. [Leonard Welsted] 1711, folio, price 1*s.*

The Battle of Poets, an heroic poem. By Tho. Cooke, printed for J. Roberts, folio, 1725.

Memoirs of Lilliput. Anon. [Eliza Haywood] octavo, printed in 1727.

An Essay on Criticism, in prose. By the Author of the Critical History of England [J. Oldmixon] octavo, printed 1728.

Gulliveriana and Alexandriana; with an ample preface and critique on Swift and Pope's Miscellanies. By Jonathan Smedley, printed by J. Roberts, octavo, 1728.

Characters of the Times; or, an account of the writings, characters, &c., of several gentlemen libelled by S—— and P——, in a late Miscellany. Octavo, 1728.

Remarks on Mr. Pope's Rape of the Lock, in letters to a friend. By Mr. Dennis; written in 1724, though not printed till 1728, octavo.

VERSES, LETTERS, ESSAYS, OR ADVERTISEMENTS, IN THE PUBLIC PRINTS.

British Journal, Nov. 25, 1727. A Letter on Swift and Pope's Miscellanies. [Writ by M. Concanen.]

Daily Journal, March 18, 1728. A Letter by Philomauri. James-Moore Smith.

Id. March 29. A Letter about Thersites; accusing the author of disaffection to the Government. By James-Moore Smith.

Mist's Weekly Journal, March 30. An Essay on the Arts of a Poet sinking in reputation; or, a Supplement to the Art of Sinking in Poetry. [Supposed by Mr. Theobald.]

Daily Journal, April 3. A Letter under the name of Philoditto. By James-Moore Smith.

Flying Post, April 4. A Letter against Gulliver and Mr. P. [by Mr. Oldmixon.]

Daily Journal, April 5. An Auction of Goods at Twickenham. By James-Moore Smith.

The Flying Post, April 6. A Fragment of a Treatise upon Swift and Pope. By Mr. Oldmixon.

The Senator, April 9. On the same. By Edward Roome.

Daily Journal, April 8. Advertisement by James-Moore Smith.

Flying Post, April 13. Verses against Dr. Smith, and against M. P—'s Homer. By J. Oldmixon.

Daily Journal, April 23. Letter about the translation of the character of Thersites in Homer. By Thomas Cooke, &c.

Mist's Weekly Journal, April 27. A Letter of Lewis Theobald.

Daily Journal, May 11. A Letter against Mr. P. at large. Anon. [John Dennis.]

All these were afterwards reprinted in a pamphlet, entitled A Collection of all the Verses, Essays, Letters, and Advertisements, occasioned by Mr. Pope and Swift's Miscellanies, prefaced by Concanen, Anonymous, octavo, and printed for A. Moore, 1728, price 1*s*. Others of an elder date, having lain as waste paper many years, were, upon the publication of the Dunciad, brought out, and their authors betrayed by the mercenary booksellers (in hope of some possibility of vending a few) by advertising them in this manner—"The Confederates, a farce. By Captain Breval (for which he was put into the Dunciad). An Epilogue to Powel's Puppet-show. By Col. Ducket (for which he is put into the Dunciad). Essays, &c. By Sir Richard Blackmore. (N.B. It was for a passage of this book that Sir Richard was put into the Dunciad)." And so of others.

AFTER THE DUNCIAD, 1728.

An Essay on the Dunciad. Octavo, printed for J. Roberts. [In this book, p. 9, it was formally declared, "That the complaint of the aforesaid libels and advertisements was forged and untrue; that all mouths had been silent, except in Mr. Pope's praise; and nothing against him published, but by Mr. Theobald."]

Sawney, in blank verse, occasioned by the Dunciad: with a Critique on that poem. By J. Ralph [a person never mentioned in it at first, but inserted after], printed for J. Roberts, octavo.

A complete Key to the Dunciad. By E. Curl, 12mo, price 6*d.*

A second and third edition of the same, with additions, 12mo.

The Popiad. By E. Curl, extracted from J. Dennis, Sir Richard Blackmore, &c. 12mo, price 6*d.*

The Curliad. By the same E. Curl.

The Female Dunciad. Collected by the same Mr. Curl, 12mo, price 6*d.* With the Metamorphosis of P. into a stinging nettle. By Mr. Foxton, 12mo.

The Metamorphosis of Scriblerus into Snarlerus. By. J. Smedley, printed for A. Moore, folio, price 6*d.*

The Dunciad Dissected. By Curl and Mrs. Thomas, 12mo.

An Essay on the Taste and Writings of the present times. Said to be writ by a gentleman of C. C. C. Oxon, printed for J. Roberts, octavo.

The Arts of Logic and Rhetoric, partly taken from Bouhours, with new reflections, &c. By John Oldmixon, octavo.

Remarks on the Dunciad. By Mr. Dennis, dedicated to Theobald, octavo.

A Supplement to the Profund. Anon. [by Matthew Concanen], octavo.

Mist's Weekly Journal, June 8. A long Letter, signed W. A. Writ by some or other of the club of Theobald, Dennis, Moore, Concanen, Cooke, who for some time held constant weekly meetings for these kind of performances.

Daily Journal, June 11. A Letter, signed Philoscriblerus, on the name of Pope.—Letter to Mr. Theobald, in verse, signed B. M. (Bezaleel Morris) against Mr. P.—Many other little epigrams about this time in the same papers, by James Moore, and others.

Mist's Journal, June 22. A Letter by Lewis Theobald.

Flying Post, August 8. Letter on Pope and Swift.

Daily Journal, August 8. Letter charging the Author of the Dunciad with Treason.

Durgen; a plain satyr on a pompous satyrist. By Edward Ward, with a little of James Moore.

Apollo's Maggot in his cups. By E. Ward.

Gulliveriana secunda. Being a collection of many of the Libels in the Newspapers, like the former volume, under the same title, by Smedley. Advertised in the Craftsman, Nov. 9, 1728, with this remarkable promise, that "*any thing* which *any body* should send as Mr. Pope's or Dr. Swift's, should be inserted and published as theirs."

Pope Alexander's supremacy and infallibility examined, &c. By George Ducket and John Dennis, quarto.

Dean Jonathan's paraphrase on the 4th chapter of Genesis. Writ by E. Roome, folio, 1729.

Labeo. A paper of verses by Leonard Welsted, which after came into *one epistle*, and was published by James Moore. quarto, 1730. Another part of it came out in Welsted's own name, under the just title of Dulness and Scandal, folio, 1731.

There have been since published:

Verses on the Imitator of Horace. By a Lady (or between a Lady, a Lord, and a Court-'squire.) Printed for J. Roberts, folio.

An Epistle from a Nobleman to a Doctor of Divinity, from Hampton-court (Lord H——y). Printed for J. Roberts also, folio.

A Letter from Mr. Cibber to Mr. Pope. Printed for W. Lewis in Covent-garden, octavo.

III.

ADVERTISEMENT TO THE FIRST EDITION,

WITH NOTES, IN QUARTO, 1729.

It will be sufficient to say of this edition, that the reader has here a much more correct and complete copy of the Dunciad, than has hitherto appeared. I cannot answer but some mistakes may have slipt into it, but a vast number of others will be prevented by the names being now not only set at length, but justified by the authorities and reasons given. I make no doubt, the author's own motive to use real rather than feigned names, was his care to preserve the innocent from any false application; whereas, in the former editions, which had no more than the initial letters, he was made, by keys printed here, to hurt the inoffensive; and (what was worse) to abuse his friends, by an impression at Dublin.

The commentary which attends this poem was sent me from several hands, and consequently must be unequally written; yet will have one advantage over most commentaries, that it is not made upon conjectures, or at a remote distance of time: and the reader cannot but derive one pleasure from the very *obscurity* of the persons it treats of, that it partakes of the nature of a *secret*, which most people love to be let into, though the men or the things be ever so inconsiderable or trivial.

Of the *persons* it was judged proper to give some account: for since it is only in this monument that they must expect to survive (and here survive they will, as long as the English tongue shall remain such as it was in the reigns of queen ANNE and king GEORGE), it seemed but humanity to bestow a word or two upon each, just to tell what he was, what he writ, when he lived, and when he died.

If a word or two more are added upon the chief offenders, it is only as a paper pinned upon the breast, to mark the enormities for which they suffered; lest the correction only should be remembered, and the crime forgotten.

In some articles it was thought sufficient, barely to transcribe from Jacob, Curl, and other writers of their own rank, who were much better acquainted with them than any of the authors of this comment can pretend to be. Most of them had drawn each other's characters on certain occasions; but the few here inserted are all that could be saved from the general destruction of such works.

Of the part of Scriblerus I need say nothing; his manner is well enough known, and approved by all but those who are too much concerned to be judges.

The imitations of the ancients are added to gratify those who either never read, or may have forgotten them; together with some of the parodies and allusions to the most excellent of the moderns. If, from the frequency of the former, any man think the poem too much a cento, our poet will but appear to have done the same thing in jest which Boileau did in earnest; and upon which Vida Fracastorius, and many of the most eminent Latin poets, professedly valued themselves.

IV.

ADVERTISEMENT TO THE FIRST EDITION,

SEPARATE, OF THE FOURTH BOOK OF THE DUNCIAD.

We apprehend it can be deemed no injury to the author of the three first books of the Dunciad, that we publish this fourth. It was found merely by accident, in taking a survey of the *library* of a late eminent nobleman; but in so blotted a condition, and in so many detached pieces, as plainly showed it to be not only *incorrect* but *unfinished*. That the author of the three first books had a design to extend and complete his poem in this manner, appears from the dissertation prefixed to it, where it is said, that *the design is more extensive, and that we may expect other episodes to complete it:* and from the declaration in the argument to the third book, that *the accomplishment of the prophecies therein, would be the theme hereafter of a greater Dunciad.* But whether or no he be the author of this, we declare ourselves ignorant. If he be, we are no more to be blamed for the publication of it, than Tucca and Varius for that of the last six books of the Æneid, though perhaps inferior to the former.

If any person be possessed of a more perfect copy of this work, or of any other fragments of it, and will communicate them to the publisher, we shall make the next edition more complete: in which, we also promise to insert any *criticisms* that shall be published (if at all to the purpose) with the *names* of the *authors;* or any letters sent us (though not to the purpose) shall yet be printed under the title of *Epistolæ Obscurorum Virorum;* which, together with some others of the same kind formerly laid by for that end, may make no unpleasant addition to the future impressions of this poem.

V.

THE GUARDIAN.

BEING A CONTINUATION OF SOME FORMER PAPERS ON THE SUBJECT OF PASTORALS.

Monday, April 27, 1713.

Compulerantque greges Corydon et Thyrsis in unum.—
Ex illo Corydon, Corydon est tempore nobis.

I DESIGNED to have troubled the reader with no farther discourse of pastoral; but being informed that I am taxed of partiality, in not mentioning an author whose Eclogues are published in the same volume with Mr. Philips's; I shall employ this paper in observations upon him, written in the free spirit of criticism, and without any apprehension of offending that gentleman, whose character it is, that he takes the greatest care of his works before they are published, and has the least concern for them afterwards.

I have laid it down as the first rule of Pastoral, that its ideas should be taken from the manners of the *golden age*, and the moral formed upon the representation of innocence; it is therefore plain that any deviations from that design degrade a poem from being truly pastoral. In this view it will appear that Virgil can only have two of his Eclogues allowed to be such: his first and ninth must be rejected, because they describe the ravages of armies, and oppressions of the innocent; Corydon's criminal passion for Alexis throws out the second; the calumny and railing in the third are not proper to that state of concord; the eighth represents unlawful ways of procuring love by enchantments, and introduces a shepherd whom an inviting precipice tempts to self-murder: as to the fourth, sixth, and tenth, they are given up by Heinsius, Salmasius, Rapin, and the critics in general. They likewise observe that but eleven of all the Idyllia of Theocritus are to be admitted as Pastorals; and even out of that number the greater part will be excluded for one or other of the reasons above mentioned. So that when I remarked in a former paper, that Virgil's Eclogues, taken altogether, are rather select poems than pastorals, I might have said the same thing, with no less truth, of Theocritus. The reason of this I take to be yet unobserved by the critics, viz., they never meant them all for pastorals.

Now it is plain Philips hath done this, and in that particular excelled both Theocritus and Virgil.

As simplicity is the distinguishing characteristic of pastoral, Virgil hath been thought guilty of too courtly a style; his language is perfectly pure, and he often forgets he is among peasants. I have frequently wondered that since he was so conversant in the writings of Ennius, he had not imitated the rusticity of the Doric, as well by the help of the old obsolete Roman language, as Philips hath by the antiquated English: for example, might not he have said *quoi* instead of *cui, quoijum* for *cujum, volt* for *vult, &c.*, as well as our modern hath *welladay* for *alas, whilome* for *of old, make mock* for *deride,* and *witless younglings* for *simple lambs, &c.*, by which means he had attained as much of the air of Theocritus, as Phillips hath of Spenser.

Mr. Pope hath fallen into the same error with Virgil. His clowns do not converse in all the simplicity proper to the country; his names are borrowed from Theocritus and Virgil, which are improper to the scene of his pastorals: he introduces Daphnis, Alexis, and Thyrsis on British plains, as Virgil hath done before him on the Mantuan. Whereas Philips, who hath the strictest regard to propriety, makes choice of names peculiar to the country, and more agreeable to a reader of delicacy, such as Hobbinol, Lobbin, Cuddy, and Colin-Clout.

So easy as pastoral writing may seem (in the simplicity we have described it), yet it requires great reading, both of the ancients and moderns, to be a master of it. Philips hath given us manifest proofs of his knowledge of books. It must be confessed his competitor hath imitated *some single thoughts* of the ancients well enough (if we consider he had not the happiness of an University education), but he hath dispersed them, here and there, without that order and method which Mr. Philips observes, whose *whole* third pastoral is an instance how well he hath studied the fifth of Virgil, and how judiciously reduced Virgil's thoughts to the standard of pastoral; as his contention of Colin-Clout and the Nightingale shows with what exactness he hath imitated every line in Strada.

When I remarked it as a principal fault to introduce fruits and flowers of a foreign growth, in the descriptions where the scene lies in our own country, I did not design that observation should extend also to animals, or the sensitive life; for Mr. Philips hath with great judgment described wolves in England in his first pastoral. Nor would I have a poet slavishly confine himself (as Mr. Pope hath done) to one particular season of the year, one certain time of the day, and one unbroken scene in each eclogue. 'Tis plain Spenser neglected this pedantry, who in his pastoral of November mentions the mournful song of the nightingale:

Sad Philomel her song in tears doth steep.

And Mr. Philips, by a poetical creation, hath raised up finer beds of flowers than the most industrious gardener; his roses, endives, lilies, king-cups, and daffodils, blow all in the same season.

But the better to discover the merits of our two contemporary pastoral writers, I shall endeavour to draw a parallel of them, by setting several of their particular thoughts in the same light, whereby it will be obvious how much Philips hath the advantage. With what simplicity he introduces two shepherds singing alternately!

Hobb. *Come, Rosalind, O come, for without thee*
What pleasure can the country have for me!
Come, Rosalind, O come! my brinded kine,
My snowy sheep, my farm, and all are thine.

Lanq. *Come, Rosalind, O come; here shady bowers,*
Here are cool fountains, and here springing flowers,
Come, Rosalind; here ever let us stay,
And sweetly waste our live-long time away.

Our other pastoral writer, in expressing the same thought, deviates into downright poetry:

Streph. *In spring the fields, in autumn hills I love;*
At morn the plains, at noon the shady grove;
But Delia always; forced from Delia's sight,
Nor plains at morn, nor groves at noon delight.

Daph. *Sylvia's like autumn ripe, yet mild as May,*
More bright than noon, yet fresh as early day;
Even spring displeases when she shines not here;
But blest with her, 'tis spring throughout the year.

In the first of these authors, two shepherds thus innocently describe the behaviour of their mistresses:

Hobb. *As Marian bathed, by chance I passed by,*
She blush'd, and at me cast a side-long eye;
Then swift beneath the crystal wave she tried
Her beauteous form, but all in vain, to hide.

Lanq. *As I to cool me, bathed one sultry day,*
Fond Lydia lurking in the sedges lay;
The wanton laugh'd, and seem'd in haste to fly;
Yet often stopp'd, and often turn'd her eye.

The other modern (who, it must be confessed, hath a knack of versifying) hath it as follows:

Streph. *Me gentle Delia beckons from the plain,*
Then, hid in shades, eludes her eager swain;
But feigns a laugh, to see me search around,
And by that laugh the willing fair is found.

Daph. *The sprightly Sylvia trips along the green,*
She runs, but hopes she does not run unseen,
While a kind glance at her pursuer flies,
How much at variance are her feet and eyes!

There is nothing the writers of this kind of poetry are fonder of, than descriptions of pastoral presents. Philips says thus of a sheep-hook:

Of season'd elm, where studs of brass appear,
To speak the giver's name, the month, and year;
The hook of polish'd steel, the handle turn'd,
And richly by the graver's skill adorn'd.

The other of a bowl embossed with figures:

——— *where wanton ivy twines,*
And swelling clusters bend the curling vines;
Four figures rising from the work appear,
The various seasons of the rolling year;
And what is that which binds the radiant sky,
Where twelve bright signs in beauteous order lie?

The simplicity of the swain in this place, who forgets the name of the zodiac, is no ill imitation of Virgil: but how much more plainly and unaffectedly would Philips have dressed this thought in his Doric:

And what that hight which girds the welkin sheen,
Where twelve gay signs in meet array are seen?

If the reader would indulge his curiosity any farther in the comparison of particulars, he may read the first Pastoral of Philips with the second of his contemporary; and the fourth and sixth of the former with the fourth and first of the latter; where several parallel places will occur to every one.

Having now shown some parts in which these two writers may be compared, it is a justice I owe to Mr. Philips, to discover those in which no man can compare with him. First, that beautiful rusticity, of which I shall only produce two instances of an hundred not yet quoted:

O woeful day! O day of woe! quoth he;
And woeful I, who live the day to see!

The simplicity of the diction, the melancholy flowing of the numbers, the solemnity of the sound, and the easy turn of the words in this dirge (to make use of our author's expression), are extremely elegant.

In another of his Pastorals, a shepherd utters a dirge not much inferior to the former, in the following lines:

Ah me, the while! ah me! the luckless day!
Ah luckless lad! the rather might I say!
Ah silly I! more silly than my sheep,
Which on the flowery plain I once did keep.

How he still charms the ear with these artful repetitions of the epithets; and how significant is the last verse! I defy the most common reader to repeat them without feeling some motions of compassion.

In the next place I shall rank his Proverbs, in which I formerly observed he excels. For example:

A rolling stone is ever bare of moss;
And, to their cost, green years old proverbs cross.

— He that latē lies down, as late will rise,
And sluggard-like, till noon-day snoring lies.

— Against ill luck all cunning foresight fails;
Whether we sleep or wake, it nought avails.

— Nor fear, from upright sentence, wrong.

Lastly, his elegant dialect, which alone might prove him the eldest born of Spenser, and our only true Arcadian. I should think it proper for the several writers of Pastoral to confine themselves to their several counties. Spenser seems to have been of this opinion; for he hath laid the scene of one of his Pastorals in Wales; where, with all the simplicity natural to that part of our island, one shepherd bids the other good-morrow, in an unusual and elegant manner:

Diggon Davy, I bid hur God-day;
Or Diggon hur is, or I mis-say.

Diggon answers,

Hur was hur while it was day-light;
But now hur is a most wretched wight, &c.

But the most beautiful example of this kind that I ever met with, is in a very valuable piece which I chanced to find among some old manuscripts, entitled a Pastoral Ballad: which I think, for its nature and simplicity, may (notwithstanding the modesty of the title) be allowed a perfect Pastoral. It is composed in the Somersetshire dialect, and the names such as are proper to the country people. It may be observed, as a farther beauty of this Pastoral, the words Nymph, Dryad, Naiad, Fawn, Cupid, or Satyr, are not once mentioned throughout the whole. I shall make no apology for inserting some few lines of this excellent piece. Cicily breaks thus into the subject as she is going a milking:

Cicily. *Rager, go vetch tha kee, or else tha zun*
Will quite be go, bevore c'have half a don.
Roger. *Thou shouldst not ax ma tweece, but I've a bee*
To dreave our bull to bull tha parson's kee.

It is to be observed, that this whole dialogue is formed upon the passion of *jealousy;* and his mentioning the parson's kine naturally revives the jealousy of the shepherdess Cicily, which she expresses as follows:

Cicily. *Ah Rager, Rager! ches was zore avraid*
When in yon vield you kiss'd the parson's maid;
Is this the love that once to me you zed,
When from the wake thou brought'st me ginger-bread!

Roger. *Cicily thou charg'st me valse,—I'll zwear to thee*
The parson's maid is still a maid for me.

In which answer of his are expressed at once that spirit of Religion, and that Innocence of the golden age, so necessary to be observed by all writers of Pastoral.

At the conclusion of this piece, the author reconciles the lovers, and ends the eclogue the most simply in the world:

So Rager parted vor to vetch tha kee,
And vor her bucket in went Cicily.

I am loth to show my fondness for antiquity so far as to prefer this ancient British author to our present English writers of Pastoral; but I cannot avoid making this obvious remark, that Philips hath hit into the same road with this old west country bard of ours.

After all that hath been said, I hope none can think it

any injustice to Mr. Pope, that I forbore to mention him as a Pastoral writer; since, upon the whole, he is of the same class with Moschus and Bion, whom we have excluded that rank; and of whose eclogues, as well as some of Virgil's, it may be said, that (according to the description we have given of this sort of poetry) they are by no means Pastorals, but something better.

VI.

OF THE POET LAUREATE.

November 19, 1729.

THE time of the election of a Poet Laureate being now at hand, it may be proper to give some account of the *rites* and *ceremonies* anciently used at that solemnity, and only discontinued through the neglect and degeneracy of later times. These we have extracted from an historian of undoubted credit, a reverend bishop, the learned Paulus Jovius; and are the same that were practised under the pontificate of Leo X., the great restorer of learning.

As we now see an *age* and a *court*, that for the encouragement of poetry rivals, if not exceeds, that of this famous Pope, we cannot but wish a restoration of all its *honours* to *poesy;* the rather, since there are so many parallel circumstances in the *person* who was then honoured with the laurel, and in *him,* who (in all probability) is now to wear it.

I shall translate my author exactly as I find it in the 82nd chapter of his Elogia Vir. Doct. He begins with the character of the poet himself, who was the original and father of all Laureates, and called Camillo. He was a plain country-man of Apulia, whether a *shepherd* or *thresher*, is not material. "This man (says Jovius), excited by the fame of the great encouragement given to poets at court, and the high honour in which they were held, came to the city, bringing with him a strange kind of lyre in his hand, and at least some *twenty thousand of verses.* All the wits and critics of the court flocked about him, delighted to see a *clown,* with a ruddy, hale complexion, and in his own long hair, so top full of poetry; and at the first sight of him all agreed he was born to be *Poet Laureate.* He had a most hearty welcome in an *island* of the river Tiber (an agreeable place, not unlike our Richmond), where he was first made to *eat* and *drink plentifully*, and *to repeat his verses to everybody.* Then they adorned him with a new and elegant garland, composed of *vine-leaves, laurel,* and *brassica* (a sort of cabbage), so composed, says my author, emblematically, *ut tam sales, quam lepida ejus temulentia, Brassicæ remedio cohibenda, notaretur.* He was then saluted by common consent with the title of *archi-poeta*, or *arch-poet*, in the style of those days, in ours *Poet Laureate.* This honour the poor man received with the most sensible demonstrations of joy, his eyes drunk with tears and gladness. Next the public acclamation was expressed in a *canticle*, which is transmitted to us, as follows·

Salve, brassicea virens corona,
Et lauro, archipoeta, pampinoque!
Dignus principis auribus Leonis.

All hail, arch-poet without peer!
Vine, bay, or cabbage fit to wear,
And worthy of the prince's ear.

From hence he was conducted in pomp to the *capitol* of Rome, mounted on an *elephant*, through the shouts of the populace, where the ceremony ended.

The historian tells us farther, "That at his introduction to Leo, he not only poured forth verses innumerable, like a torrent, but also *sung* them with *open mouth.* Nor was he only *once* introduced, or on *stated* days (like our Laureates), but made a *companion* to his *master*, and entertained as one of the instruments of his *most elegant pleasures.* When the prince was at table, the poet had his place at the window. When the prince had half eaten his meat, he gave with his own hands the rest to the poet. When the poet drank, it was out of the prince's own flagon, insomuch (says the historian) that through so great good eating and drinking he contracted a most terrible gout." Sorry I am to relate what follows, but that I cannot leave my reader's curiosity unsatisfied in the catastrophe of this extraordinary man. To use my author's words, which are remarkable, *mortuo Leone, profligatisque poetis, &c.* "When Leo died, and poets were no more" (for I would not understand *profligatis* literally, as if poets then were *profligate*), this unhappy Laureate was forthwith reduced to return to his country, where, oppressed with *old age* and *want*, he miserably perished in a *common hospital*.

We see from this sad conclusion (which may be of example to the poets of our time) that it were happier to meet with no encouragement at all, to remain at the plough, or other lawful occupation, than to be elevated above their condition, and taken out of the common means of life, without a surer support than the *temporary*, or, at best, *mortal* favours of the great. It was doubtless for this consideration, that when the Royal Bounty was lately extended to a *rural genius*, care was taken to *settle it upon him for life*. And it hath been the practice of our Princes, never to remove from the station of Poet Laureate any man who hath once been chosen, though never so much greater geniuses might arise in his time. A noble instance, how much the *charity* of our monarchs hath exceeded their *love of fame*.

To come now to the intent of this paper. We have here the whole ancient *ceremonial* of the Laureate. In the first place the crown is to be mixed with *vine-leaves*, as the vine is the plant of Bacchus, and full as essential to the honour, as the *butt of sack* to the salary.

Secondly, the *brassica* must be made use of as a qualifier of the former. It seems the *cabbage* was anciently accounted a remedy for *drunkenness*; a power the French now ascribe to the onion, and style a soup made of it, *soupe d'yvrogne*. I would recommend a large mixture of the *brassica* if Mr. Dennis be chosen; but if Mr. Tibbald, it is not so necessary, unless the cabbage be supposed to signify the same thing with respect to *poets* as to *tailors*, viz. *stealing*. I should judge it not amiss to add another plant to this garland, to wit, *ivy*: not only as it anciently belonged to poets in general, but as it is emblematical of the three virtues of a court poet in particular; it is *creeping*, *dirty*, and *dangling*.

In the next place, a *canticle* must be composed and sung in laud and praise of the new poet. If Mr. Cibber be laureated, it is my opinion no man can *write* this but himself: and no man, I am sure, can *sing* it so affectingly. But what this canticle should be, either in his or the other candidate's case, I shall not pretend to determine.

Thirdly, there ought to be a *public show*, or entry of the poet. To settle the order or procession of which, Mr. Anstis and Mr. DENNIS ought to have a conference. I apprehend here two difficulties: one, of procuring an *elephant*, the other of teaching the poet to ride him: therefore I should imagine the next animal in size or dignity would do best; either a *mule* or a large *ass;* particularly if that noble one could be had, whose portraiture makes so great an ornament of the *Dunciad*, and which (unless I am misinformed) is yet in the park of a nobleman near this city:——Unless Mr. CIBBER be the man, who may, with great propriety and beauty, ride on a *dragon*, if he goes by land; or if he chuse the water, upon one of his own *swans* from *Cæsar in Egypt.*

We have spoken sufficiently of the *ceremony;* let us now speak of the *qualifications* and *privileges* of the Laureate. First, we see he must be able to make verses *extempore*, and to pour forth innumerable, if required. In this I doubt Mr. TIBBALD. Secondly, he ought to *sing*, and intrepidly, *patulo ore:* here, I confess the excellency of Mr. CIBBER. Thirdly, he ought to carry a *lyre* about with him: if a large one be thought too cumbersome, a small one may be contrived to hang about the neck, like an order, and be very much a grace to the person. Fourthly, he ought to have a good *stomach*, to eat and drink whatever his betters think fit; and therefore it is in this high office as in many others, no puny constitution can discharge it. I do not think CIBBER or TIBBALD here so happy: but rather a stanch, vigorous, seasoned, and dry *old gentleman*, whom I have in my eye.

I could also wish at this juncture, such a person as is truly jealous of the *honour* and *dignity* of *poetry;* no joker, or trifler, but a bard in *good earnest;* nay, not amiss if a critic, and the better if a little *obstinate.* For when we consider what great privileges have been lost from this office (as we see from the forecited authentic record of Jovius), namely, those of *feeding* from the *prince's table*, *drinking* out of his *own flagon*, becoming even his *domestic* and *companion;* it requires a man warm and resolute to be able to claim and obtain the restoring of these high honours. I have cause to fear the most of the candidates would be liable, either through the influence of ministers, or for rewards or favours, to give up the glorious rights of the Laureate: yet I am not without hopes, there is *one*, from whom a *serious* and *steady* assertion of these privileges may be expected; and, if there be such a one, I must do him the justice to say, it is Mr. DENNIS, the worthy president of our society.

VII.

ADVERTISEMENT.

PRINTED IN THE JOURNALS, 1730.

WHEREAS, upon occasion of certain pieces relating to the gentlemen of the Dunciad, some have been willing to suggest, as if they looked upon them as an *abuse:* we can do no less than own, it is our opinion, that to call these gentlemen *bad authors* is no sort of *abuse*, but a great *truth.* We cannot alter this opinion without some reason; but we promise to do it in respect to every person who thinks it an injury to be represented as no *wit*, or *poet*, provided he procures a certificate of his being really such, from any *three of his companions* in the Dunciad, or from Mr. Dennis *singly*, who is esteemed equal to any three of the number.

www.ingramcontent.com/pod-product-compliance
Lightning Source LLC
LaVergne TN
LVHW021315110826
845150LV00003B/579

* 9 7 8 1 4 2 5 5 5 7 7 8 2 *